MultiCurrency Capabilities in PeopleSoft

Anil Goel
Gaurav Singhal

MultiCurrency Capabilities in PeopleSoft
by Anil Goel, Gaurav Singhal

Published by Anil Goel

Printed in China

Front and back cover design: Front and back cover design by Revo Yanson (www.byrevo.com)

Sept 2010 First Edition

For error reporting or feedback please use this link: http://groups.google.com/group/Screen_By_Screen

ISBN: 978-0-615-39567-8

To Neena, Deepak and Arjun

and

www.cacharcancerhospital.org

Table of Contents

Preface iv

Part I

1. The Big Picture 1
2. Market Rates and Journals 10
3. Currency Precision & Rounding 29
4. Currency Triangulation 48
5. Currency Controls 56

Part II

6. Multi-Book Ledgers and Keep Ledgers in Sync 85
7. Revalue Ledger Balances 101
8. Ledger Translations 133
9. Translate Within Ledgers 151
10. Misc Functionalities 166

Appendix A –PeopleTools Objects 172

Appendix B –TableSet Control 175

Appendix C –Message Catalog 177

Appendix D –PeopleBooks 180

Preface

The book discusses PeopleSoft's *multi-currency* capabilities from the perspective of its General Ledger module. The book is divided into two parts. Part I discusses basic multi-currency topics such as currency codes, market rates, rounding, triangulation etc. Part II discusses advanced topics such as ledger re-valuations and translations.

The Book's Audience

This book is primarily addressed to two groups of users:

- Users who already use some multi-currency functionalities can take advantage of learning new functionalities that they may not currently use
- Users who are new to multi-currency processing can benefit by sequentially reading through the book and learning basic to advanced topics

All the examples and screen shots used in this book have been tested in PeopleSoft demo environment versions 9.0 and/or 9.1.

It is assumed that the readers have some prior knowledge of PeopleSoft General Ledger module.

Conventions used in this book

Throughout the book we have tried to use the following typographical convention:

- Most text is Arial, 10 pt
- User data entry values on PeopleSoft screens are in `courier new, 10 pt`
- Name of screens, field names, processes, reports etc are in *Arial Italics, 10 pt*
- Date references are in mm/dd/yyyy format
- This book employs the usage of a second-person voice. That is, you, the reader, will be frequently addressed and instructed what to do to simulate a classroom learning environment.

How to Contact us

We have tested and verified the concepts and examples used in this book to best of our ability, but you may still find mistakes. Please let us know about any errors you find, suggestions for future editions or technical questions you may have, by writing to anil.goel1@gmail.com.

Acknowledgments

We would like to thank William Brydges, Matt Habibi, Neena Goel, and John Hoebler for reviewing and providing valuable feedback. John also initially helped edit the book.

Part I

The Big Picture

This chapter summarizes the different components of Oracle's PeopleSoft which enable multi-currency processing. These components can be grouped into five main areas:

1. Currency Configuration: This has screens to maintain currencies. These include: *Currency Code, Currency Quotation Method, Currency Codes - Euro, Currency Denominations, Currency Code Report, Currency Exchange Calculator* etc.

2. Market Rates: Setup screens to capture currency exchange rates. These screens include: *Market Rate Index, Market Rate Type, Market Rate Definitions, Market Rates, plus Cross/Reciprocal Rate calc* etc.

3. Ledger Group: Use this screen to group detail ledger(s) into a *Ledger Group* and optionally choose to synchronize journal postings to all ledgers in the group. Each ledger in the ledger group can have its own base currency.

4. Currency Controls Configuration: The three screens in this area are: *General Ledger Definition* (i.e. GL business unit), *Ledgers For A Unit* and *Journal Source*. These screens allow you to configure the following currency controls: *Currency Balancing, Base Currency Adjustment, Foreign Currencies Per Journal, Translate Ledger Exchange Rate* and *Rounding Adjustment Option.*

5. Multi-Currency Transactions and Processes: The configurations from the previous four areas come together when you enter and post journals. The screens in this area allow you to configure and run ledger revaluation and translations on ledger balances. These multi-currency processes create adjustment journals. The screens include: *Journals*, *Sub system transactions*, *Ledger Translation*, *Ledger Revaluation*, and *Translation Within Ledger.*

The diagram below shows data flow between these five areas, and their interdependencies:

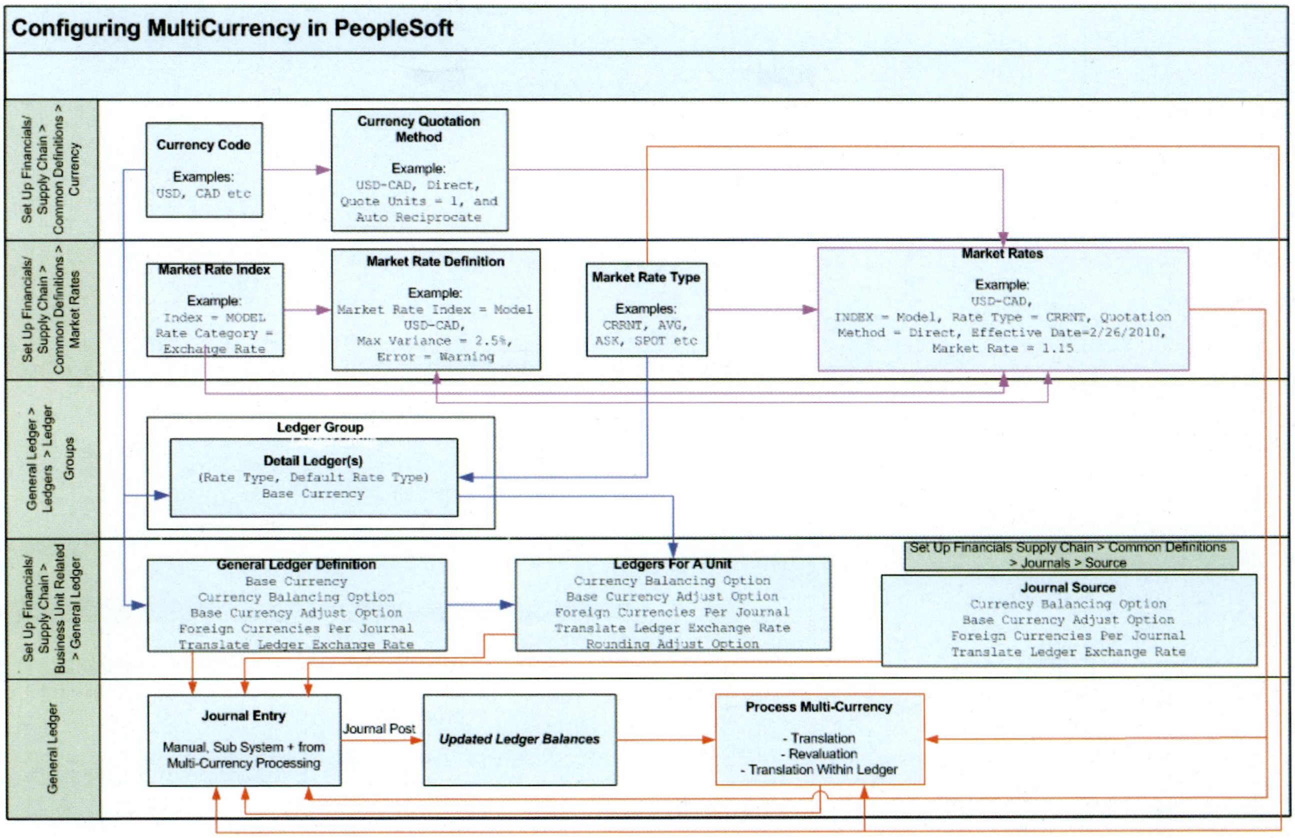

The individual functionalities are briefly discussed below.

#	Functionality	Description
1	Currency Code	Use this page to maintain currency codes (e.g. `USD, CAD, BRL, JPY, EUR, INR, AUD`). PeopleSoft uses CURRENCY_CD field to track individual currencies. Although not required by the system, it is a good practice to use International Standards Organization (ISO) currency codes. You can specify currency symbols, country, decimal position precision and scale positions. 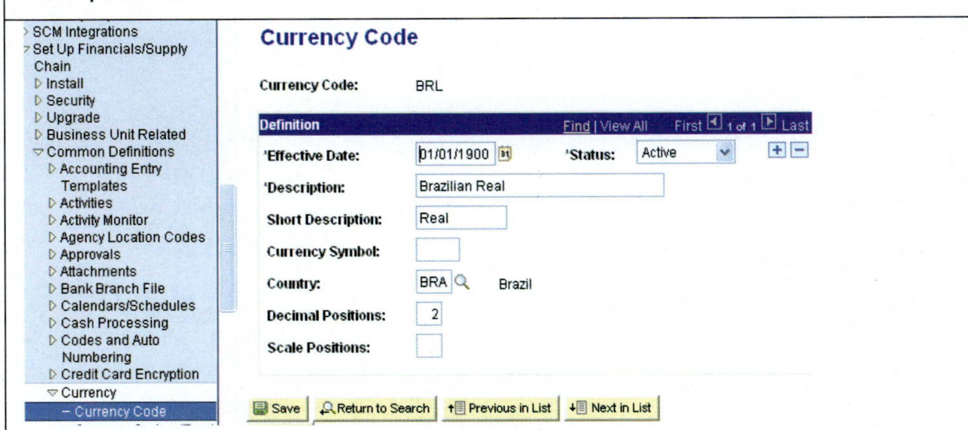

<table>
<tr><th>#</th><th>Functionality</th><th>Description</th></tr>
<tr><td>2</td><td>Currency Codes (Euro)</td><td>Allows you to maintain a Euro participating currency's status as active or inactive.
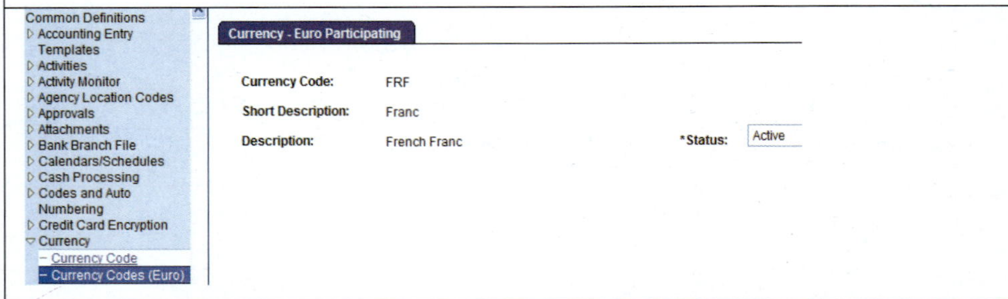
</td></tr>
<tr><td>3</td><td>Currency Quotation Method</td><td>PeopleSoft supports direct and indirect rate quotation, quote units, and triangulation.
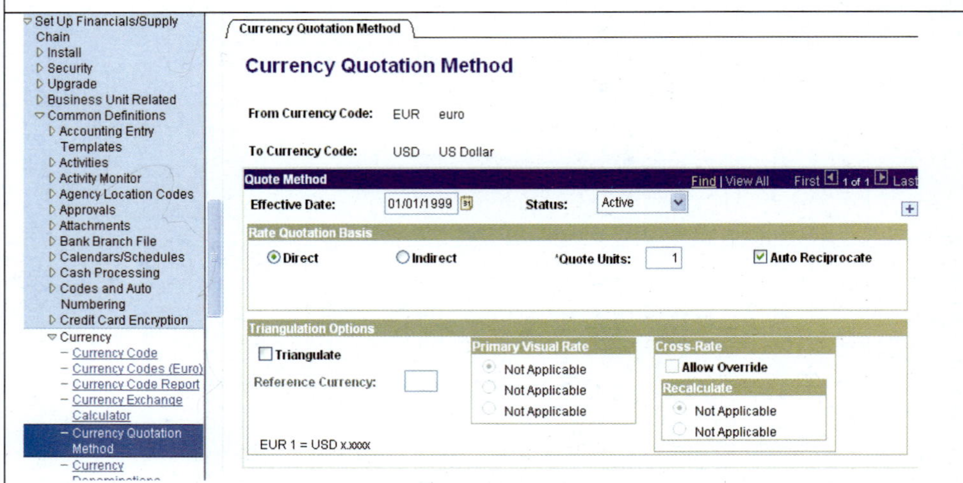
</td></tr>
<tr><td>4</td><td>Denominations</td><td>Describes currency amounts, usually for coins or banknotes, for example: $100 (one hundred dollars), $1 (one dollar), Quarter (twenty five cents), Penny (one cent) etc.
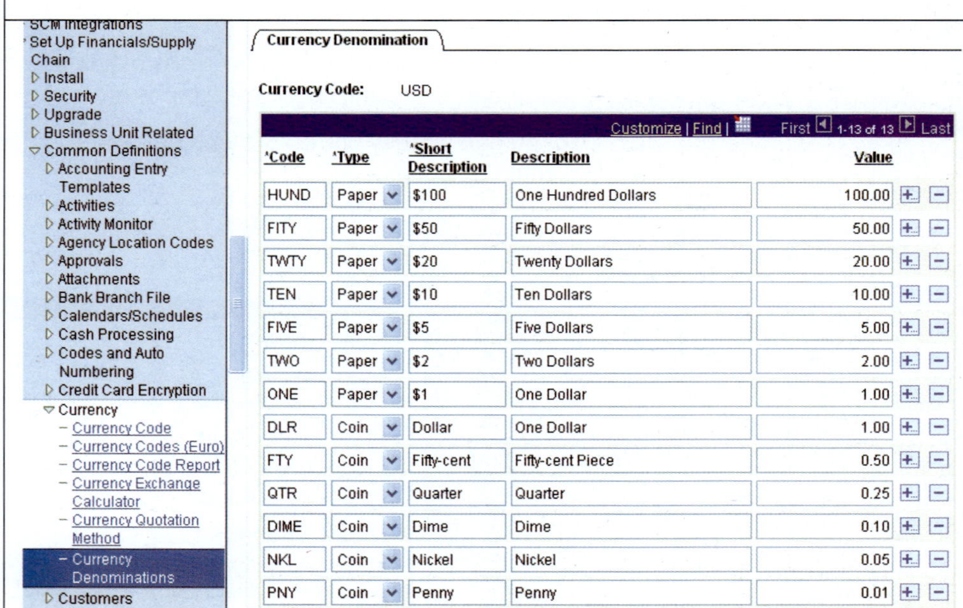
</td></tr>
</table>

<table>
<tr><th>#</th><th>Functionality</th><th>Description</th></tr>
<tr><td>5</td><td>Market Rate Definition</td><td>

Use this screen to define valid combinations of *Term*, *From Currency, To Currency* and other fields (depending on the rate category specified on the market rate index).

For example, the system will allow you to enter a rate (on the *Market Rate* page) using the combination *Term* = 30, *From Currency* = USD, and *To Currency* = CAD only if you first setup a *Market Rate Definition* of the same values. If you do not have a market rate definition already setup, the system will create a market rate definition using default values when you setup the market rate.

The *Maximum Variance* field specifies percentage variance allowed (default 2.5%) for manual overrides of system retrieved market rates. Depending upon the configuration, you get either an error or warning message (warning message by default) if the override exceeds the tolerance.

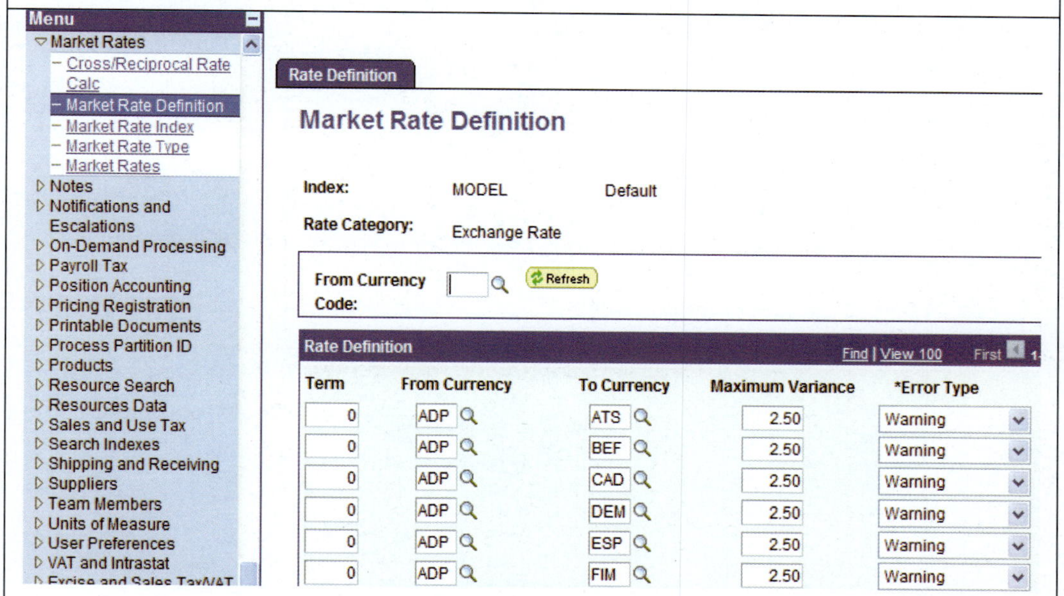

</td></tr>
</table>

<table>
<tr>
<td>6</td>
<td>Market Rate Index</td>
<td>
An index categorizes the various market rates that you track. Typical market rate indexes include LIBOR (London Interbank Offered Rate), BBFX (Bloomberg FX rates), RTFX (Reuters FX rates) exchange etc.

Use this screen to maintain the indexes for which you track rates. This screen also allows you to select a *Rate Category* (for an index) from the following list: `Commodity Price`, `Economic Indicator`, `Exchange Rate`, `Future Price`, `Interest Rate`, `Other`, `Stock Exchange Index`, or `Stock Price`. You can specify one index as the default for rate category of type `Exchange Rate`.

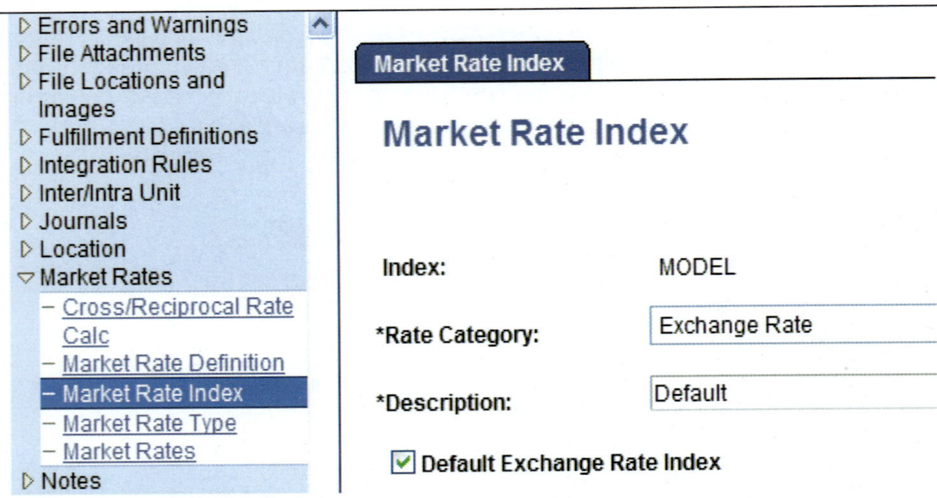

</td>
</tr>
<tr>
<td>7</td>
<td>Market Rate Type</td>
<td>
Use this to define market rate types (e.g. `AVG`, `BID`, `CRRNT`, `HIST`, `MID`, `SPOT`).

</td>
</tr>
</table>

<table>
<tr>
<td>8</td>
<td>Market Rates</td>
<td>Use this page to maintain market rates.
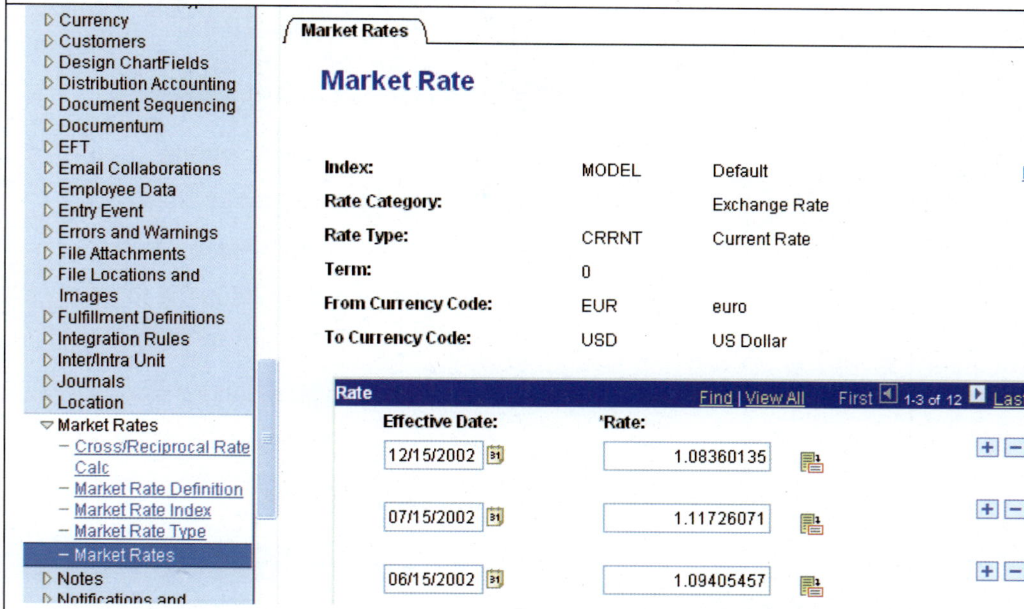

</td>
</tr>
<tr>
<td>9</td>
<td>Ledger Group (and multibook)</td>
<td>Allows a GL business unit to have multiple ledgers (books) each with their own base currency.

Configuration options in a ledger group are:
<ul>
<li>detail ledgers can inherit the base currency from the GL business unit or can have their own base currency</li>
<li>configure the system to post transactions to a selected detail ledger or all ledgers in the ledger group (in real time using Keep Ledgers in Sync option)</li>
<li>mark a detail ledger as a Translation ledger</li>
<li>Rate Type</li>
</ul>
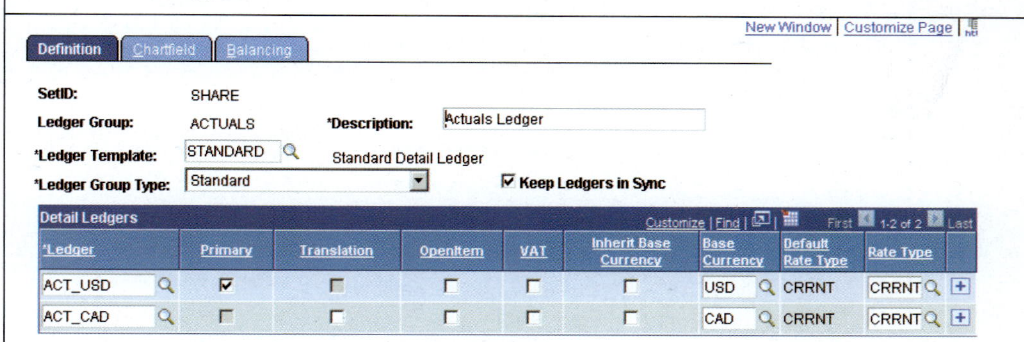

</td>
</tr>
</table>

<table>
<tr><td rowspan="4">10</td><td>Currency Controls</td><td>PeopleSoft allows you to configure the following currency controls in the General Ledger:
• Currency Balancing Options
• Base Currency Adjust Option
• Foreign Currencies Per Journal
• Translate Ledger Exchange Rate
• Rounding Adjustment Option
These controls can be configured on the following three screens:
• Journal Source
• Ledgers For A Unit (i.e. ledger groups attached to a GL business unit)
• General Ledger Definition (i.e. GL business unit)</td></tr>
<tr><td>General Ledger Definition</td><td>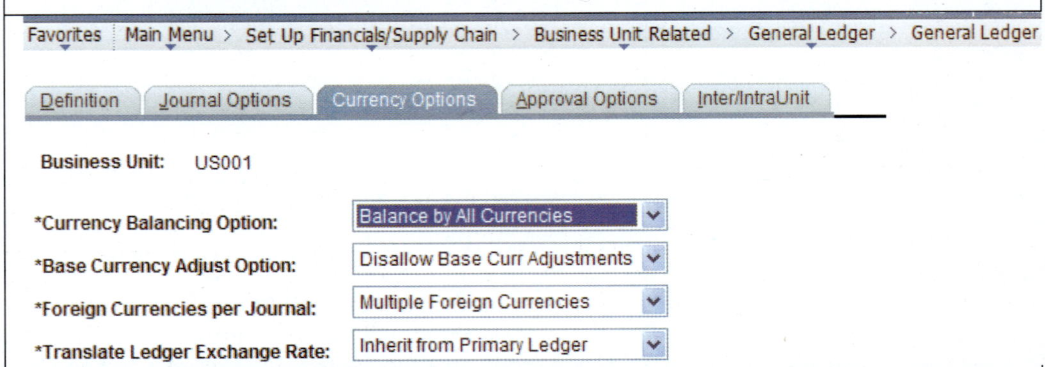
</td></tr>
<tr><td>Ledgers For A Unit</td><td>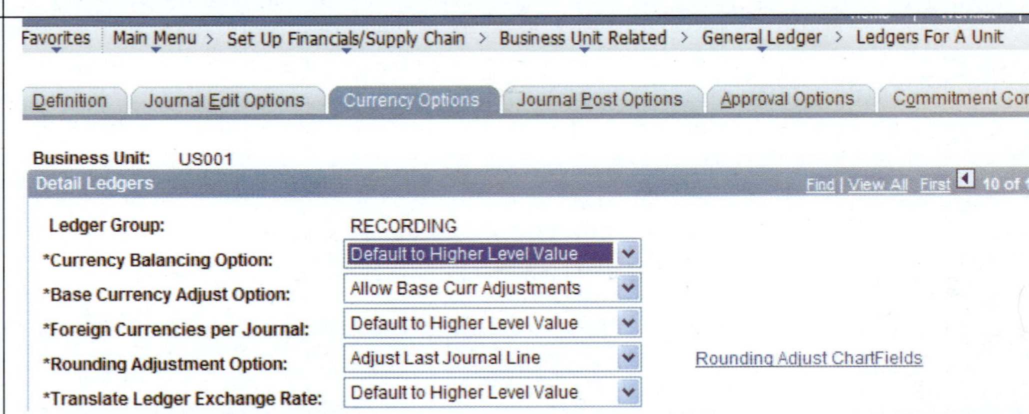
</td></tr>
<tr><td>Journal Source</td><td>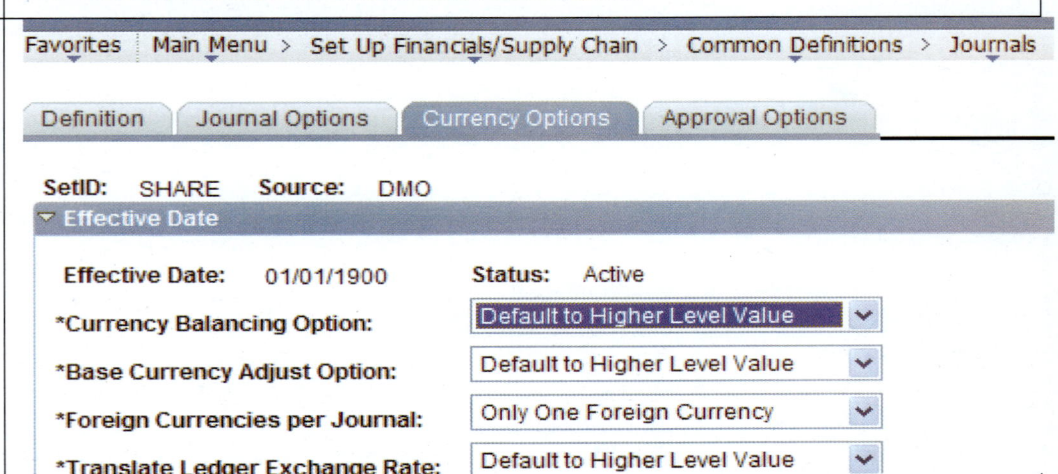
</td></tr>
</table>

<table>
<tr>
<td>11</td>
<td>Revaluation</td>
<td>The Revaluation process adjusts (by creating adjusting journal entries) the base currency ledger balances due to fluctuations in currency exchange rates. The system also creates corresponding entries for any gain or loss that results from the revaluation process.

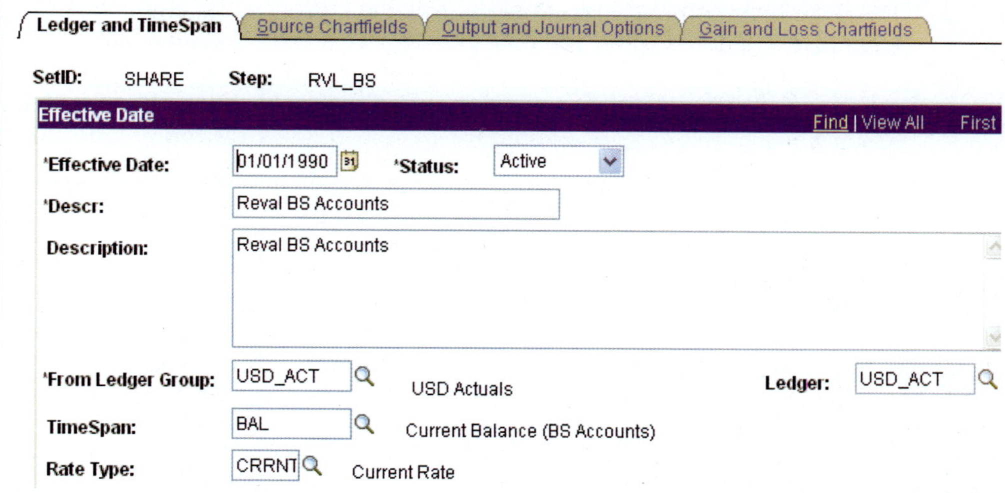

</td>
</tr>
<tr>
<td>12</td>
<td>Translation</td>
<td>Use the Translation batch process to translate ledger balances into a separate ledger with a different base currency. You can choose to run translation every night, every month-end depending or as needed by the business.

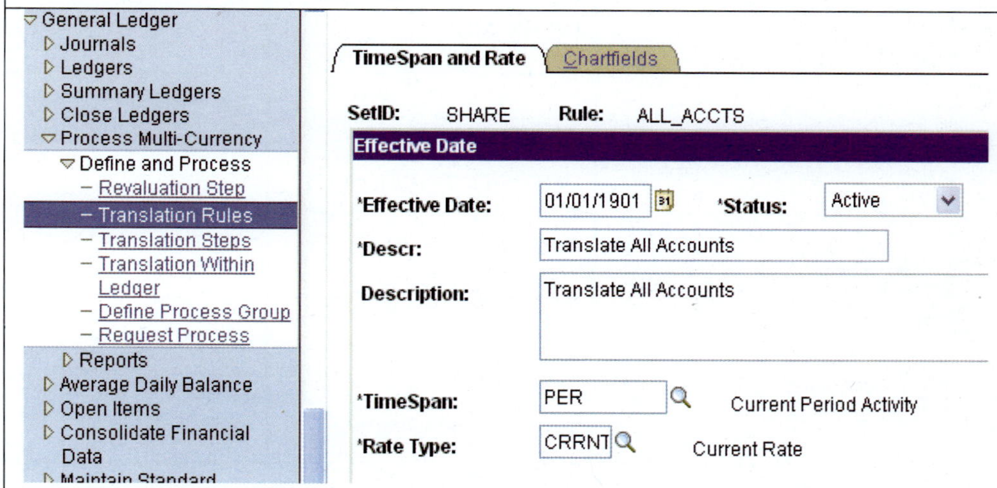

</td>
</tr>
<tr>
<td>13</td>
<td>Translation Within Ledger</td>
<td>The Translation Within Ledger batch process is used to revalue translation ledgers. This process works only for translation ledgers, whereas the Revaluation process works only for secondary ledgers in a ledger group.

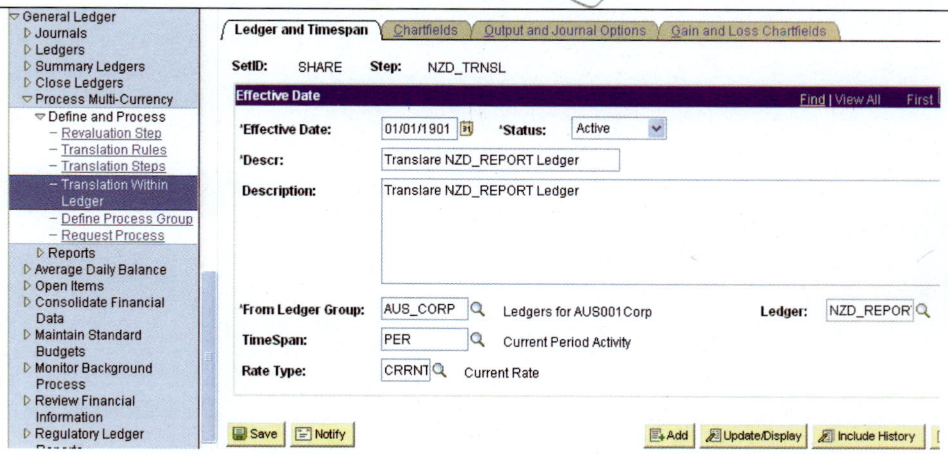

</td>
</tr>
</table>

The next nine chapters discuss each of these (and related) functionalities in detail. Each chapter uses examples to discuss the functionalities. In most of these examples you will enter journals to create test data.

The table below shows an example of how the currency and amount fields in the JRNL_LN and LEDGER records are updated when you post journals. This is discussed in detail in the next few chapters.

Record	Fields	Journal line with base cu rency amount (= 100 USD)	Journal line with foreign currency amount (= 200 CAD)	
JRNL_LN	CURRENCY_CD	USD	USD	
	MONETARY_AMOUNT	100.00	157.20	
	FOREIGN_CURRENCY	USD	CAD	
	FOREIGN_AMOUNT	100.00	200.00	
	RT_TYPE	CRRNT	CRRNT	
	RATE_DIV	1.00	1.27223090	
	RATE_MULT	1.00	1.00	
LEDGER			**CAD ledger row**	**USD ledger row**
	POSTED_TOTAL_AMT	100.00	200.00	157.20
	POSTED_BASE_AMT	100.00	157.20	0.00
	POSTED_TRAN_AMT	100.00	200.00	0.00
	CURRENCY_CD	USD	CAD	USD
	BASE_CURRENCY	USD	USD	USD

Market Rates and Journals

In this chapter we will discuss how foreign currency amounts, base currency amounts and currency exchange rates are calculated for foreign currency transactions.

By default, the journal date determines the market rate system will use. To gain a detailed understanding of this topic, follow the steps below:

#	Step	Step Description
1	review *Currency Quotation Method*	review *Currency Quotation Method* for EUR-USD
2	review *Market Rates*	review effective-dated market rates for USD-EUR conversion
3	enter journals	enter journals with different dates to confirm that the correct effective-dated market rates are used

1. Review Currency Quotation Method

    a. Navigate to *Set Up Financials/Supply Chain > Common Definitions > Currency > Currency Quotation Method*

    b. Review the following *Currency Quotation Method*:

    - `From Currency Code: EUR, To Currency Code: USD`
    - `Rate Quotation Basis: Direct, Auto Reciprocate: Checked`

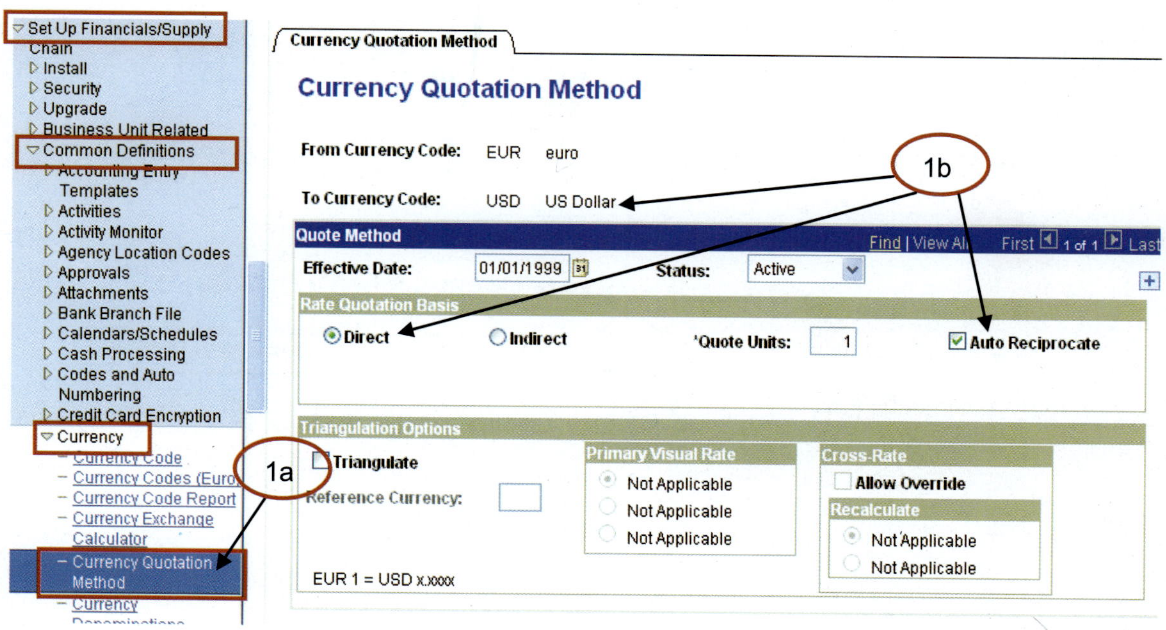

2. Review Market Rates

    a. Navigate to *Set Up Financials/Supply Chain > Common Definitions > Market Rates > Market Rates*

    b. Review the following market rates:

- Click *Include History* at the bottom of the screen (not shown)
- `Effective Date: 12/15/2002, Rate:1.08360135`
- `Effective Date: 07/15/2002, Rate:1.11726071`

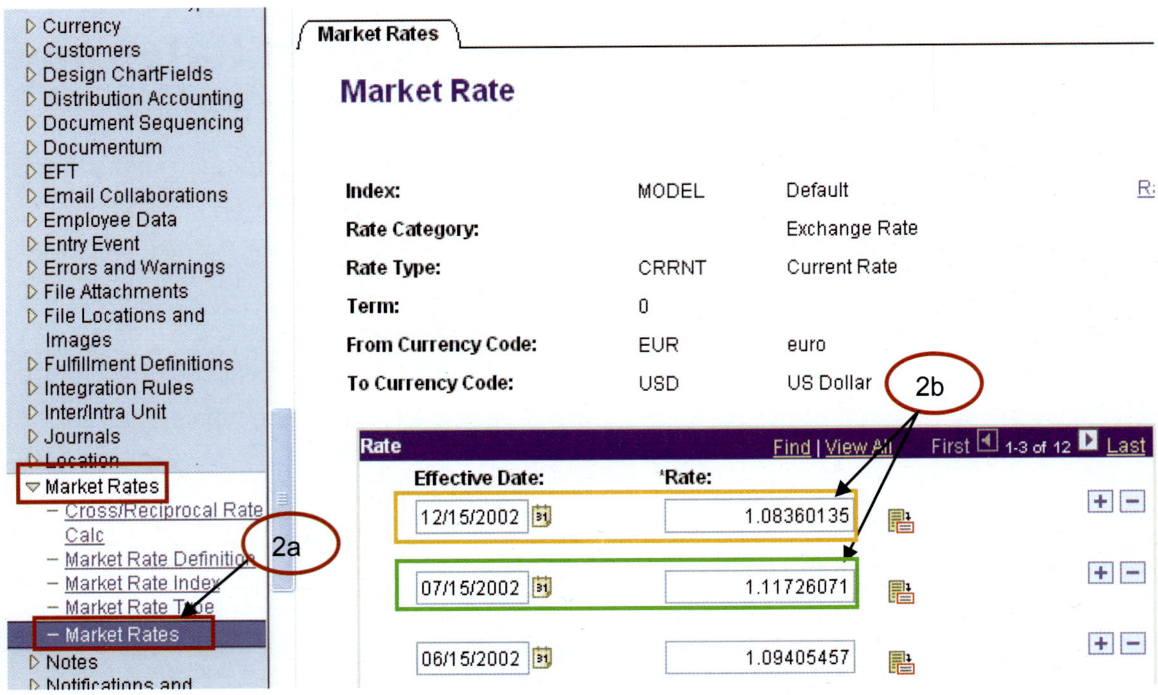

3. Enter Journals
   a. Navigate to *General Ledger > Journals > Journal Entry > Create/Update Journal Entries > Add a New Value*
   b. Specify the following values:
      - `Business Unit: US001`
      - `Journal ID: NEXT`
      - `Journal Date: 12/30/2002`
   c. Click on *Add*

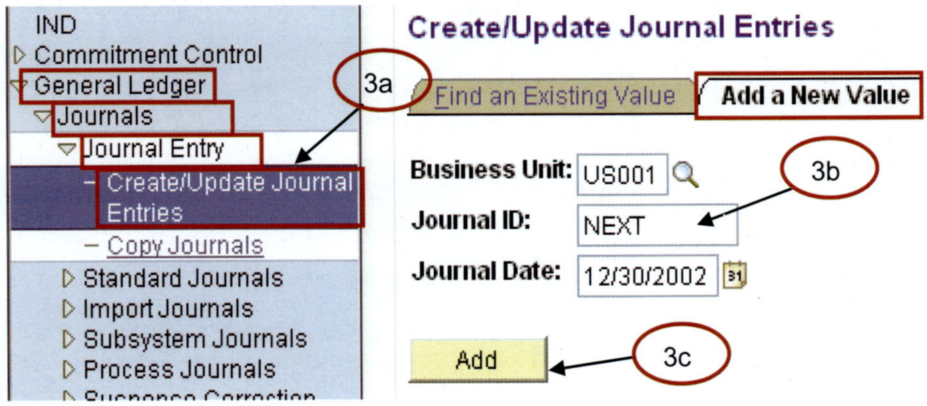

   d. Accept default values in the *Header* tab. You do not need to make additional changes.

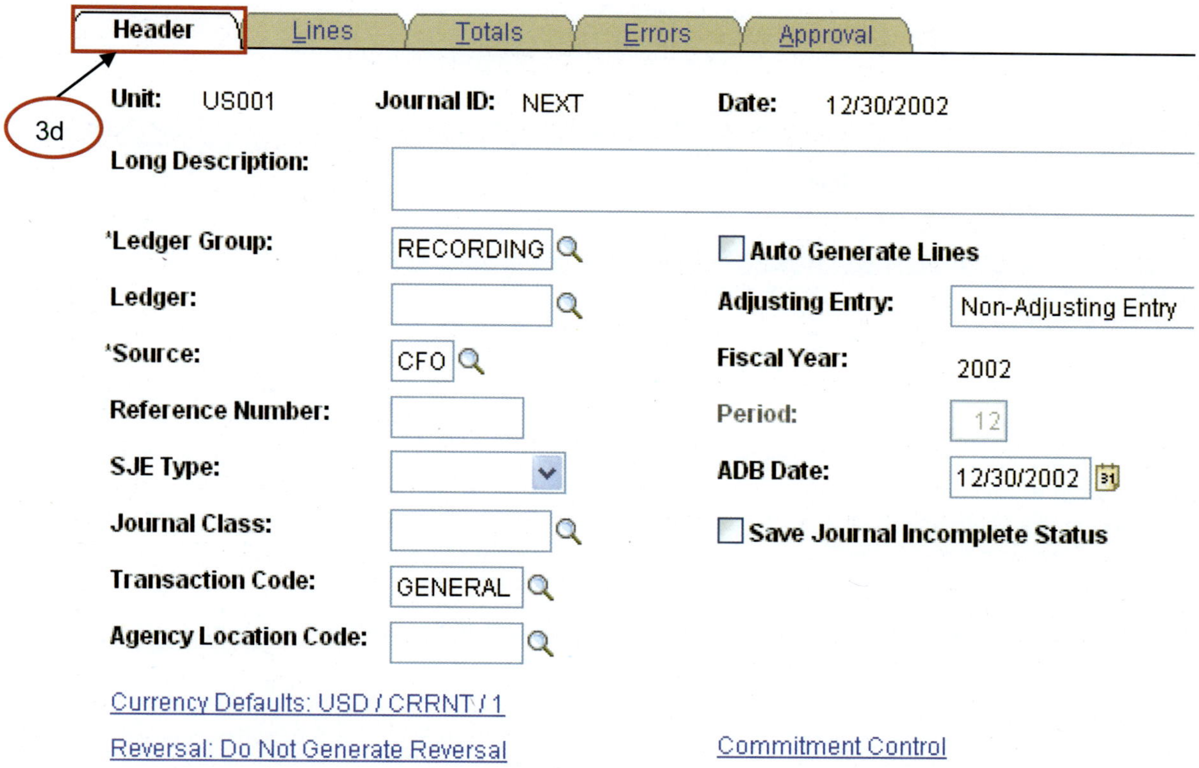

e. Click on the *Lines* tab and specify the following values for the first journal line:

- `Line 1: Account: 100000, Currency: EUR, Amount: 100`

f. Click on *Save*

For the journal date 12/30/2002, the system uses the market rate effective 12/15/2002 (i.e. the last active market rate equal or prior to the journal date).

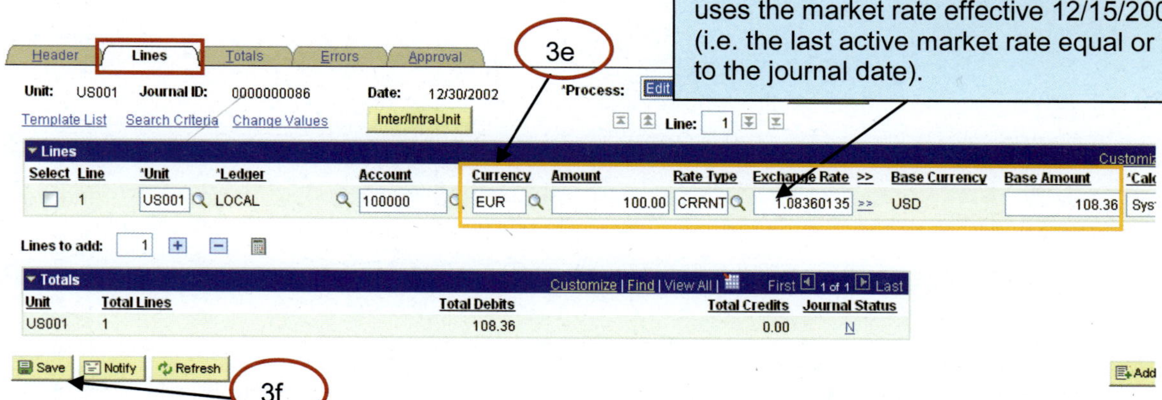

g. Enter a new journal using the following values, repeating steps 3a thru 3d:

- `Business Unit: US001`
- `Journal ID: NEXT`
- `Journal Date: 07/30/2002`
- `Line 1: Account=100000, Currency: EUR, Amount = 100`

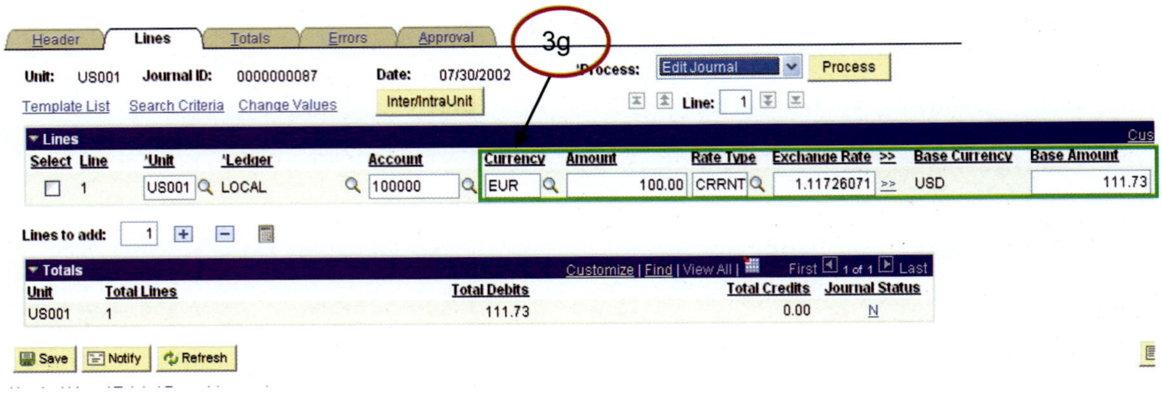

If the market rates change after entering a journal, the system gives the option to recalculate exchange rates. The system recalculates exchange rates for manual journal edits only if *Recalc Currency Exchange Rates* is checked in the *User Preference* screen. In the advent that journal edits are being performed as a batch process, *Recalc Exchange Rates* in the *Journal Edit* run control page takes precedence over *User Preference* configurations. This arrangement is tabulated below.

Manual Journal Edit	
Recalc Currency Exchange Rates in ***User Preference***	Exchange rate recalculated?
X	Y
--	N

Batch Journal Edit		
Recalc Currency Exchange Rates in ***User Preference***	*Recalc Exchange Rates* in ***Journal Edit***	Exchange rate recalculated?
X	**X**	Y
X	--	N
--	**X**	Y

To gain a detailed understanding of the topic follow the steps listed below:

#	Step	Step Description
1	review *User Preferences*	review *User Preferences* for user VP1; ensure that field *Recalc Currency Exchange Rates* is checked
2	setup a new user and configure *User Preferences*	create a new PS login called VP2; uncheck *Recalc Currency Exchange Rates*
3	enter journals	enter and edit journals
4	update *Market Rates*	update market rates for USD-EUR
5	re-edit journal	while logged in as VP1, re-edit the journal; confirm that the system recalculated the currency exchange rates
6	challenge exercises	
7	more on *Market Rates*	explore more *Market Rates* concepts

1. Review User Preferences
    a. Navigate to *Set Up Financials/Supply Chain* > *Common Definitions* > *User Preferences* > *Define User Preferences*
    b. Specify the following value:
        - `User ID: VP1`
    c. Click on *Search*
    d. Click on the *General Ledger* link
    e. Ensure that *Recalc Currency Exchange Rates* is checked

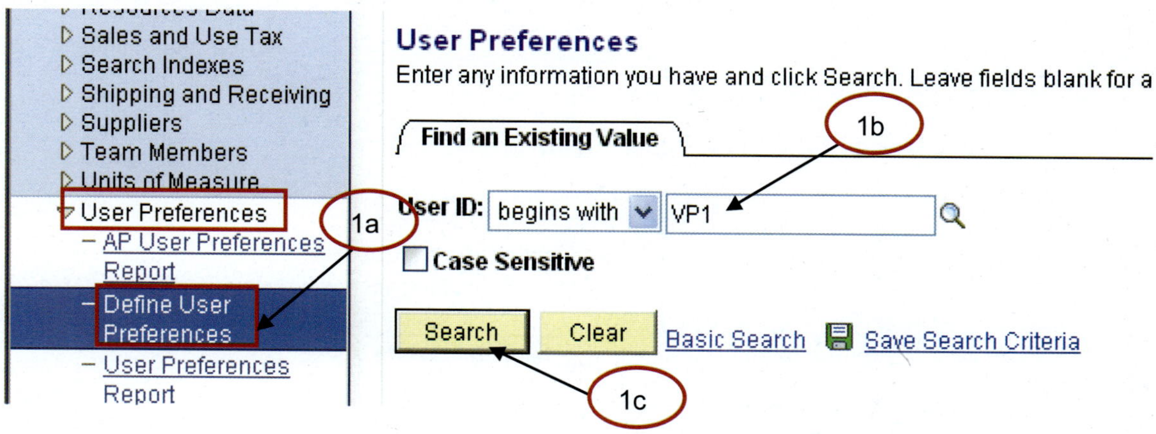

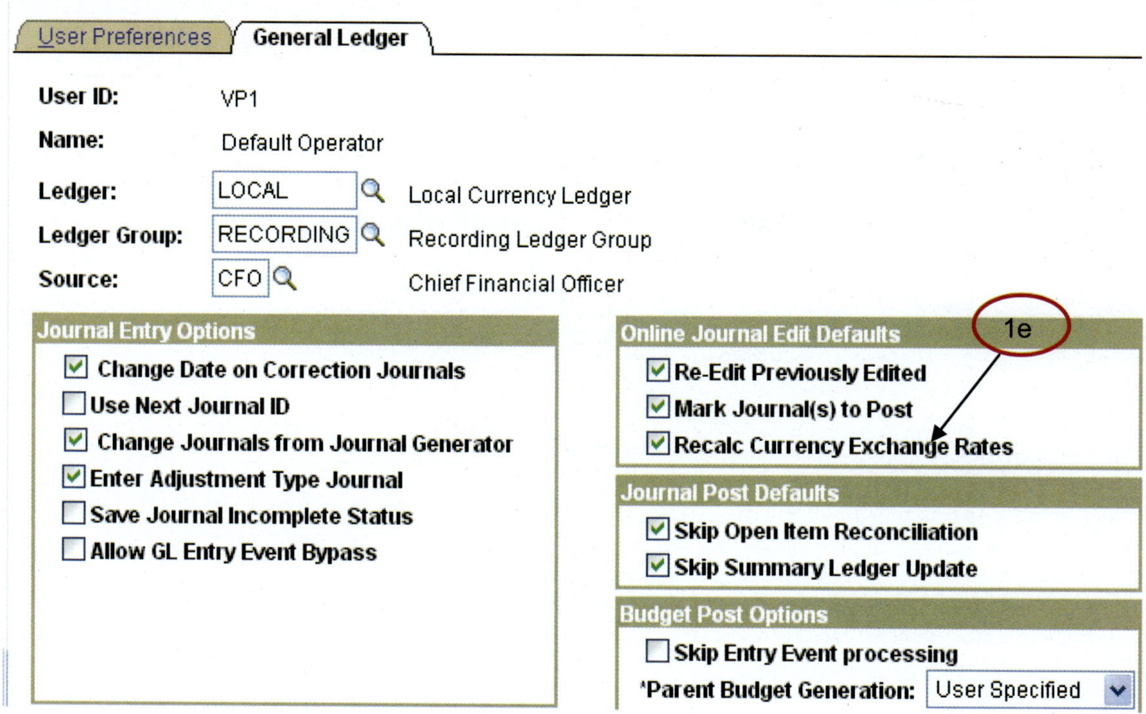

2. Setup a new user and configure his User Preferences
    a. Navigate to *PeopleTools > Security > Copy User Profile*
    b. Specify the following values:
        - `User ID: VP1`
    c. Click on *Search*
    d. On the *Copy User Profiles* screen specify the following values:
        - `New User ID: VP2`
        - `Description: VP2`
        - `New Password: VP2`
        - `Confirm Password: VP2`
    e. Click on *Save* at the bottom of the screen

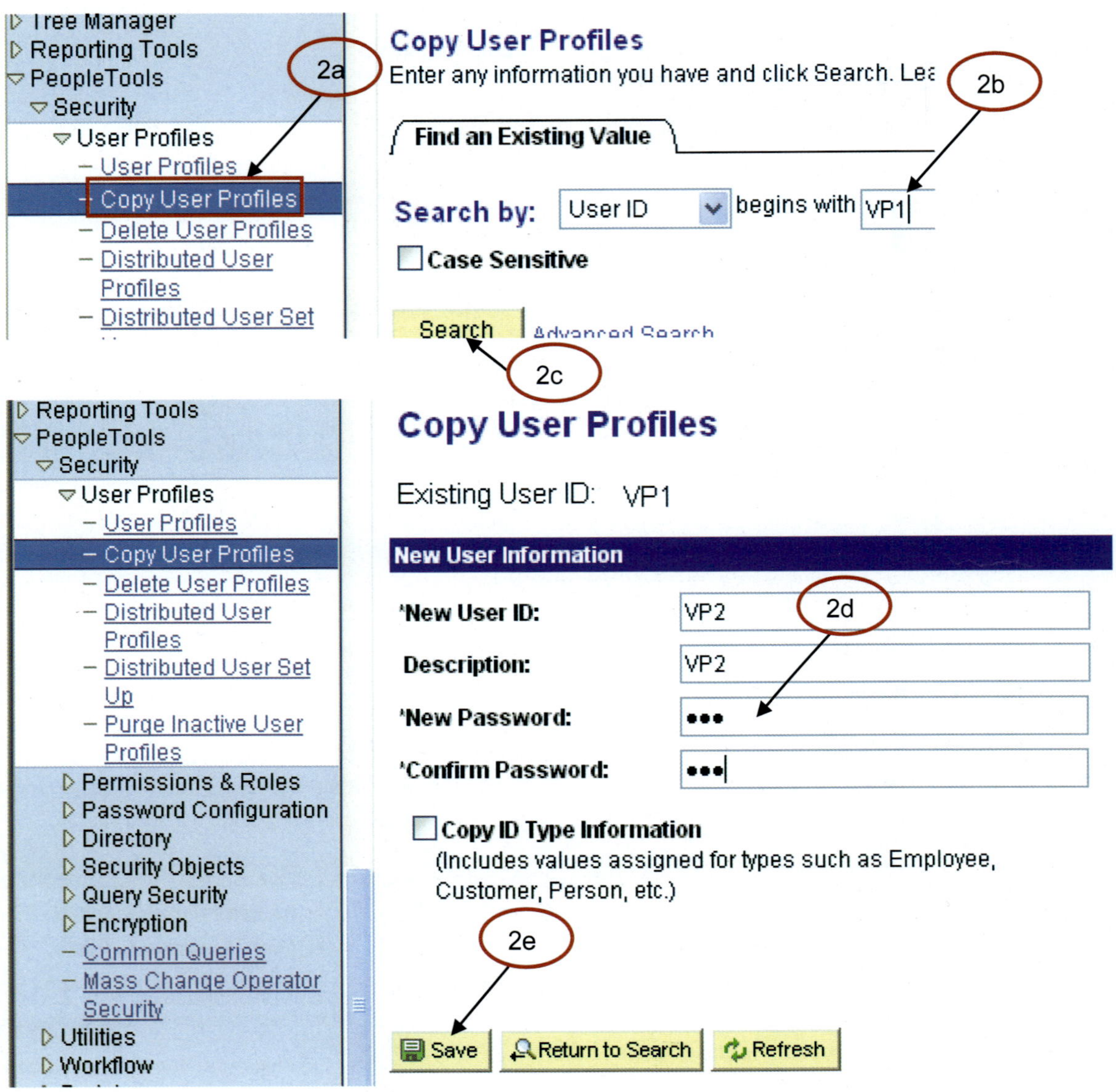

    f. Navigate to *Set Up Financials/Supply Chain > Common Definitions > User Preferences > Define User Preferences*

g. Specify the following value:
   - `User ID: VP2`
h. Click on *Search*
i. Click on the *Overall Preferences* link
j. Specify the following values:
   - `Name: VP2, Business Unit: US001, SetID: SHARE`
   - `As of Date: 01/01/1901, Localization Country: USA`
   - `Accept default values for other options`
k. Select the *User Preferences* tab and click on the *General Ledger* link
l. Specify the following values:
   - `Ledger: LOCAL, Ledger Group: RECORDING, Source: CFO`
   - `Recalc Currency Exchange Rates: Uncheck`
   - `Accept default values for other options`
m. Click on *Save* at the bottom of the screen

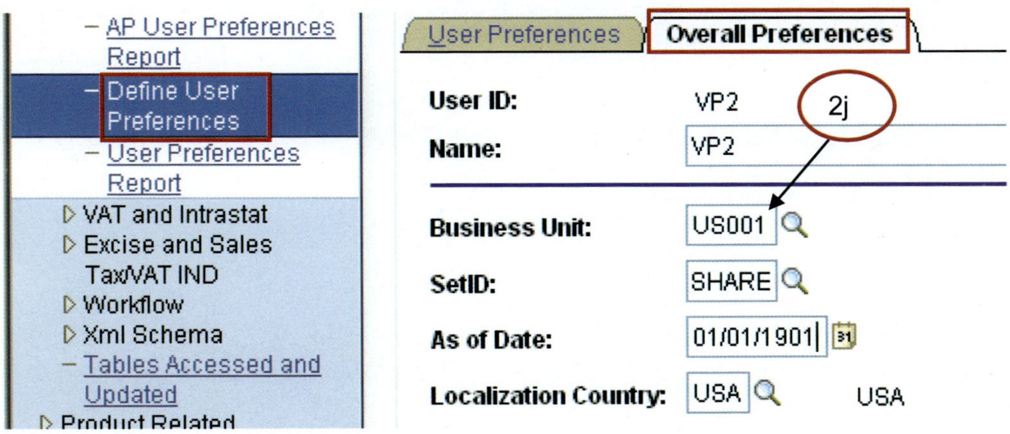

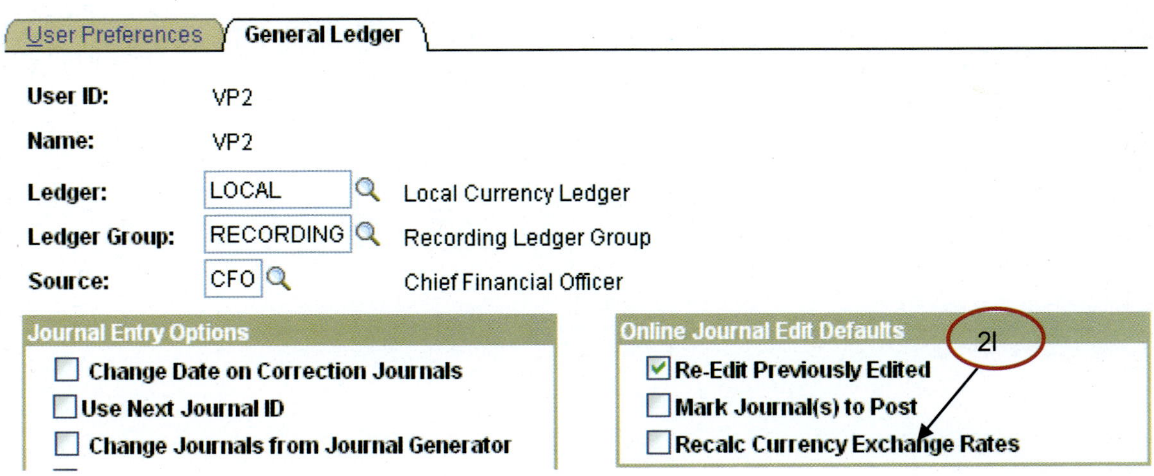

3. Enter Journals
   a. Navigate to *General Ledger > Journals > Journal Entry > Create/Update Journal Entries > Find An Existing Value*

b. Search for the journal added in step 3f in the previous section (*0000000086* in the screen shot below)

c. Use *Copy Journal* to create four new journals, each with the journal date 12/15/2002. One such journal is shown below.

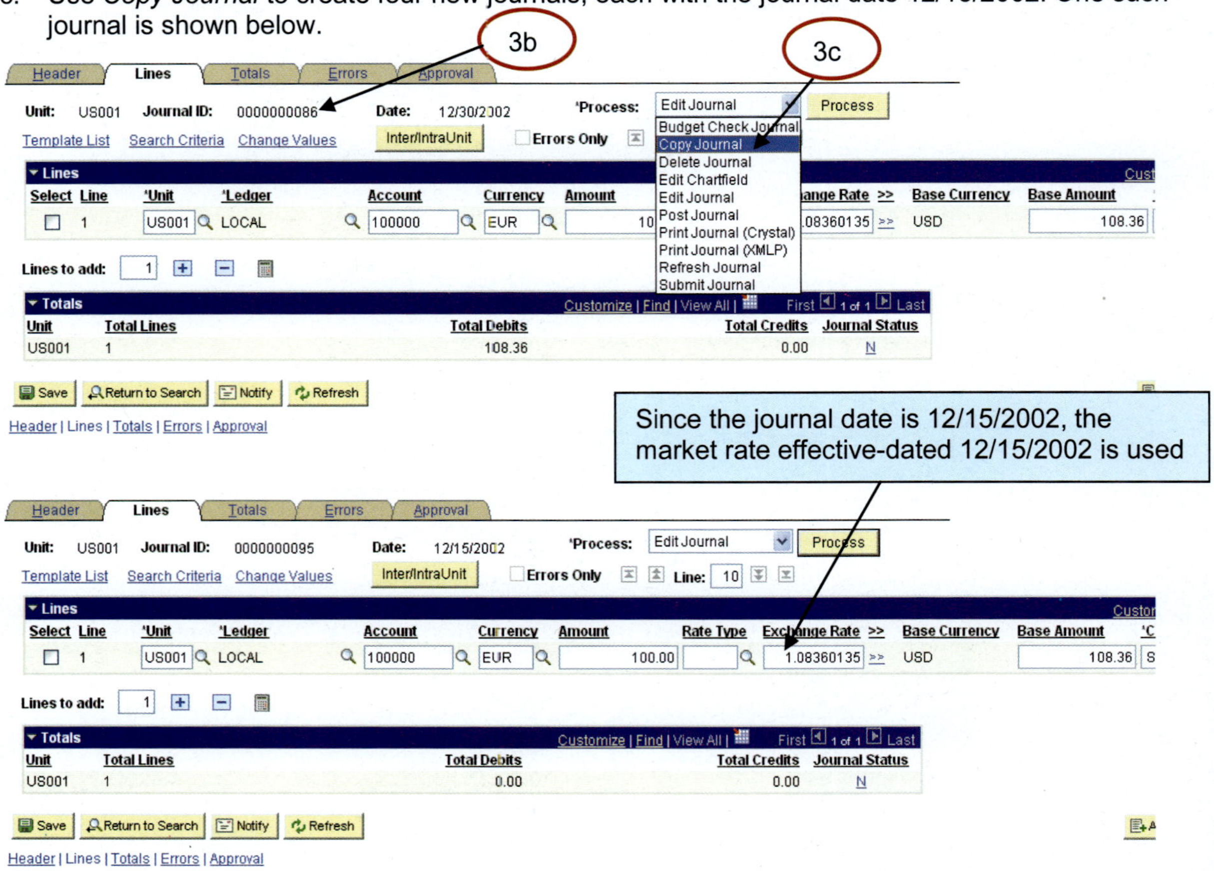

4. Update Market Rates

   a. Navigate to *Set Up Financials/Supply Chain* > *Common Definitions* > *Market Rates* > *Market Rates*

   b. Add a new market rate for USD-EUR for *Rate Type* `CRRNT`

      - `Effective Date: 12/30/2002, Rate:1.09120342`

   c. And update market rate for effective-date `12/15/2002` to `1.06`

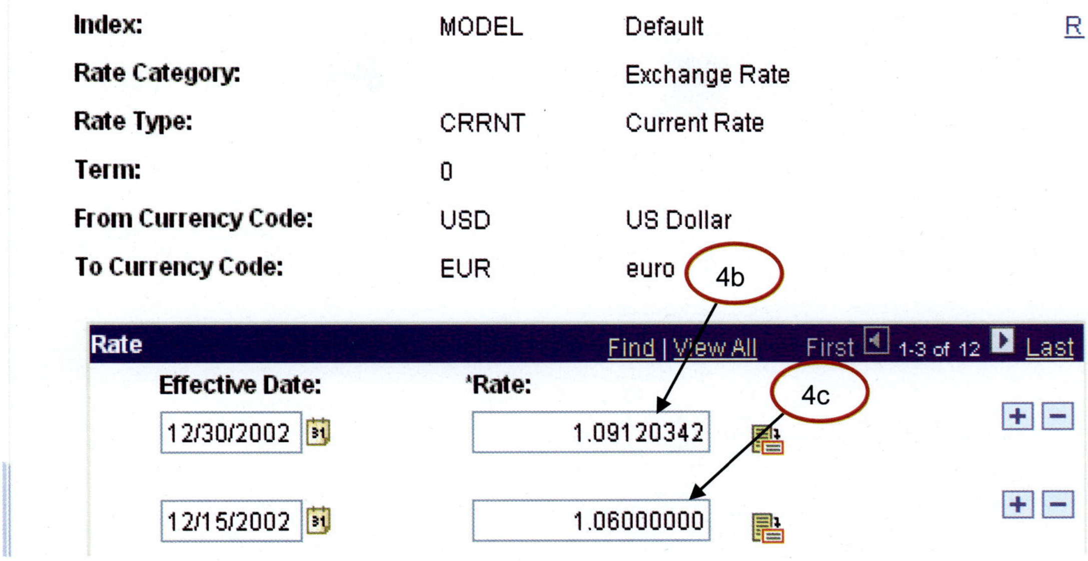

5. Re-Edit Journal
    a. Still logged in as VP1 navigate to: *General Ledger* > *Journals* > *Journal Entry* > *Create/Update Journal Entries* > *Find An Existing Value*
    b. Search for the journal created in step 3c for this section (*0000000095* in the screen shot below)
    c. Click on *Process* to re-edit the journal
    d. Note that the system recalculated the currency exchange rate using the updated rate of 1.06

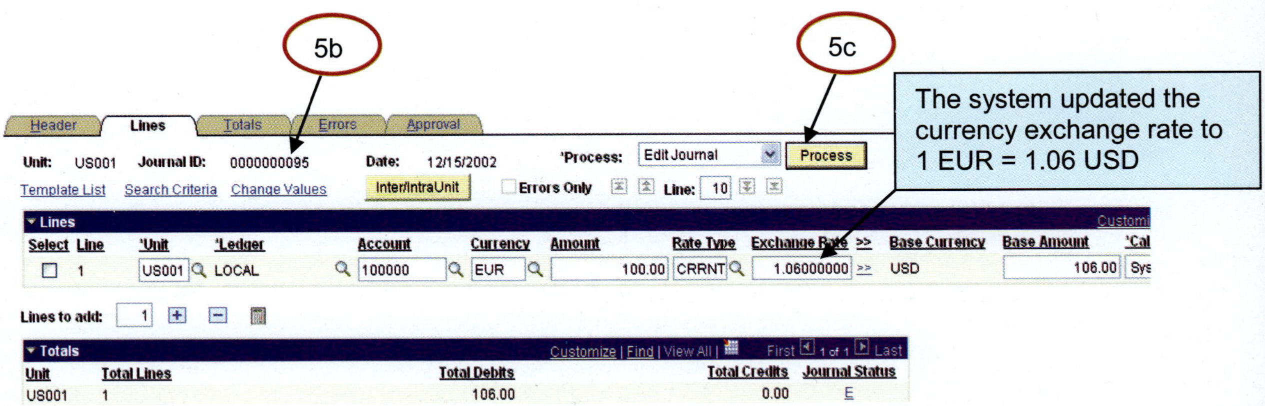

6. Challenge Exercises
    a. Log out. Log in as VP2/VP2
    b. Navigate to: *General Ledger* > *Journals* > *Journal Entry* > *Create/Update Journal Entries* > *Find An Existing Value*
    c. Search for one of the journal copied earlier in step 3c
    d. Click on *Process* to re-edit the journal
    e. Confirm that system did not recalculate currency exchange rate
    f. Navigate to *General Ledger* > *Journals* > *Process Journals* > *Edit Journals*
    g. Run the *Journal Edit* process for one of the journals added in step 3c. Ensure *Re-Edit* and *Recalc Exchange Rates* are both checked. See the screen shot below for details.
    h. Confirm that the system recalculated the currency exchange rate

i. Log out. Log in as VP1/VP1

j. Navigate to *General Ledger* > *Journals* > *Process Journals* > *Edit Journals*

k. Run the *Journal Edit* process for another journal added in step 3c. Ensure *Re-Edit* and *Recalc Exchange Rates* are both unchecked.

l. Confirm that the system did not recalculate the currency exchange rate

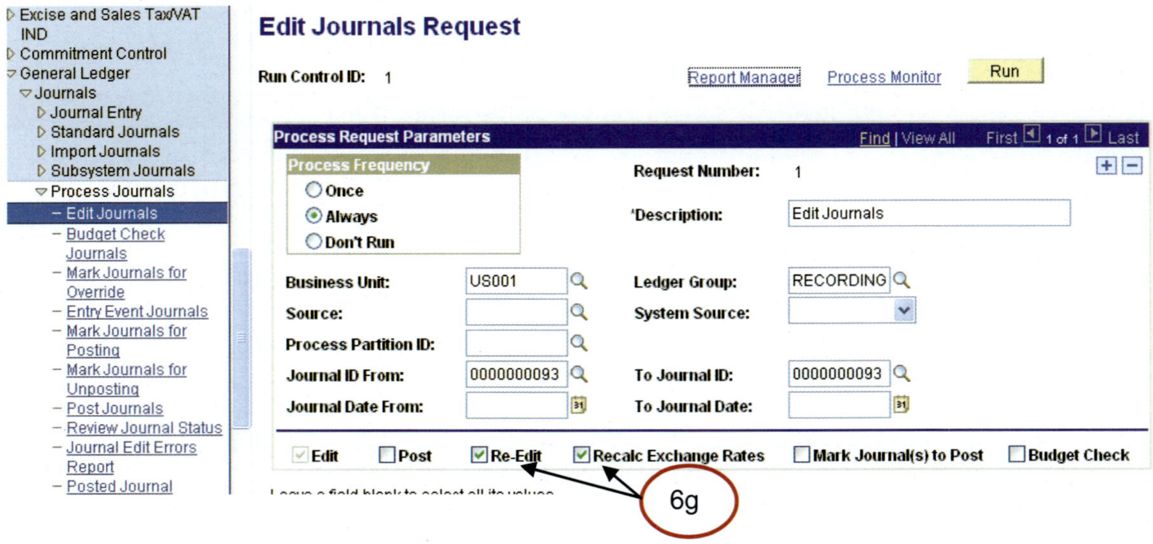

7. More on Market Rates

In the examples above, the system cannot retrieve the exchange rates if any of the below four values are missing:

- *From Currency* (e.g. EUR)
- *To Currency* (e.g. USD)
- *Rate Type* (e.g. CRRNT)
- *Currency Effective-Date* (e.g. 12/15/2002)

Hence how does the system retrieve the exchange rates when one or more of the values are missing? Or if the market rate is not setup at all?

If there is no market rate defined for the transaction currency, the system retrieves an exchange rate of zero, and a warning message is issued. In the example below, the market rate is not setup for USD-AMD, resulting in a zero currency exchange rate on the journal line.

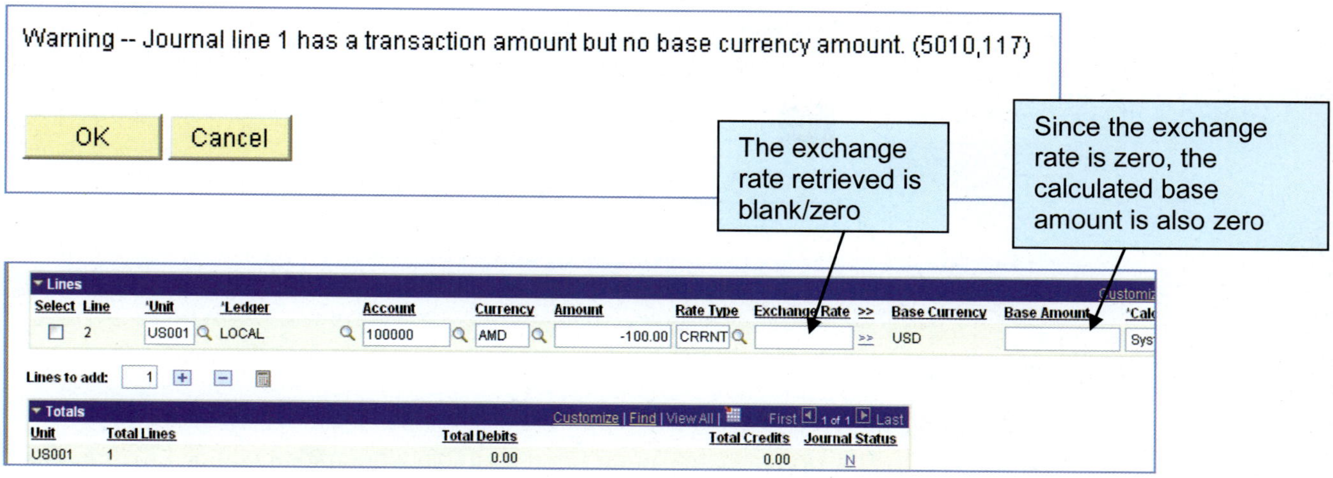

If there is no *Rate Type* specified on the line, the exchange rate is set to zero. Refer to the screenshot below:

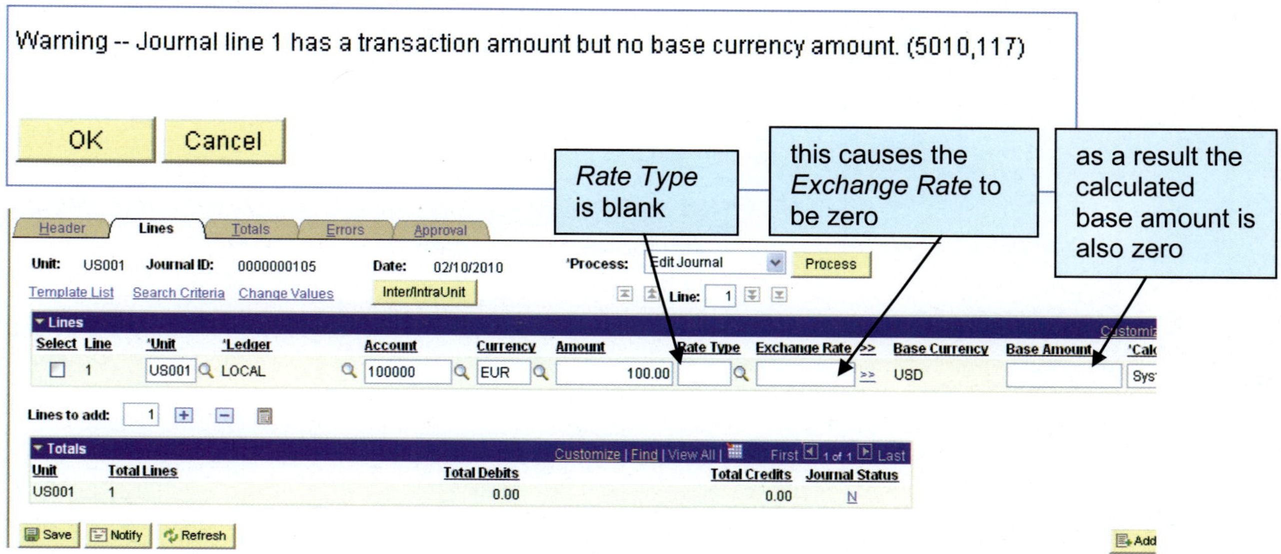

You can manually override system-generated exchange rates. In doing so the system blanks out the *Rate Type* field. However, based on the following two tests, the system may not accept the manually-entered rates:

- You cannot enter a manual rate if all three of the following options are selected on the *Currency Quotation Method* page: *Triangulation, Cross Rate as the Primary Visual Rate,* and *Do Not Allow Cross Rate Override*. If you try to enter a manual rate, the system generates an error message appears and ignores the entered manual rate.
- Either a stop-error or warning-message is generated if the difference between the system-generated rate and manual rate exceeds the tolerance defined in the *Rate Definition page* (see screen shot below). A warning-message is informational only, but for a stop-error you must change the manual rate as to not exceed the *Maximum Variance* to continue.

In the example below, note that EUR-USD has a *Maximum Variance* of 2.5.

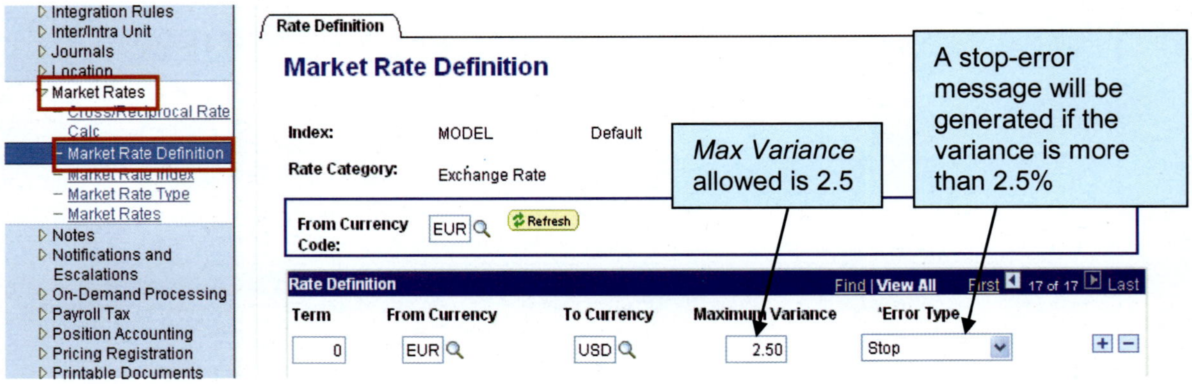

The system generates a stop-error message when overriding the market rate of 1.07 (for effective date 12/10/2010) with 1.25, as this value exceeds the *Max Variance* allowed (1.07 X 1.025 = 1.09675).

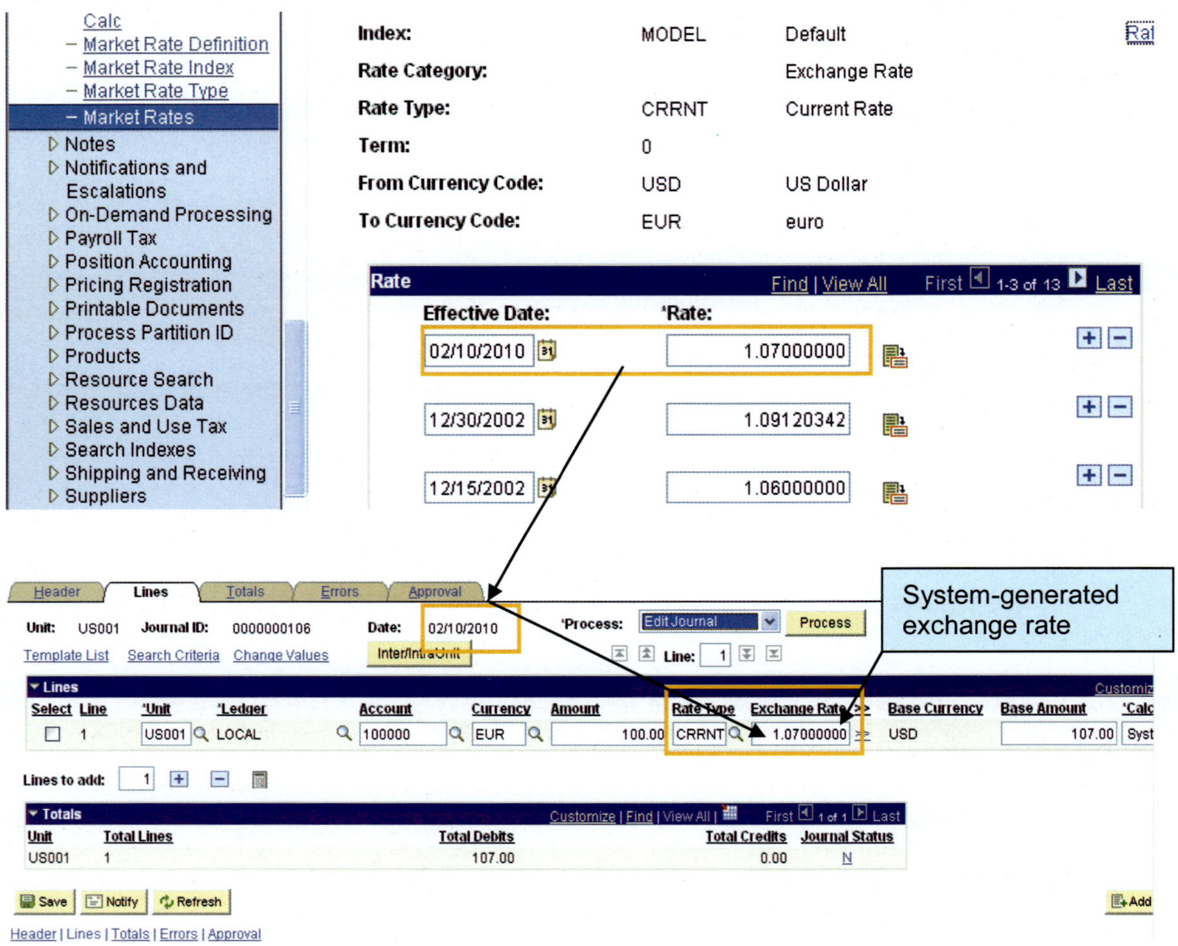

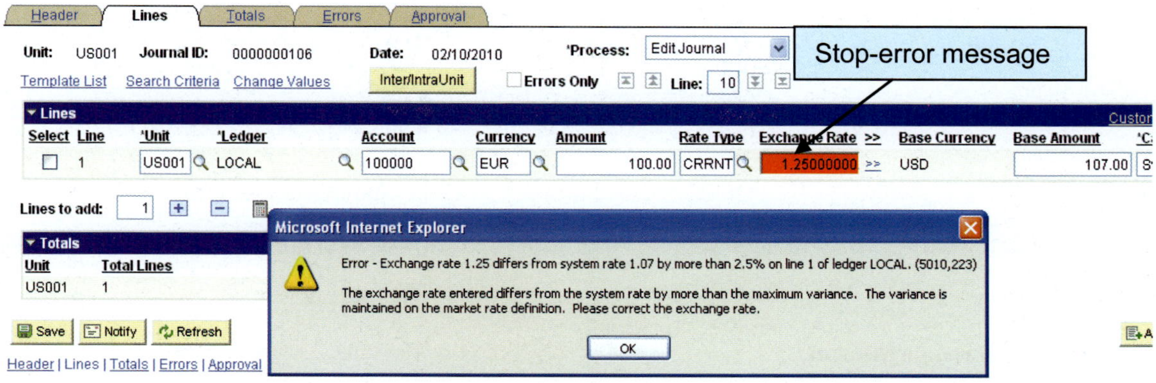

Regardless of any manual overrides for the market rate, the system must be able to retrieve a *rate type* in order to establish the system rate (for variance checking). The system uses the following hierarchy to retrieve the rate type:

1) The rate type specified on the journal line

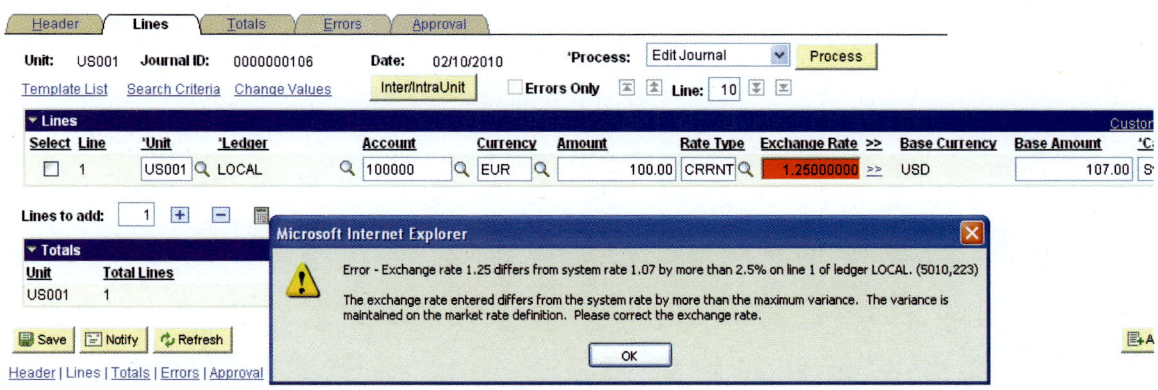

2) If the rate type on the journal line is blank use the rate type from the journal header

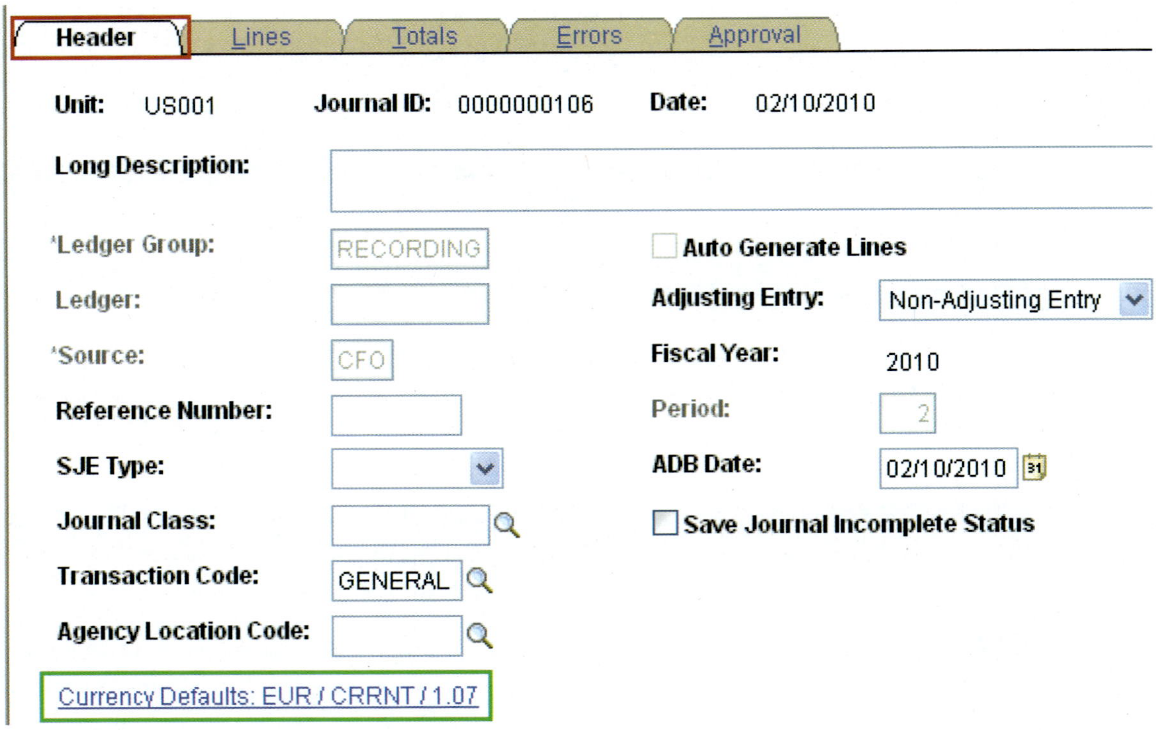

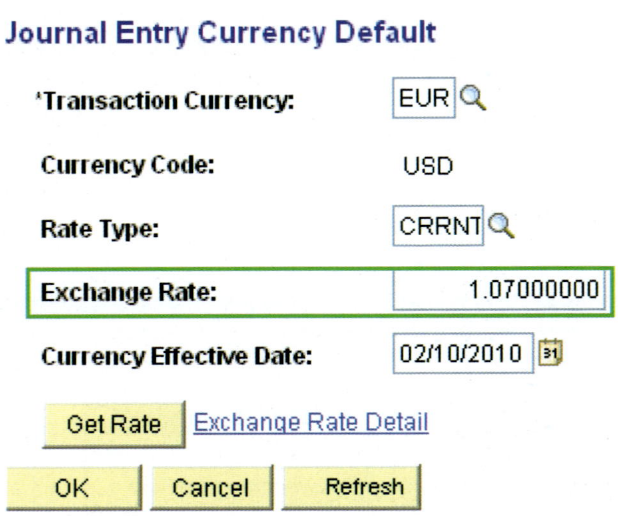

The rate type on journal line is blank; therefore, the system uses the rate type from the journal header.

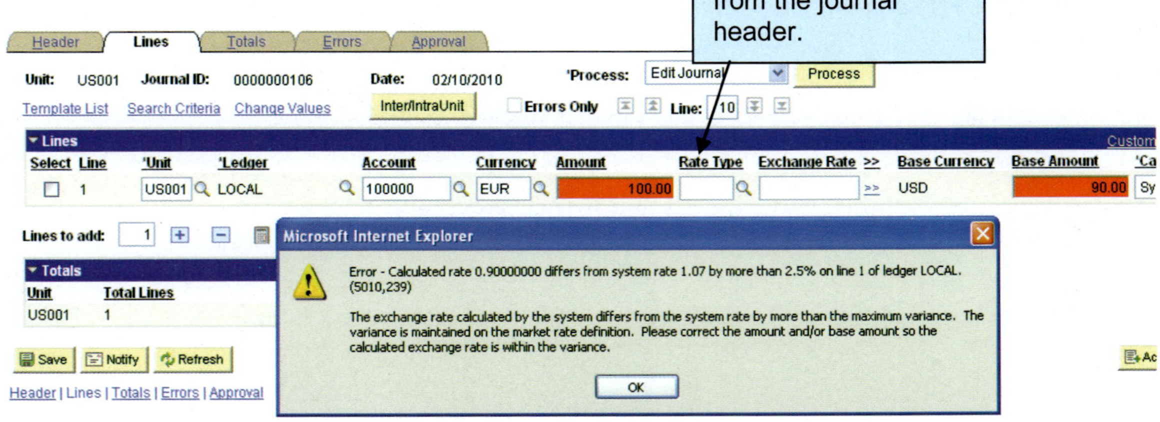

3) If the rate type is blank on the journal line and header, use the rate type specified for the ledger in its ledger group.

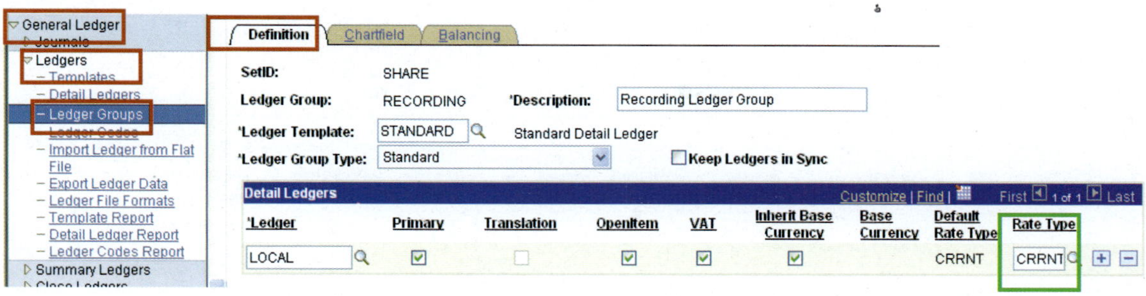

4) Use the *Default Rate Type* if the *Rate Type* fields are blank in the ledger group, journal header, and journal line.

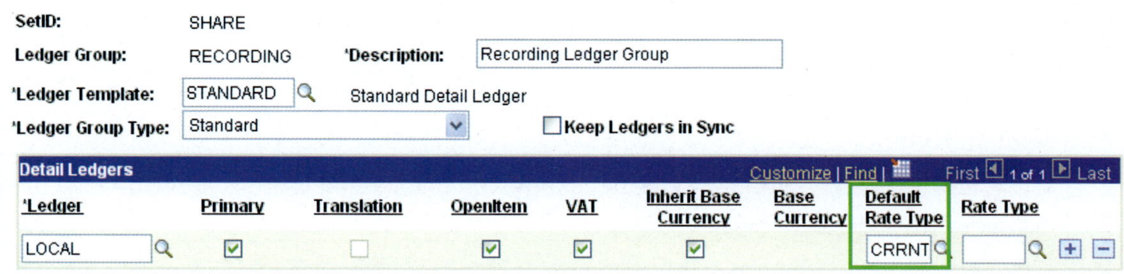

Calculation Rules: The *Calculate Rules* field in the journal entry page determines how the following three fields are calculated:

- Foreign Amount
- Exchange Rate
- Base Amount

System Rule is the default *Calculation Rule*. If the values generated by *System Rule* are undesired and need frequent manual changes, you can instead use other calculation rules.

The *Calculation Rules* and their subsequent actions are as follows:

Calculate Rule	**Fields on the journal entry page**		
	Exchange Rate	***Foreign Amount***	***Base Amount***
Amount	User specified	System Calculated	User specified
Base Amount	User specified	User specified	System Calculated
Exchange Rate	System Calculated	User specified	User specified

The screen shot below illustrates examples for the above three calculate rules. Note that when the user enters values for any two fields, the system calculates the missing third field.

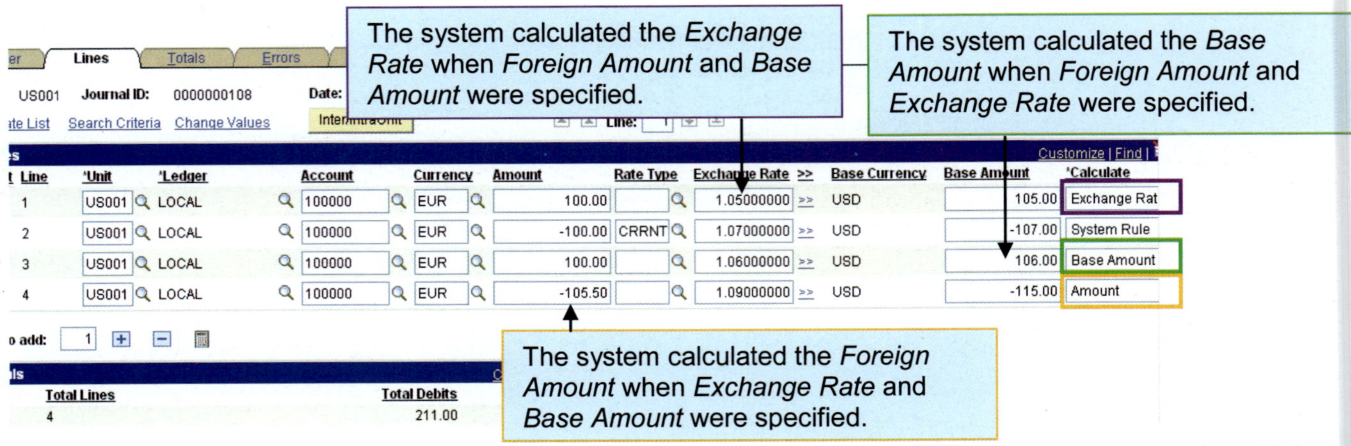

System Rule:

1. When two of the three field values change, the unchanged value is subsequently recalcula

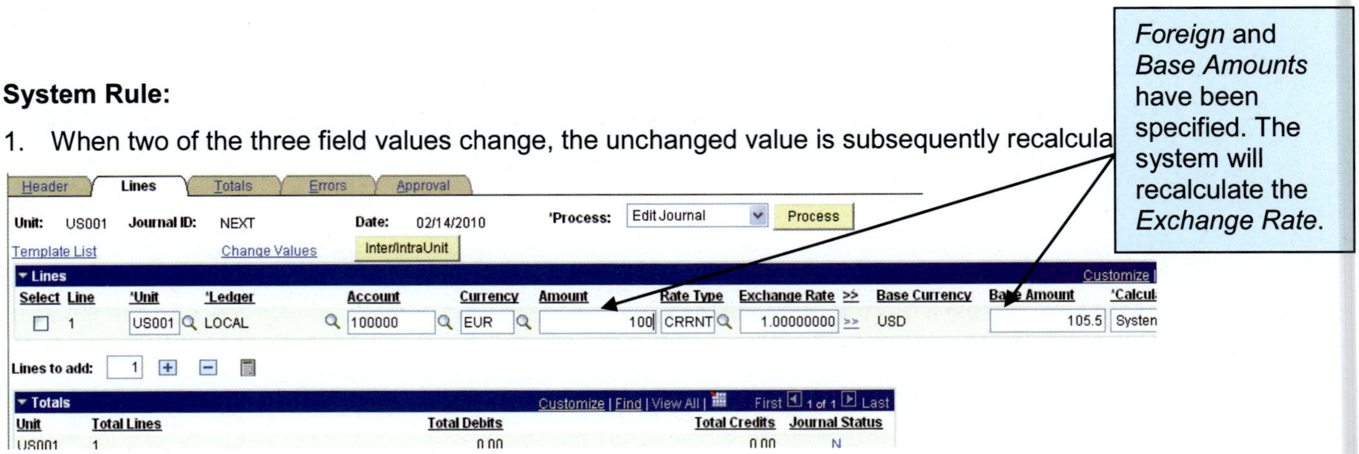

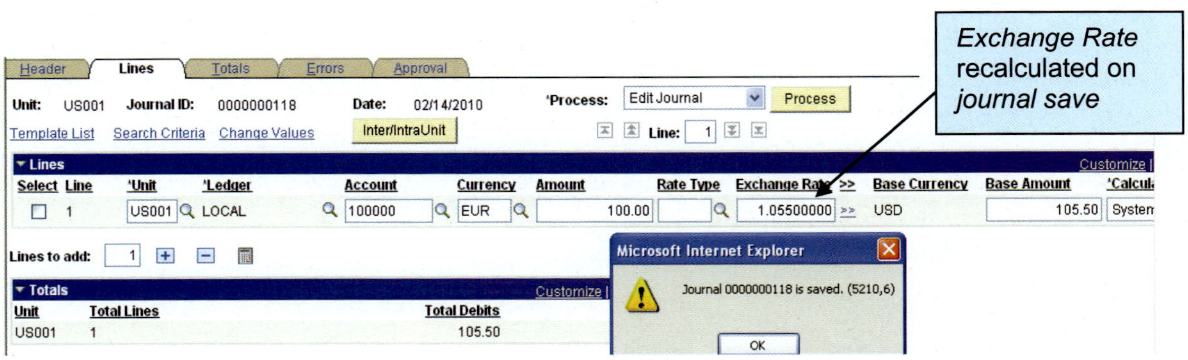

2. When the *Exchange Rate* is populated, the system recalculates the *Base Amount* whenever the *Foreign Amount* is changed.

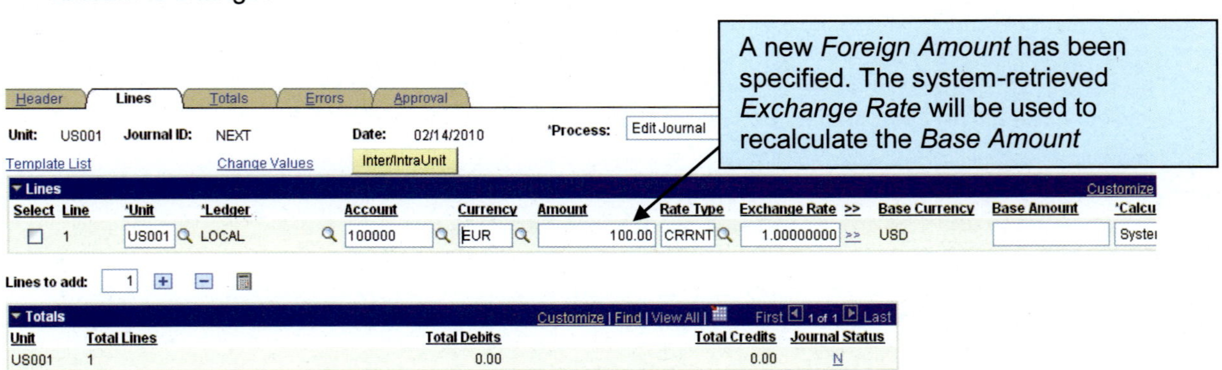

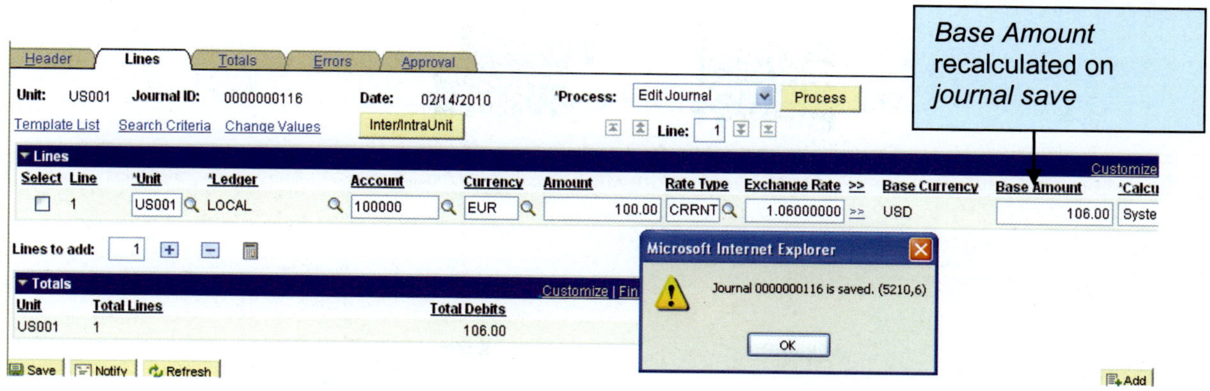

3. When the *Exchange Rate* is populated, the system recalculates the *Foreign Amount* whenever the Base *Amount* is changed.

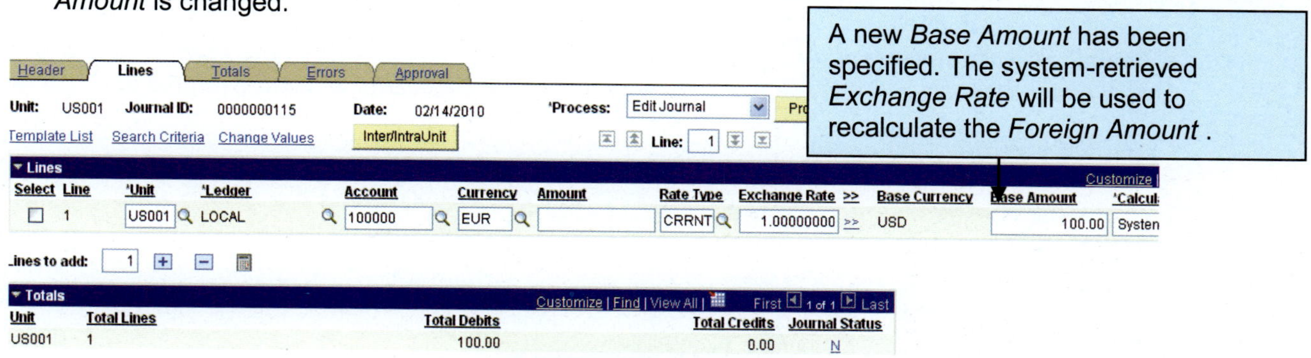

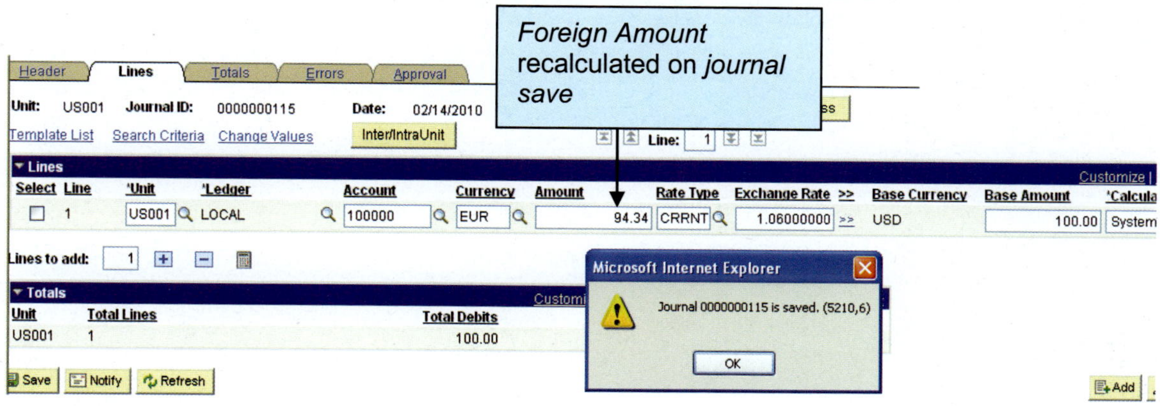

4. When the *Foreign Amount* is non-zero, the system recalculates the *Base Amount* whenever the Exchange Rate is changed.

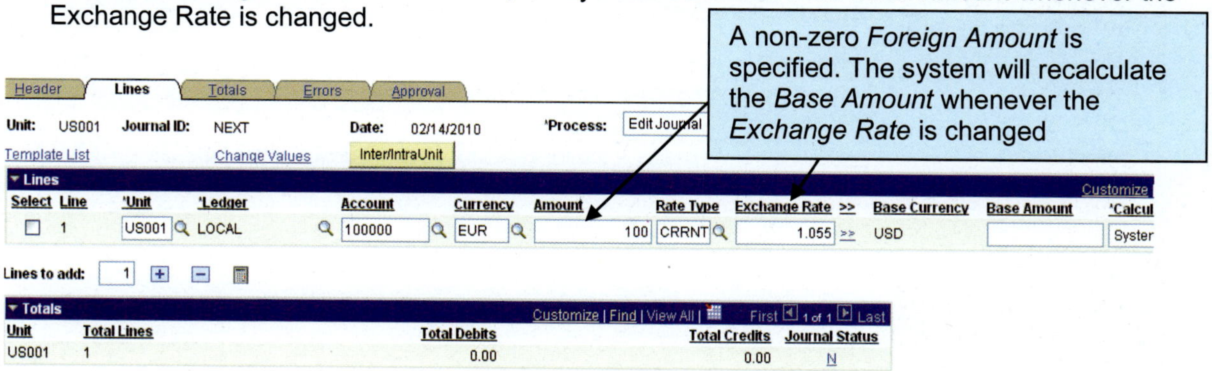

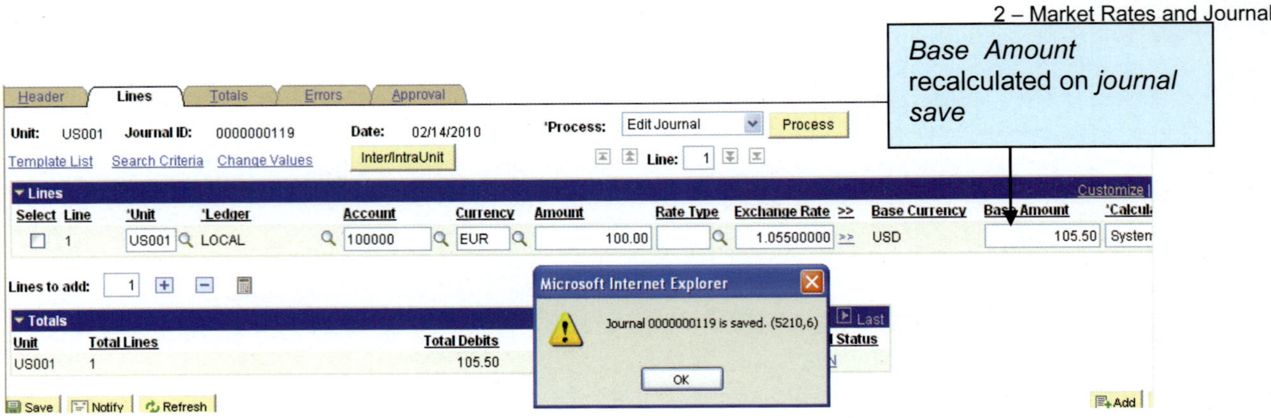

5. The system allows manual overrides of all three fields as long as the values are valid. If any one of the three entered values is zero, the system will automatically calculate its value.

Note that, you can use the *Journal Entry Template* (accessed by *Set Up Financials/Supply Chain* > *Common Definitions* > *Journals* > *Entry Template)* to hide/unhide the *Calculate* field in the journal entry page.

In the example below for `Template Type: All Users` and `Template ID: STANDARD` the *Calculate* field has been unchecked.

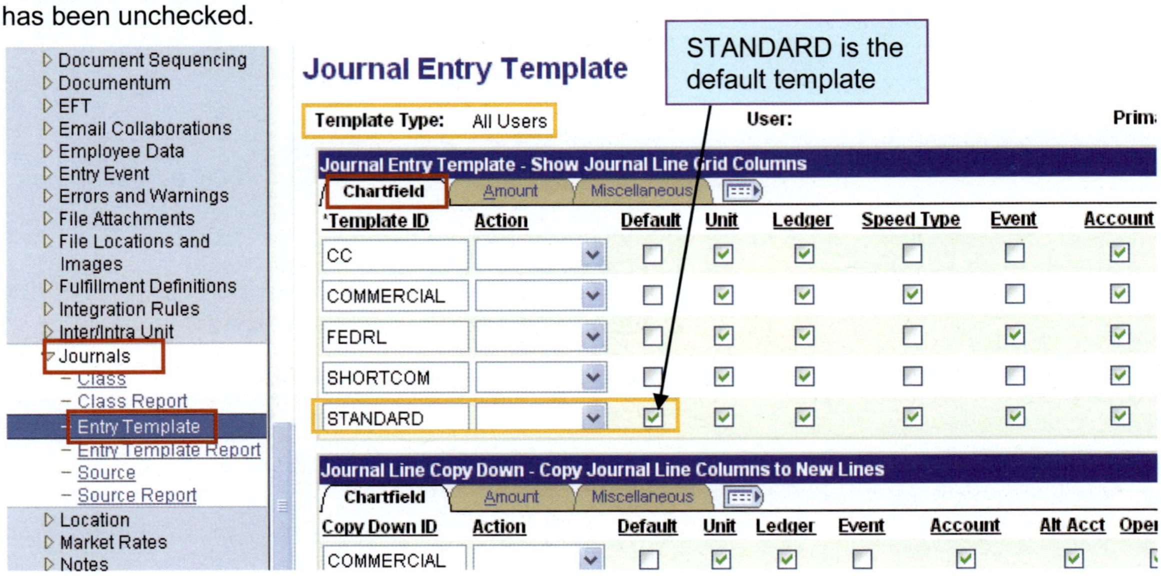

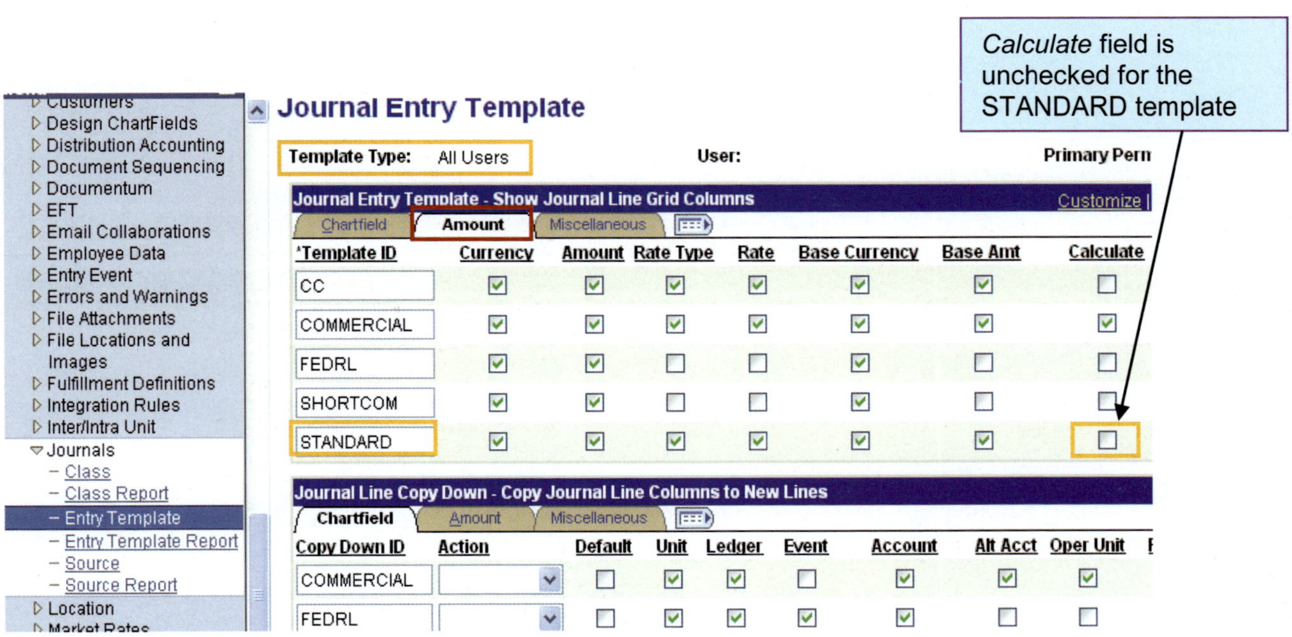

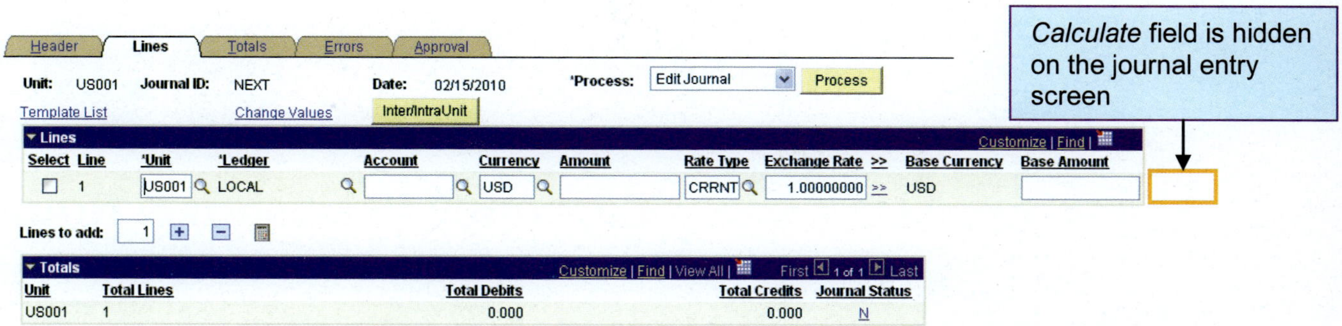
Header
Lines
Totals
Errors
Approval
Unit: US001
Journal ID: NEXT
Date: 02/15/2010
*Process: Edit Journal
Process
Template List
Change Values
Inter/IntraUnit
Lines
Customize | Find |
Select
Line
*Unit
*Ledger
Account
Currency
Amount
Rate Type
Exchange Rate
Base Currency
Base Amount
1
US001
LOCAL
USD
CRRNT
1.00000000
USD
Lines to add: 1
Totals
Customize | Find | View All |
First 1 of 1 Last
Unit
Total Lines
Total Debits
Total Credits
Journal Status
US001
1
0.000
0.000
N
Calculate field is hidden on the journal entry screen

Currency Precision & Rounding

Currency precision ranges from zero to three decimal places in PeopleSoft, as defined by currencies' ISO standards. For example per ISO standards, US dollar amounts have two digits to the right of the decimal and Japanese yen have none.

PeopleSoft handles currency precision as follows:

- All *currency sensitive amount fields* have a standard length of 23.3. That is 23 digits to the left of the decimal point and 3 digits to the right of the decimal point.
- All amount fields on PeopleSoft delivered SQR reports are currency sensitive.
- Amount fields on Crystal and nVision reports are not currency sensitive. Instead, the number of decimals displayed is equal to the field precision specified on the report.
- Out-of-the-box PeopleSoft processes round all currency sensitive amount fields to currency specific precisions.

Follow the steps below to gain a detailed understanding of the above concepts:

#	Step	Step Description
1	review currency sensitive amount fields	review amount fields on JRNL_LN and LEDGER records
2	review currency precision configuration	review *Decimal Positions* field in the *Currency Code* page for Brazilian Real
3	setup business unit and enter journals	setup a Brazilian business unit BRZ01 and enter journals in BRL currency
4	learn about *Currency Control Field*	blank out *Currency Control Field* in the MONETARY_AMOUNT and FOREIGN_AMOUNT fields and enter journals
5	learn about currency precision on SQRs, Crystals and nVisions	run SQRs, Crystals and nVisions.
6	learn about currency rounding in PeopleSoft	enter journals

1. Review Currency Sensitive Amount Fields
   a. Start *Application Designer*, open the following records, and review the currency sensitive amount fields
      - Record = JRNL_LN, Fields = MONETARY_AMOUNT and FOREIGN_AMOUNT
      - Record = LEDGER, Fields = POSTED_TOTAL_AMT, POSTED_TRAN_AMT and POSTED_BASE_AMT

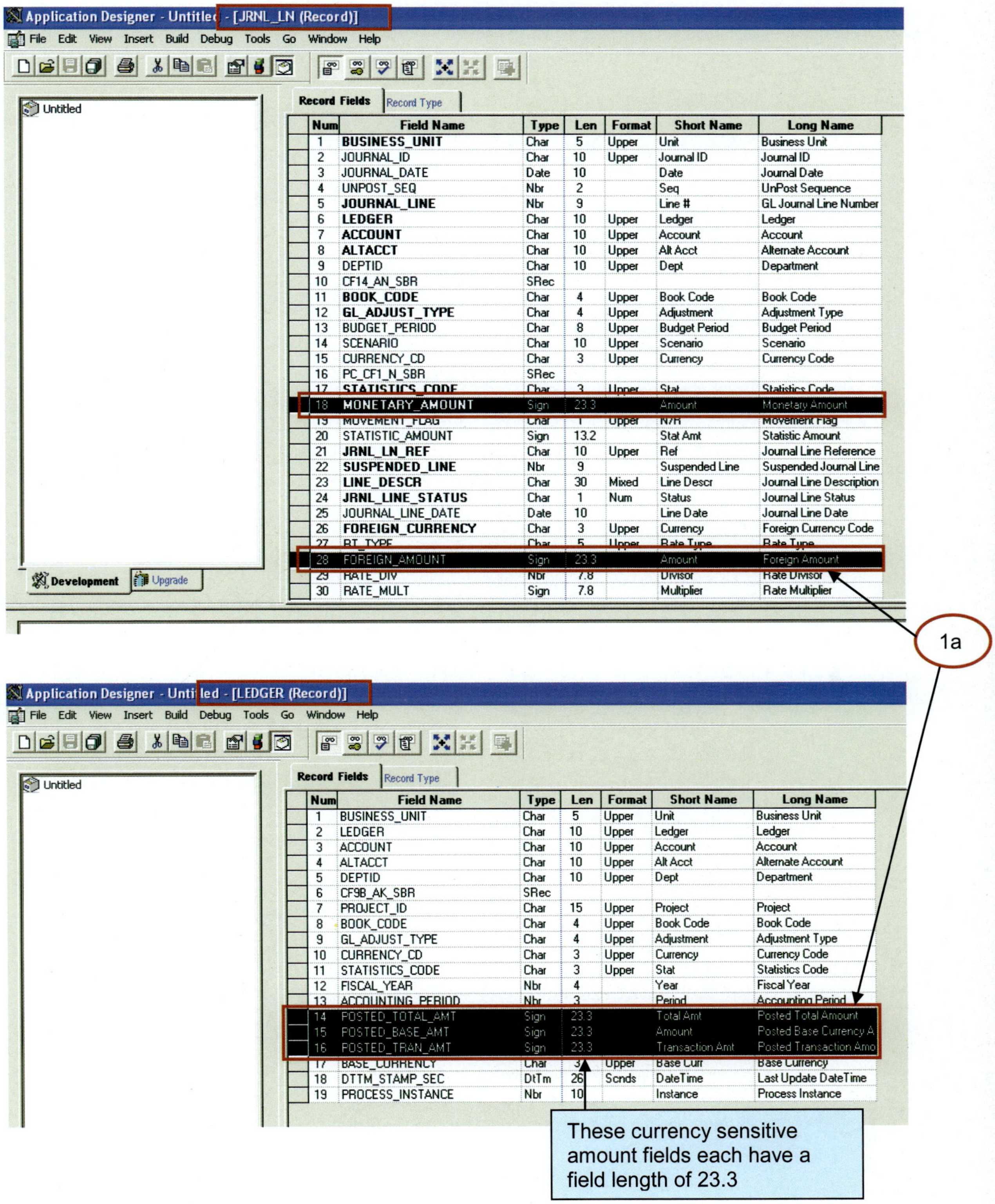

2. Review Currency Precision Configuration

   a. Navigate to *Set Up Financials/Supply Chain* > *Common Definitions* > *Currency* > *Currency Code* and search for the currency *BRL* (Brazilian Real).

   b. The field *Decimal Positions* defines the precision of a currency. Per ISO standards, PeopleSoft delivers Brazilian Real with a precision of 2 decimal places.

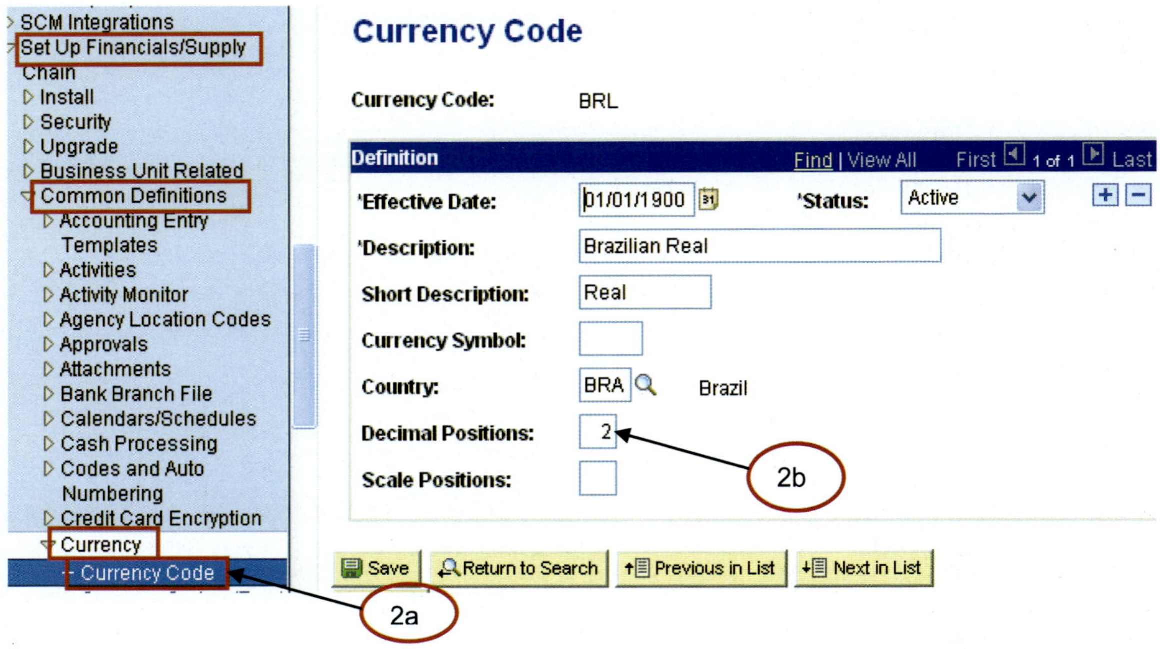

3. Setup Business Unit and Enter Journals

   a. Navigate to *Set Up Financials/Supply Chain > Business Unit Related > General Ledger > General Ledger Definition > Add a New Value*

   b. Specify `Business Unit: BRZ01` and click on *Add*

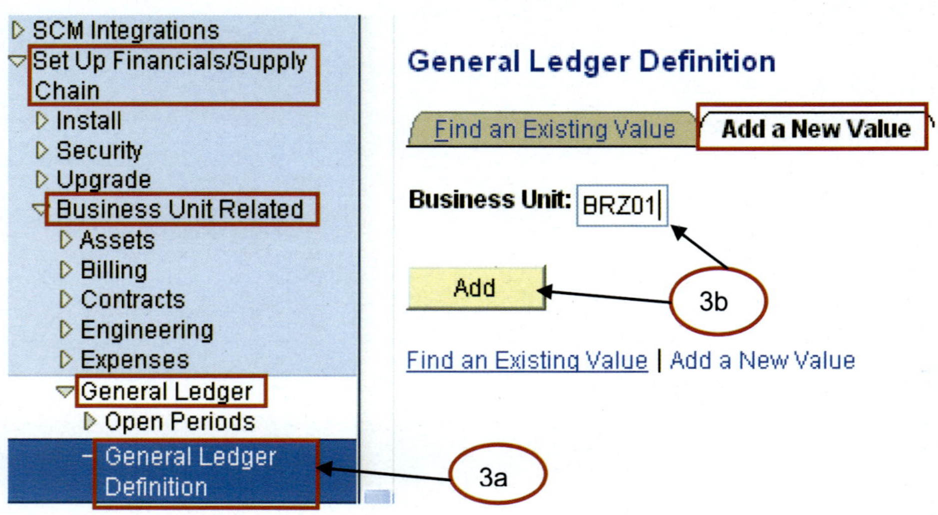

   c. Specify the following values on the *Definition* tab and click on *Create BU*:

      - `Business Unit: BRZ01`
      - `Description: Brazil Corporation`
      - `Short Desc: BRZ01`
      - `Base Currency: BRL`
      - `As of Date: 01/01/1990`
      - `Default SetID: SHARE`

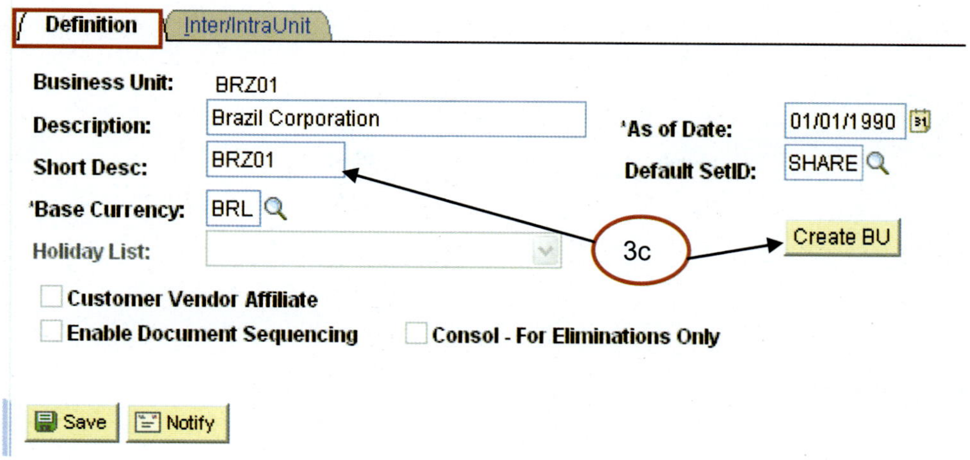

d. The above step may take a few seconds to complete. Note that the system added new tabs at the top of the screen. Do not change any of the values that defaulted in. Click on *Save* (not shown).

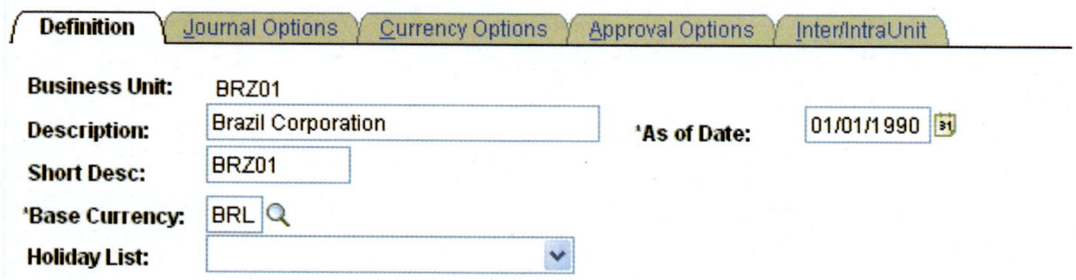

e. Navigate to *General Ledger > Ledgers > Detail Ledgers*. You will use the PeopleSoft pre-configured detail ledger called *LOCAL*.

f. Navigate to *General Ledger > Ledgers > Ledger Groups*. You will use a PeopleSoft pre-configured ledger group called *RECORDING*.

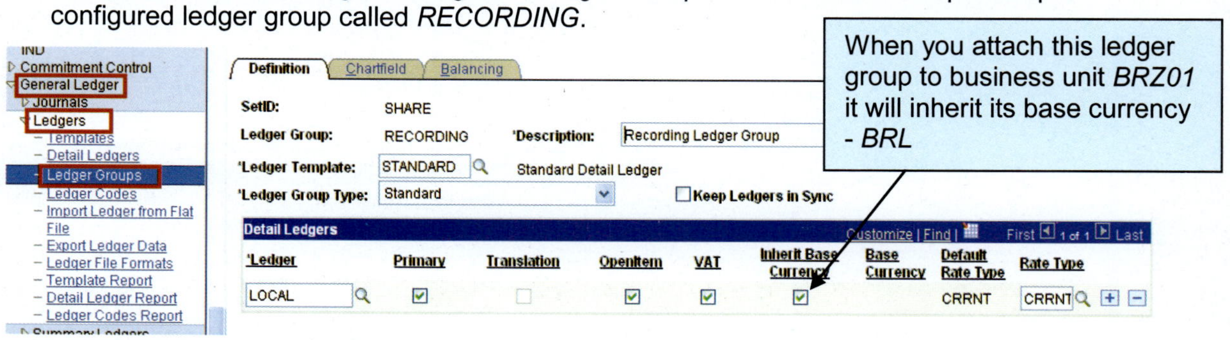

g. Now attach ledger group *RECORDING* to *BRZ01* business unit. Navigate to *Set Up Financials/Supply Chain > Business Unit Related > General Ledger > Ledgers For A Unit > Find an Existing Value*. Specify Business Unit: `BRZ01` and click on *Search*.

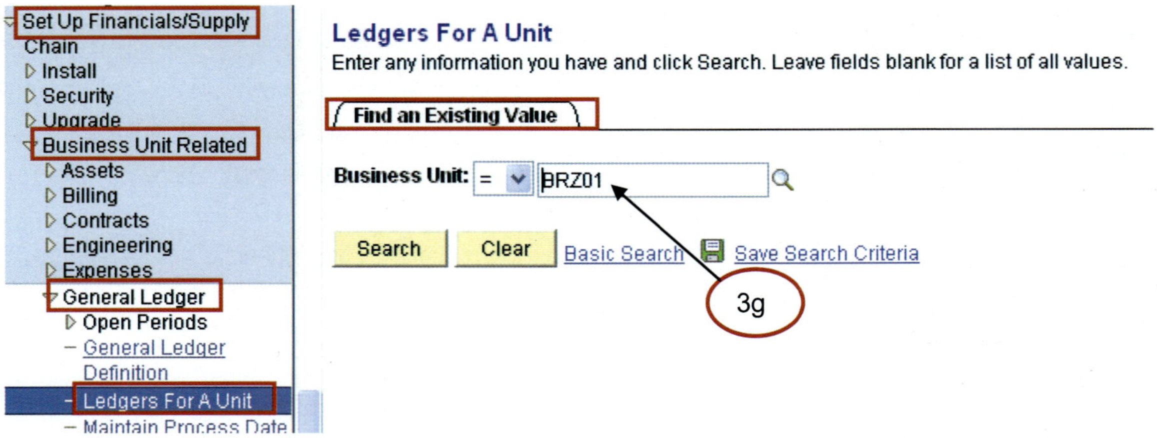

h. Specify the following values on the *Definition* tab and then click on *Save*. Accept default values for the fields not listed below:

- `Ledger Type: Detail Ledger`
- `Ledger Group: RECORDING`
- `Calendar ID: 01`
- `Balanced Ledger: Checked`
- `Journal Generator Default: Checked`

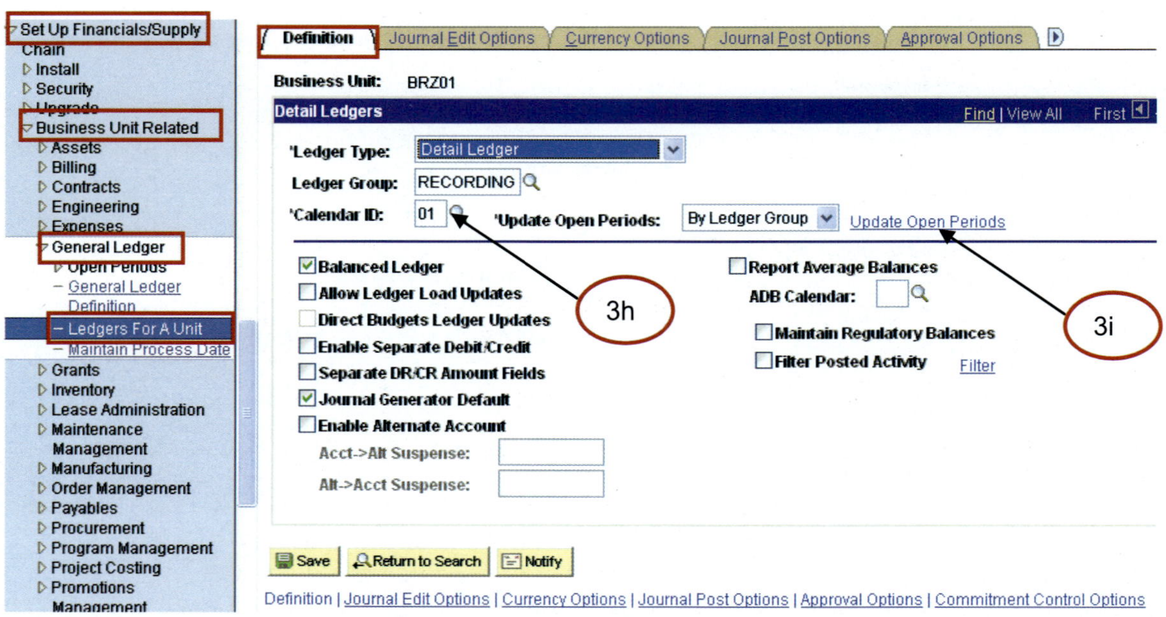

i. Click on the *Update Open Periods* link. Open periods 2010/1 thru 2010/12.Click on *Save* (not shown).

j. Next, enter journals to *BRZ01* business unit and *LOCAL* ledger. Navigate to *General Ledger > Journals > Journal Entry > Create/Update Journal Entries*. Specify the following values and click on *Add*:

- `Business Unit: BRZ01`
- `Journal ID: CP1`
- `Journal Date: 02/01/2010`

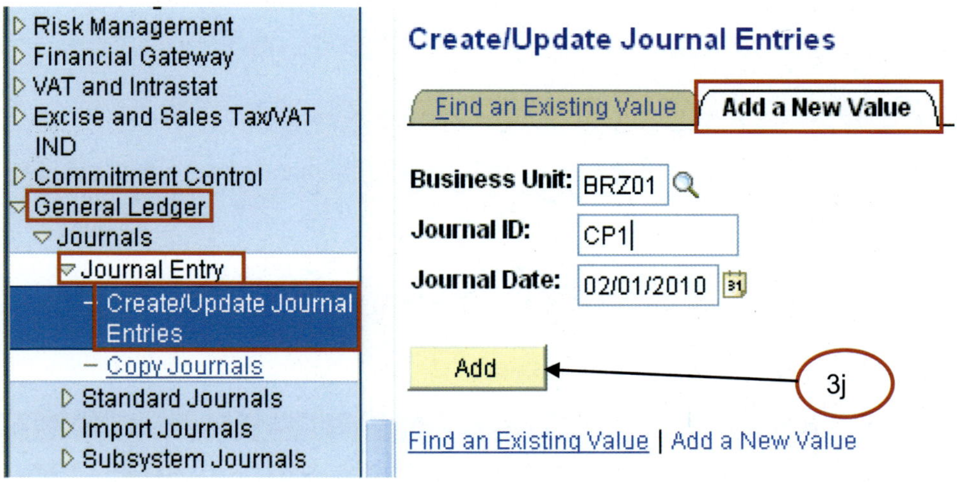

k. Accept default values on the *Header* tab. Click on the *Lines* tab and enter the following values:

- `Account: 100000`
- `Amount: 100.123` (which is more than two decimal places allowed for BRL currency)

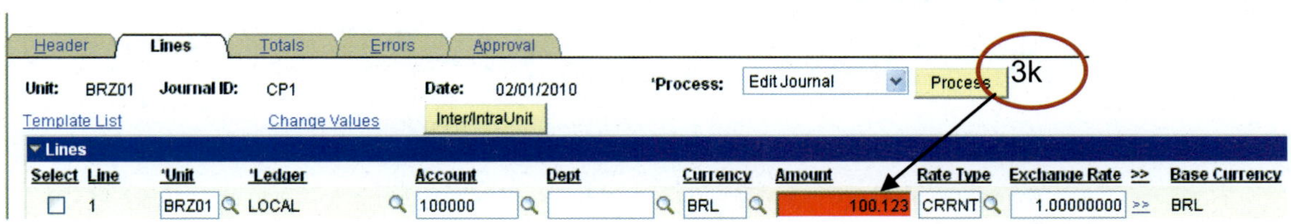

l. Click on *Save* (not shown). The system generates the error message shown below.

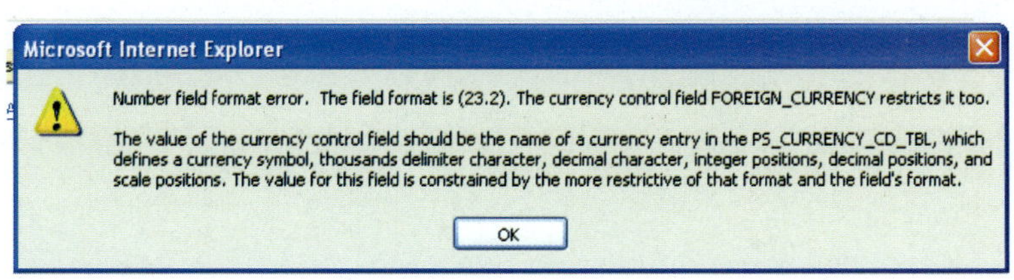

m. Next, change the amount field on the journal line to `100.12` (two decimal places) and click on the **+** icon to add another journal line. Enter `Account: 620003` and `Amount: -100.12` on the second line. Click on *Save*. Note that no errors are generated.

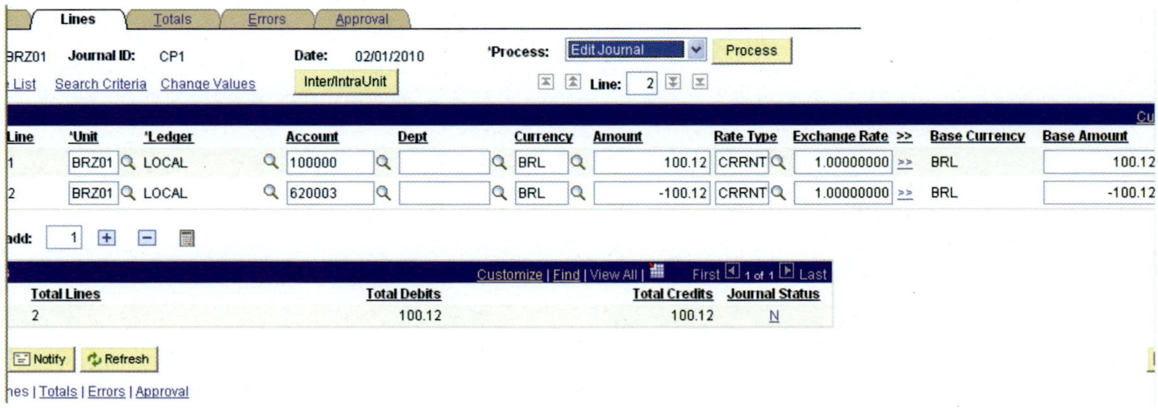

n. Next, on the *Currency Code* page, change the *Decimal Positions* field value to `3` for `BRL` currency.

o. Re-enter the above journal, but change the amounts to `100.123` and `-100.123` (three decimal places) on the journal lines. Unlike the previous journal, the system will let you save and not generate an error message.

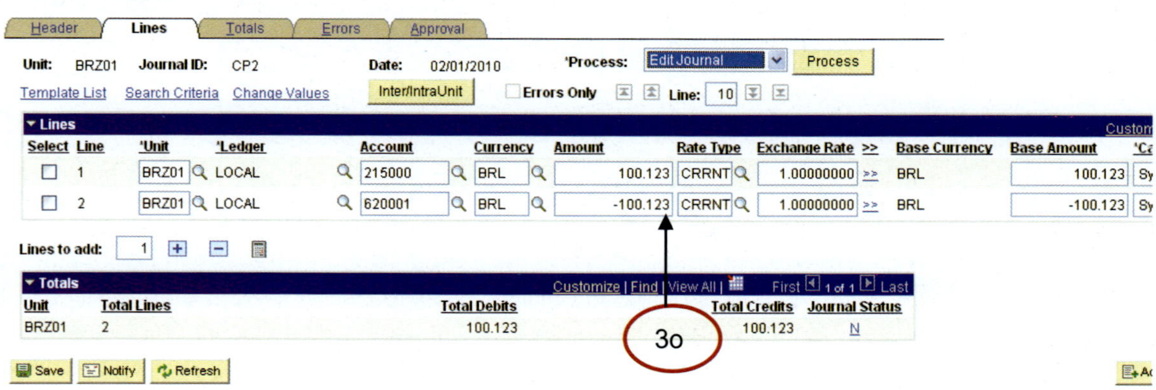

p. Select *Post Journal* from the drop down menu and click on *Process*. This will post the CP2 journal to the ledger. Repeat this step to post the CP1 journal.

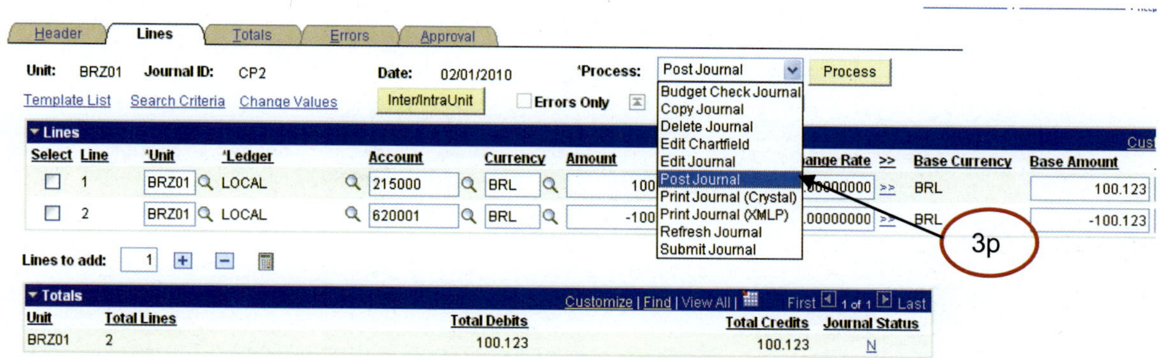

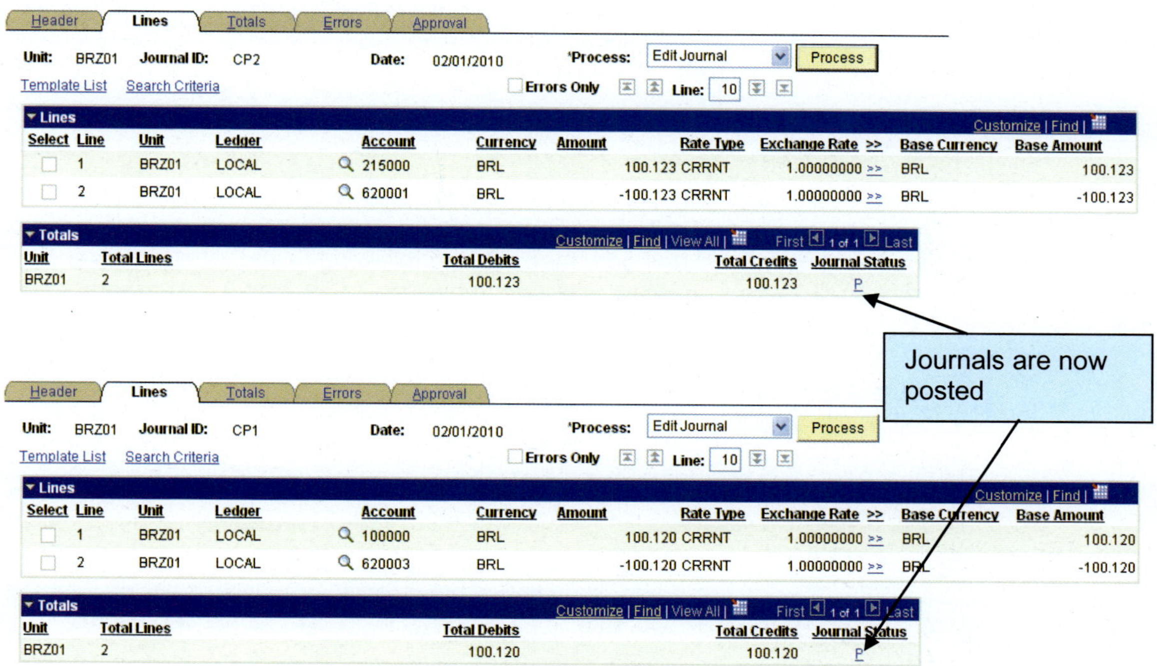

q. On the *Currency Code* page, change the `Decimal Positions` field value to `4` for BRL currency, and enter a new journal with amount fields set to four decimal places. The system generates an error message when you save the journal. Why? This time you are limited by the amount field length of 23.3 (specified in the JRNL_LN record). Fix the journal lines to three decimal places. Then save and post the journal. Refer to the screen shots below for details.

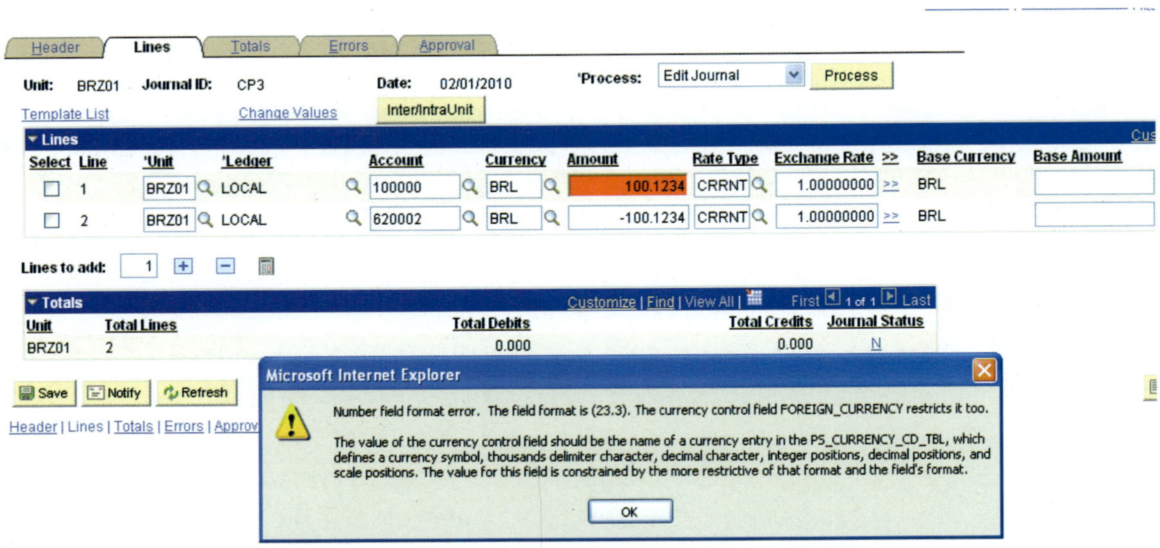

r. Next, query the JRNL_LN record to see the journal lines that you added in the previous steps. Navigate to *Reporting Tools* > *Query* > *Query Manager* and click on *Create New Query*. Search for `JRNL_LN` record and add; then add the following fields: `BUSINESS_UNT`, `JOURNAL_ID`, `JOURNAL_DATE`, `JOURNAL_LINE`, `LEDGER`, `ACCOUNT`, `CURRENCY_CD` and `MONETARY_AMOUNT`.

On the *Criteria* tab specify `Business Unit = BRZ01` and run the query. See the screen shots below for details.

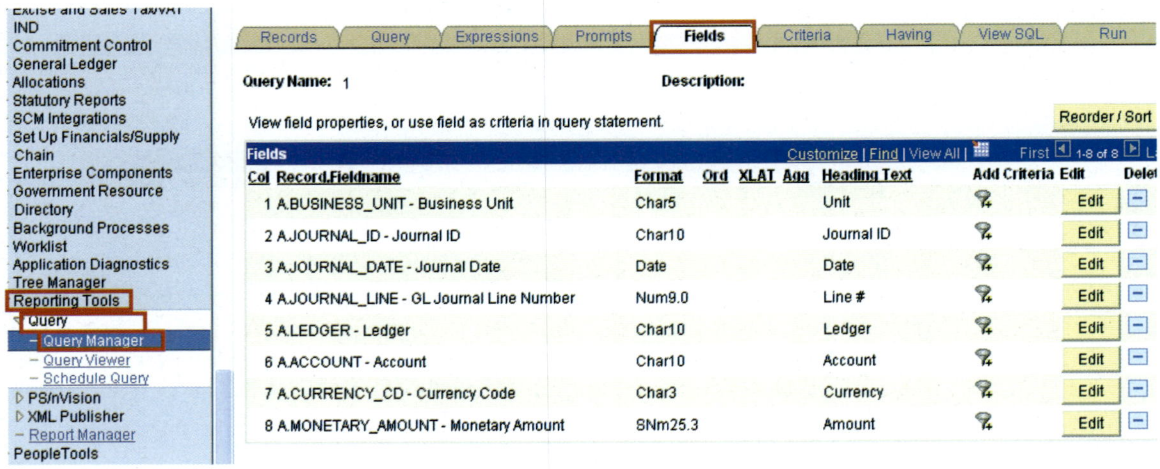

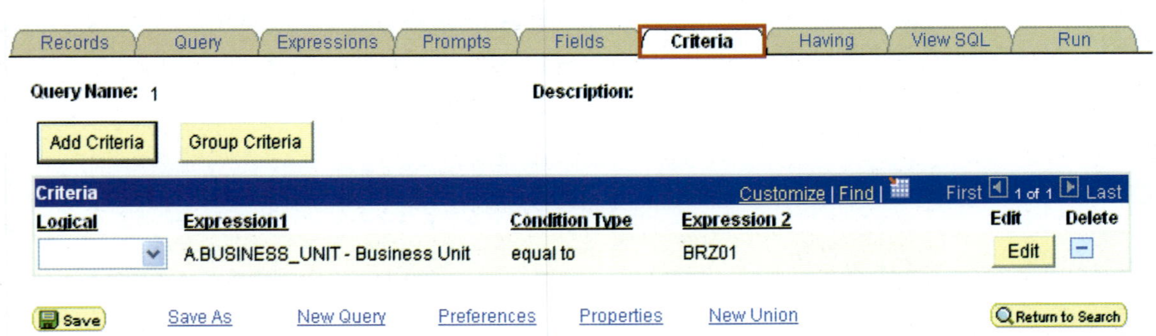

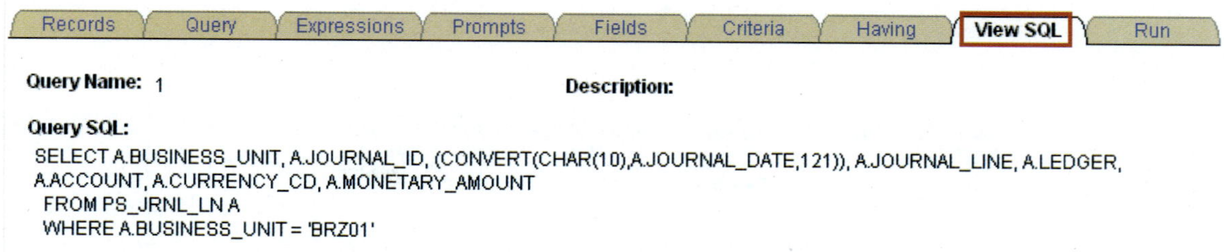

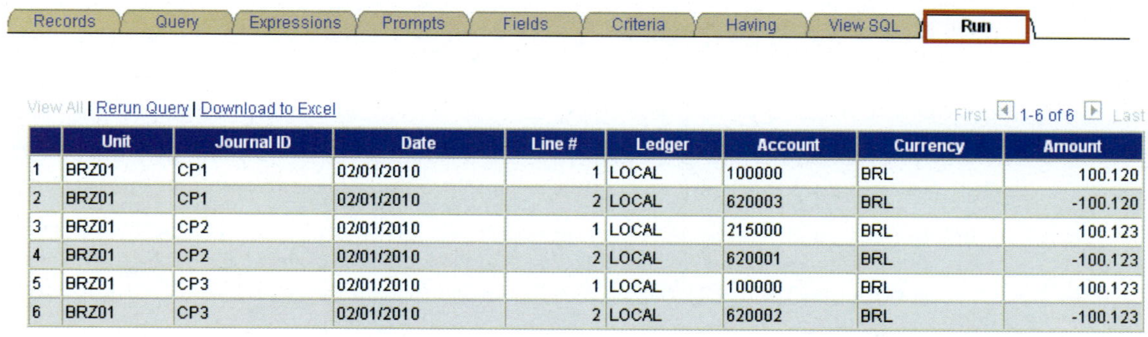

s. Optionally, enter the following two journals to BRZ01 business unit and LOCAL ledger per details below:

- `Journal ID: CP5 and Journal Date: 02/01/2010`
- `Line 1: Account: 215000, Amount:100.128`
- `Line 2: Account: 620001, Amount:-100.128`

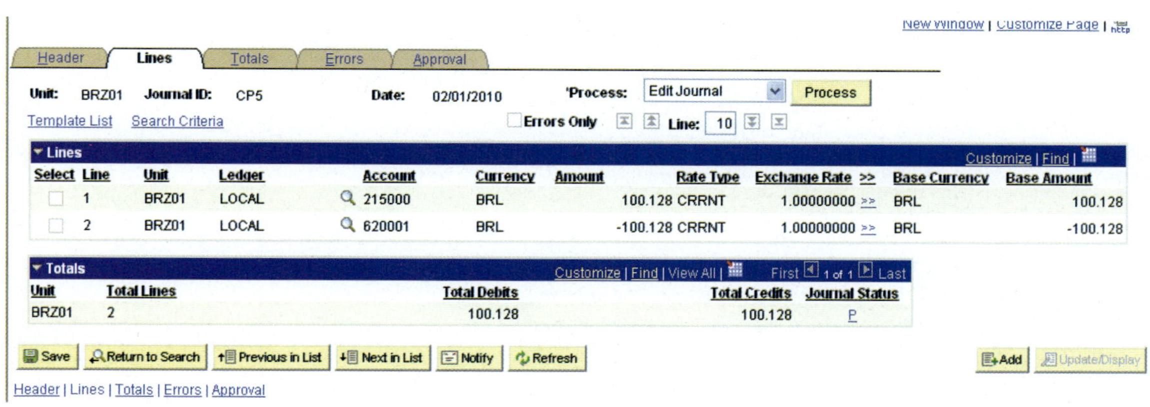

- `Journal ID: CP6 and Journal Date: 02/01/2010`
- `Line 1: Account: 215002, Amount:100.128`
- `Line 2: Account: 620004, Amount:-100.128`

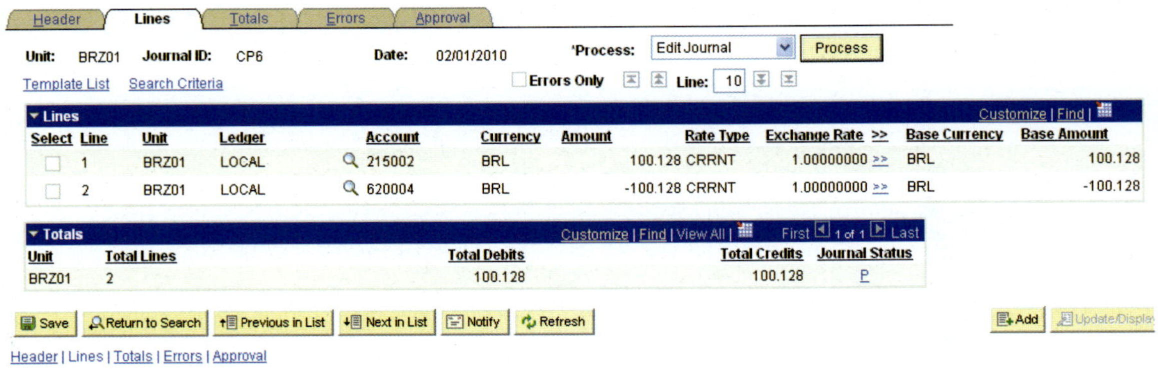

4. Learn about the Currency Control Field

   The *Currency Control Field* is used to define if amount fields created in the Application Designer are currency sensitive. Follow the steps below to gain a detailed understanding of this topic:

   a. In Application Designer open record JRNL_LN and double click on the MONETARY_AMOUNT field. This will open up the *Record Field Properties* dialog box. Note that *Currency Control Field* is populated with CURRENCY_CD, which makes the MONETARY_AMOUNT field currency sensitive.

      Repeat the above step for the FOREIGN_AMOUNT field. Note that the *Currency Control Field* is set to FOREIGN_CURRENCY. See screen shots below.

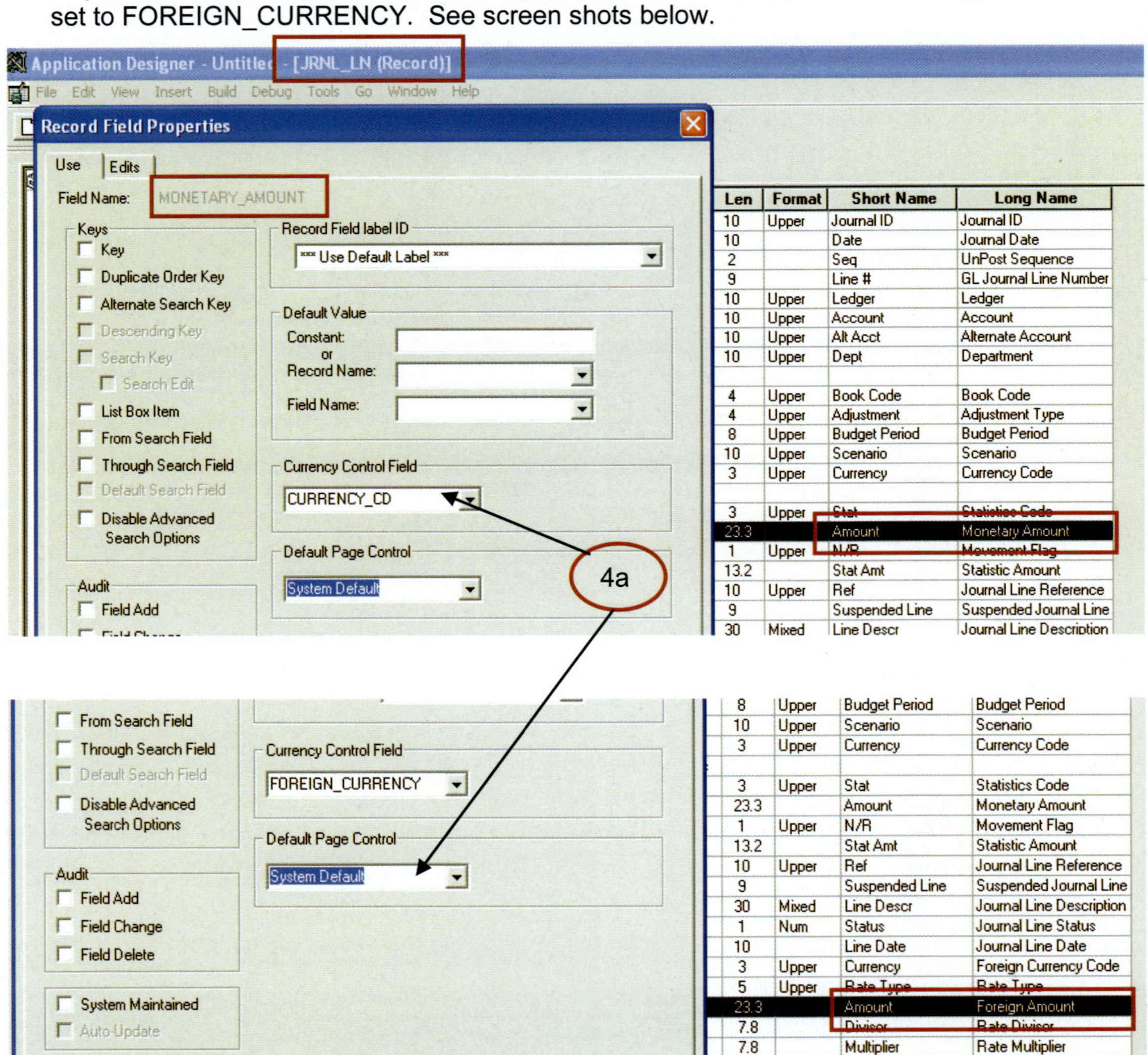

In the example below, you will blank out the *Currency Control Field* and confirm that the system does not restrict the decimal places (on the journal line page) to the value specified in the *Currency Code* page. Refer the steps below:

b. In Application Designer open record JRNL_LN. Double click on the MONETARY_AMOUNT field. On the *Record Field Properties* dialog box blank out the *Currency Control Field.*

Repeat the above step for field FOREIGN_AMOUNT. Save the record. See screen shots below for details:

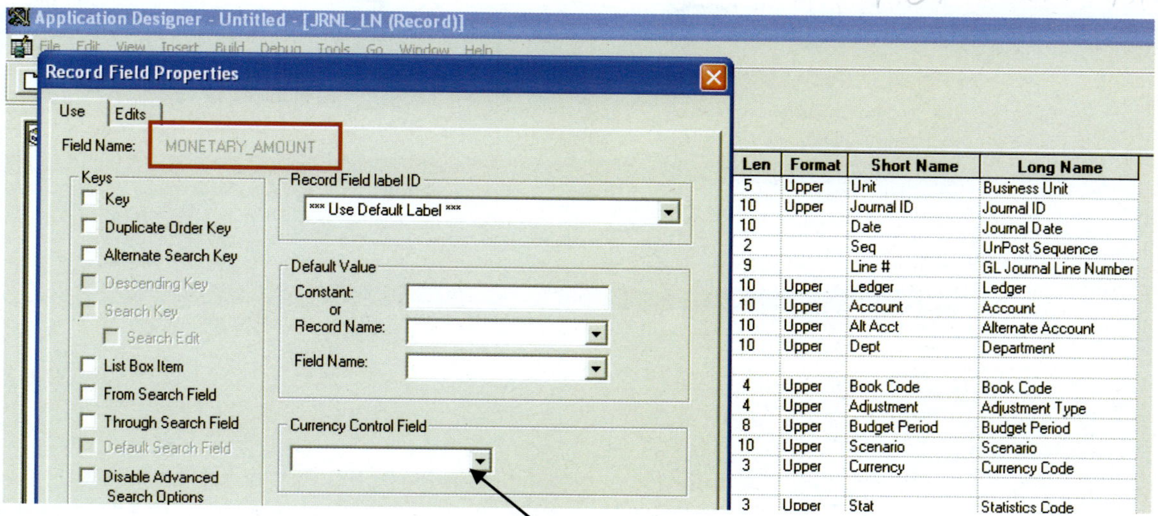

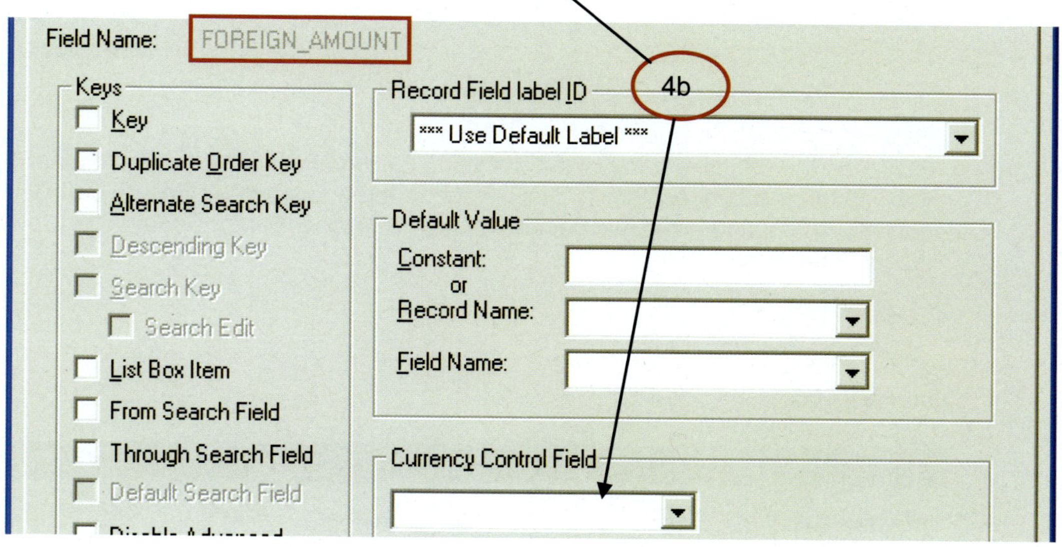

c. Verify that currency USD is configured to two decimal places.

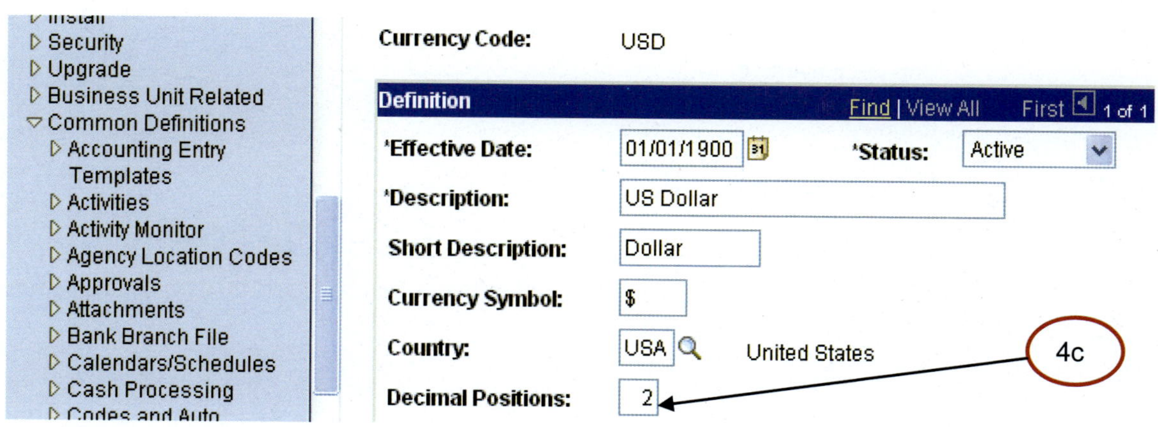

d. Enter a new journal per details below:

- `Business Unit: US001, Journal ID: Next, Journal Date: 02/25/2010`
- `Line 1: Account: 100001, Currency: USD, Amount: 123.123`

e. Click on *Save*. The system saved the journal without any errors. It allowed you to enter USD amounts with three decimal places even though USD currency is configured to two decimal places. Why? Because the journal amount fields are no longer currency sensitive per updates you performed in step b.

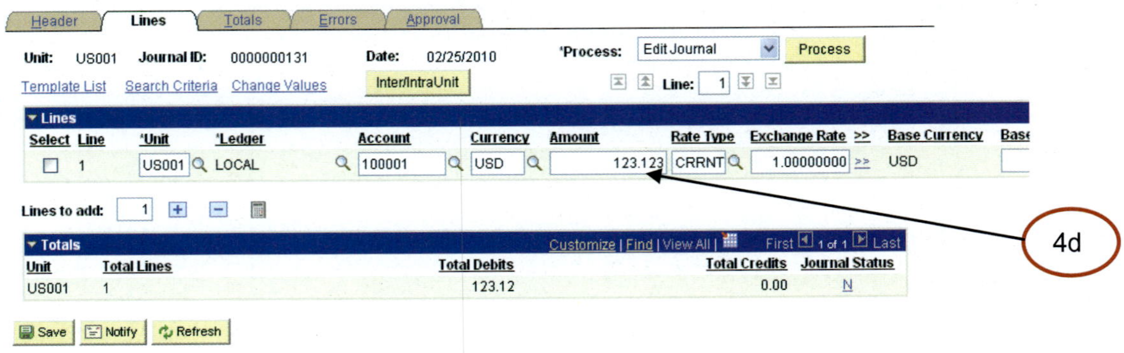

f. Re-populate the currency control fields that you blanked out in Step b (for MONETARY_AMOUNT and FOREIGN_AMOUNT) and enter a new journal with same information as in Step d. Note that the system will not allow you to save the journal.

5. Learn about Currency Precision on SQRs, Crystals and nVision reports

   a. PeopleSoft SQRs are currency sensitive if they include the code `#include number.sqc`. SQC has the necessary code for formatting currency sensitive amount fields. To understand this you will run the *Ledger Activity* SQR report in the steps below. Ensure beforehand that the BRL currency is configured to two decimal places on the *Currency Code* page. Update to two decimal places if necessary.

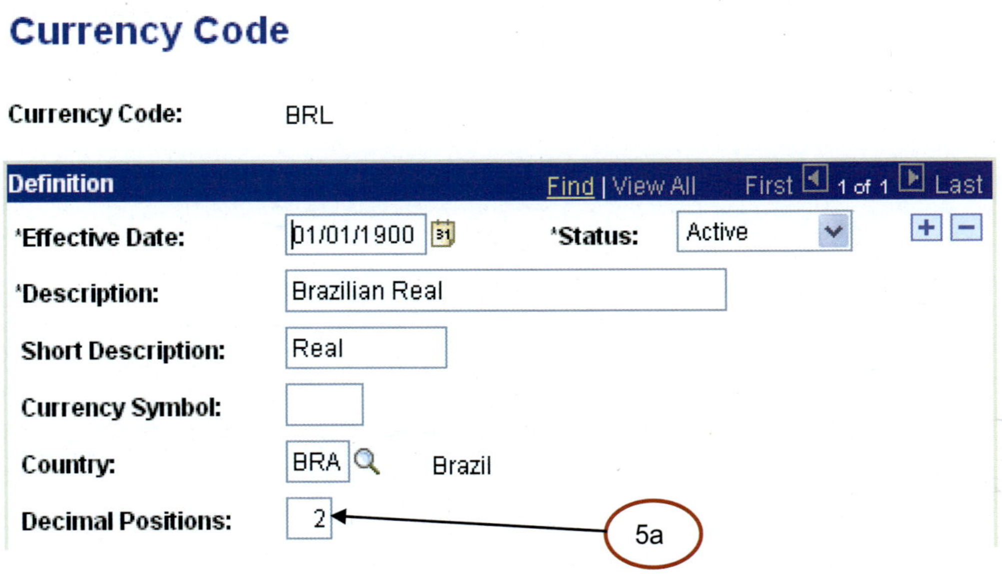

   b. Navigate to *General Ledger > General Reports > Ledger Activity*. On the run control page specify the following values:

      - `Unit: BRZ01, Ledger: LOCAL, Fiscal Year: 2010, From Period: 2, To Period: 2, Currency: BRL, Show Journal Detail: Checked`
      - Click on *Refresh*. On the *Chartfield Selection* grid select the following checkboxes for Account chartfield: `Include CF, Summarize, Detail, All Values.`
      - Click on *Run*

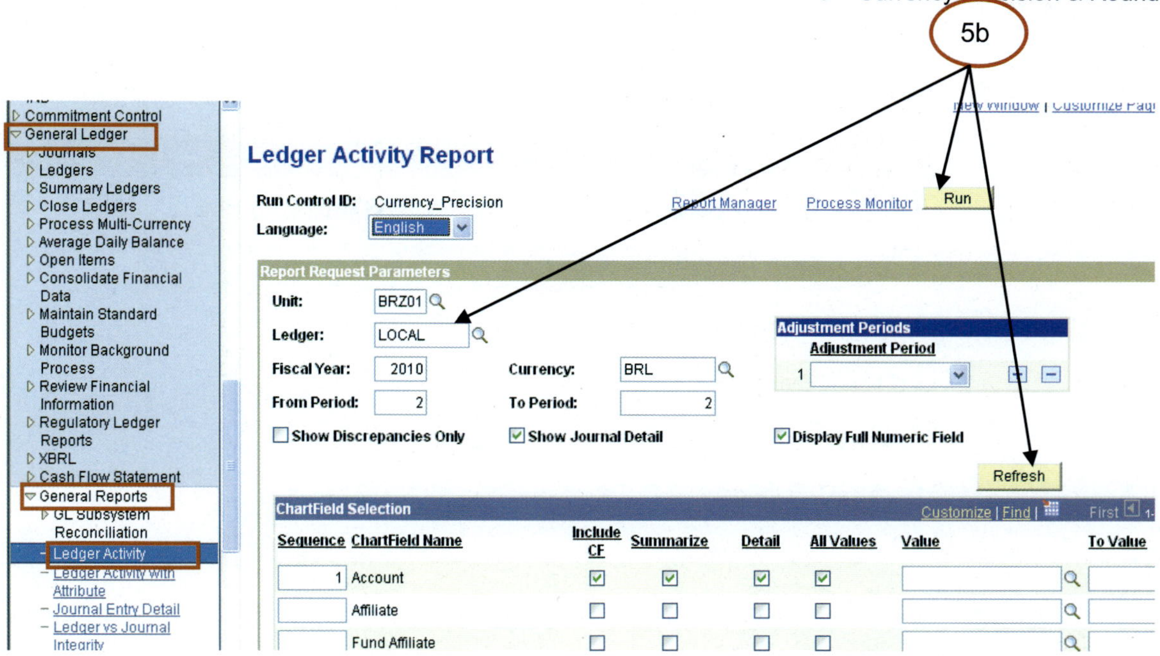

c. On the *Process Scheduler Request* page select `Type: Web` and `Format: PDF.` Click on *OK* (not shown).

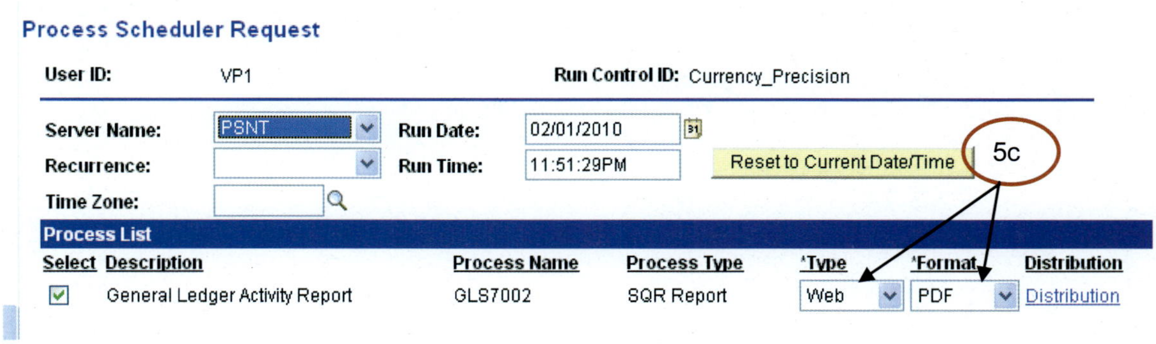

d. The PDF report shows amount fields rounded to two decimal places.

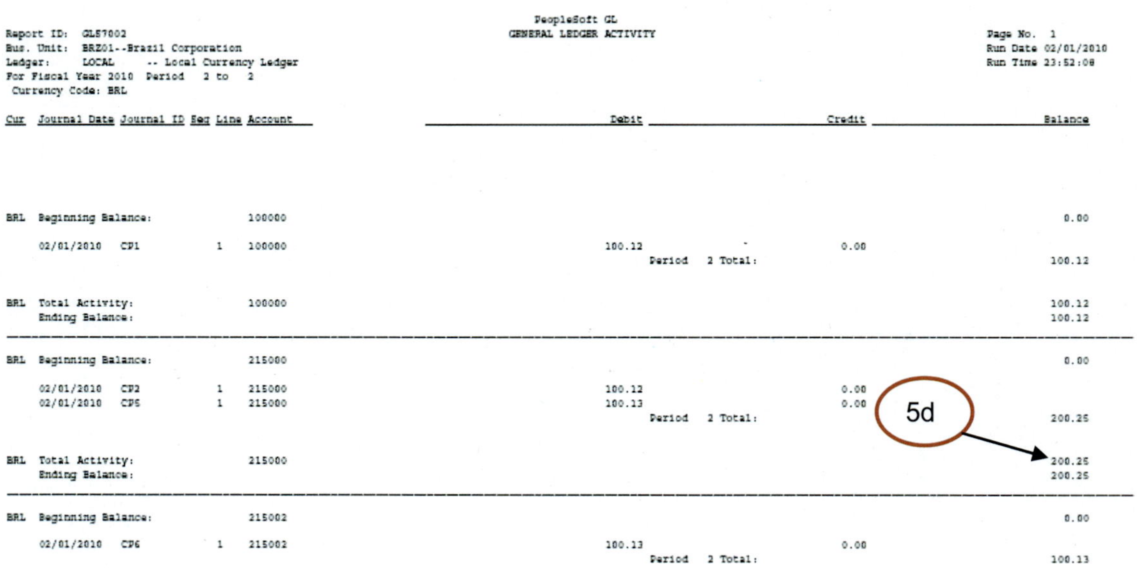

e. Next, for BRL currency change the *Decimal Positions* to three.

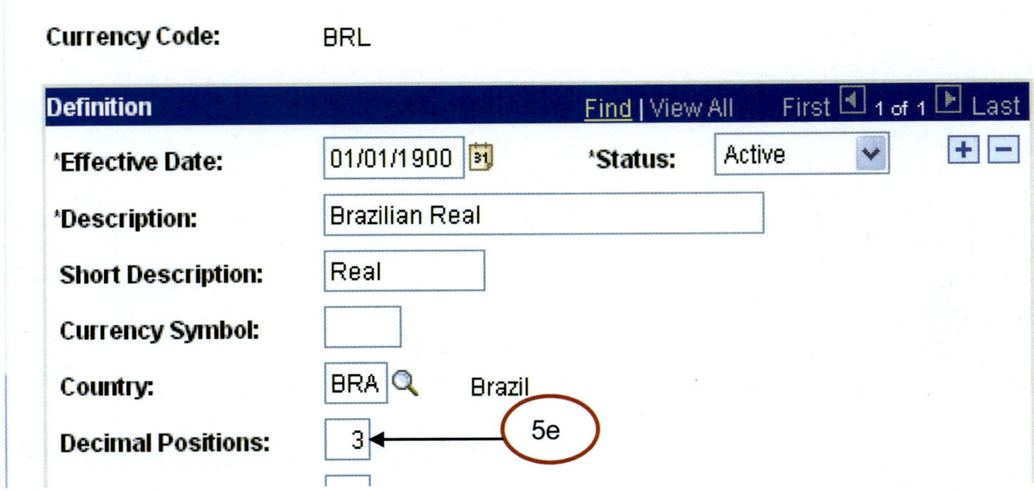

f. Re-run the *Ledger Activity* report. The report output now shows amount fields with three decimal places.

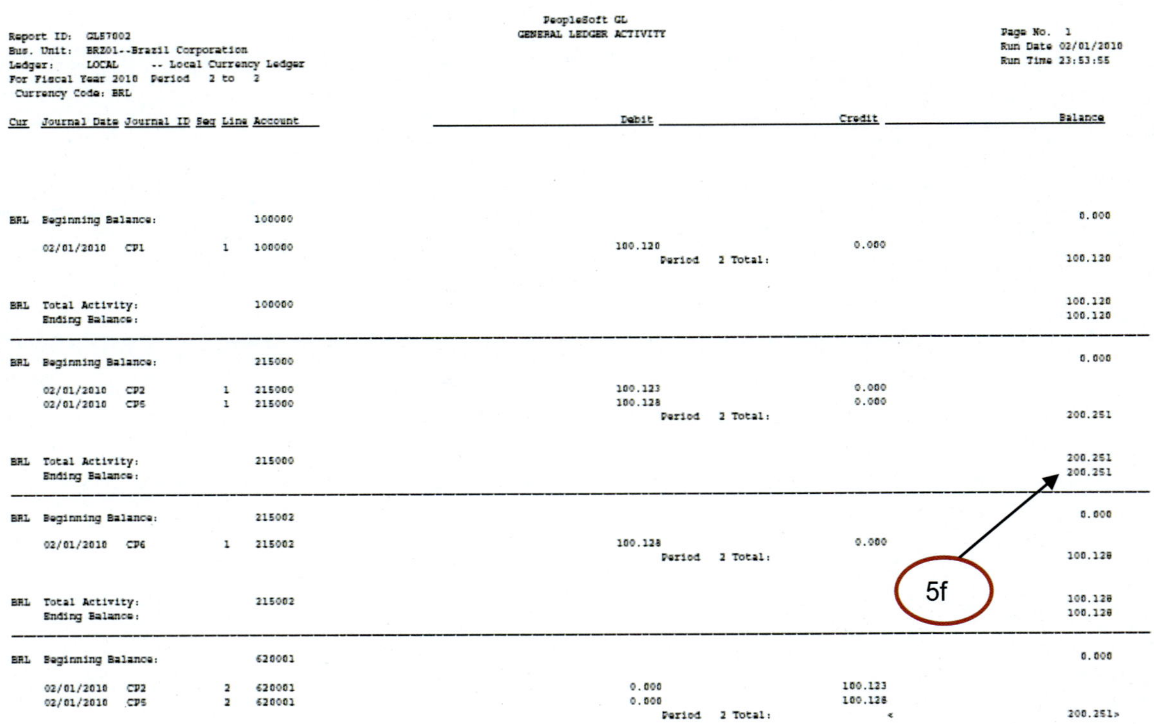

```
                                   PeopleSoft GL
Report ID:  GLS7002             GENERAL LEDGER ACTIVITY                      Page No.  1
Bus. Unit:  BRZ01--Brazil Corporation                                        Run Date 02/01/2010
Ledger:     LOCAL    -- Local Currency Ledger                                Run Time 23:53:55
For Fiscal Year 2010  Period   2 to   2
 Currency Code: BRL

Cur  Journal Date Journal ID Seq Line Account         Debit          Credit          Balance

BRL  Beginning Balance:             100000                                           0.000
     02/01/2010   CP1          1    100000          100.120           0.000
                                                   Period   2 Total:                100.120

BRL  Total Activity:                100000                                         100.120
     Ending Balance:                                                               100.120
---------------------------------------------------------------------------------------------
BRL  Beginning Balance:             215000                                           0.000
     02/01/2010   CP2          1    215000          100.123           0.000
     02/01/2010   CP5          1    215000          100.128           0.000
                                                   Period   2 Total:                200.251

BRL  Total Activity:                215000                                         200.251
     Ending Balance:                                                               200.251
---------------------------------------------------------------------------------------------
BRL  Beginning Balance:             215002                                           0.000
     02/01/2010   CP6          1    215002          100.128           0.000
                                                   Period   2 Total:                100.128

BRL  Total Activity:                215002                                         100.128
     Ending Balance:                                                               100.128
---------------------------------------------------------------------------------------------
BRL  Beginning Balance:             620001                                           0.000
     02/01/2010   CP2          2    620001            0.000         100.123
     02/01/2010   CP5          2    620001            0.000         100.128
                                                   Period   2 Total:        <       200.251>
```


g. *Field Precision* (and not the *Decimal Positions* on the *Currency Code* page) determines the decimal places displayed on Crystal reports. The steps below explain this. Open journal `CP6` that you entered in Step 3s. On the *Lines* tab select *Print Journal (Crystal)* and click on Process to run the GLC7501 Crystal report.

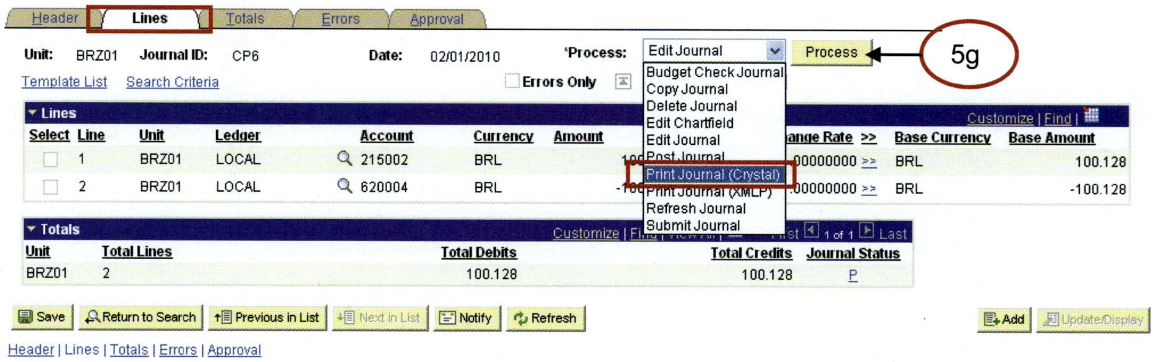

h. The report output displays numbers rounded to two decimal places.

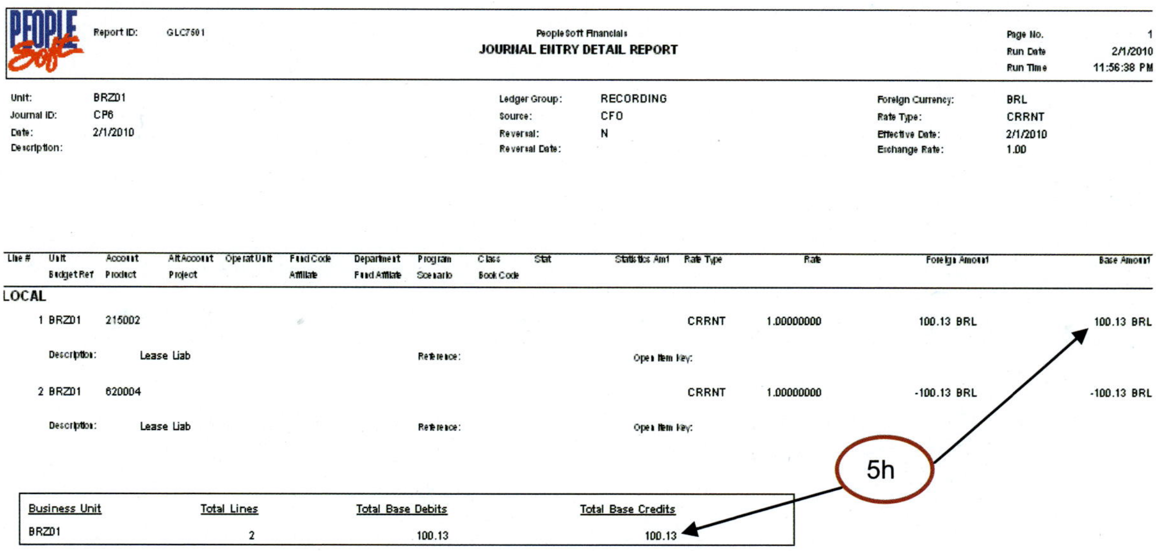

i. Next you will change field precision on MONETARY_AMOUNT field on the Crystal report GLC7501. Right click on the MONETARY_AMOUNT field and select *Format Field…*

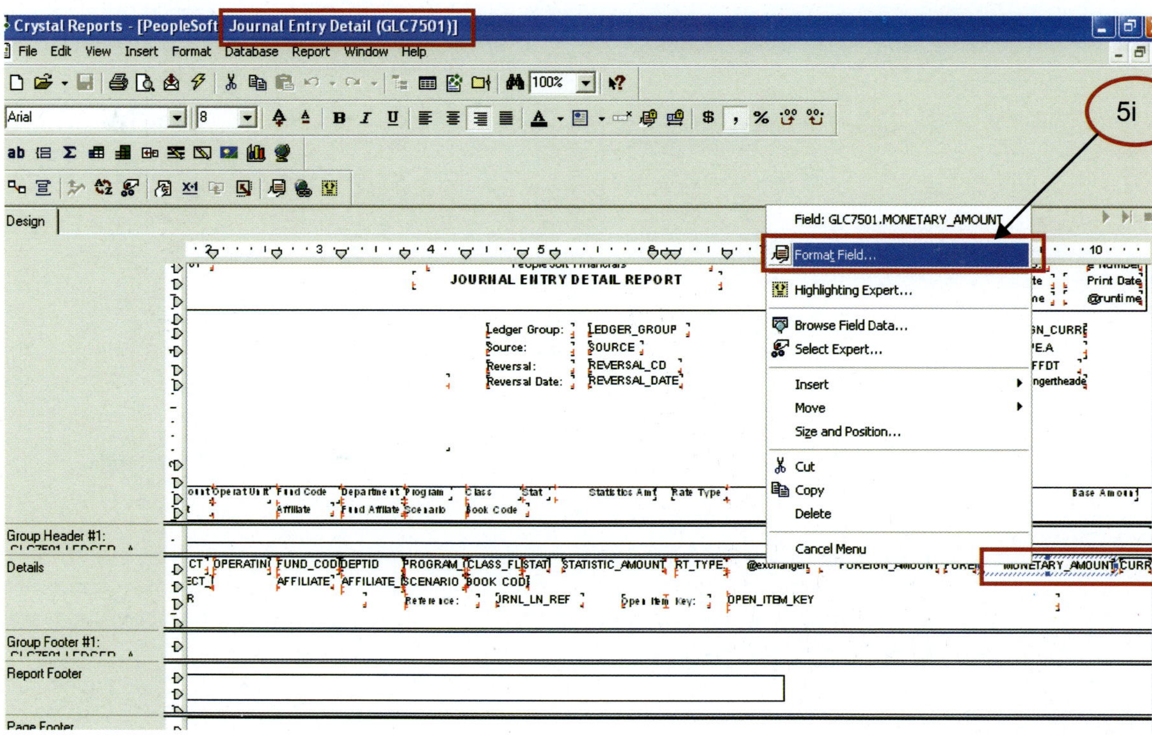

j. On the *Format Editor* dialog box select *Custom Style* and click on *Customize…*

k. On the *Custom Style* dialog box note that the *Rounding* is set to `0.01`. Change the value to `0.001`. Save the Crystal report.

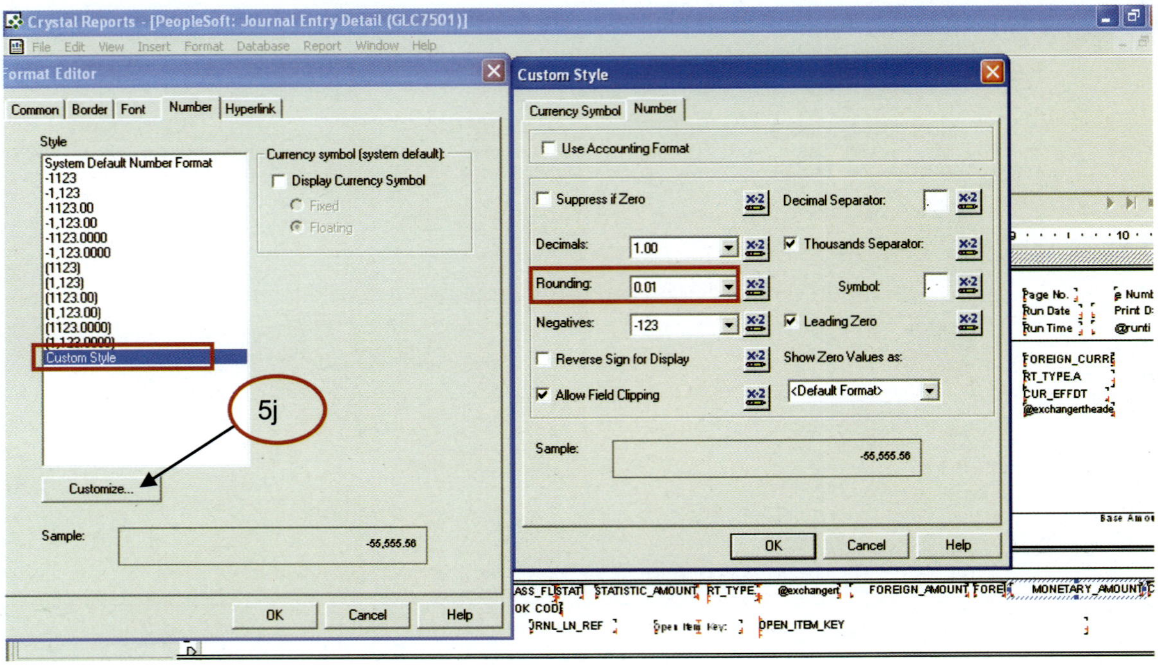

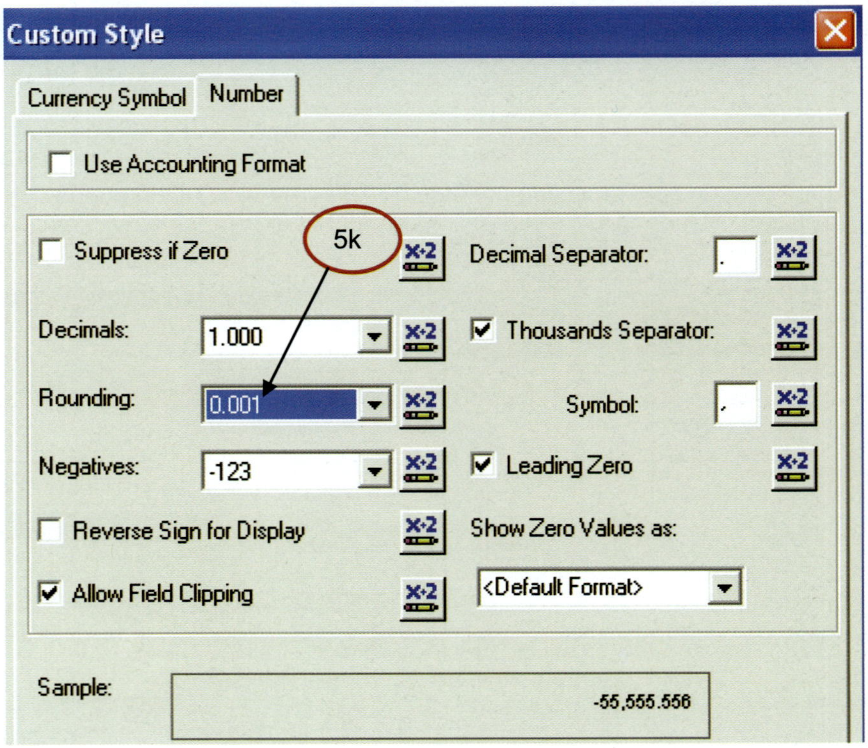

l. Re-run the GLC7501 Crystal - *Journal Entry Detail* report. Note that the amount field that you changed in the previous step now displays numbers to three decimal places. However, the amount fields at the bottom of the Crystal report, which you did not change, still display numbers to two decimal places.

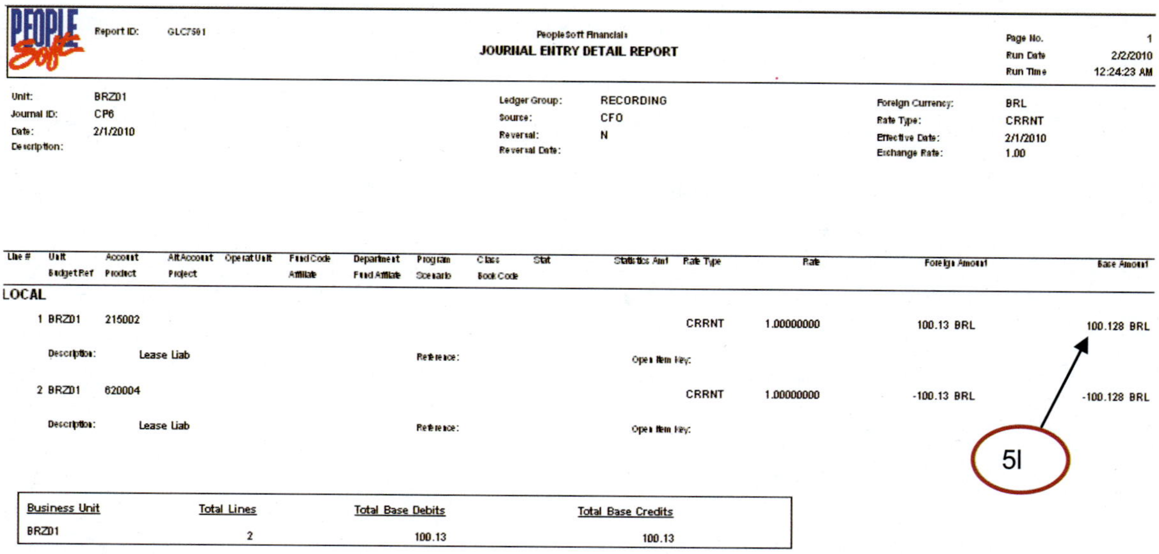

m. For nVision reports, Excel cell formatting determines the number of decimal places displayed. The steps below explain this. Create the nVision layout shown below in PeopleSoft's demo environment. Do not apply any Excel formatting.

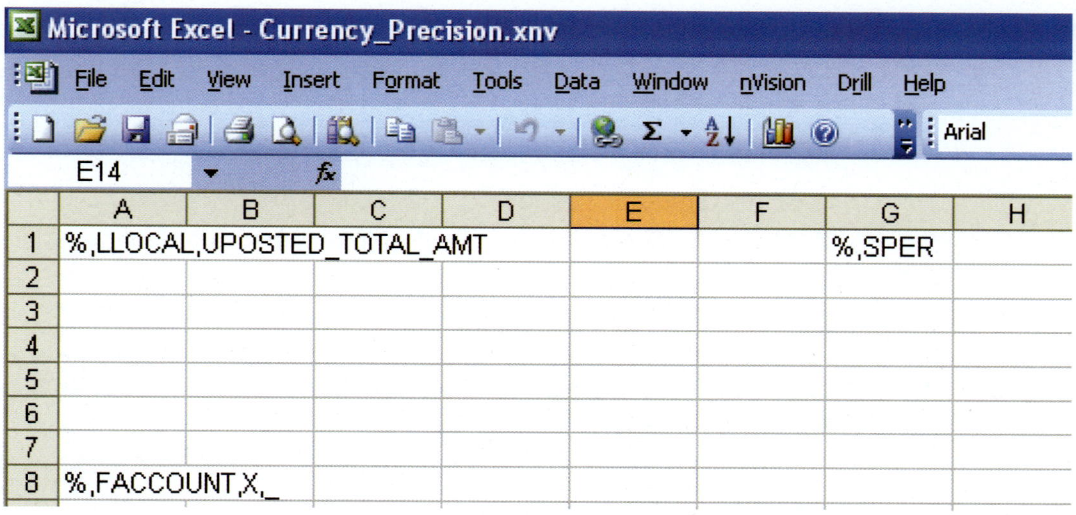

n. The report output below shows ledger balances in col G. Note that no Excel number formatting was applied.

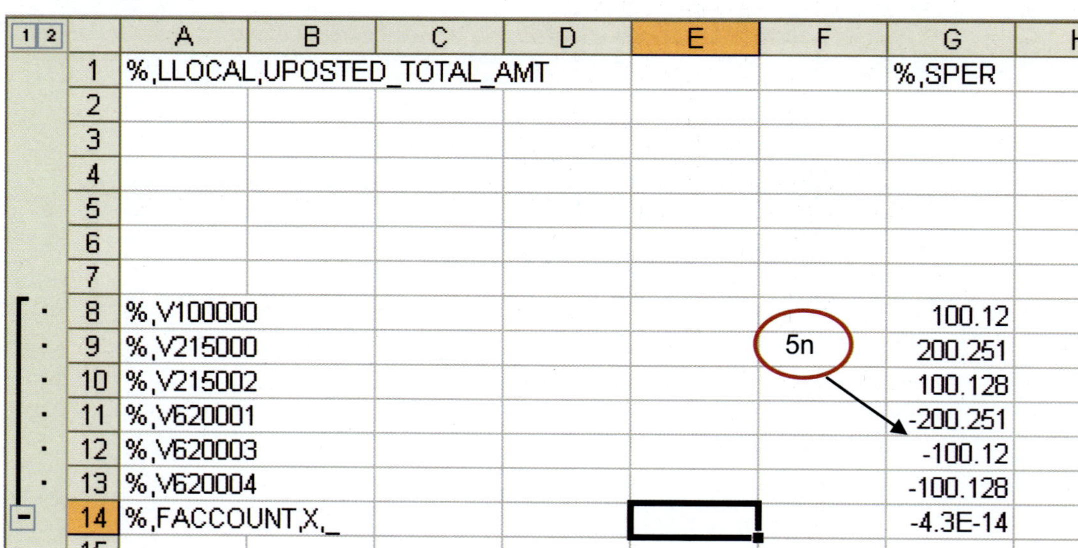

o. The nVision report output below shows ledger balances after number formatting the .XNV layout to one decimal place prior to running the report.

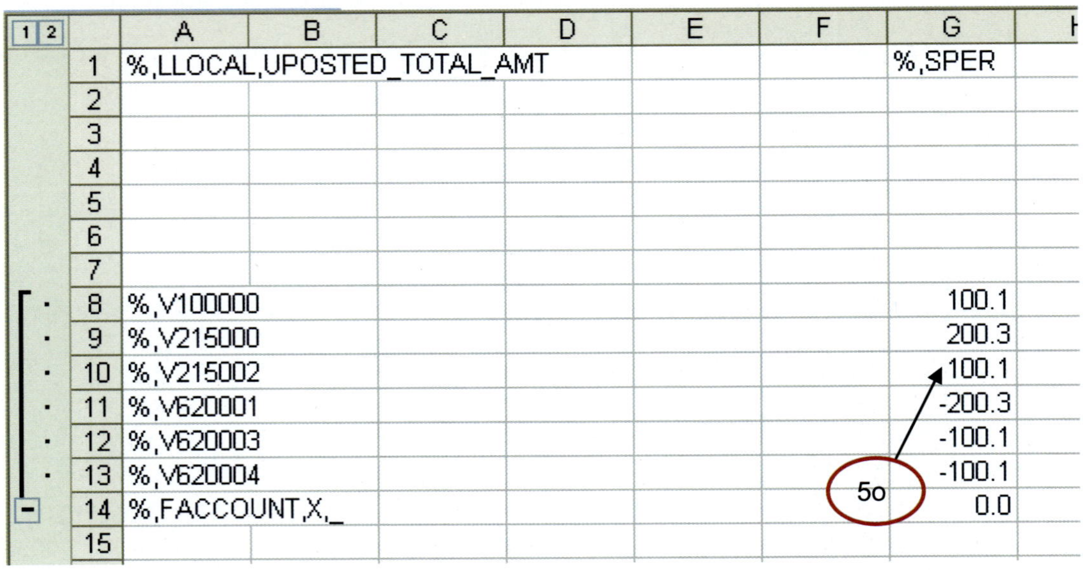

6. Learn about Currency Rounding in PeopleSoft

   a. All PeopleSoft processes round currency sensitive amount fields to their respective currency precisions. Enter the following journal to get a detailed understanding of this concept:

      - `Business Unit: US001, Journal ID: Next, Journal Date: 02/24/2010`
      - `Line 1: Account: 620002, Currency: CAD, Amount: -1.21, Exchange Rate: 1.191867`
      - `Line 2: Account: 620001, Currency: CAD, Amount: 1.21, Exchange Rate: 1.190767`

Note that the system calculated the base amounts of 1.02 for the same foreign amounts (1.21 and -1.21) using two different exchange rates. It rounded *1.21/1.191867 = 1.0152139* as well as *1.21./1.190767 = 1.0161517* to 1.02 (two decimal places).

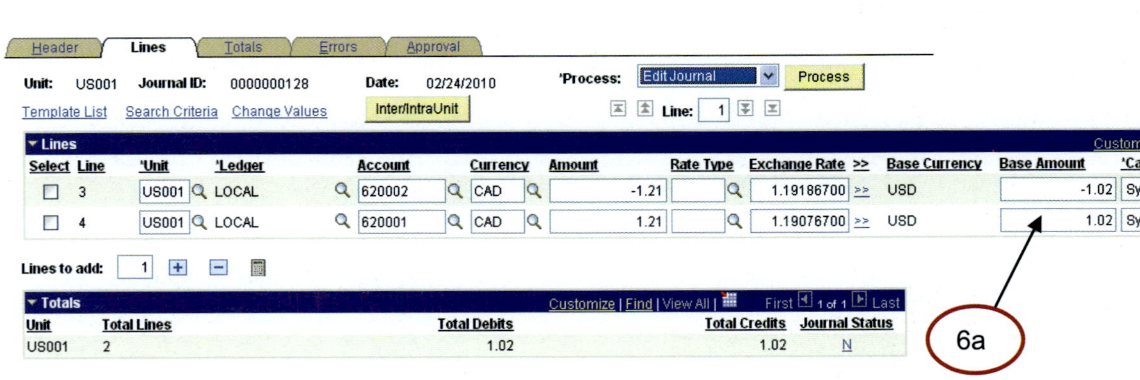

We will review currency rounding in other multi-currency processes later in this book.

Currency Triangulation

Cross currency triangulation allows you to convert two currency pairs using a third currency as a reference.

For example, cross currency triangulation is used to convert a country's native currency to euro upon its entry into the European Monetary Union. During the replacement period, the native currency is quoted directly against the euro (EUR) using a fixed exchange rate. When the euro completely displaces the currency, the native currency no longer exists and is no longer quoted.

The *Currency Quotation Method* page below shows the configuration to convert USD to FRF using EUR as the reference currency. Note that the *Triangulate* checkbox is checked.

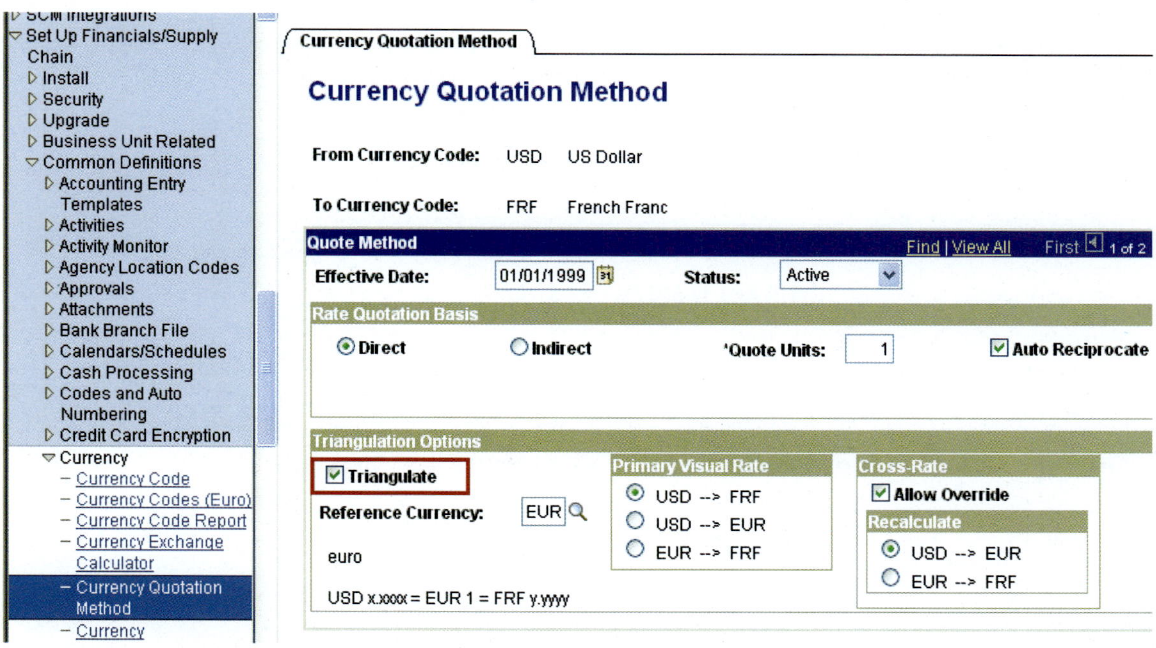

The system performs two conversions to convert USD amounts to FRF:

1. Converts USD to EUR (the reference currency)
2. Next, converts EUR to FRF

Currency pairs that triangulate (USD–EUR and EUR–FRF in the above example) must be setup on the *Currency Quotation Method* page either as *Direct* or *Indirect*.

In the example below USD-EUR is setup as *Indirect*.

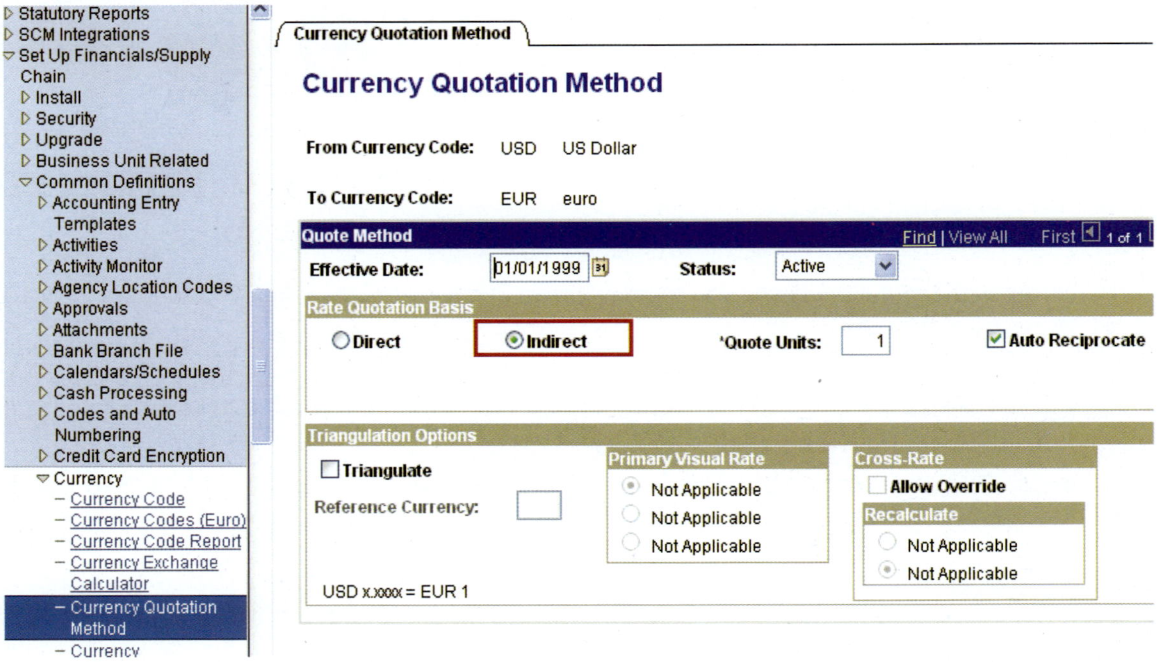

The screen shot below shows market rate for USD-EUR.

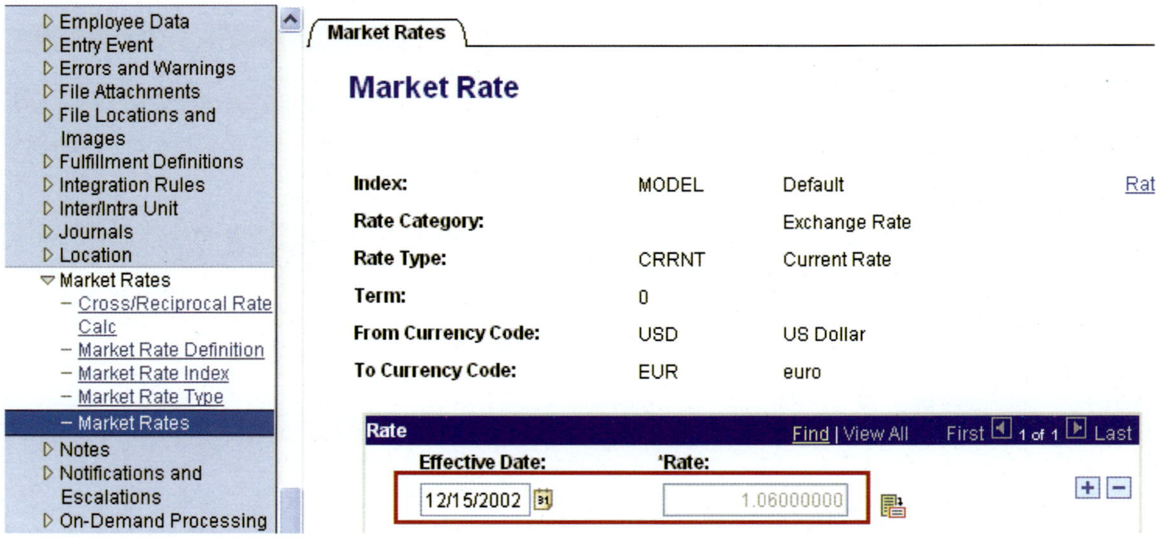

Market rates that you enter are called *visual rates.* Visual rates are stored in the table RT_RATE_TBL in the fields RATE_MULT (for *Direct*) or RATE_DIV (for *Indirect*). The *Quote Units* are stored in the field not containing the visual rate. As a result, the formula for currency conversion is always:

(*from-currency* ÷ RATE_DIV) × RATE_MULT = *to-currency*

The query below on the RT_RATE_TBL table shows market rates highlighted for EUR-USD and USD-EUR currency pairs.

Records | Query | Expressions | Prompts | Fields | Criteria | Having | View SQL | Run

View All | Rerun Query | Download to Excel — First 1-9 of 9 Last

	Index	Term	From Cur	To Cur	Rate Type	Eff Date	Multiplier	Divisor
1	MODEL	0	EUR	EUR	CRRNT	12/15/2002	1.00000000	1.00000000
2	MODEL	0	EUR	FRF	CRRNT	12/15/2002	6.55957000	1.00000000
3	MODEL	0	EUR	USD	CRRNT	12/15/2002	1.06000000	1.00000000
4	MODEL	0	FRF	EUR	CRRNT	12/15/2002	1.00000000	6.55957000
5	MODEL	0	FRF	FRF	CRRNT	12/15/2002	1.00000000	1.00000000
6	MODEL	0	FRF	USD	CRRNT	12/15/2002	1.08360135	6.55957000
7	MODEL	0	USD	EUR	CRRNT	12/15/2002	1.00000000	1.06000000
8	MODEL	0	USD	FRF	CRRNT	12/15/2002	6.55957000	1.08360135
9	MODEL	0	USD	USD	CRRNT	12/15/2002	1.00000000	1.00000000

Since EUR-USD is quoted *Direct*
RATE_MULT = 1.060 and
RATE_DIV = *Quote Units* = 1.00

Since USD-EUR is quoted *Indirect*
RATE_DIV = 1.060 and
RATE_MULT = *Quote Units* = 1.00

The screen shot below show that EUR-FRF is setup as *Direct*.

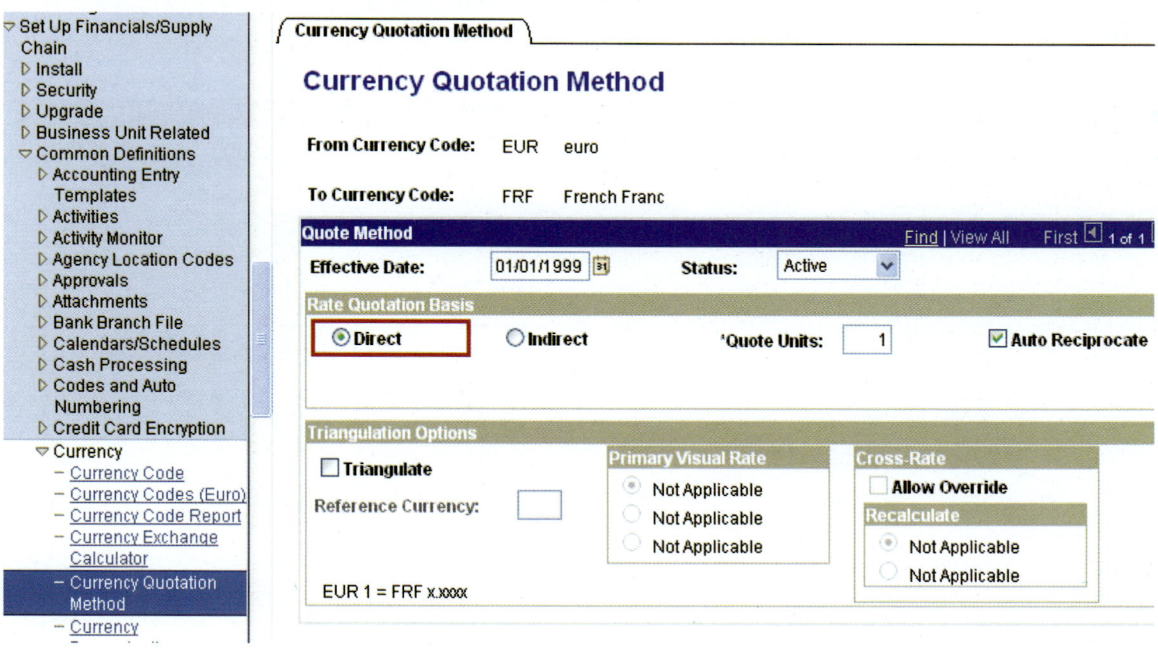

The screen shot below shows market rate for EUR-FRF conversion.

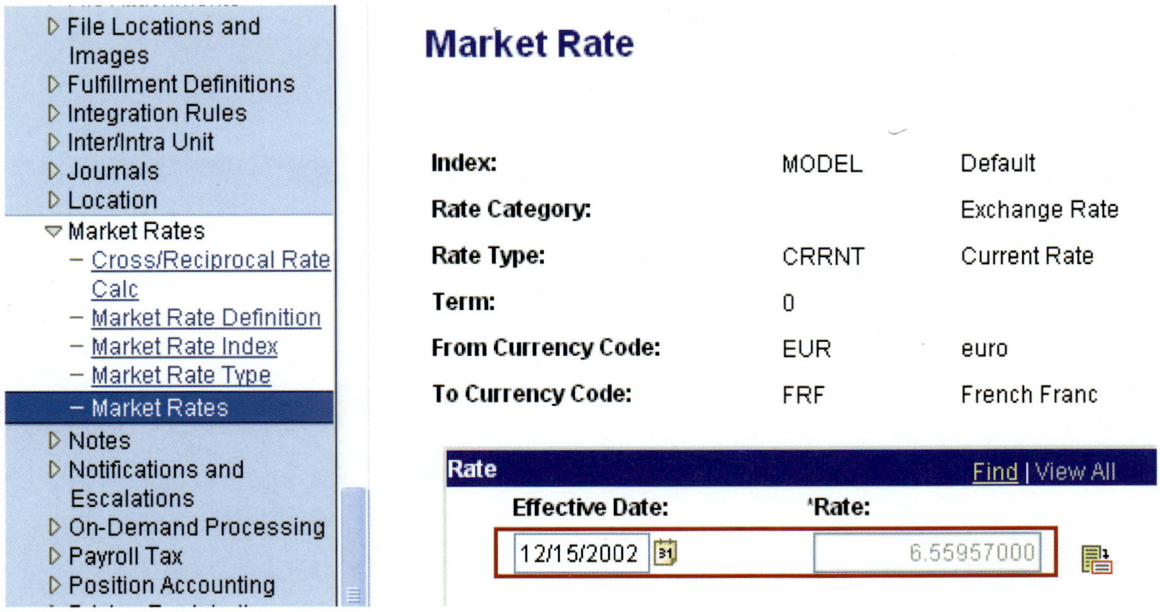

The query below on RT_RATE_TBL table shows market rates highlighted for EUR-FRF and FRF-EUR currency pairs.

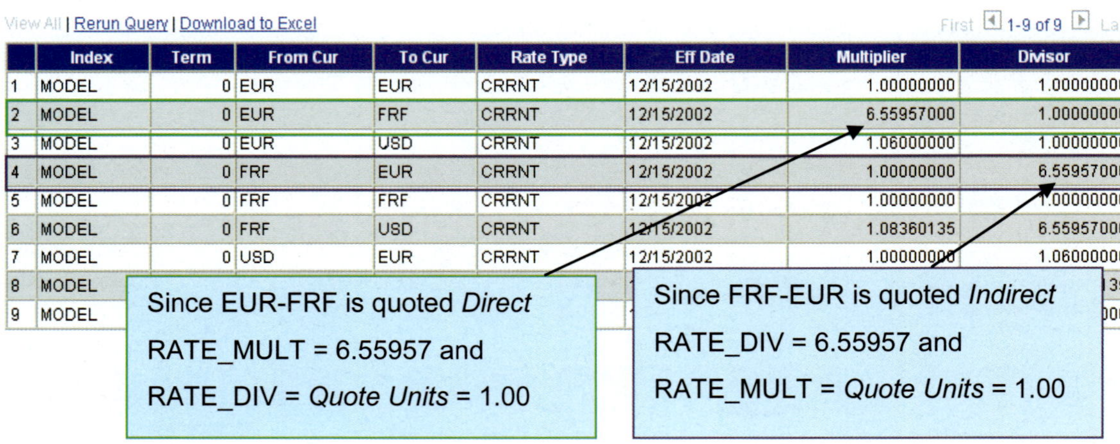

View All | Rerun Query | Download to Excel — First 1-9 of 9 Last

	Index	Term	From Cur	To Cur	Rate Type	Eff Date	Multiplier	Divisor
1	MODEL	0	EUR	EUR	CRRNT	12/15/2002	1.00000000	1.00000000
2	MODEL	0	EUR	FRF	CRRNT	12/15/2002	6.55957000	1.00000000
3	MODEL	0	EUR	USD	CRRNT	12/15/2002	1.06000000	1.00000000
4	MODEL	0	FRF	EUR	CRRNT	12/15/2002	1.00000000	6.55957000
5	MODEL	0	FRF	FRF	CRRNT	12/15/2002	1.00000000	1.00000000
6	MODEL	0	FRF	USD	CRRNT	12/15/2002	1.08360135	6.55957000
7	MODEL	0	USD	EUR	CRRNT	12/15/2002	1.00000000	1.06000000
8	MODEL	[illegible]	[illegible]	[illegible]	[illegible]	[illegible]	[illegible]	[illegible]35
9	MODEL	[illegible]	[illegible]	[illegible]	[illegible]	[illegible]	[illegible]	[illegible]000

Let us try to convert 1000 FRF to USD using currency cross triangulation.

The system performs two conversions using the formula:

(*from-currency* ÷ RATE_DIV) × RATE_MULT = *to-currency*

1. Converts FRF amount to EUR (the reference currency)

   (1000 ÷ 6.55957) X 1 = 152.44901 EUR

2. Converts EUR amount to USD

   (152.44901 ÷ 1) X 1.06 = 161.59595 USD

Note that you do not maintain triangulated rates online. Instead, you only maintain the from-currency to reference-currency and the reference-currency to to-currency rates. Run the Cr*oss-Rate Reciprocal* SQR (*EO9030.SQR*) to calculate the triangulated exchange rates.

To wind up this chapter, let us now discuss the other configurable pieces in the *Currency Quotation Method* screen as they relate to currency triangulation.

The *Currency Quotation Method* screen contains the *Primary Visual Rate*, determining the primary rate that appears in screens and reports. In the screen below the primary visual rate is set to USD -- > FRF.

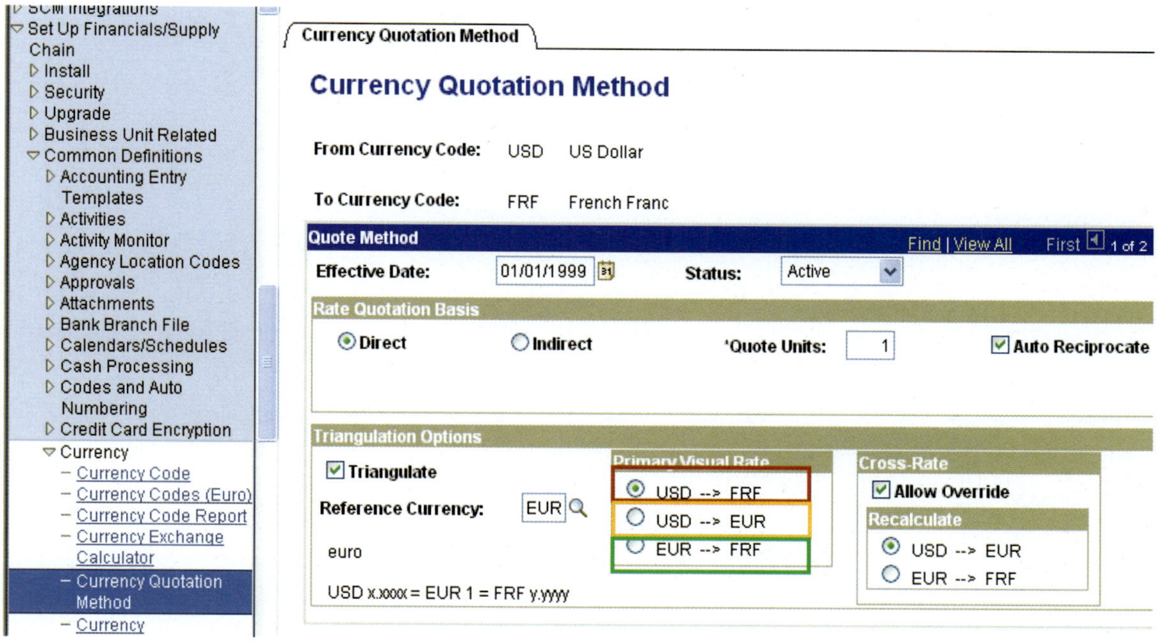

Now, when you enter a journal into business unit FRA01 (base currency FRF) with foreign currency lines in USD, the system displays the *Visual Rate* of **USD -- > FRF**.

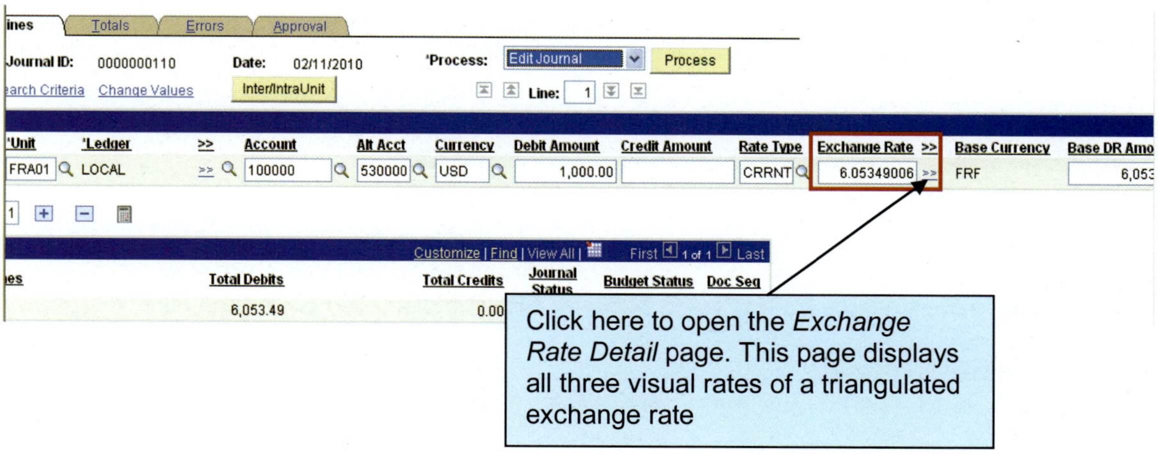

Exchange Rate Detail

Rate Quotation Basis: Direct
Quote Units: 1
Triangulate: Y
Reference Currency: EUR

Current Quote

1.08360135 USD = 1 EUR = 6.55957 FRF

Historic Quote

Not Applicable

Exchange Rate

From	To	Rate
USD	FRF	6.05349006
USD	EUR	1.08360135
EUR	FRF	6.55957000

OK Cancel Refresh

When the *Primary Visual Rate* is set to USD -- > EUR the displayed *Exchange Rate* is 1.08360135.

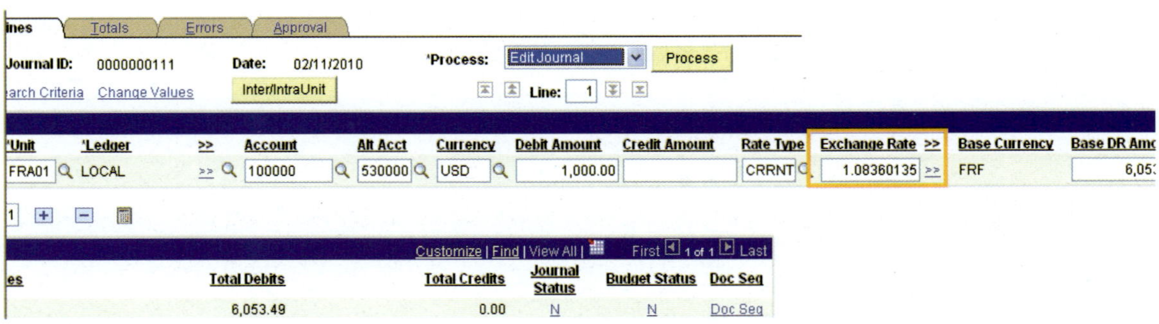

And when the *Primary Visual Rate* is set to EUR -- > FRF the displayed *Exchange Rate* is 6.55957.

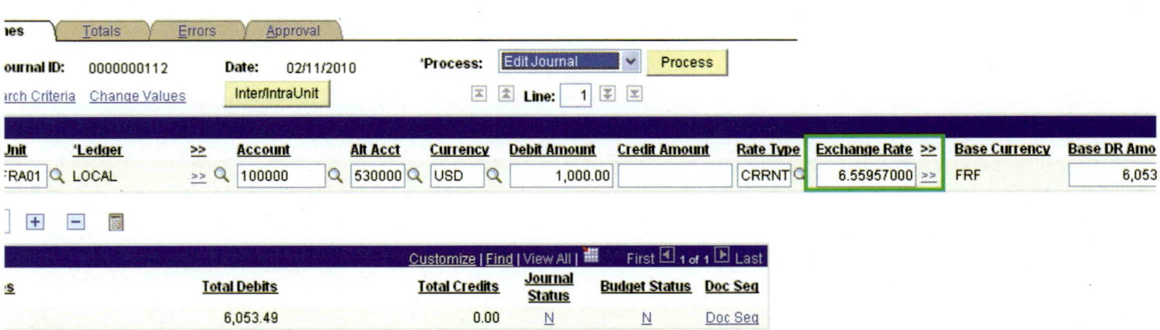

If you clear *Allow Override* checkbox, the system will not allow you to change the cross rates. See the error message below when you try to change the rate.

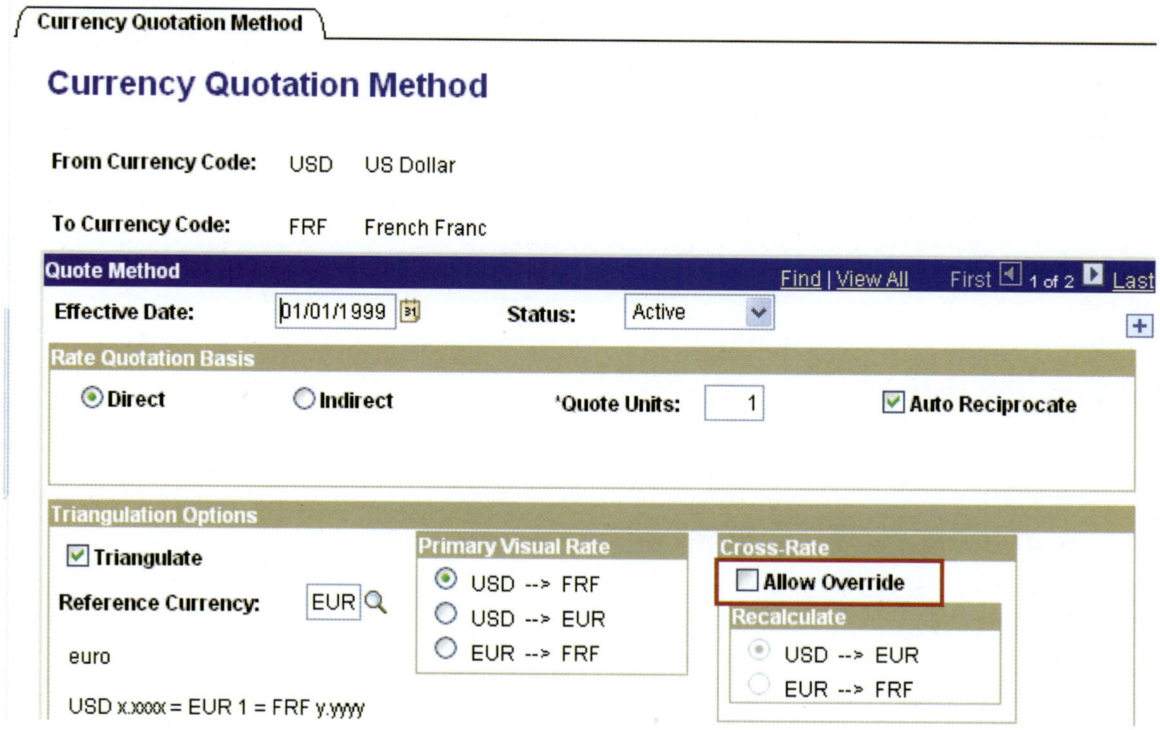

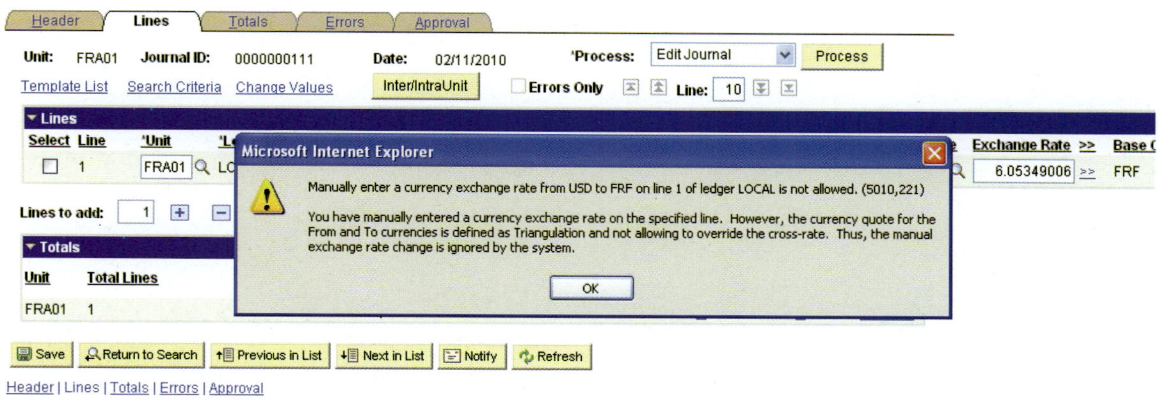

Selecting the *Allow Override* checkbox enables you to override the system retrieved exchange rate of a triangulated currency pair. As a prerequisite, you must configure the currency pair the system will use to recalculate the exchange rate. This will allow you to maintain triangulation accuracy.

For a triangulated rate where RATE_MULT = 6.55957, RATE_DIV = 1, and the cross rate is 6.55957, if you change the cross rate to 6.565 then:

- the system first recalculates RATE_DIV = 0.99917288
- the system then recalculates the cross rate to 6.56500004 based on the first recalculation

A warning message on the journal entry screen will give you the opportunity to override triangulation and to use the exact rate that you entered.

The table below shows the *Reciprocal* values using USD-FRF-USD as an example. *Reciprocal* is discussed in *Chapter 7*.

Field	Value (USD to FRF)	Reciprocal Value (FRF to USD)
Quotation Basis	Direct Indirect	Indirect Direct
Quote Units	Any valid value	Same value
Rate Decimal Positions	Default	Default
Auto Reciprocate	Yes No	Yes No
Triangulate	Yes No	Yes No
Reference Currency	Any valid value	Same value
Primary Visual Rate	From - To (USD - FRF) From - Ref (USD - EUR) Ref - To (EUR - FRF)	From - To (FRF - USD) Ref - To (EUR - USD) From - Ref (FRF - EUR)
Cross-Rate Allow Override	Yes No	Yes No
Cross-Rate Recalculate	From - Ref (USD - EUR) Ref - To (EUR - FRF)	Ref - To (EUR - USD) From - Ref (FRF - EUR)

Currency Controls

Currency Controls define currency related system behavior. For example, you can configure PeopleSoft to define a predetermined behavior (based on business needs) in the case of a journal getting out of balance due to rounding issues.

PeopleSoft allows you to configure the following currency controls in the General Ledger:

- Currency Balancing Options
- Base Currency Adjust Option
- Foreign Currencies Per Journal
- Translate Ledger Exchange Rate
- Rounding Adjustment Option

These controls can be attached to either of the following three screens:

- Journal Source
- Ledgers For A Unit (i.e. ledger groups attached to a business unit)
- General Ledger Definition (i.e. GL business unit)

If the same control is configured differently across any two or more of the above screens then the system uses the hierarchy defined by the sequence listed above (i.e. *Journal Source, Ledger For A Unit, General Ledger Definition*).

Note that not all currency controls are available in all three screens. Follow the steps below to familiarize yourself with the above currency controls:

#	Step
1	Review currency controls defined on *General Ledger Definition* (i.e. GL business unit)
2	Review currency controls defined on *Ledgers For A Unit* (i.e. ledger groups attached to a GL business unit)
3	Review currency controls defined on *Journal Source*

1. Review currency controls defined by *General Ledger Definition*

    a. Navigate to *Set Up Financials/Supply Chain > Business Unit Related> General Ledger > General Ledger Definition > Currency Options*

    b. Verify that the controls match the below table:

Currency Controls	General Ledger Definition	Ledger For A Unit	Journal Source
Currency Balancing Options	Y	Y	Y
Base Currency Adjust Option	Y	Y	Y
Foreign Currencies Per Journal	Y	Y	Y
Translate Ledger Exchange Rate	Y	Y	Y
Rounding Adjustment Option	N	Y	N

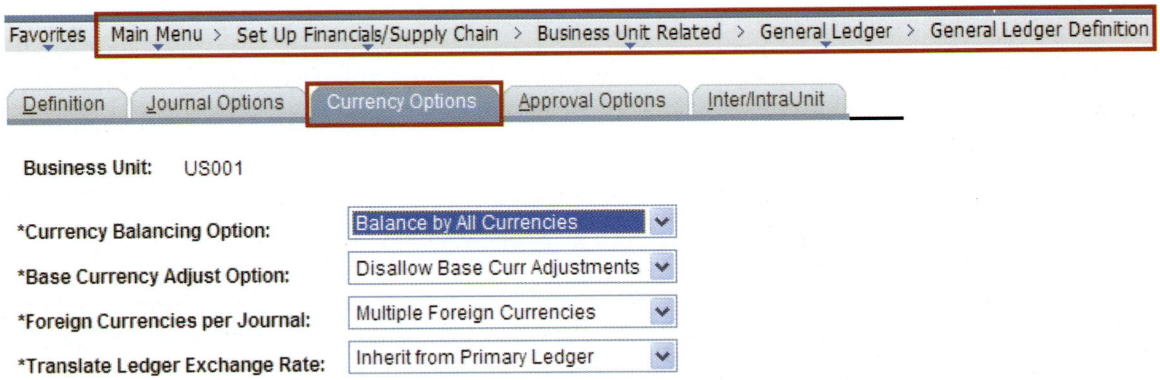

2. Review currency controls defined by *Ledgers For a Unit*

   a. Navigate to *Set Up Financials/Supply Chain > Business Unit Related> General Ledger > Ledgers For A Unit > Currency Options* and verify that the currency controls match the above table.

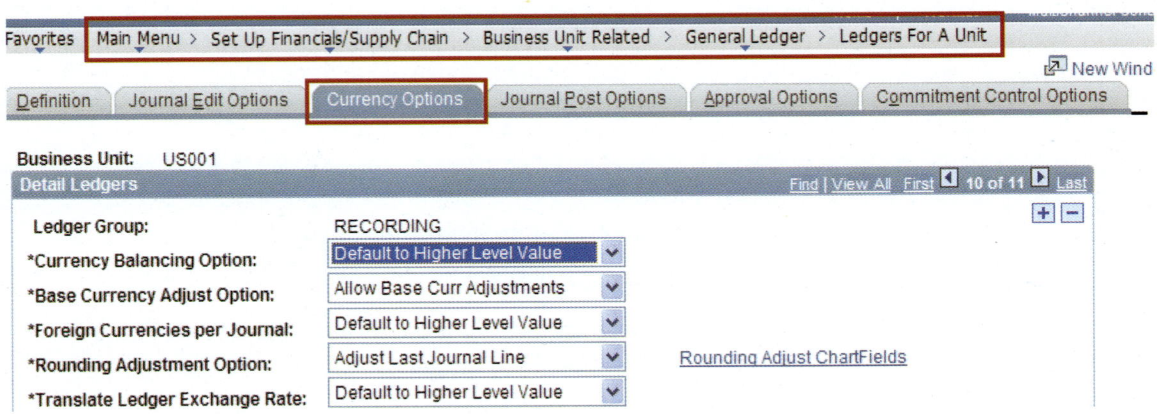

3. Review currency controls defined by *Journal Sources*

   a. Navigate to *Set Up Financials/Supply Chain > Common Definitions> Journals > Source > Currency Options* and verify that the currency controls match the above table.

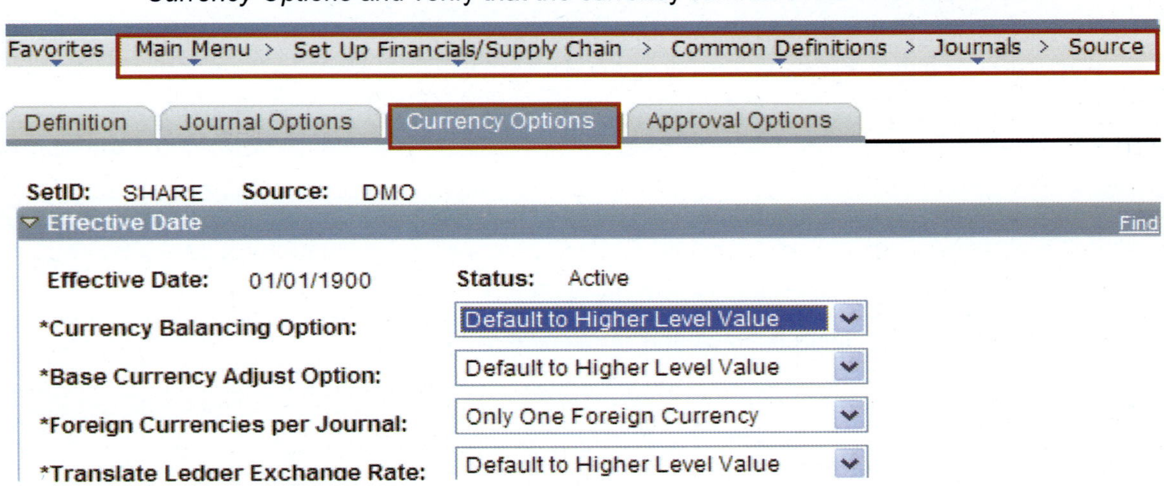

The table below explains these currency controls:

Currency Control	Description
Currency Balancing Options	Specify how journal lines are balanced. Allowed values are: • *Balance by All Currencies:* A journal must balance by all individual transaction currencies. Use this option when the *Keep Ledgers in Sync* option is selected on the ledger group. • *Balance by Base Currency Only:* Balances journals by the base currency only
Base Currency Adjust Option	Allows you to control manual adjustments to the base currency amounts on foreign currency journal lines. Allowed values are: • *Allow Base Curr Adjustments*: allows user change base currency amount on foreign currency journal lines. • *Disallow Base Curr Adjustments:* prevents user changes to the base currency amount on foreign currency journal lines.
Foreign Currencies Per Journal	Allows you to control the number of foreign currencies in a journal. Allowed values are: • *Multiple Foreign Currencies:* allows multiple foreign currencies in a journal • *Only One Foreign Currency:* allows lines in base currency and a single foreign currency only; the allowed foreign currency must be specified on the journal header • *No Foreign Currencies:* only allows lines in the base currency of a journal
Translate Ledger Exchange Rate	Allows you to consistently control the default exchange rate for the translate ledger during both online and batch edit: • *Inherit from Primary Ledger:* translate ledger inherits the currency exchange rate of the primary ledger within the ledger group. • *Retain Exchange Rate:* translate ledger retains the currency exchange rate from the rate type specified by its ledger group
Rounding Adjustment Option	This option is only available in the *Ledgers For A Unit* page. Base currency totals are often out of balance due to rounding caused by individual journal line conversions. This control defines how the system corrects out-of-balance conditions caused by these rounding differences: • *Adjust Last Journal Line:* applies a rounding adjustment to the last base currency line in the journal • *Add Adjusting Journal Line*: inserts a new journal line with the adjustment amount in the base currency.

In addition to the above controls, for each ledger in the ledger group you can choose to either inherit the ledger's base currency from the business unit or define the ledger's base currency manually. Refer to the screen shot below for details.

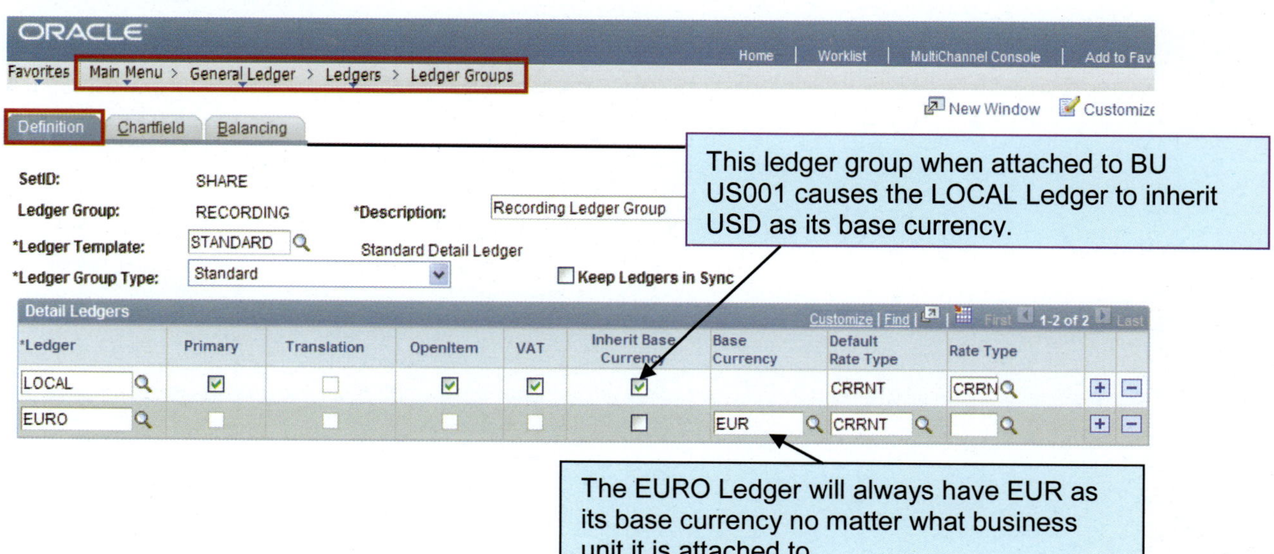

The table below shows the configuration that you will setup to learn the currency controls. The colors used in the table match the graphics below.

	BU = US001	**Ledger Group = RECORDING**	**Ledger Group = REPORTING**	**Source = DMO**	**Source = CFO**	**Source = ONL**
Currency Balancing Options	Balance by All Currencies	Default to Higher Level	Balance by Base Currency Only	Default to Higher Level	Default to Higher Level	Default to Higher Level
Base Currency Adjust Option	Disallow Base Currency Adjustments	Allow Base Curr Adjustments	Default to Higher Level	Default to Higher Level	Default to Higher Level	Default to Higher Level
Foreign Currencies Per Journal	Multiple Foreign Currencies	Default to Higher Level	Default to Higher Level	Only one Foreign Currency	Default to Higher Level	No Foreign Currencies
Translate Ledger Exchange Rate	Inherit Primary Ledger	Default to Higher Level	Retain Exchange Rate	Default to Higher Level	Default to Higher Level	Default to Higher Level
Rounding Adjustment Option	N/A	Adjust Last Journal Line	Add Adjusting Journal Line	N/A	N/A	N/A

Follow these steps to understand the concepts further:

#	Step	Step Description
1	Configure *Currency Options* for the General Ledger business unit	Configure *Currency Controls* in GL business unit US001
2	Configure *Currency Options* for *Ledgers For A Unit*	Configure *Currency Controls* on RECORDING and REPORTING ledger groups for the GL business unit US001
3	Configure *Currency Options* for *Journal Source*	Configure *Currency Controls* for *Journal Sources*: *DMO*, *CFO* and *ONL*
4 - 10	Enter and edit journals	Enter and edit journals to understand each of the currency controls tabulated above

1. Configure *Currency Options* for the GL business unit
    a. Navigate to *Set Up Financials/Supply Chain* > *Business Unit Related* > *General Ledger* > *General Ledger Definition* and search for BU US001
    b. Specify the following values on the *Currency Options* tab:
        - `Currency Balancing Options: Balance by All Currencies`
        - `Base Currency Adjust Option: Disallow Base Curr Adjustments`
        - `Foreign Currencies Per Journal: Multiple Foreign Currencies`
        - `Translate Ledger Exchange Rate: Inherit Primary Ledger`

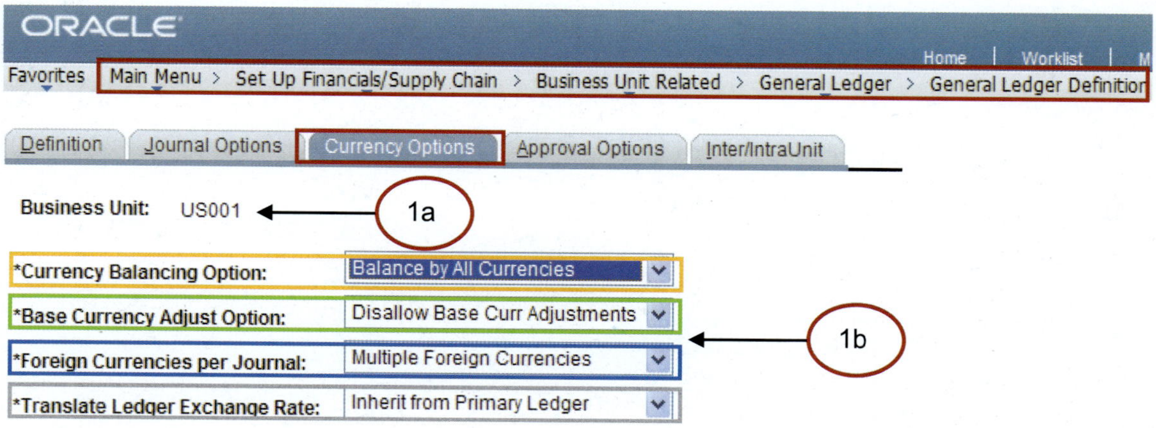

2. Configure *Currency Options* for *Ledgers For A Unit*
   a. Navigate to *Set Up Financials/Supply Chain > Business Unit Related > General Ledger > Ledgers For A Unit* and search for business unit US001
   b. Ensure that on the *Definition* page the RECORDING ledger group (ledger 10 of 11 in the example below) is <u>balanced</u>. Check the *Balanced Ledger* field if needed.
   c. Specify the following values in the *Currency Options* tab:
      - `Currency Balancing Options: Default to Higher Level`
      - `Base Currency Adjust Option: Allow Base Curr Adjustments`
      - `Foreign Currencies Per Journal: Default to Higher Level`
      - `Rounding Adjustment Option: Adjust Last Journal Line`
      - `Translate Ledger Exchange Rate: Default to Higher Level`

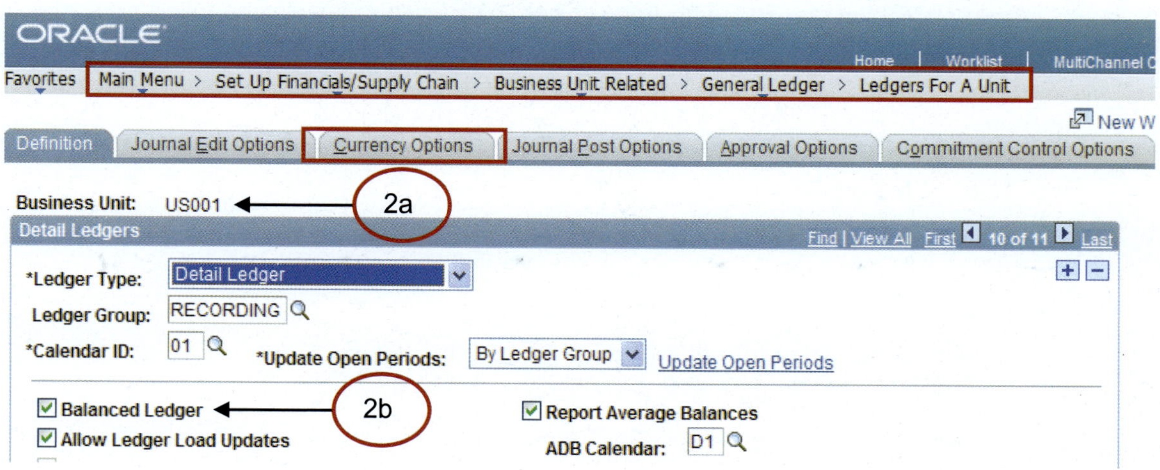

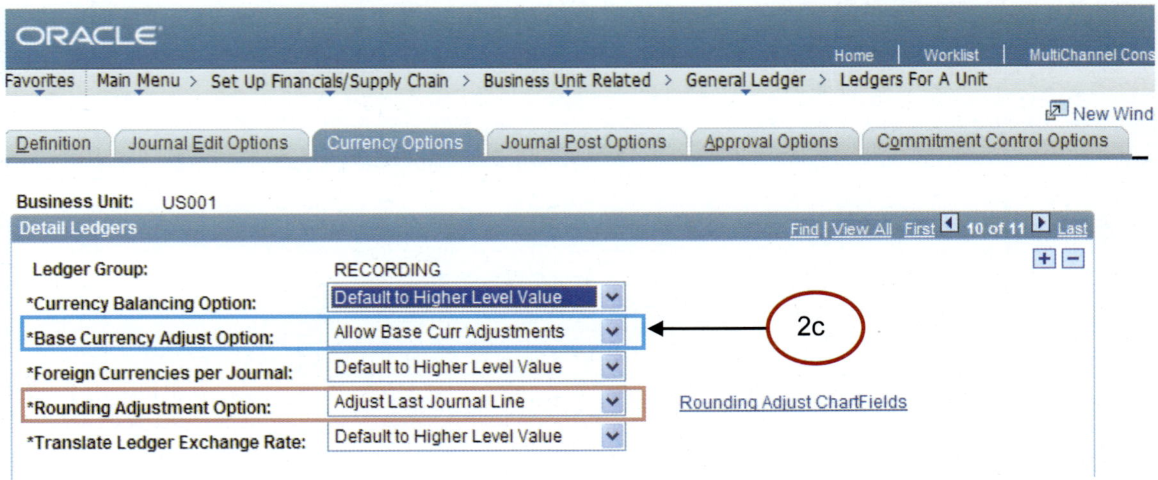

d. Navigate to the REPORTING ledger group (ledger group 11 of 11 in this example):

e. Ensure that on the *Definition* page the REPORTING ledger group (ledger 11 of 11 in the example below) is balanced. Check the *Balanced Ledger* field if needed.

f. Specify the following values in the *Currency Options* tab:

- `Currency Balancing Options: Balance by Base Currency Only`
- `Base Currency Adjust Option: Default to Higher Level`
- `Foreign Currencies Per Journal: Default to Higher Level`
- `Rounding Adjustment Option: Add Adjusting Journal Line`
- `Translate Ledger Exchange Rate: Retain Exchange Rate`

g. Click on the *Rounding Adjust Chartfields* link and specify the following values in the page that opens:

- `Group: Default`
- `Chartfield: Account, Chartfield Value: 693000`

h. Click on *OK*

i. Save the configuration

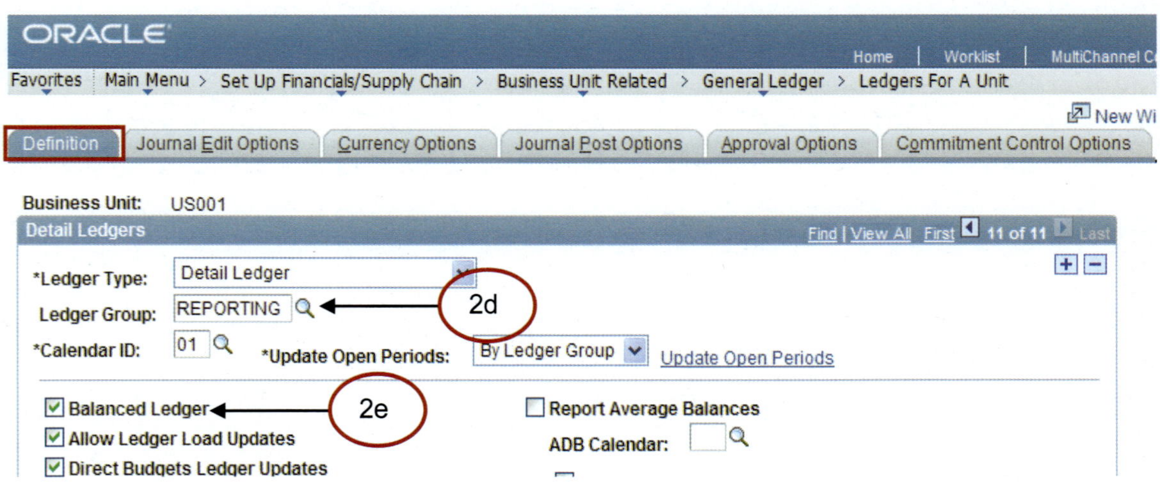

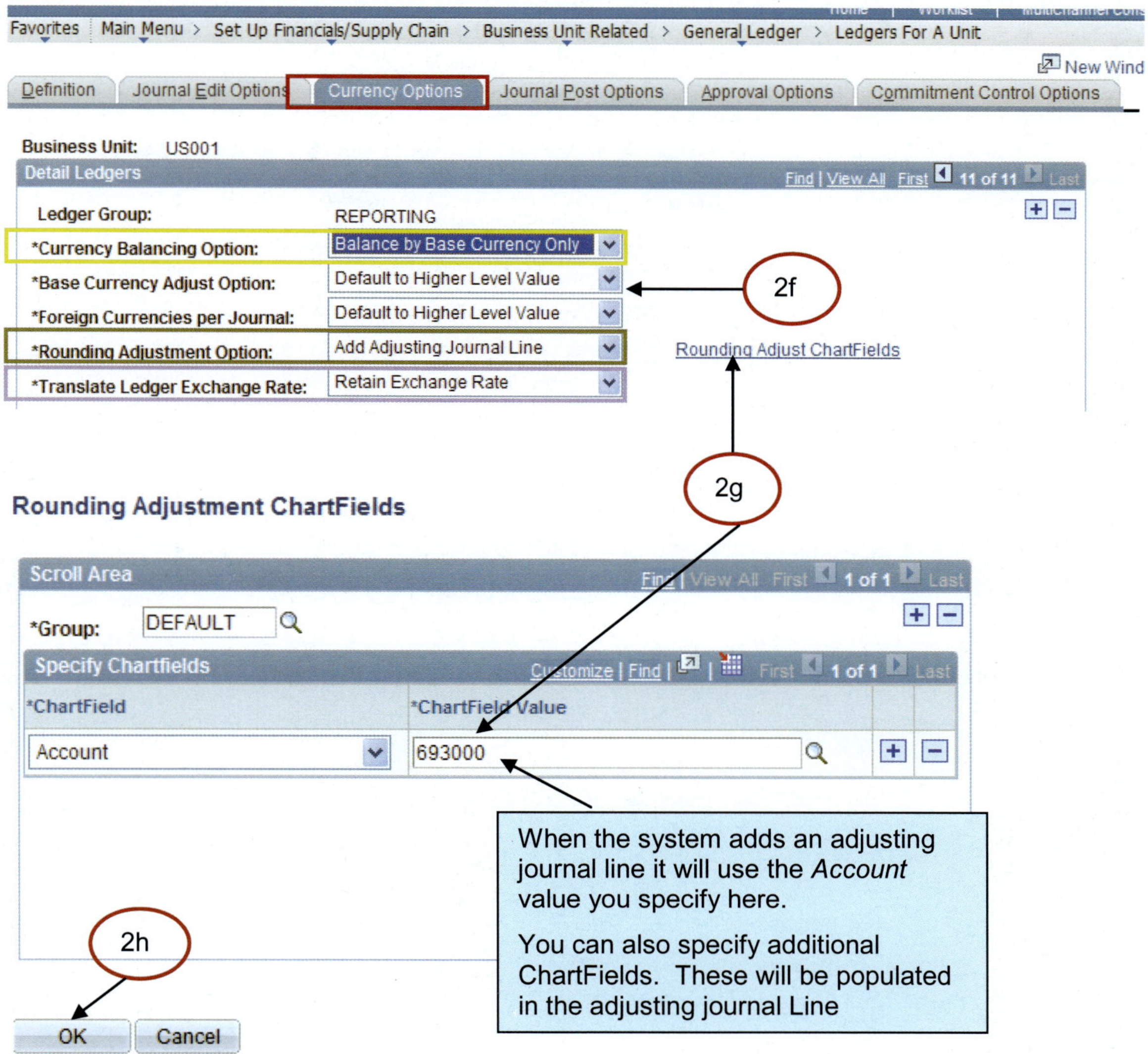

j. Click on the *Update Open Periods* link in the *Definition* page. For each of the ledger groups RECORDING and REPORTING, ensure that the entire fiscal year 2010 is open.

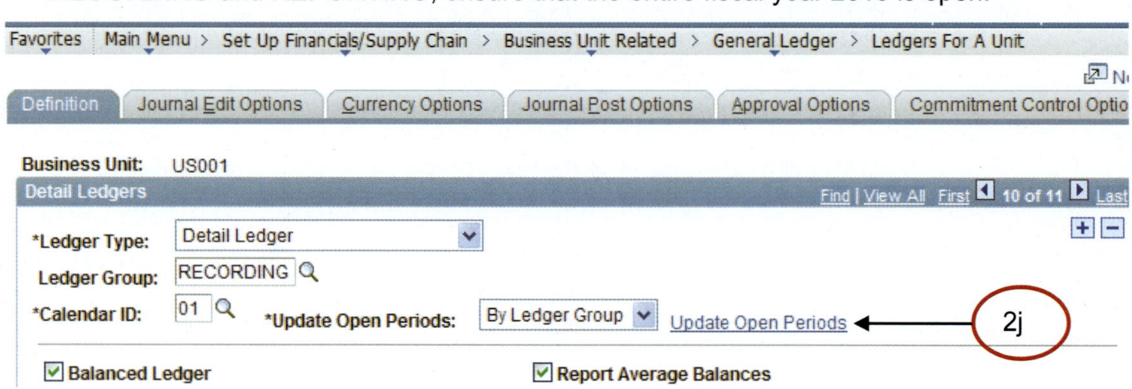

Favorites | Main Menu > Set Up Financials/Supply Chain > Business Unit Related > General Ledger > Ledgers For A Unit

Open Period Update

PeopleSoft Product: GL **Business Unit:** US001 **Ledger Group:** RECORDING

☑ Show all transaction types

Ledgers for a Unit

Open Period(s) — Customize | Find | First 1-6 of 6

Trans Type	Description	From Year	From Period	First Open	To Year	To Period	Last Open
DEF	Default	1998	1	01/01/1998	2020	12	12/31/2020
PCA	Procurement Car	1998	1	01/01/1998	2020	12	12/31/2020
POR	Purchase Order	1998	1	01/01/1998	2020	12	12/31/2020
RCA	Receipt Accrual	1998	1	01/01/1998	2020	12	12/31/2020
REQ	Requisition	1998	1	01/01/1998	2020	12	12/31/2020
UNP	GL Journal Unpost	1998	1	01/01/1998	2020	12	12/31/2020

Fiscal Year 2010 is open for business unit: US001 and both ledger groups.

PeopleSoft Product: GL **Business Unit:** US001 **Ledger Group:** REPORTING

☑ Show all transaction types

Ledgers for a Unit

Open Period(s) — Customize | Find | First 1-6 of 6

Trans Type	Description	From Year	From Period	First Open	To Year	To Period	Last Open
DEF	Default	2002	1	01/01/2002	2015	12	12/31/2015
PCA	Procurement Car	2002	1	01/01/2002	2015	12	12/31/2015
POR	Purchase Order	2002	1	01/01/2002	2015	12	12/31/2015
RCA	Receipt Accrual	2002	1	01/01/2002	2015	12	12/31/2015
REQ	Requisition	2002	1	01/01/2002	2015	12	12/31/2015
UNP	GL Journal Unpost	2002	1	01/01/2002	2015	12	12/31/2015

3. Configure Currency Options on Journal Sources

   k. Navigate to *Set Up Financials/Supply Chain* > *Common Definitions* > *Journals* > *Source* and search for journal source *DMO*

   l. On the *Currency Options* tab specify the following values for journal source *DMO*:

      - `Currency Balancing Options: Default to Higher Level Value`
      - `Base Currency Adjust Option: Default to Higher Level Value`
      - `Foreign Currencies Per Journal: Only one Foreign Currency`
      - `Translate Ledger Exchange Rate: Default to Higher Level Value`

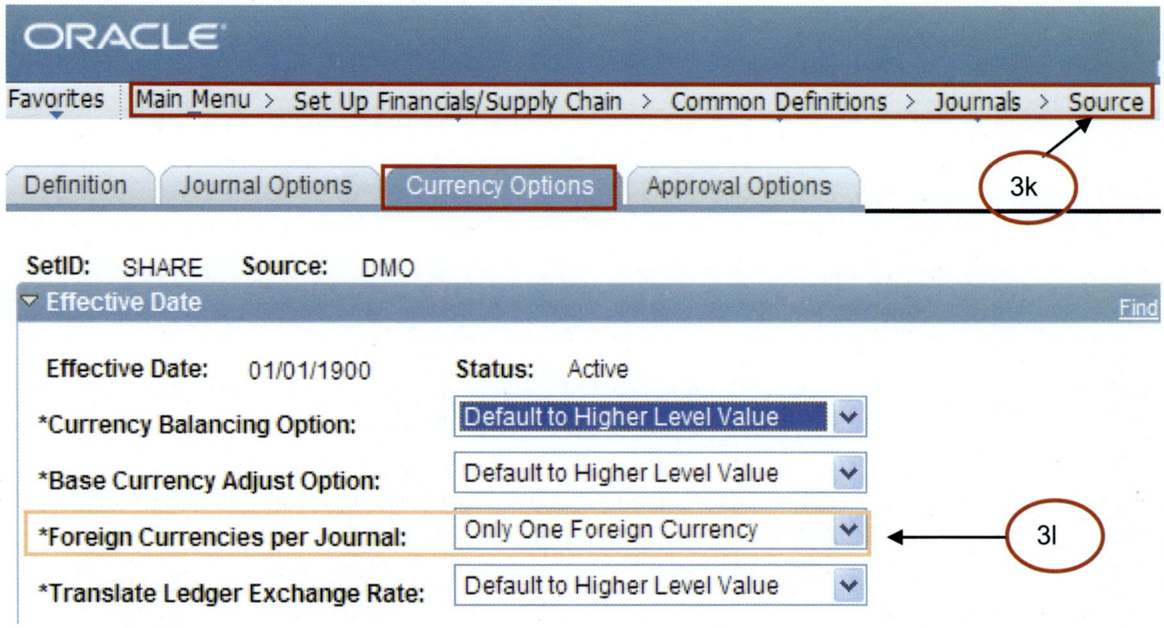

m. Repeat the previous step for journal source *CFO*. Specify `Default to Higher Level Value` for all currency options.

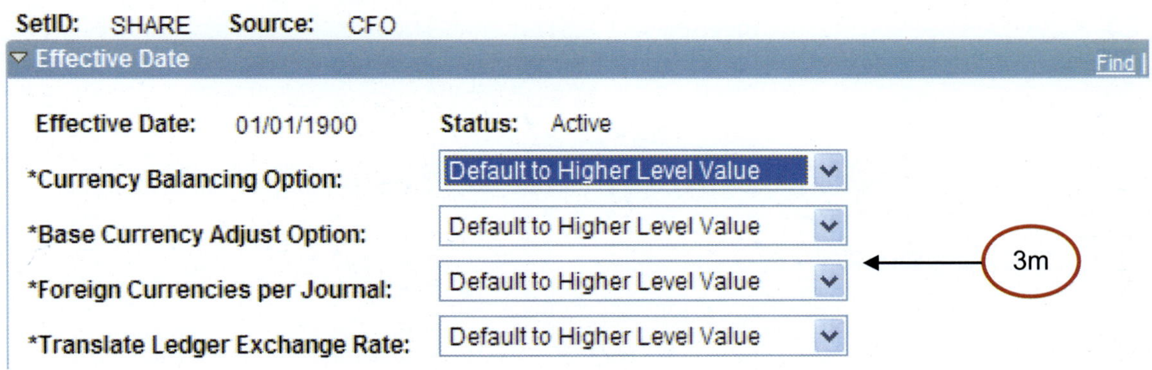

n. For journal source *ONL* specify `Default to Higher Level Value` for all currency options except for the one shown below:

- `Foreign Currencies Per Journal: No Foreign Currencies`

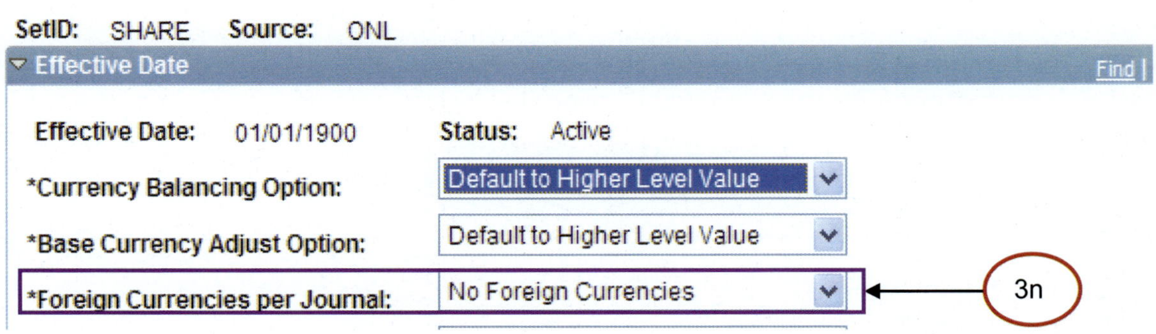

4. Enter and Edit Journals

   a. In the first journal entry, you will explore the following two concepts:

      - `Balance by All Currencies`
      - `Allow Base Currency Adjustments`

   b. You will use business unit US001, ledger group RECORDING, and journal source *CFO*

   c. Review the currency control configuration that you did in the previous steps:

      - `Currency Balancing Options` will use `Balance by All Currencies` as specified at the business unit level. Ledger group and journal source are set to `Default to Higher Level`
      - `Base Currency Adjust Option` will use `Allow Base Curr Adjustments as` specified in the ledger group RECORDING. It will override the business unit level configuration. And journal source is set to `Default to Higher Level.`

	BU = US001	**Ledger Group = RECORDING**	**Source = CFO**
Currency Balancing Options	Balance by All Currencies	Default to Higher Level	Default to Higher Level
Base Currency Adjust Option	Disallow Base Currency Adjustments	Allow Base Curr Adjustments	Default to Higher Level

4c

   d. Navigate to *General Ledger > Journals > General Ledger > Journal Entry > Create/Update Journal Entries*

   e. Specify the following values in the *Add a New Value* tab and click on *Add*

      - `Business Unit: US001`
      - `Journal ID: NEXT`
      - `Journal Date: 02/07/2010`

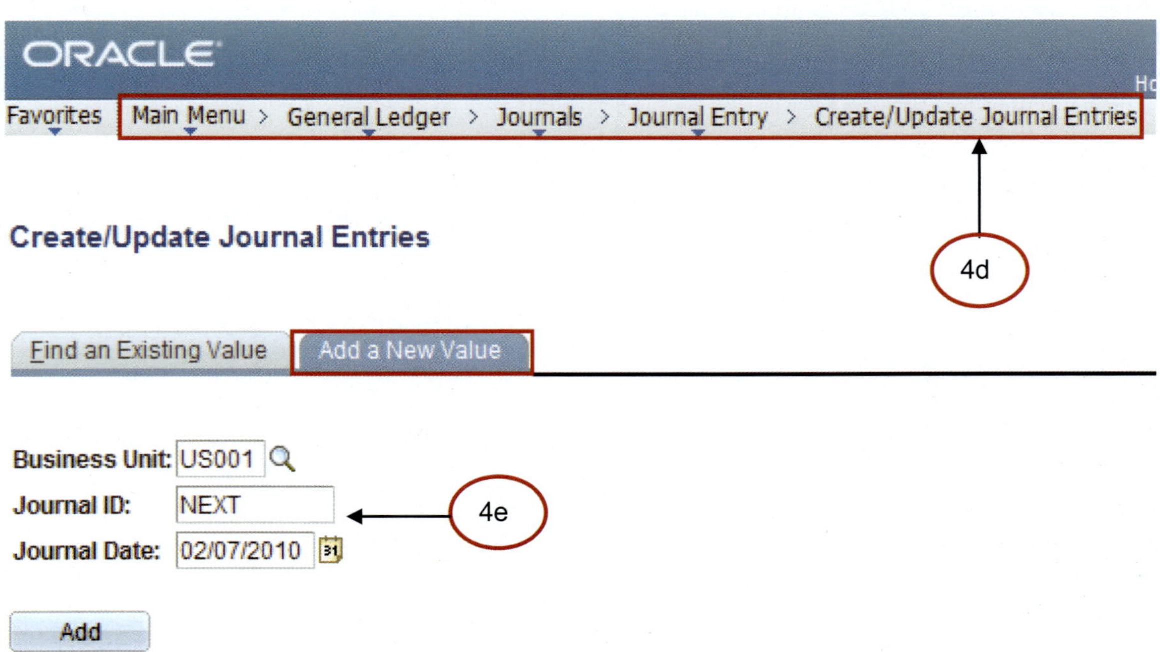

f. In the *Header* tab, by default, the *Ledger Group* and *Source* should respectively be `RECORDING` and `CFO`. If not, update the values.

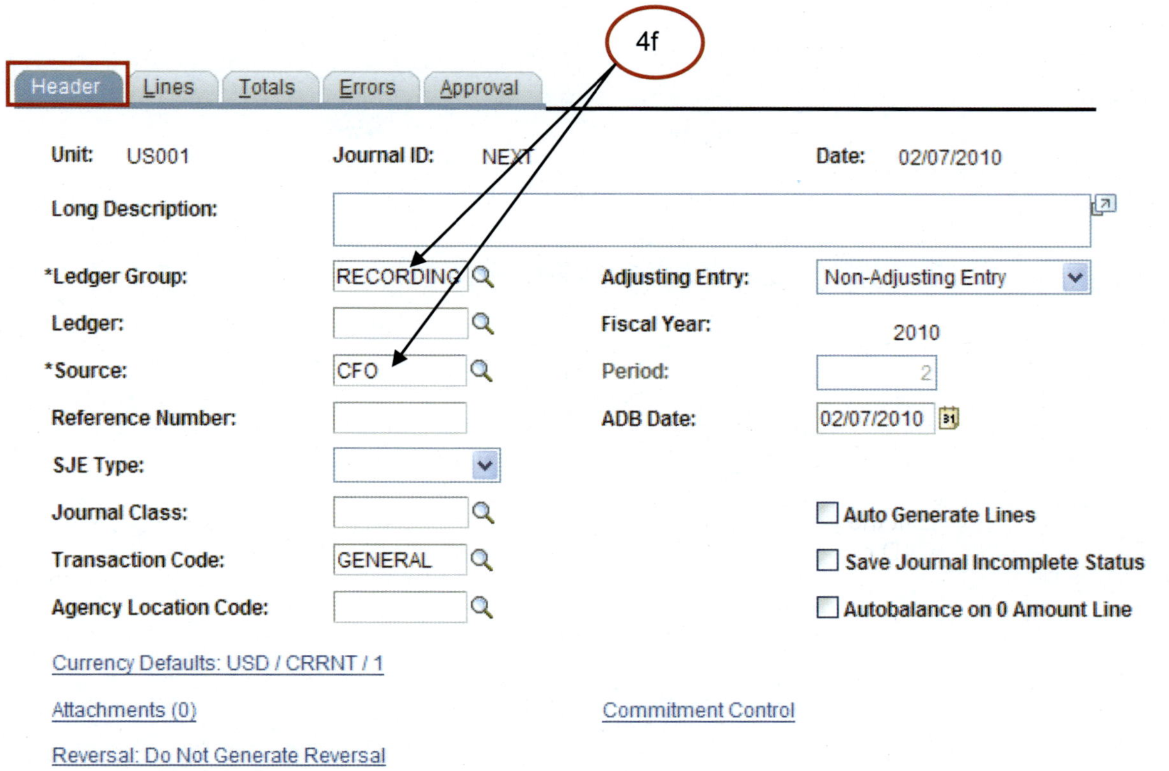

g. Specify the following values in the *Lines* tab and click *Save*

- `Line: 1, Account: 100000, Currency: CAD, Amount: 100`
- `Line: 2, Account: 600010, Currency: CAD, Amount: -98.99`

h. The system automatically calculates the respective base amounts `78.60` and `-77.81`

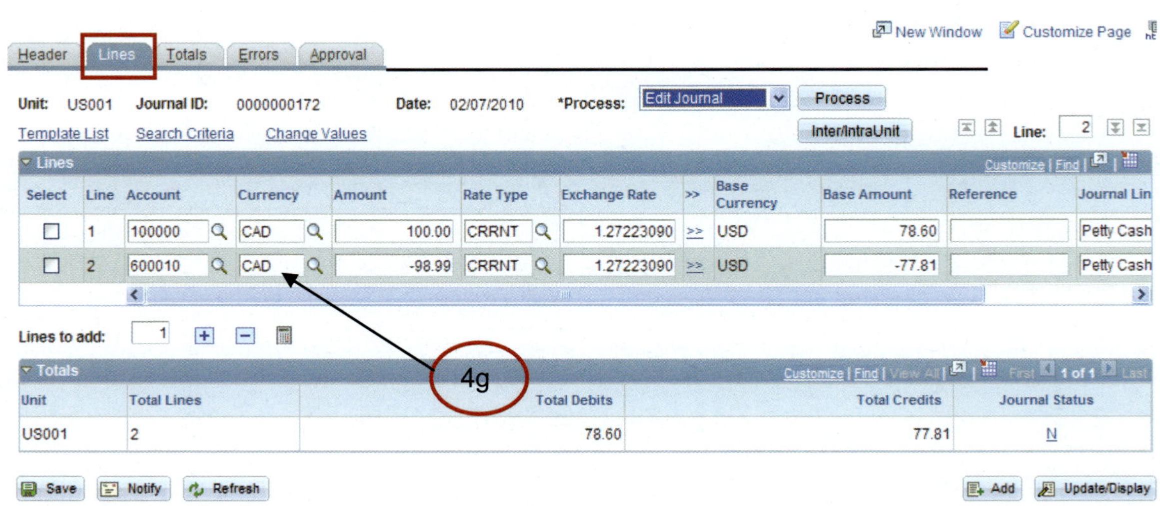

i. Click on *Process* to edit the journal. The journal status displays *E* (Error) because it is neither balanced by USD nor by CAD currency. To be valid, this journal must *balance by all currencies*.

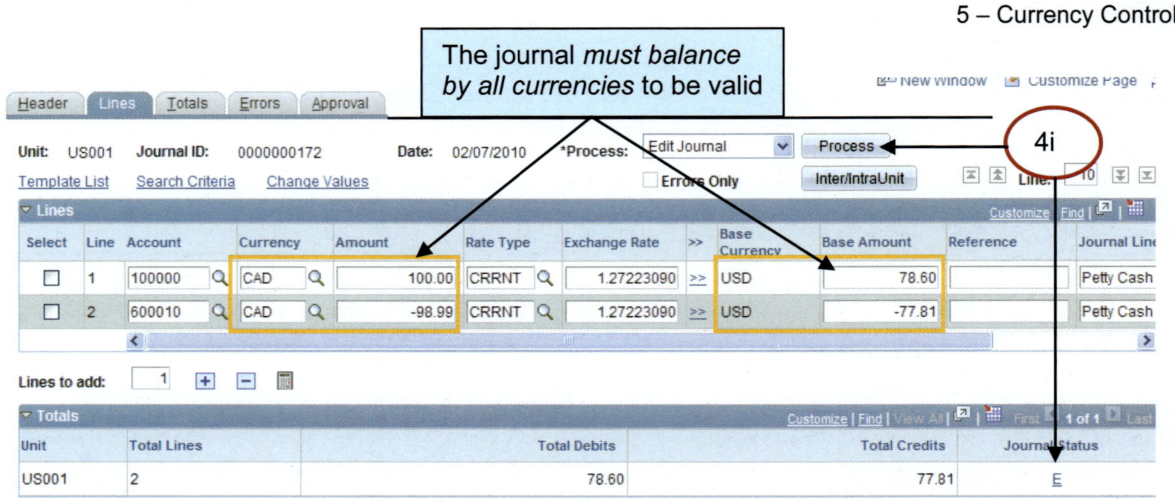

j. Leveraging the functionality *Allow Base Curr Adjustments*, change the *Base Amount* on the second journal line to `-78.60`. The journal is now balanced by USD currency. Save the journal. Note that the system blanked out the *Rate Type* field.

k. Edit the journal again. The journal status displays *E* (Error) because it is not balanced by the CAD currency. To be valid, this journal must *balance by all currencies*.

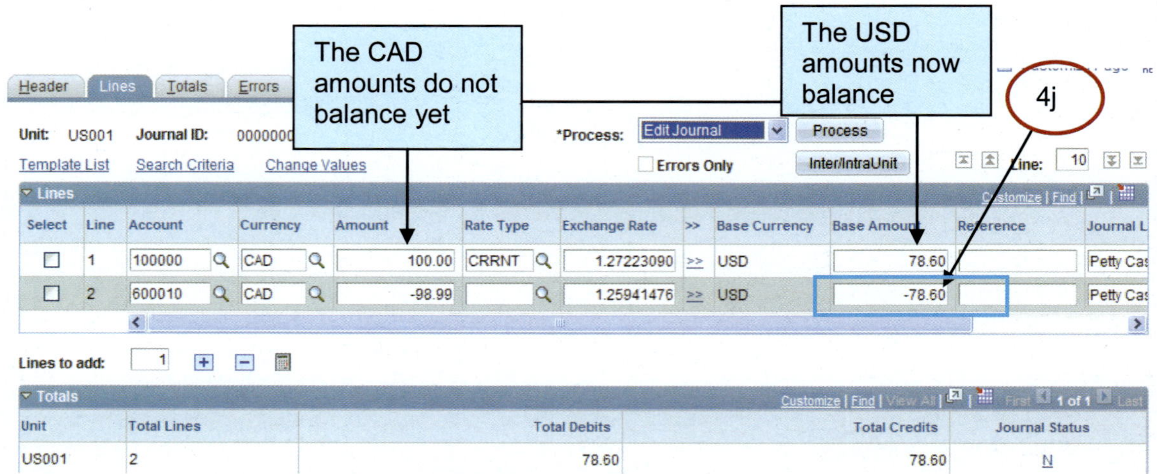

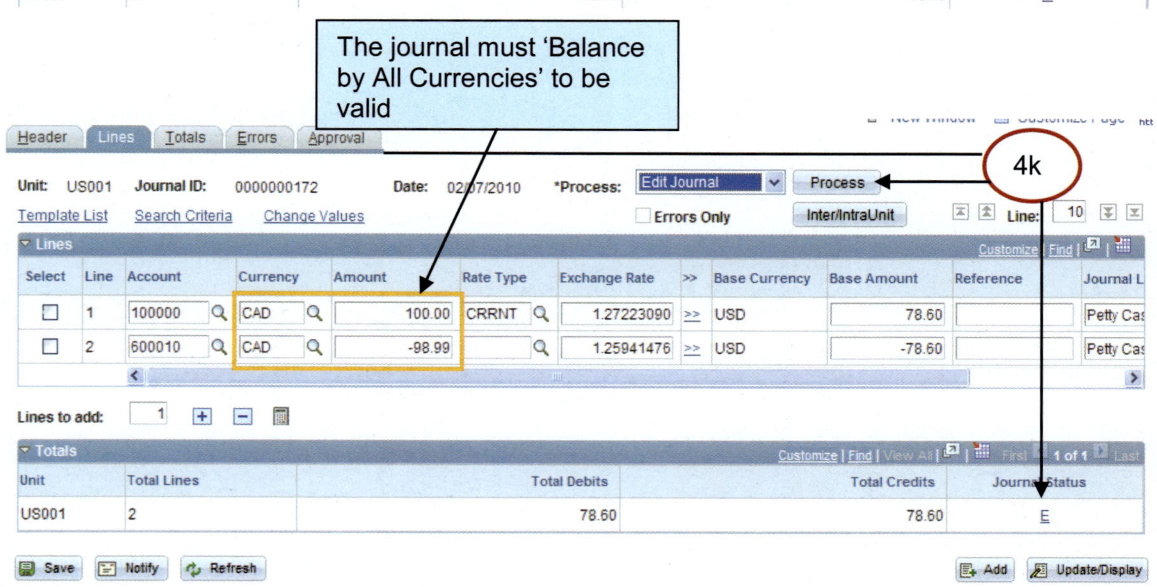

l. Now change the *CAD Foreign Currency Amount* on the second journal line to `-100.00`, balancing the CAD journal lines. When you save the journal, the system repopulates the *Rate Type* field to `CRRNT` and recalculates the *Base Amount* to `100` on the second journal line.

m. Edit the journal again. The journal status displays *V* (Valid) because it is now *balanced by all currencies*.

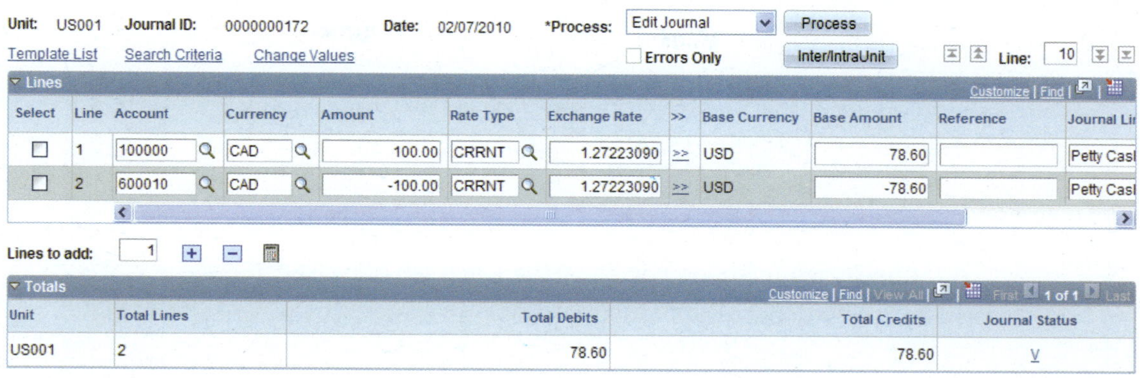

Unit: US001 Journal ID: 0000000172 Date: 02/07/2010 *Process: Edit Journal Process

Template List Search Criteria Change Values Errors Only Inter/IntraUnit Line: 10

Lines

Select	Line	Account	Currency	Amount	Rate Type	Exchange Rate	>>	Base Currency	Base Amount	Reference	Journal Li
☐	1	100000	CAD	100.00	CRRNT	1.27223090	>>	USD	78.60		Petty Casl
☐	2	600010	CAD	-100.00	CRRNT	1.27223090	>>	USD	-78.60		Petty Casl

Lines to add: 1

Totals

Unit	Total Lines	Total Debits	Total Credits	Journal Status
US001	2	78.60	78.60	V

5. Enter and Edit Journals

a. In the next journal you will explore the following two concepts:

- `Balance by Base Currency Only`
- `Disallow Base Currency Adjustments`

b. You will use business unit US001, ledger group REPORTING, and journal source *CFO*

c. Review the currency control configuration that you did in the previous steps:

- `Currency Balancing Options` will use `Balance by Base Currency Only` as specified at the ledger group level. The ledger group configuration overrides the business unit configuration. And journal source is set to `Default to Higher Level`
- `Base Currency Adjust Option` will use `Disallow Base Currency Adjustments` as specified on the business unit US001. The ledger group and journal source are set to `Default to Higher Level.`

	BU = US001	**Ledger Group = REPORTING**	**Source = CFO**
Currency Balancing Options	Balancing by All Currencies	Balance by Base Currency Only	Default to Higher Level
Base Currency Adjust Option	Disallow Base Currency Adjustments	Default to Higher Level	Default to Higher Level

5c

d. Navigate to *General Ledger > Journals > General Ledger > Journal Entry > Create/Update Journal Entries*

e. Specify the following values on the *Add a New Value* tab and then click on *Add*

- `Business Unit: US001`
- `Journal ID: NEXT`
- `Journal Date: 02/07/2010`

f. In the *Header* tab, by default, the *Ledger Group* and *Source* should respectively be `REPORTING` and `CFO`. If not, update the values.

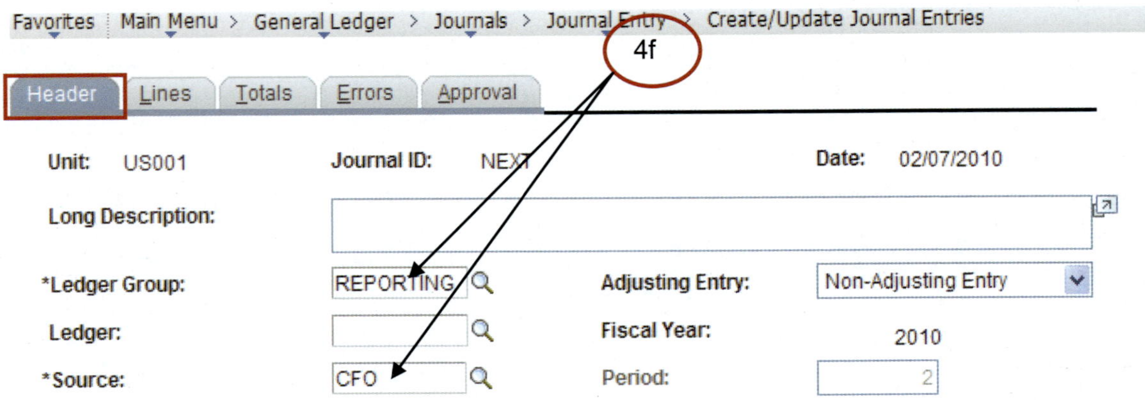

g. Specify the following values on the *Lines* tab and click on *Save*

- `Line: 1, Account: 100000, Currency: CAD, Amount: 100`
- `Line: 2, Account: 600010, Currency: CAD, Amount: -99.98`

h. The system calculates the base amounts to `78.60` and `-78.59`, respectively.

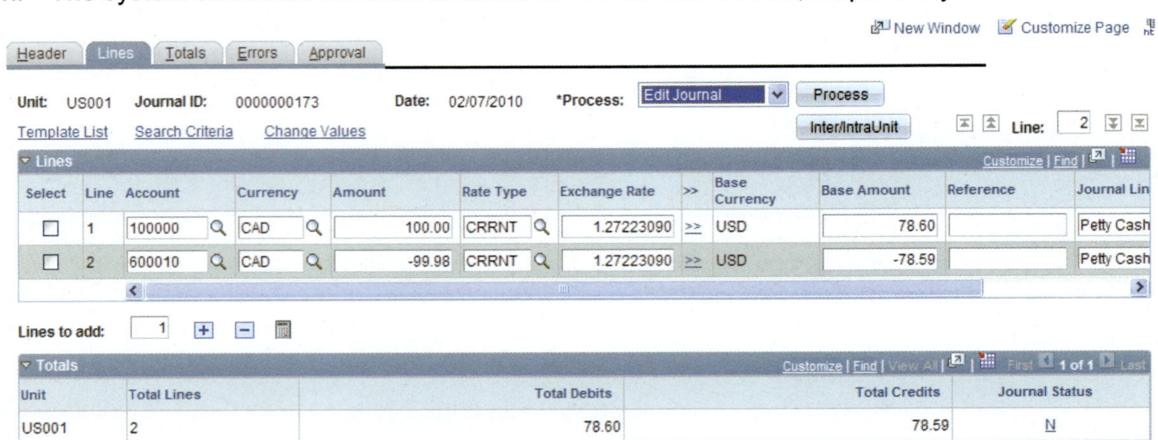

i. Change the *Base Amount* on the second journal line to `-78.60` and click on *Save* at the bottom. The system generates the error message *"You cannot make adjustments to the base monetary amount"*. Click on *OK*.

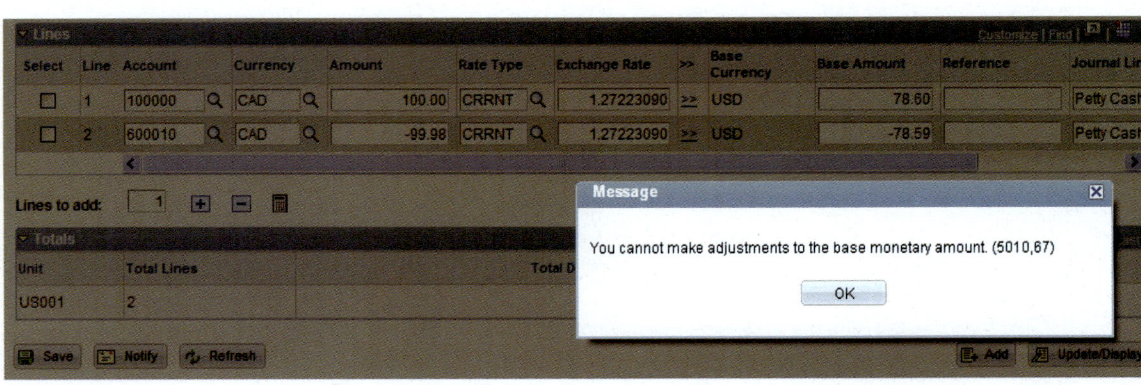

j. Enter the third journal with the values below. Save and edit the journal.

- `Line: 3, Account: 600010, Currency: USD, Amount: -0.01`

k. The journal status displays *v* (Valid). Note that the journal is only balanced by base currency (USD), but not by CAD currency.

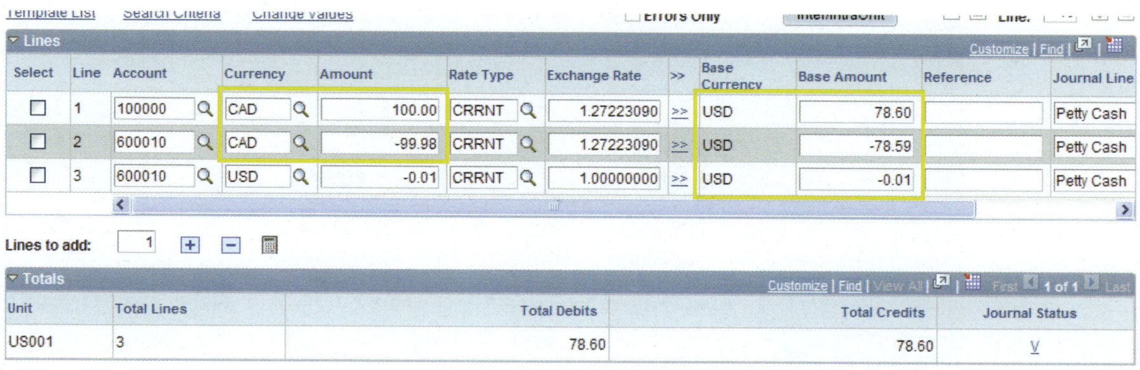

6. Enter and Edit Journals

   a. In the next journal you will explore the following concept:

      - `No Foreign Currencies`

   b. You will use business unit US001, ledger group RECORDING, and journal source *ONL*

   c. Review the currency control configuration tabulated below.

      - `Foreign Currencies Per Journal` will use `No Foreign Currencies` as specified for journal source *ONL*. It overrides the business unit level configuration of `Multiple Foreign Currencies.`

	BU = US001	**Ledger Group = RECORDING**	**Source = ONL**
Foreign Currencies Per Journal	Multiple Foreign Currencies	Default to Higher Level	No Foreign Currencies

   d. Navigate to *General Ledger* > *Journals* > *General Ledger* > *Journal Entry* > *Create/Update Journal Entries*

   e. Specify the following values on the *Add a New Value* tab and then click on *Add*

      - `Business Unit: US001`
      - `Journal ID: NEXT`
      - `Journal Date: 02/07/2010`

   f. In the *Header* tab, by default, the *Ledger Group* and *Source* should respectively be `RECORDING` and `ONL`. If not, update the values.

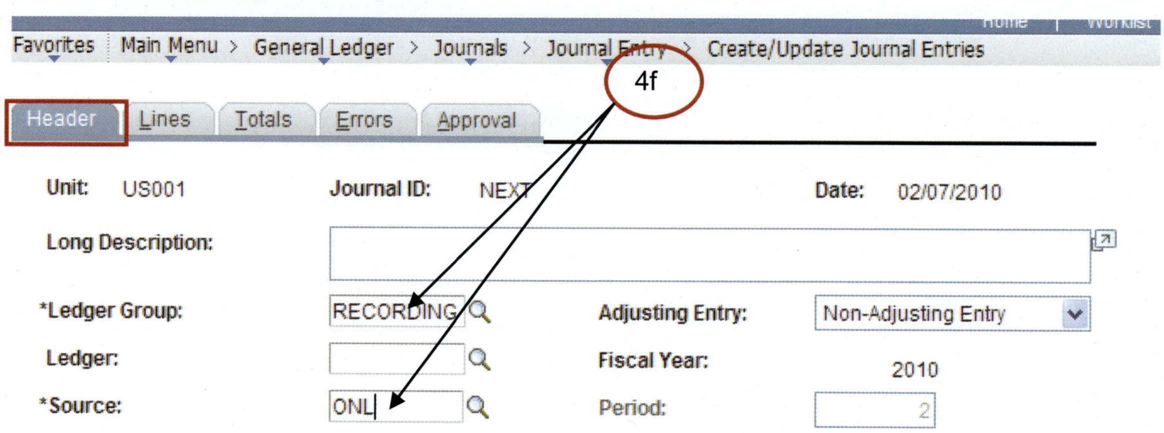

   g. On the *Line* tab as soon as you specify the foreign currency of `CAD` the system generates an error message *"You cannot change foreign currency code."*

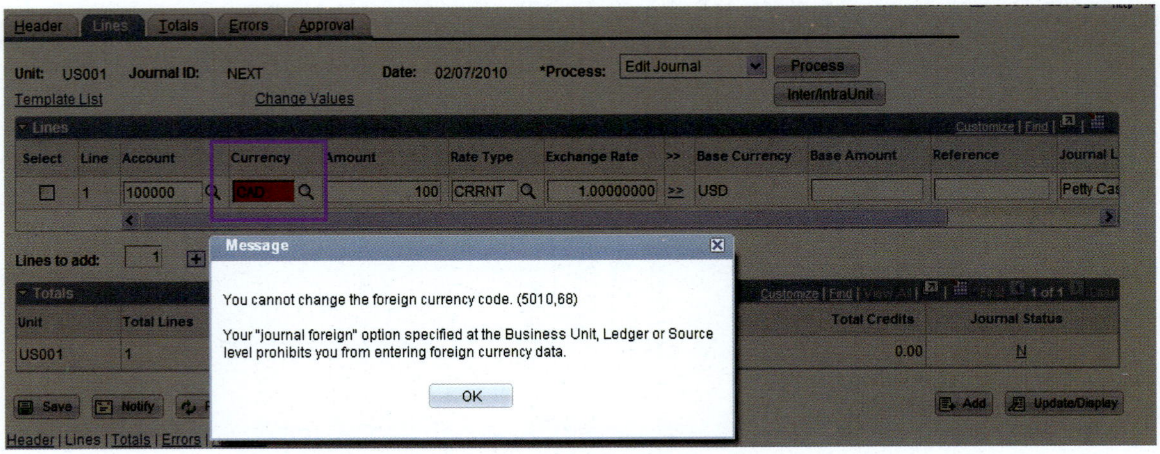

7. Enter and Edit Journals

   a. In the next journal you will explore the following concept:

      - `Only One Foreign Currency`

   b. You will use business unit: US001, Ledger Group: RECORDING and Journal Source: DMO

   c. Review the currency control configuration tabulated below:

      - `Foreign Currencies Per Journal` will use `Only One Foreign Currency` as specified for journal source *DMO*. It overrides the business unit level configuration of `Multiple Foreign Currencies`.

	BU = US001	**Ledger Group = RECORDING**	**Source = DMO**
Foreign Currencies Per Journal	Multiple Foreign Currencies	Default to Higher Level	Only one Foreign Currency

   d. Navigate to *General Ledger* > *Journals* > *General Ledger* > *Journal Entry* > *Create/Update Journal Entries*

   e. Specify the following values on the *Add a New Value* tab and then click on the *Add*

      - `Business Unit: US001`
      - `Journal ID: NEXT`
      - `Journal Date: 02/07/2010`

   f. In the *Header* tab, by default, the *Ledger Group* and *Source* should respectively be `RECORDING` and `DMO`. If not, update the values.

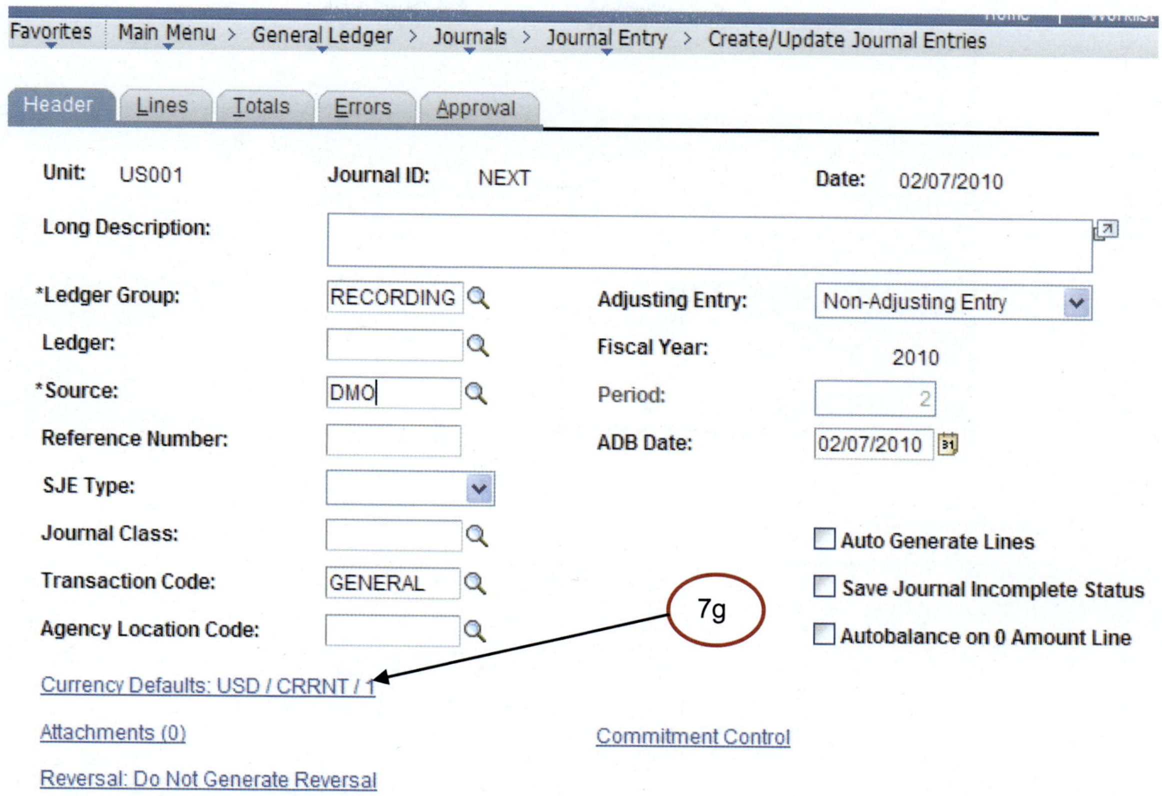

g. While on the *Header* tab click on the *Currency Defaults* link and specify `CAD`. Click on *Get Rate* followed by *OK*.

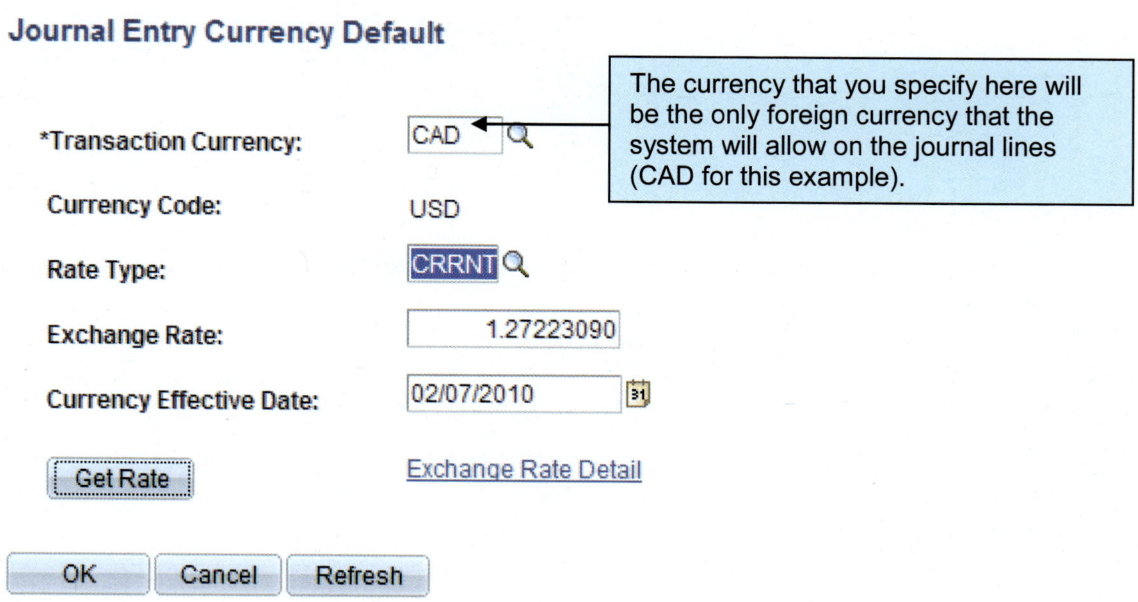

h. Note that on the *Line* tab, the system accepted the `CAD` foreign currency, but generated an error for JPY.

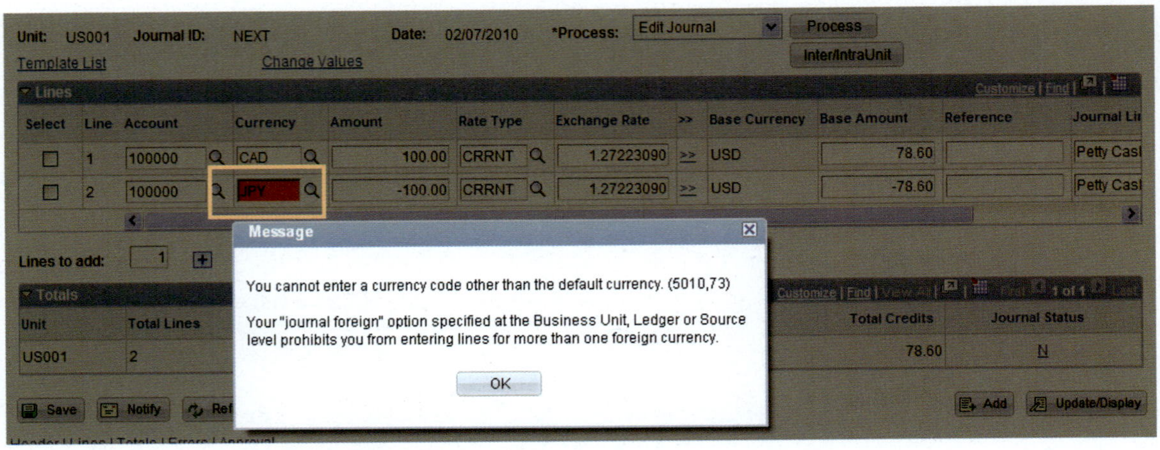

8. Enter and Edit Journals
    a. In the next journal you will explore the following concept:
        - `Multiple Foreign Currencies`
    b. You will use business unit US001, ledger group RECORDING, and journal source *CFO*
    c. Review the currency control configuration tabulated below:
        - `Foreign Currencies Per Journal` will use `Multiple Foreign Currencies` as specified in business unit `US001`. The Ledger Group and Journal Source are set to *`Default to Higher Level`*.

	BU = US001	**Ledger Group = RECORDING**	**Source = DMO**
Foreign Currencies Per Journal	Multiple Foreign Currencies	Default to Higher Level	Default to Higher Level

    d. Navigate to *General Ledger* > *Journals* > *General Ledger* > *Journal Entry* > *Create/Update Journal Entries*
    e. Specify the following values on the *Add a New Value* tab and then click on the *Add*
        - `Business Unit: US001`
        - `Journal ID: NEXT`
        - `Journal Date: 02/07/2010`
    f. In the *Header* tab, by default, the *Ledger Group* and *Source* should respectively be `RECORDING` and `DMO`. If not, update the values.
    g. While on the *Header* tab click on the *Currency Defaults* link and specify `CAD`. Click on *Get Rate* followed by *OK*.

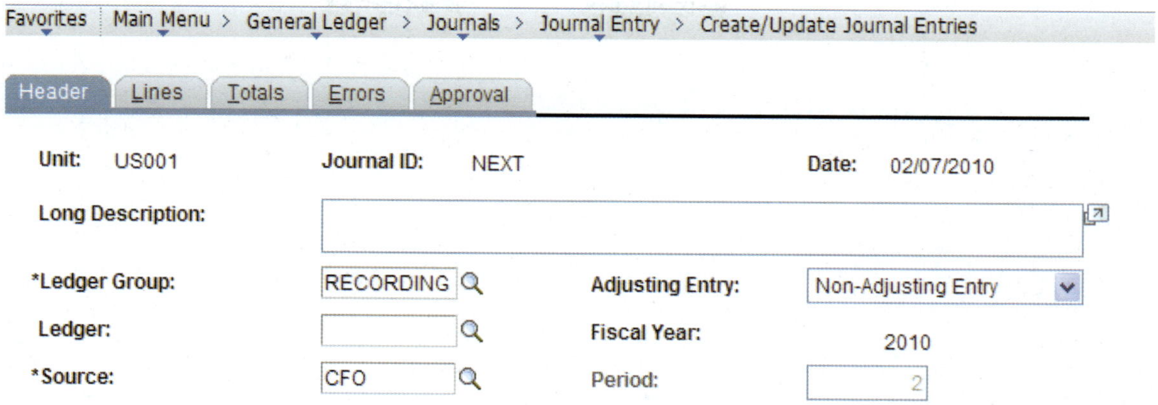

h. On the *Line* tab you can see that the system accepted both foreign currencies, CAD and JPY.

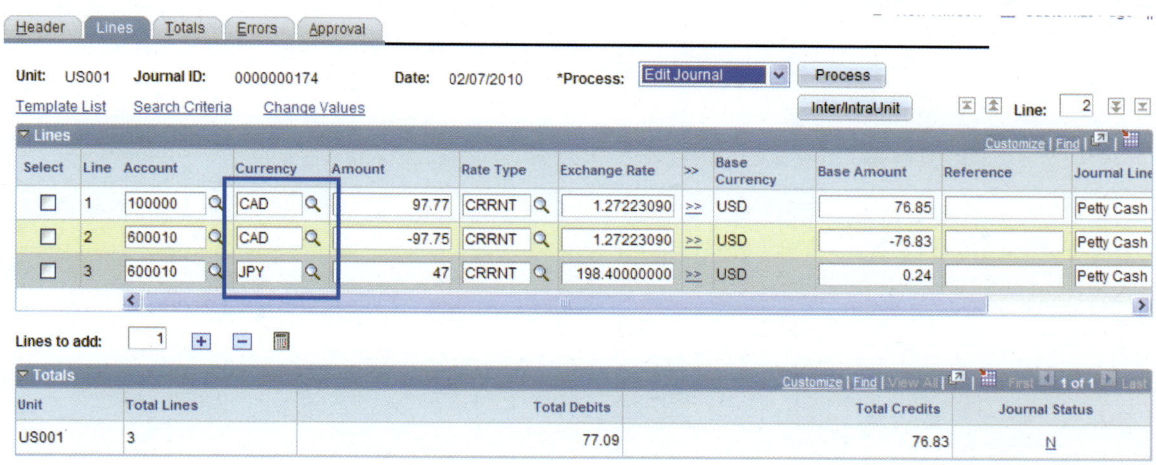

9. Enter and Edit Journals

a. In the next journal you will explore the following concept:

- `Adjust Last Journal Line`

b. You will use business unit US001, ledger group RECORDING, and journal source *CFO*

c. Review the currency control configuration tabulated below:

- `Rounding Adjustment Option` will use `Adjust Last Journal Line` as specified on the ledger group `RECORDING`. This currency control is not available in the business unit and journal source screens.

	BU = US001	**Ledger Group = RECORDING**	**Source = CFO**
Rounding Adjustment Option	N/A	Adjust Last Journal Line	N/A

d. Before adding the journal let us quickly add a market rate for USD to MXN. Navigate to *Set Up Financials/Supply Chain > Common Definitions > Market Rates > Market Rates*

e. In the *Add a New Value* page, specify the following values and click *Add*:

- `Market Rate Index: MODEL`
- `Term: 0`
- `From Currency Code: USD`
- `To Currency Code: MXN`

- `Rate Type: CRRNT`

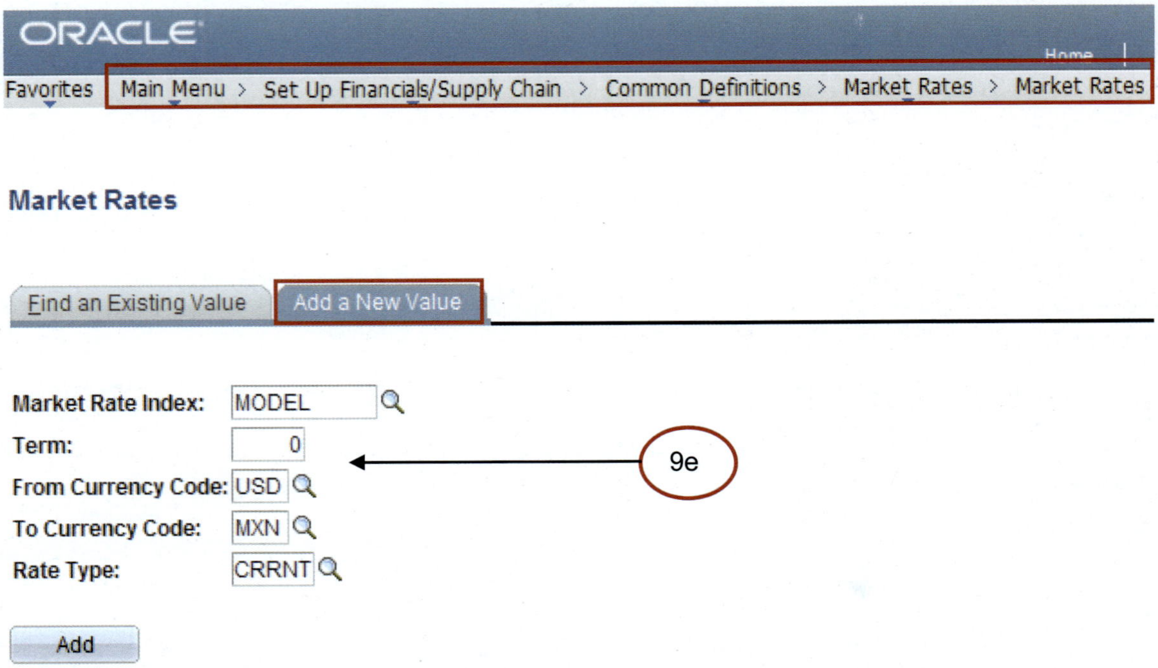

f. In the *Market Rate* page, specify the following values and save.

- `Effective Date: 02/01/2010`
- `Rate: 13.15134567`

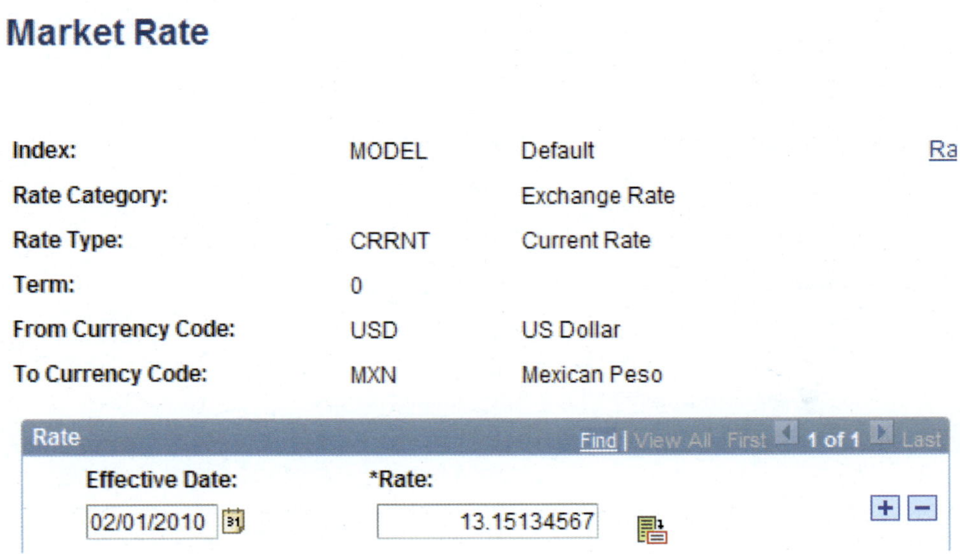

g. Navigate to *General Ledger > Journals > General Ledger > Journal Entry > Create/Update Journal Entries*

h. Specify the following values in the *Add a New Value* tab and click on *Add*

- `Business Unit: US001`
- `Journal ID: NEXT`
- `Journal Date: 02/07/2010`

i. In the *Header* tab, by default, the *Ledger Group* and *Source* should respectively be `RECORDING` and `CFO`. If not, update the values.

e. Specify the following values:

- `Effective Date: 12/01/2009`
- `Rate: 1.10`

f. Click on *Save* at the bottom

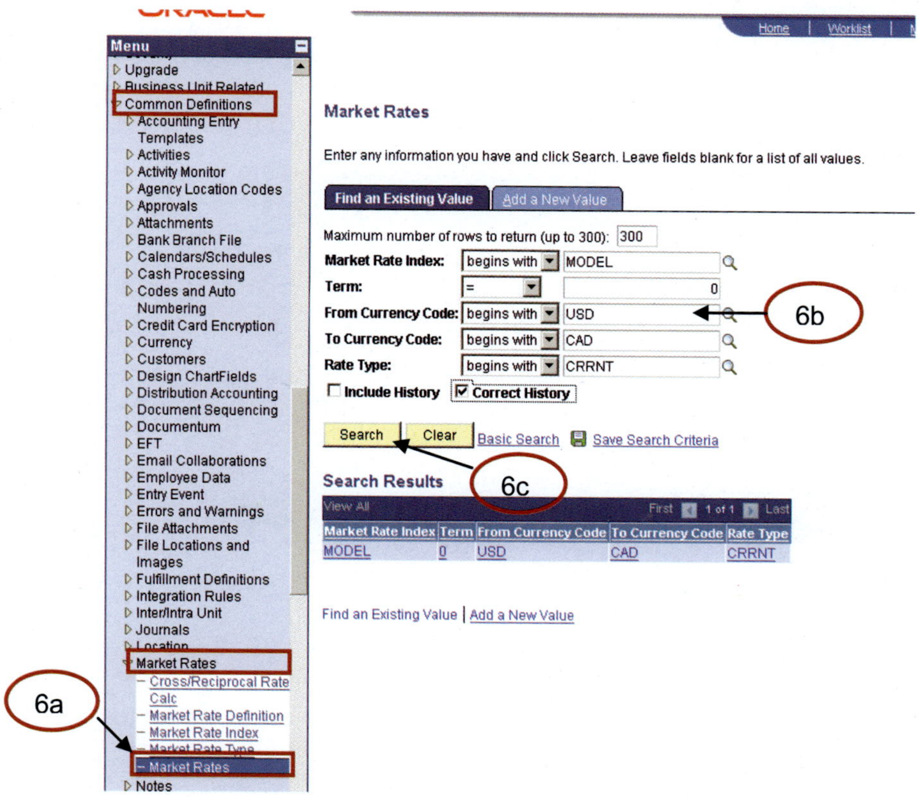

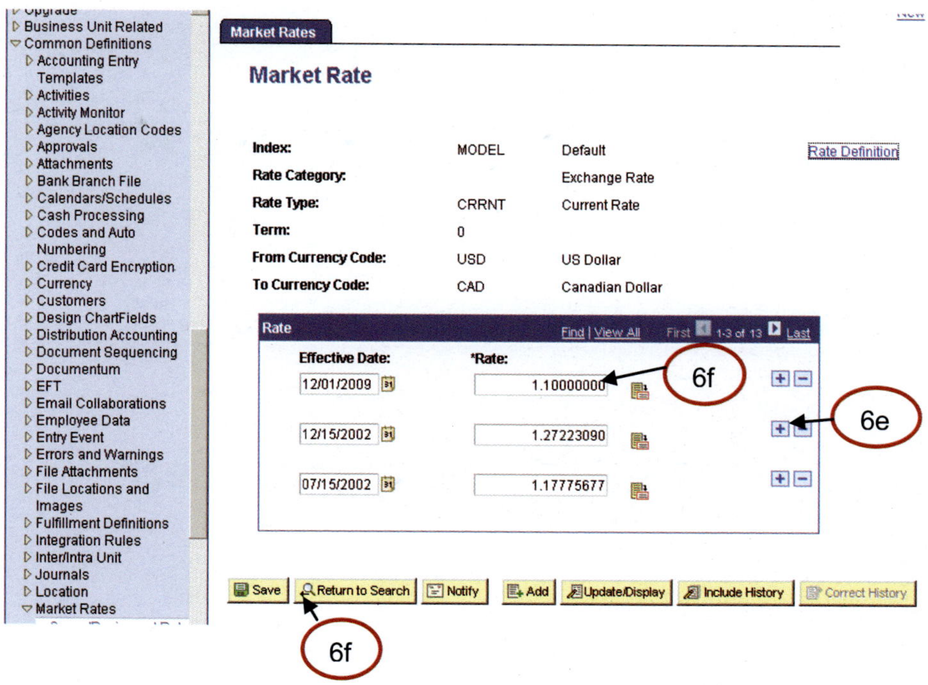

7. Enter Journal

Next you will enter a journal to create test data, run the *Journal Edit* and *Journal Post* processes. Follow the steps below to add a Journal:

a. Navigate to *Create/Update Journal Entries > Add a New Value* as highlighted in the below graphic

b. Specify the following values:

- `Business Unit: US001`
- `Journal ID: MC2`
- `Journal Date: 12/01/2009`

c. Click on *Add*

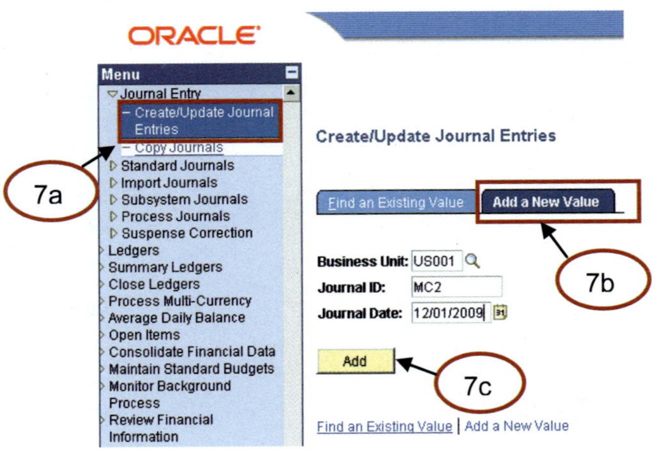

d. On the *Header* page specify the following values:

- `Ledger Group: ACTUALS`
- `Source` should be automatically updated from the default value defined on the *User Preferences* screen

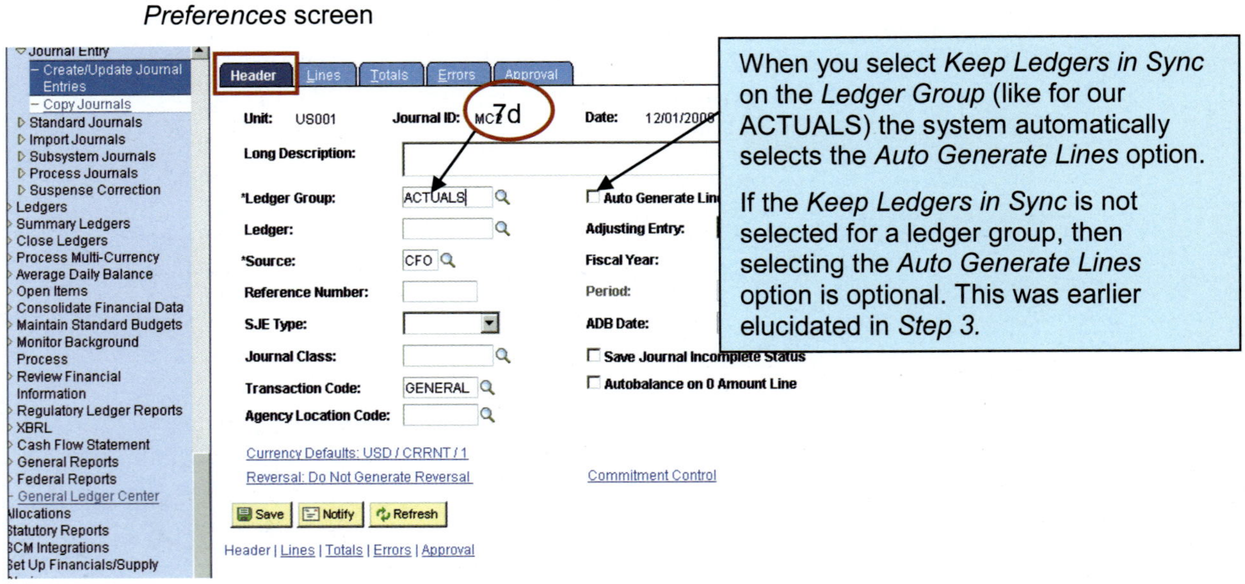

e. Click on the *Lines* tab

f. Enter the following two Journal lines:

- `Line 1: Account: 620000, Amount: 100`
- `Line 2: Account: 100000, Amount: -100`

g. Click on the *Save* at the bottom of the screen

h. Click on the *OK* button on the message box

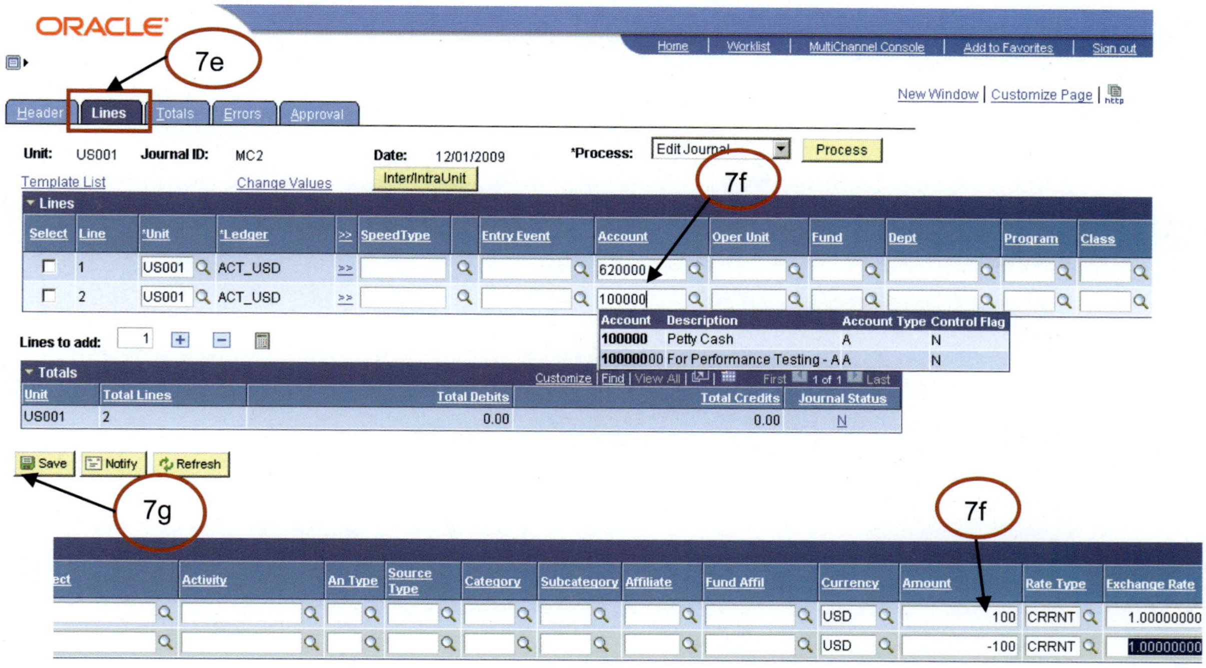

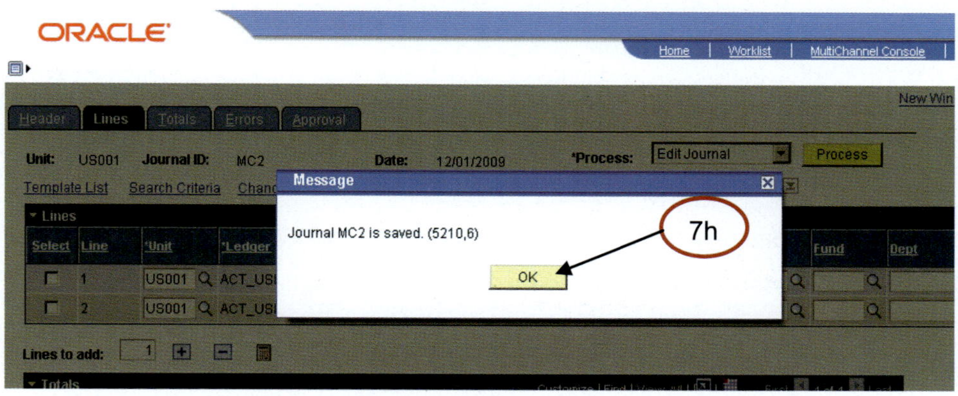

i. Click on *Process* to edit the journal. *Journal Status* will change from *N* to *V* (valid).

j. Select `Process = Post Journal` and click on *Process* to post the journal.

k. Click on *OK* in the message box. *Journal Status* will change from *V* to *P* (posted)

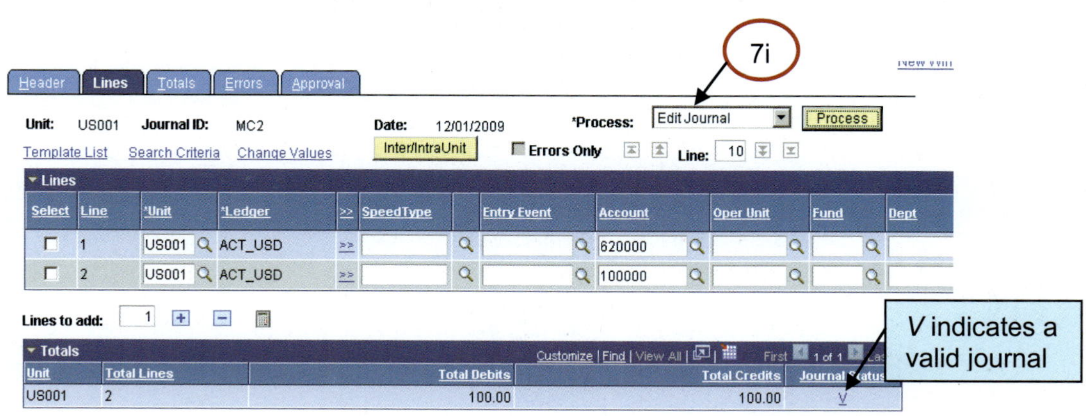

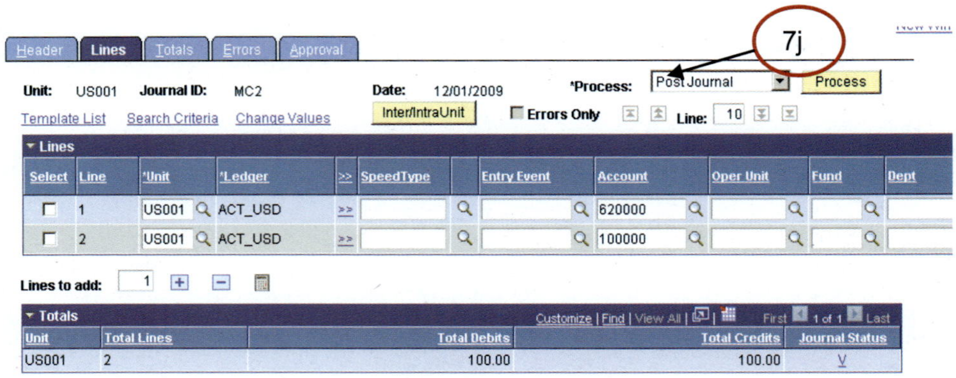

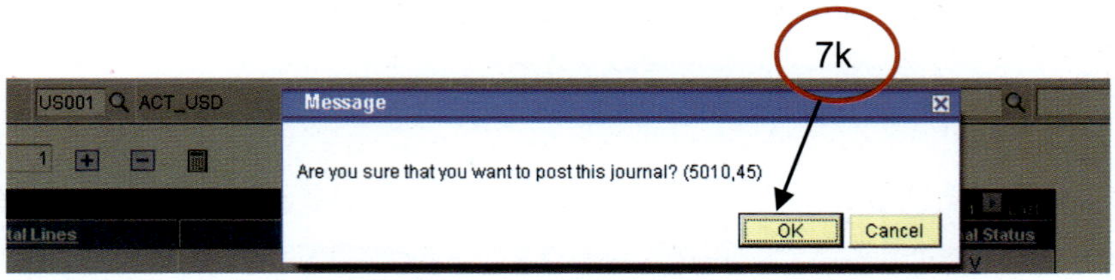

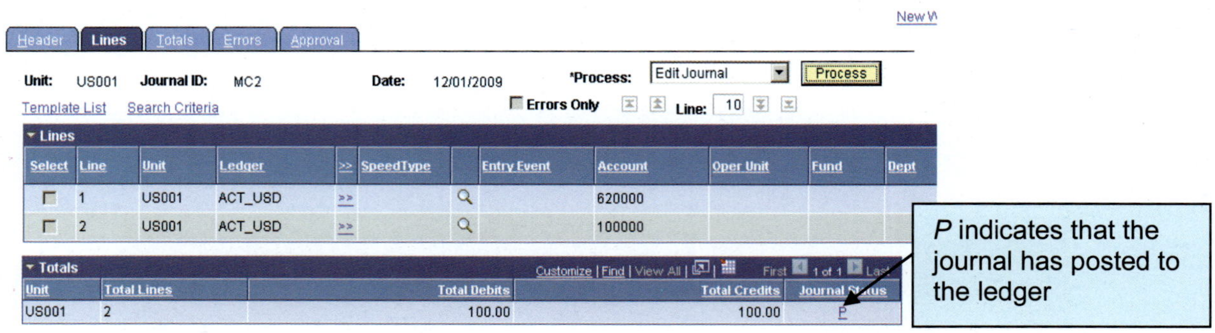

8. Review Ledger and Journal tables

Create two queries to see the tables that were updated during the journal entry.

The table that stores ledger balances is PS_LEDGER. Follow the steps below to query the ledger data:

a. Navigate to *Reporting Tools* > *Query* > *Query Manager*

b. Click on *Create New Query* link

c. Specify Record Name: `LEDGER`

d. Click on *Search*

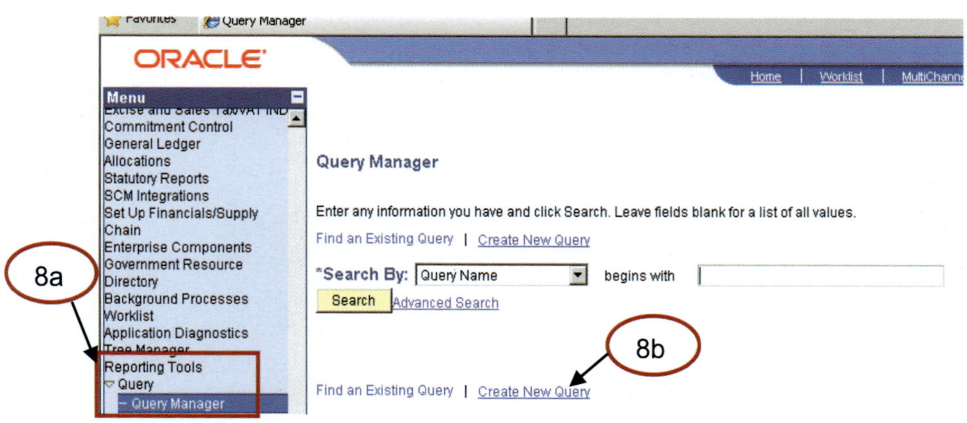

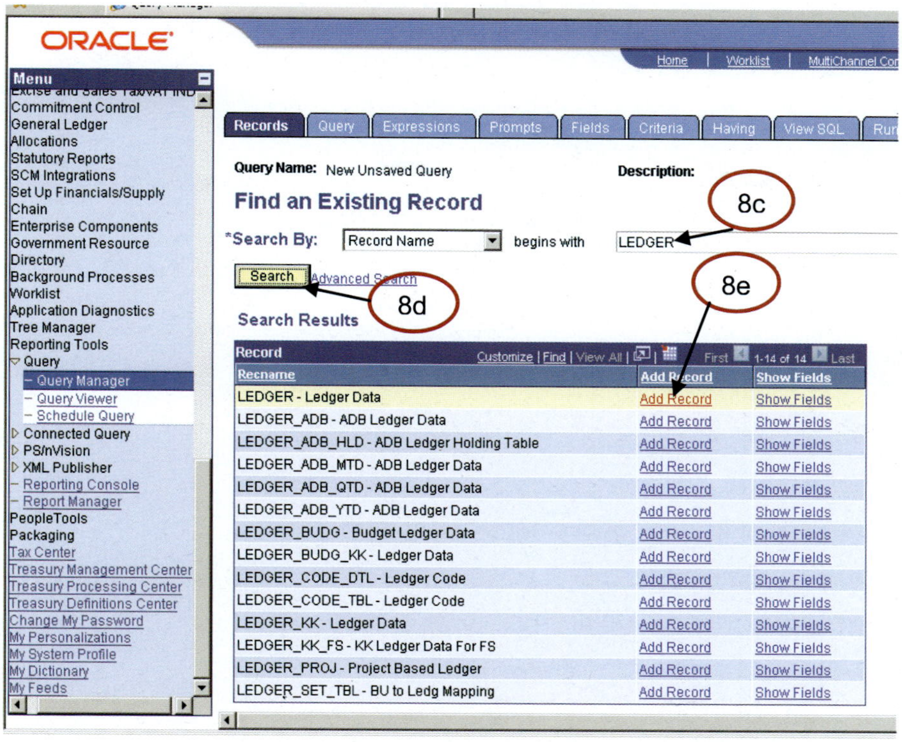

e. Click on the *Add Record* link for the LEDGER record (i.e. PS_LEDGER database table)

f. On the next screen select the following fields: `BUSINESS_UNIT`, `LEDGER`, `ACCOUNT`, `CURRENCY_CD`, `FISCAL_YEAR`, `ACCOUNTING_PERIOD`, `POSTED_TOTAL_AMT`, `POSTED_BASE_AMT`, `POSTED_TRAN_AMT`, `BASE_CURRENCY` and `DTTM_STAMP_SEC`

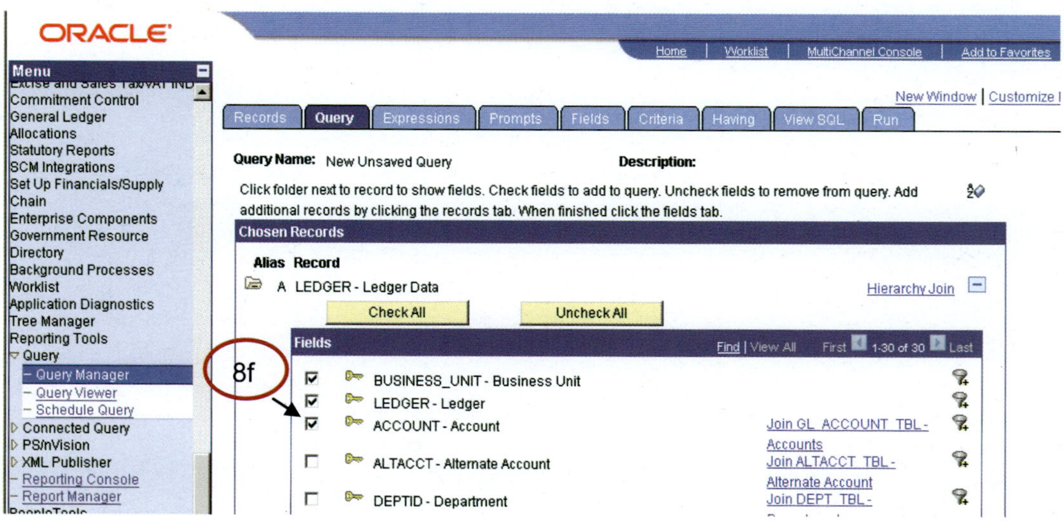

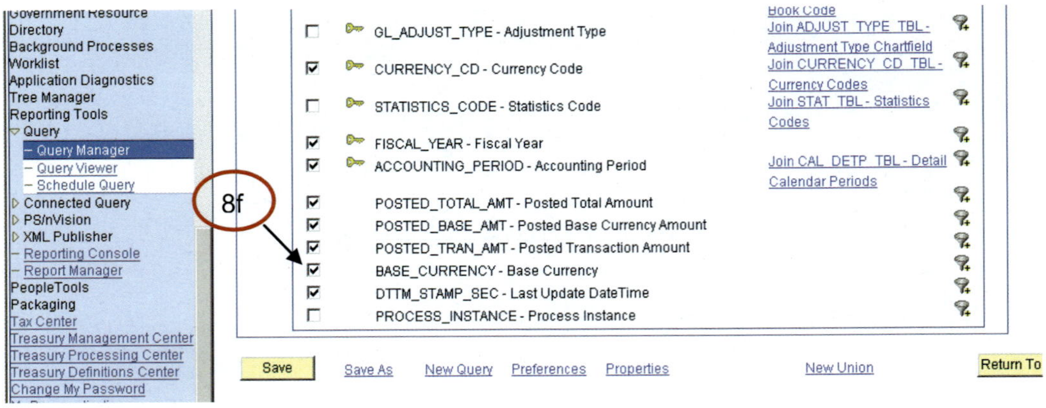

g. Click on the *Fields* tab

h. Click on *Reorder/Sort* at the top right corner of the screen

i. Specify the following sort order: `LEDGER - 1, ACCOUNT - 3` and `CURRENCY_CD - 2`

j. Click on *OK* at the bottom of the screen (not shown in the screen shot)

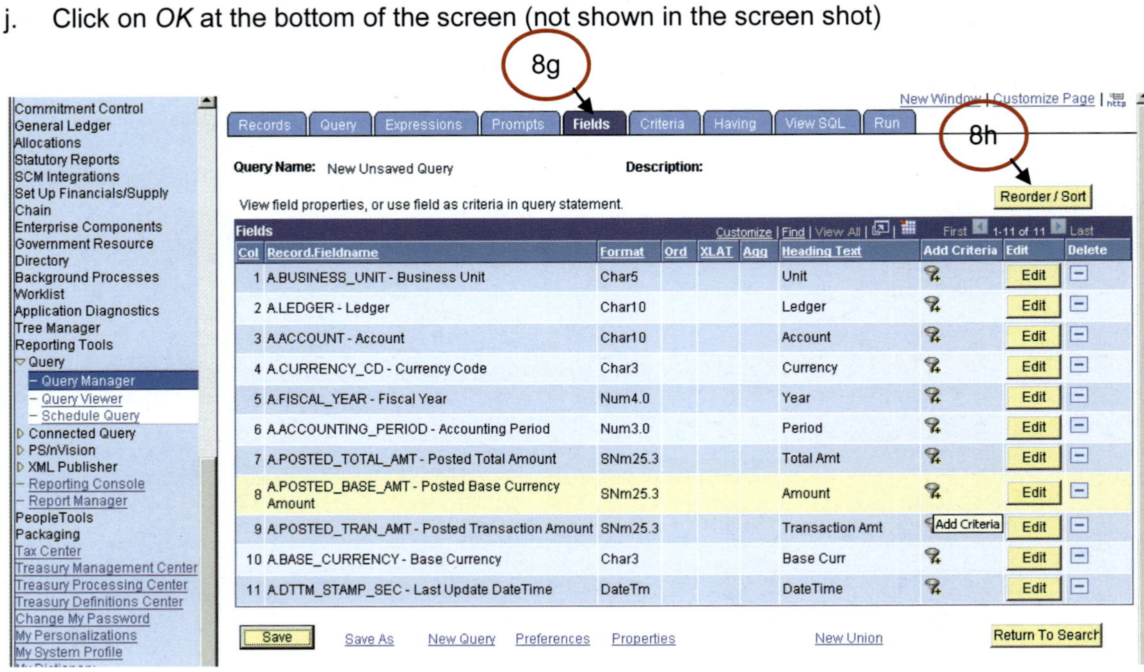

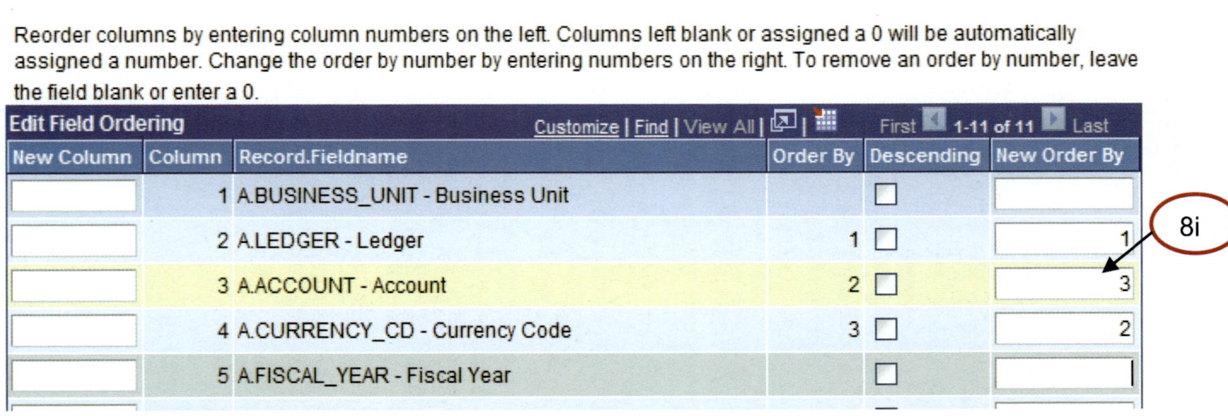

k. Click on the funnel shaped *Add Criteria* for the LEDGER field

l. On the next page select `Condition Type: like` and `Expression 2, Constant: ACT_%`. This will allow you to query only on Ledgers ACT_USD and ACT_CAD

m. Click on *OK* at the bottom of the screen

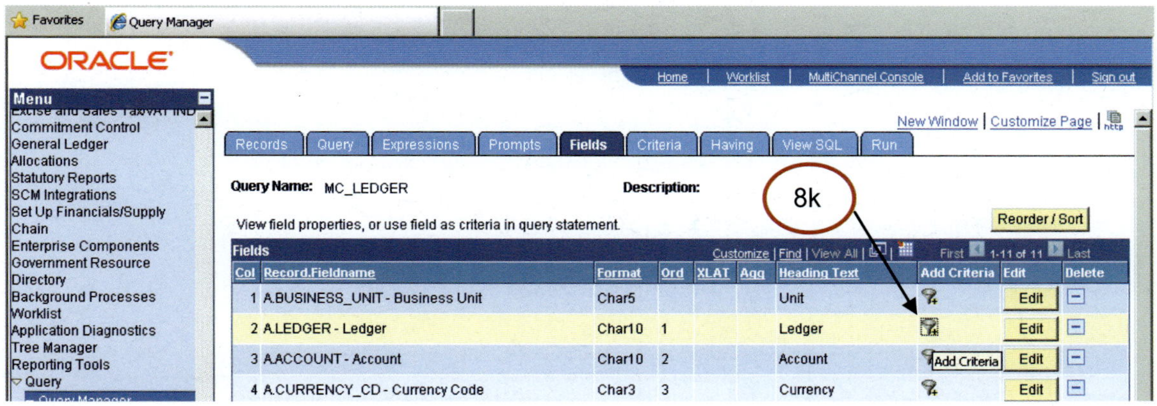

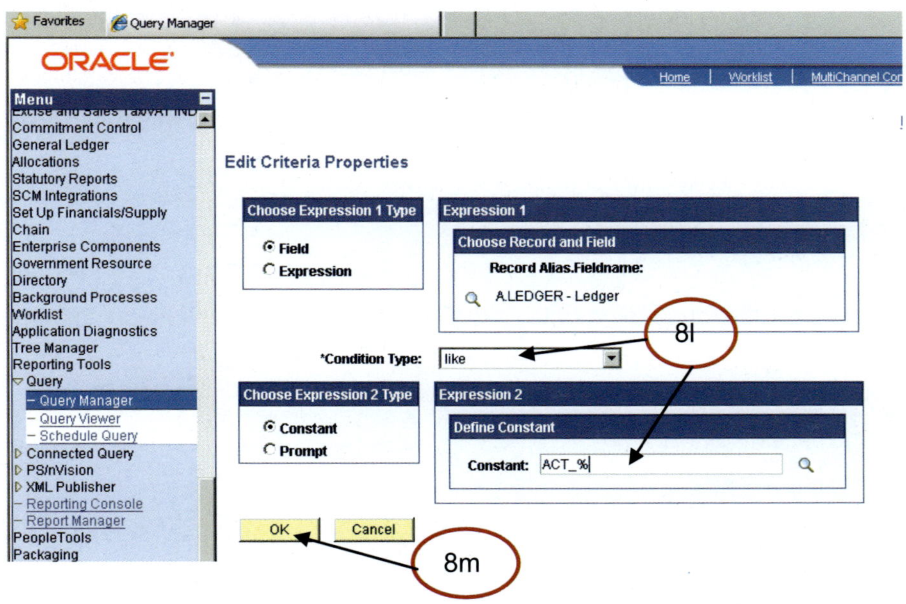

n. On the next screen, click on *Save* at the bottom of the screen (not shown in the screen shot)

o. Specify Query: `MC_LEDGER`

p. Click on *OK*

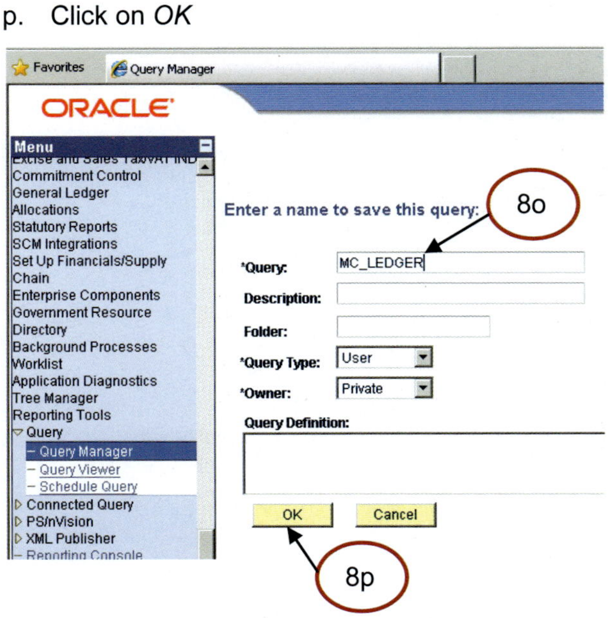

q. Click on the *Run* tab

r. Review ledger data

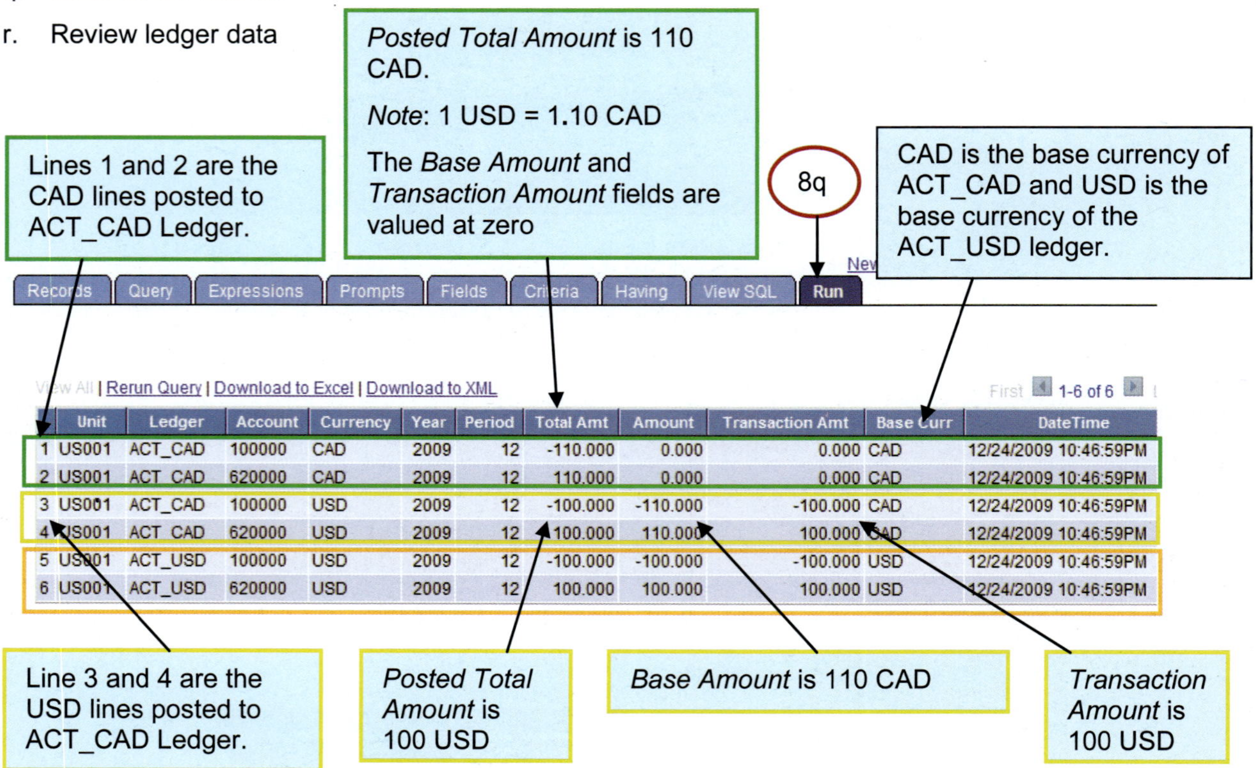

Finally, create a query to view the journal line data (JRNL_LN). Follow the steps below to create a new query.

s. Navigate to *Reporting Tools* > *Query* > *Query Manager*

t. Click on the *Create New Query* link

u. Specify Record Name: `JRNL_LN`

v. Click on *Search*

w. Click on the *Add Record* link against the JRNL_LN record (i.e. PS_JRNL_LN database table)

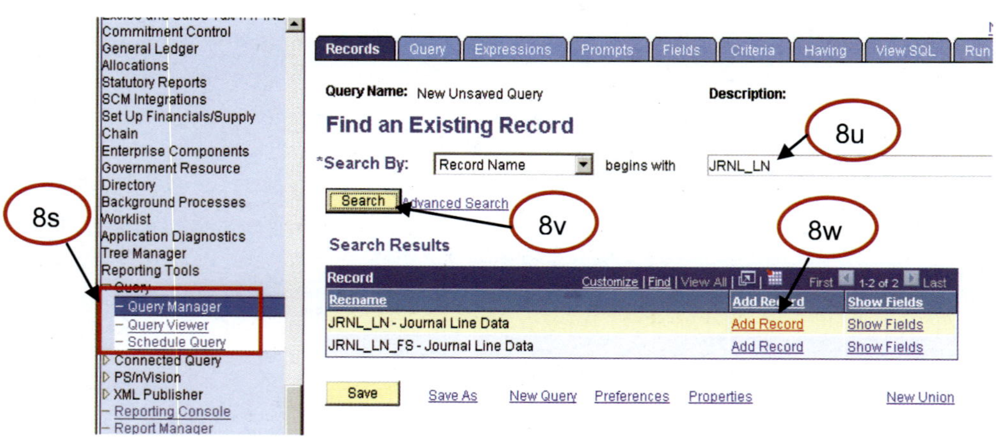

x. On the next screen, select the following fields: `BUSINESS_UNIT`, `JOURNAL_ID`, `JOURNAL_DATE`, `JOURNAL_LINE`, `LEDGER`, `ACCOUNT`, `CURRENCY_CD`, `MONETARY_AMOUNT`, `FOREIGN_CURRENCY`, `FOREIGN_AMOUNT`, `RATE_DIV`, `RATE_MULT` and `RT_TYPE`

y. Click on the *Fields* tab

z. Click on the *Reorder/Sort* button on the top right corner of the screen aa. Specify the following sort order: `LEDGER - 1`, `JOURNAL_LINE - 2`

bb. Click on *OK* at the bottom of the screen

cc. Click on the funnel shaped *Add Criteria* icon against the JOURNAL_ID field

dd. On the next page select `Condition Type: equal` to and `Expression 2, Constant: MC2` This will bring back rows from the journal that we keyed in earlier

ee. Click on *OK* at the bottom of the screen

ff. On the next screen, click on *Save* at the bottom of the screen

gg. Specify Query: `MC_JRNL_LN`

hh. Click on *OK*

ii. Click on the *Run* tab

jj. Review the journal lines data

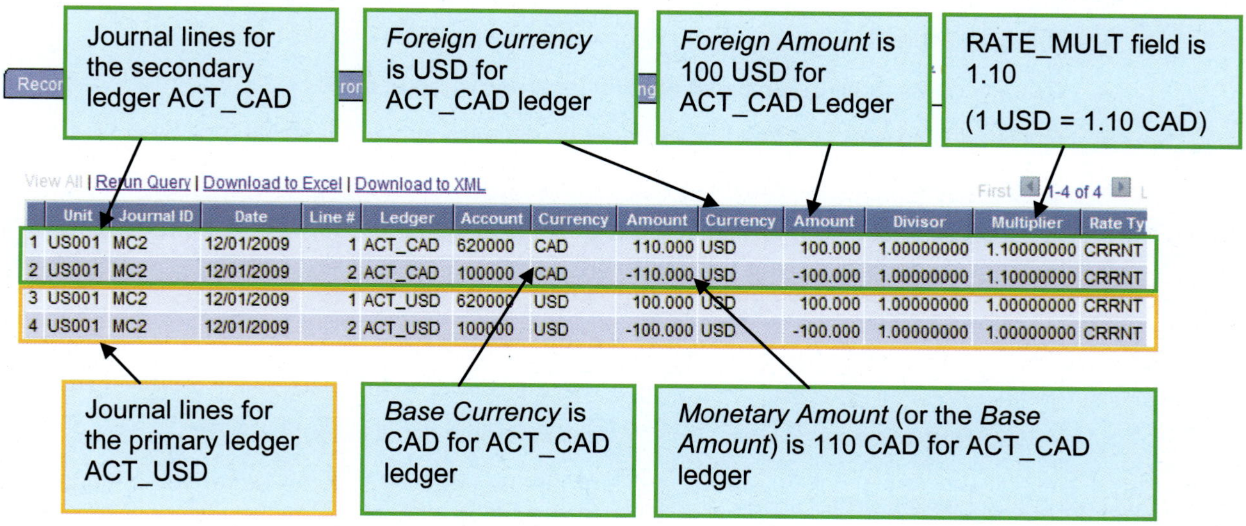

	Unit	Journal ID	Date	Line #	Ledger	Account	Currency	Amount	Currency	Amount	Divisor	Multiplier	Rate Ty
1	US001	MC2	12/01/2009	1	ACT_CAD	620000	CAD	110.000	USD	100.000	1.00000000	1.10000000	CRRNT
2	US001	MC2	12/01/2009	2	ACT_CAD	100000	CAD	-110.000	USD	-100.000	1.00000000	1.10000000	CRRNT
3	US001	MC2	12/01/2009	1	ACT_USD	620000	USD	100.000	USD	100.000	1.00000000	1.00000000	CRRNT
4	US001	MC2	12/01/2009	2	ACT_USD	100000	USD	-100.000	USD	-100.000	1.00000000	1.00000000	CRRNT

Revalue Ledger Balances

The revaluation process adjusts (by creating adjusting journal entries) the base currency ledger balances due to fluctuations in currency exchange rates. The system also creates corresponding entries for any gain or loss that results from the revaluation process.

Example: A US business (whose base currency is USD) has foreign currency transactions. It needs to revalue its foreign currency ledger balances at month-end per the following business requirements:

- Balance Sheet (BS) accounts must be revalued at CRRNT market rates
- P&L accounts must be revalued at AVG (average) market rates
- Currency gain and loss must be recorded in different account buckets for BS and P&L accounts
- Revalued transactions automatically reverse on the 1st of the next month

Solution: In this example, you will first setup a USD detail ledger called USD_ACCT, then attach it to the US GL business unit US003, and lastly configure currency conversion rules, *Market Rates* and *Revaluation Steps*. Follow these step-by-step instructions to implement the solution:

#	Step	Step Description
1	verify *Ledger Template*	use the delivered template called STANDARD
2	setup *Detail Ledger*	create a new detail ledger USD_ACT
3	setup *Ledger Group*	group the USD_ACT detail ledger into a ledger group called USD_ACT
4	setup *Ledgers For A Business Unit*	attach the ledger group USD_ACT to the GL business unit US003
5	open periods	open periods 2009/12 thru 2010/12 for the GL business unit US003 and ledger group USD_ACT
6	setup *Currency Codes* and quotations	setup currency conversion rules for USD-CAD and USD-MXN currency pairs
7	update *Market Rates*	update *Market Rates* for the USD-CAD and USD-MXN pairs
8	enter journals	enter journals to create test data
9	review journal and ledger data	query the LEDGER and JRNL_LN records
10	configure and run revaluation	create two *Revaluation Rules* RVL_BS and RVL_PL and group them into a process group called RVL_BS_PL; then run the revaluation process

1. Verify Ledger Template

Refer to *Chapter 6: Step 1* for information on STANDARD Ledger Template

2. Setup Detail Ledger

Refer to *Chapter 6: Step 2 to* setup a detail ledger called USD_ACT. See screen shot below for details:

3. Setup Ledger Group

Refer to *Chapter 6: Step 3* to setup a ledger group called USD_ACT. See screen shot below:

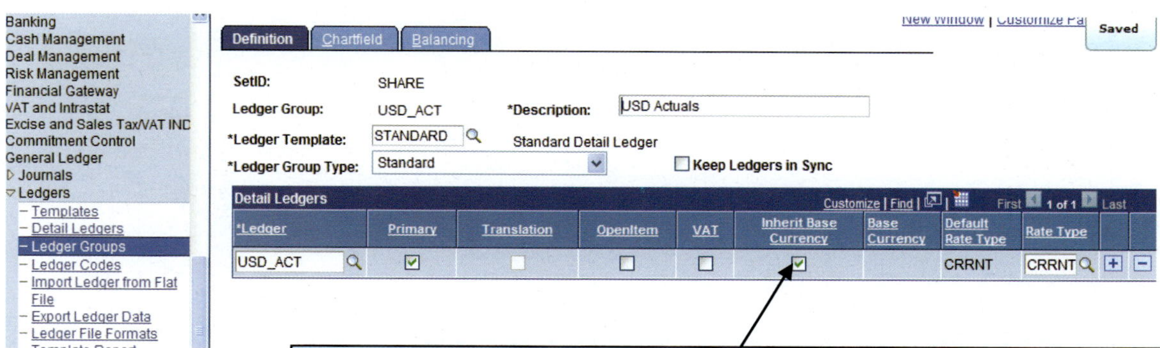

Select the check box *Inherit Base Currency*.

By attaching this ledger group to GL business unit US003 (whose base currency is USD), the detail ledger USD_ACT's base currency will automatically also be USD.

4. Setup Ledgers For A Business Unit

Refer to *Chapter 6: Step 4* to attach ledger group USD_ACT to GL business unit US003. See screen shot below for details:

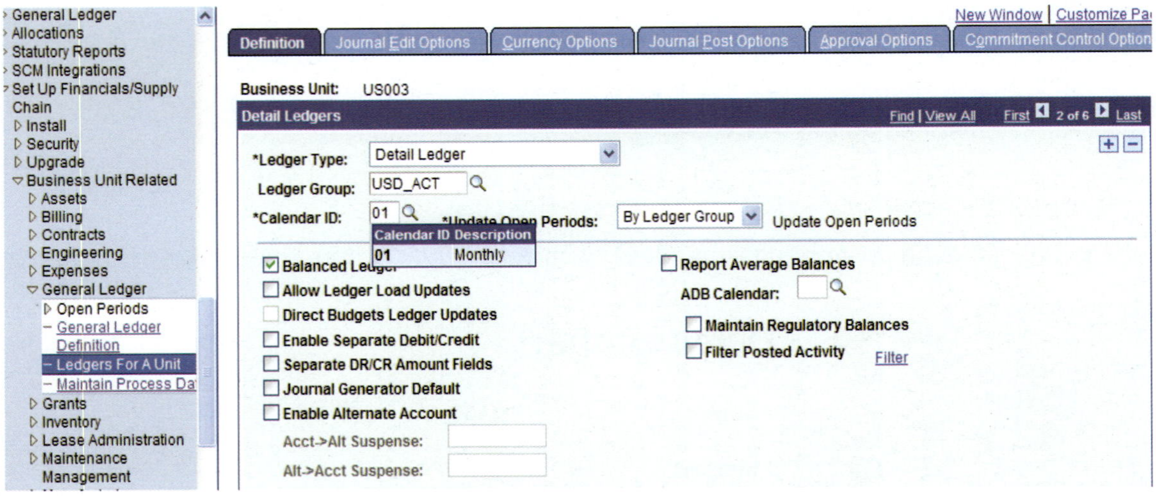

5. Open Periods

Refer to *Chapter 6: Step 5* to open periods 2009/12 through 2010/12 for GL business unit US003 and ledger group USD_ACT. See screen shot below for details:

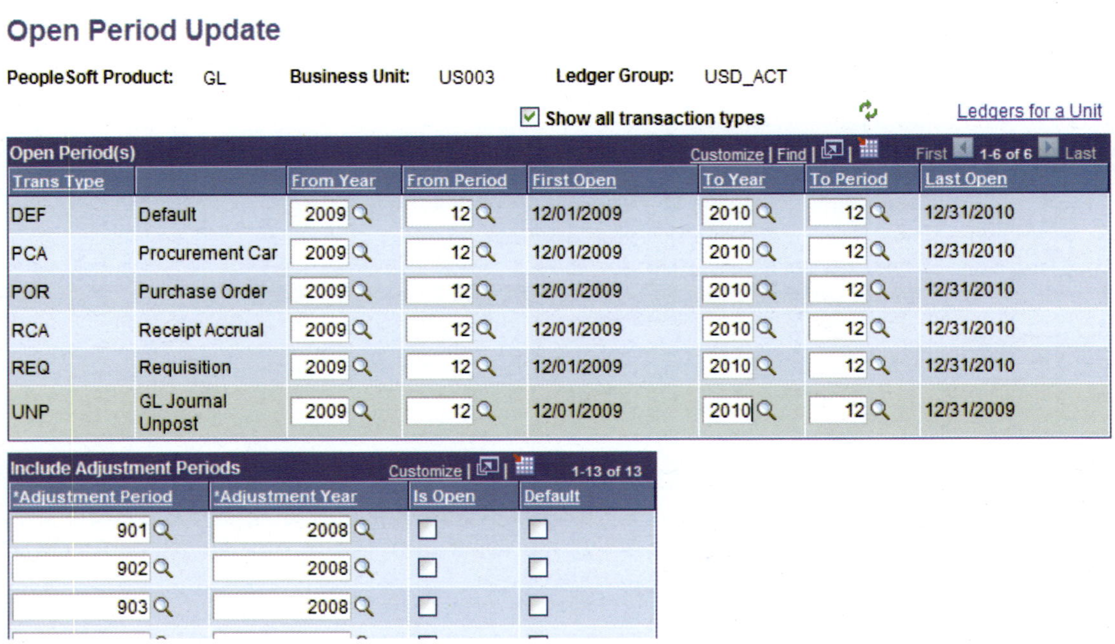

6. Review Currency Codes

The currency code table is delivered with common ISO currencies, including the three currencies in this example--USD (US Dollars), CAD (Canadian Dollars) and MXN (Mexican Peso).

Follow the steps below to review the USD, CAD and MXN currencies.

a. Navigate to *Set Up Financials/Supply Chain* > *Common Definitions* > *Currency* > *Currency Code* > *Find an Exiting Value* (full navigation not shown in screen shot below)

b. Specify the following values:

   - `Currency Code: USD`

c. Click on *Search*

d. In the *Currency Code* screen, review the USD currency

e. Click on *Return to Search* to review CAD and MXN currencies

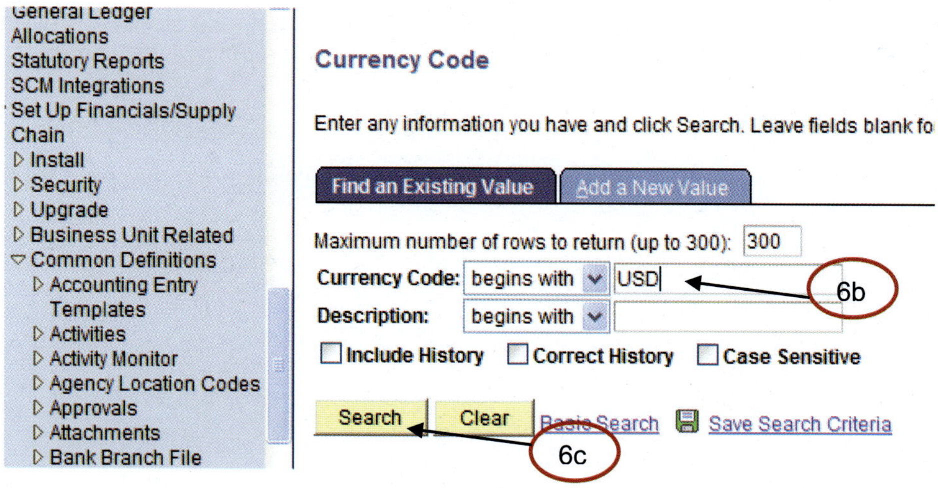

General Ledger
Allocations
Statutory Reports
SCM Integrations
Set Up Financials/Supply Chain
Install
Security
Upgrade
Business Unit Related
Common Definitions
Accounting Entry Templates
Activities
Activity Monitor
Agency Location Codes
Approvals
Attachments
Bank Branch File
Currency Code
Enter any information you have and click Search. Leave fields blank fo
Find an Existing Value
Add a New Value
Maximum number of rows to return (up to 300): 300
Currency Code: begins with USD
Description: begins with
Include History
Correct History
Case Sensitive
Search
Clear
Basic Search
Save Search Criteria
6b
6c

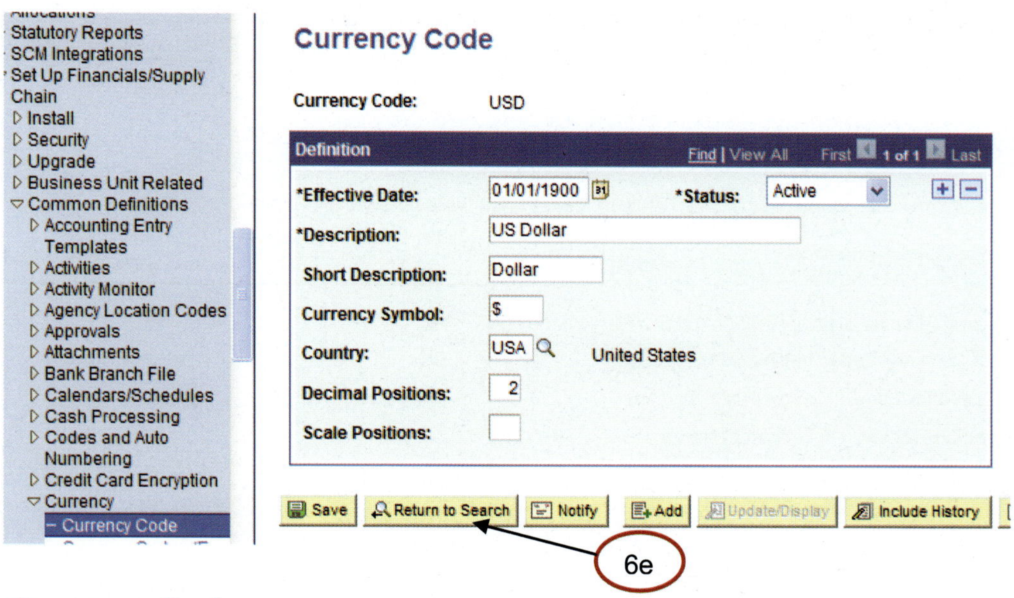

Statutory Reports
SCM Integrations
Set Up Financials/Supply Chain
Install
Security
Upgrade
Business Unit Related
Common Definitions
Accounting Entry Templates
Activities
Activity Monitor
Agency Location Codes
Approvals
Attachments
Bank Branch File
Calendars/Schedules
Cash Processing
Codes and Auto Numbering
Credit Card Encryption
Currency
– Currency Code
Currency Code
Currency Code: USD
Definition
Find | View All
First 1 of 1 Last
*Effective Date: 01/01/1900
*Status: Active
*Description: US Dollar
Short Description: Dollar
Currency Symbol: $
Country: USA United States
Decimal Positions: 2
Scale Positions:
Save
Return to Search
Notify
Add
Update/Display
Include History
6e

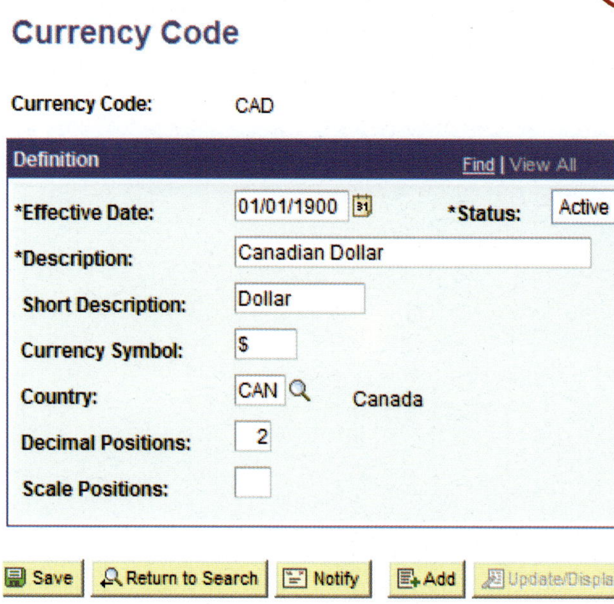

Currency Code
Currency Code: CAD
Definition
Find | View All
*Effective Date: 01/01/1900
*Status: Active
*Description: Canadian Dollar
Short Description: Dollar
Currency Symbol: $
Country: CAN Canada
Decimal Positions: 2
Scale Positions:
Save
Return to Search
Notify
Add
Update/Displa

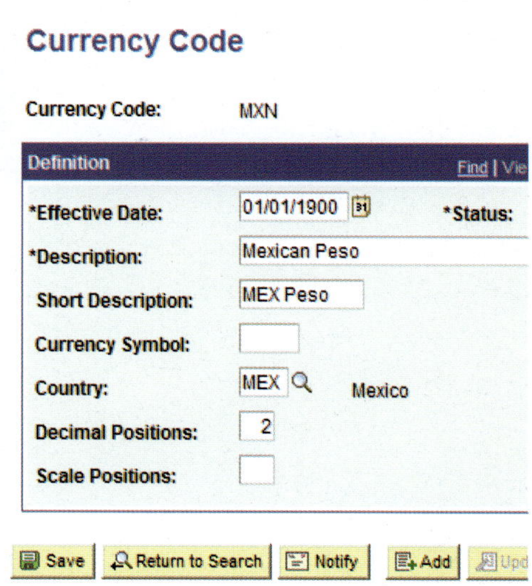

Currency Code
Currency Code: MXN
Definition
Find | Vie
*Effective Date: 01/01/1900
*Status:
*Description: Mexican Peso
Short Description: MEX Peso
Currency Symbol:
Country: MEX Mexico
Decimal Positions: 2
Scale Positions:
Save
Return to Search
Notify
Add
Upd

7. Define Currency Quotations

The currency quotation controls how stored rates are displayed, converted, and stored in the database tables. PeopleSoft supports *Direct*, *Indirect*, and *Triangulation* quotation methods. You setup a currency quotation for each currency pair.

Follow the steps below to review currency quotation methods for USD-CAD and USD-MXN currency pairs.

a. Navigate to *Set Up Financials/Supply Chain* > *Common Definitions* > *Currency* > *Currency Quotation Method*

b. Specify the following values:

- `From Currency Code: USD`
- `To Currency Code: CAD`

c. Click on *Search*

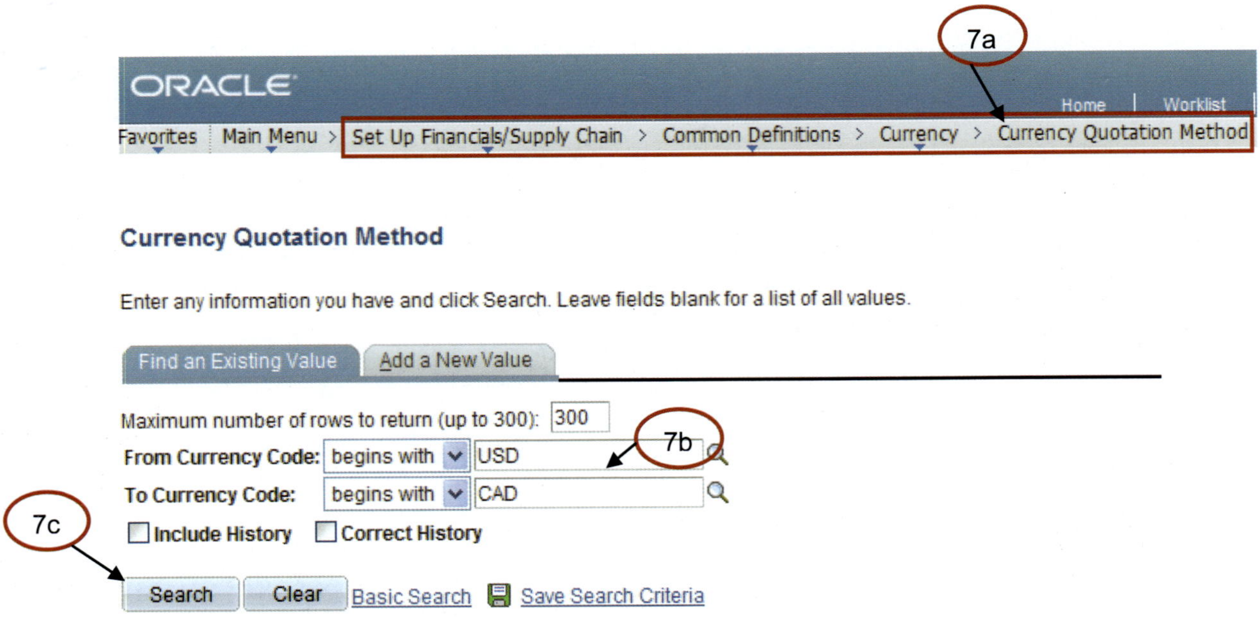

d. In the *Currency Quotation Method* page, review the USD to CAD currency quotation method

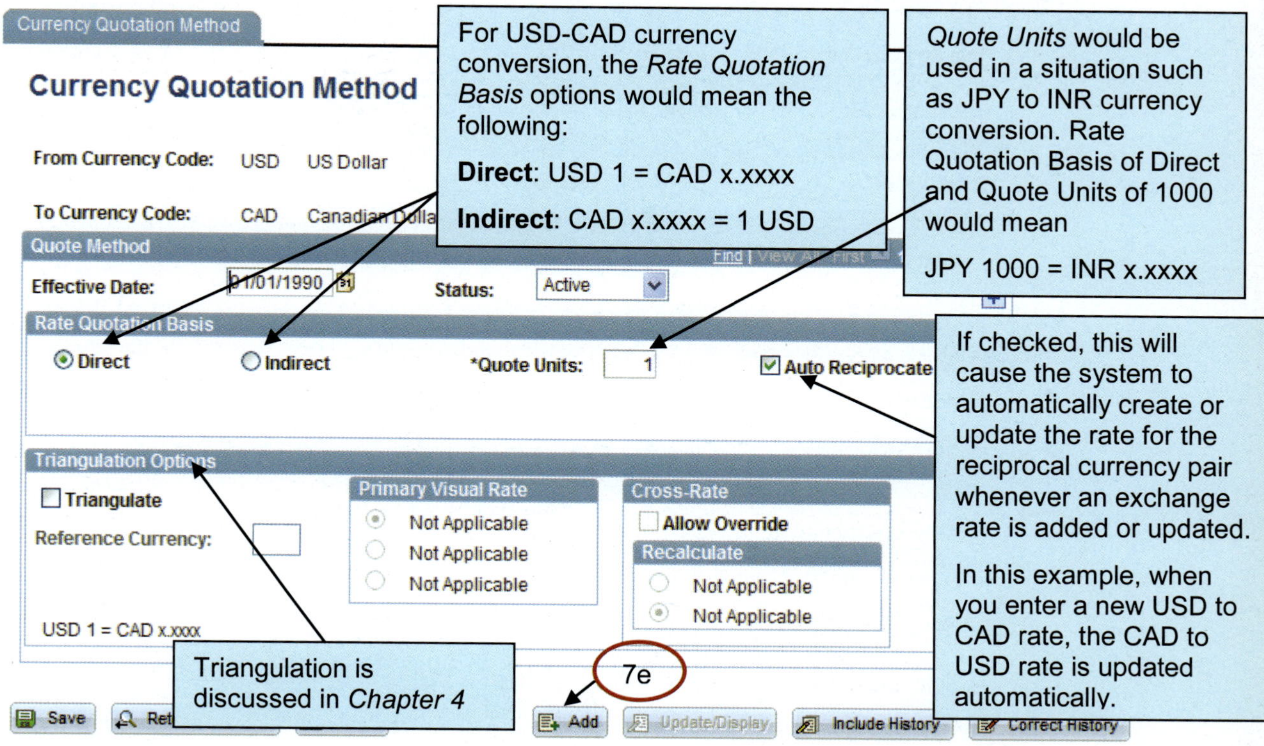

e. Click on *Add* to add the USD-MXN currency quotation:

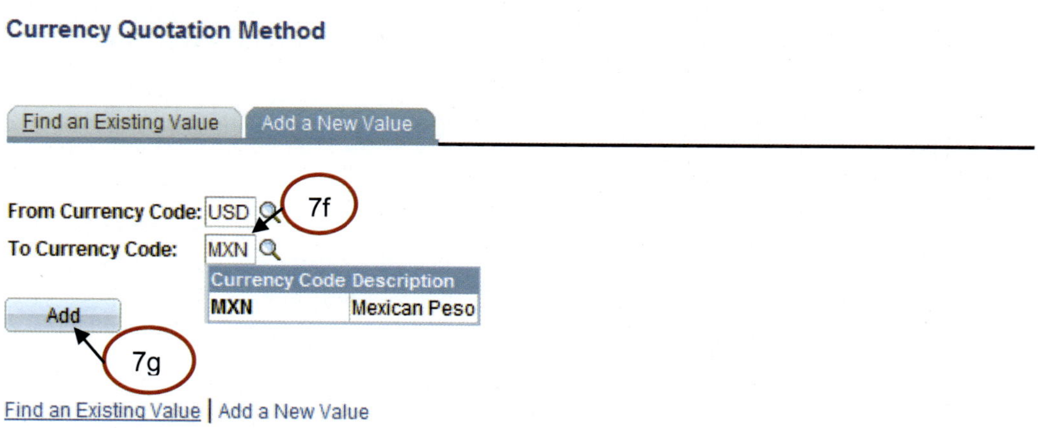

f. Specify the following values:

- `From Currency Code: USD`
- `To Currency Code: MXN`

g. Click on *Add*

h. In the *Currency Quotation Method* screen, specify the following values:

- `Effective Date: 01/01/1990`
- Accept default values for other fields as shown below:
    i. `Rate Quotation Basis = Direct,`
    ii. `Quote Units = 1`
    iii. `Auto Reciprocate = Checked`

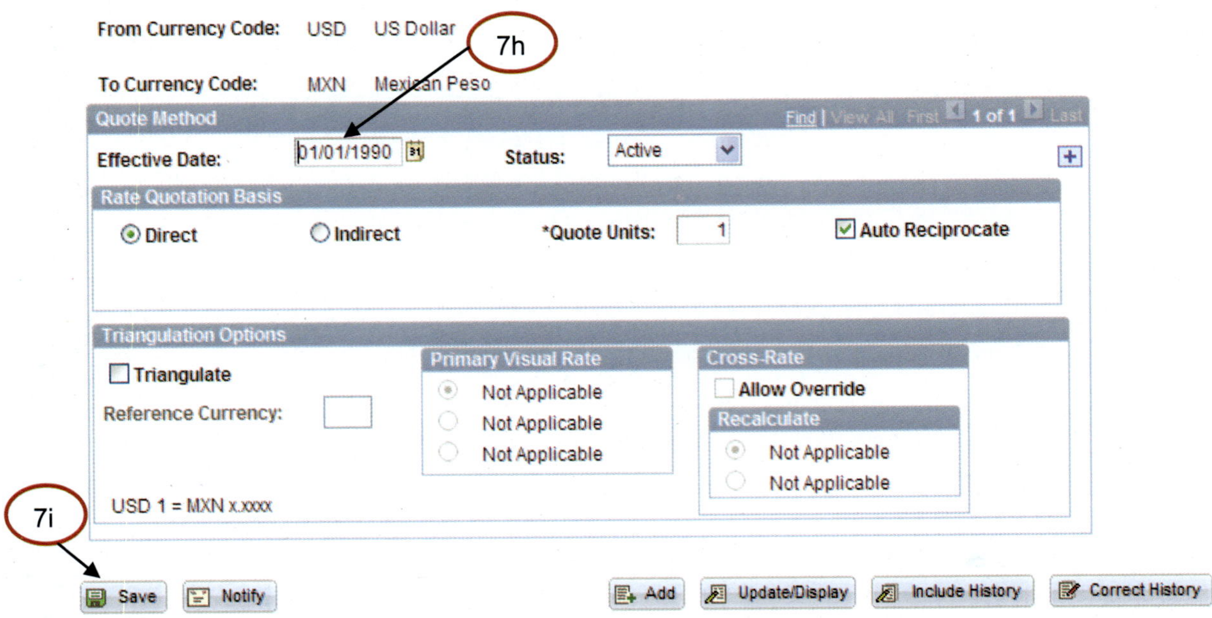

i. Click on *Save* at the bottom of the screen

j. Next you will query the CURR_QUOTE_TBL to see how the data is stored in the database

k. Navigate to *Reporting Tools* > *Query* > *Query Manager*

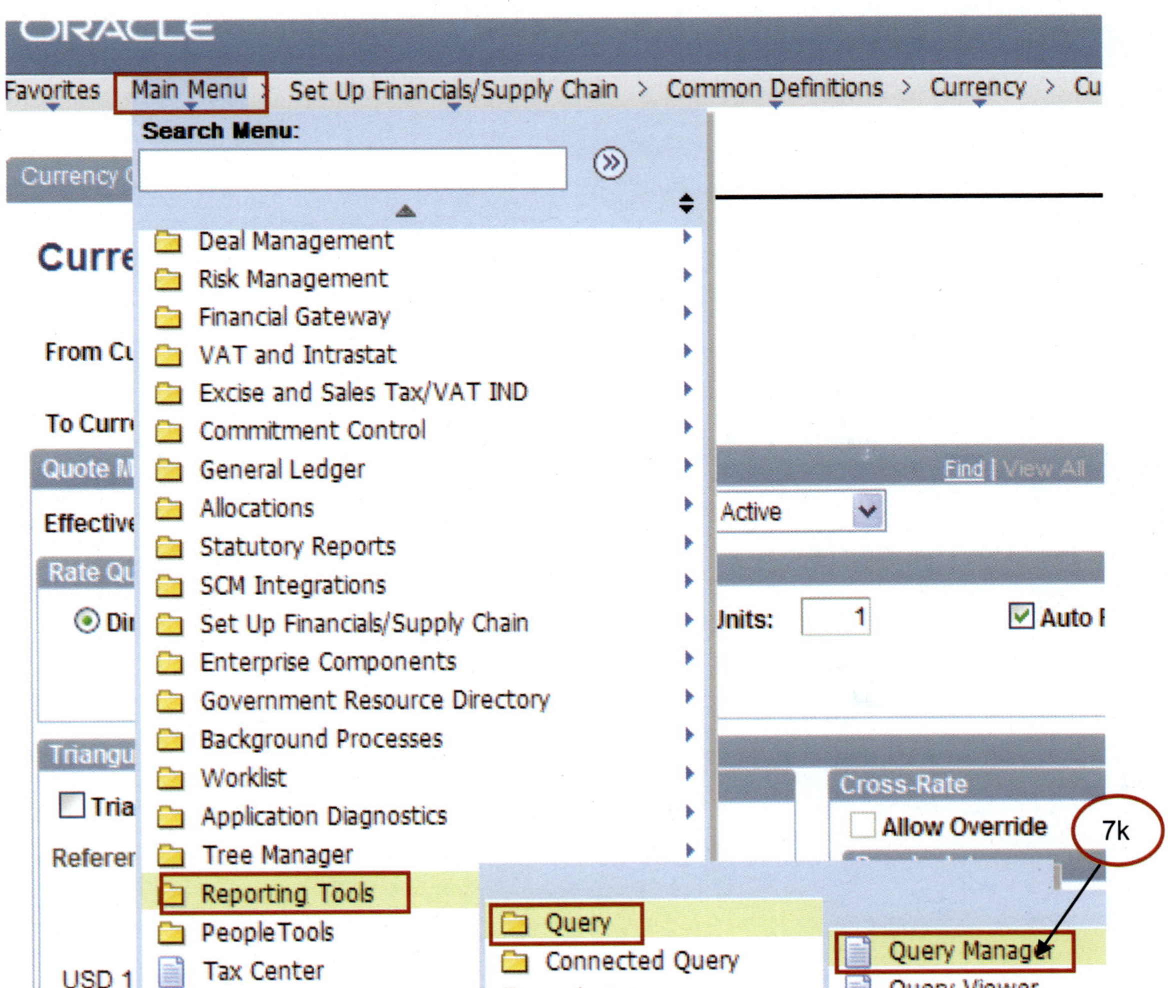

l. Click on *Create New Query* at the bottom of the *Query Manager* screen

m. Specify the following values:

- `Record Name: CURR_QUOTE_TBL`

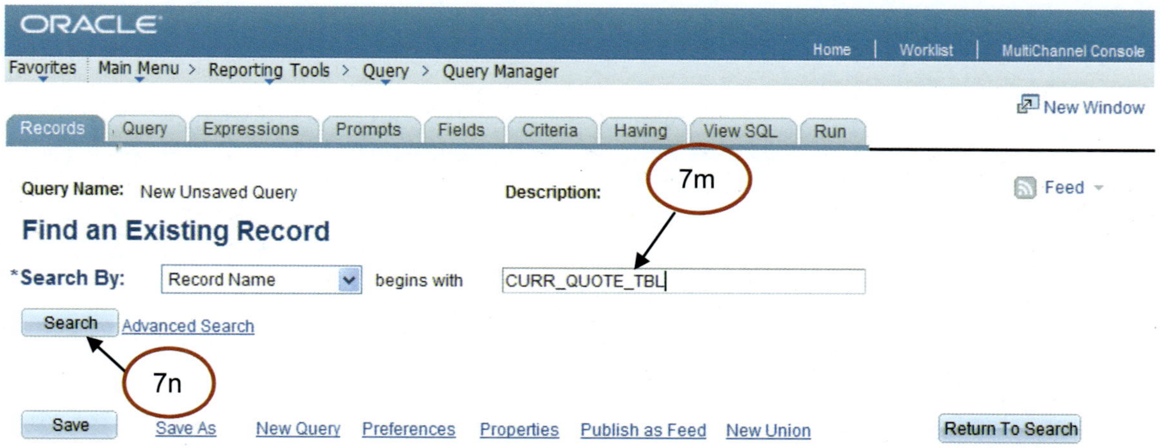

n. Click on *Search*

o. Click on *Add Record* for the CURR_QUOTE_TBL record in the *Find an Existing Record* screen

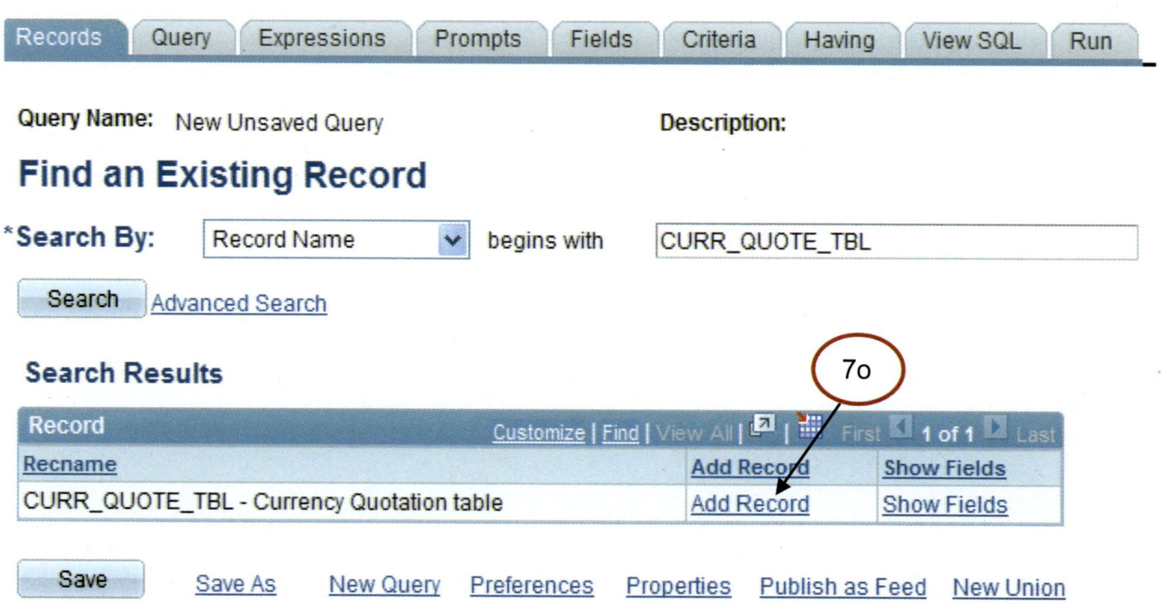

p. Click on *OK* on the dialog box that opens up

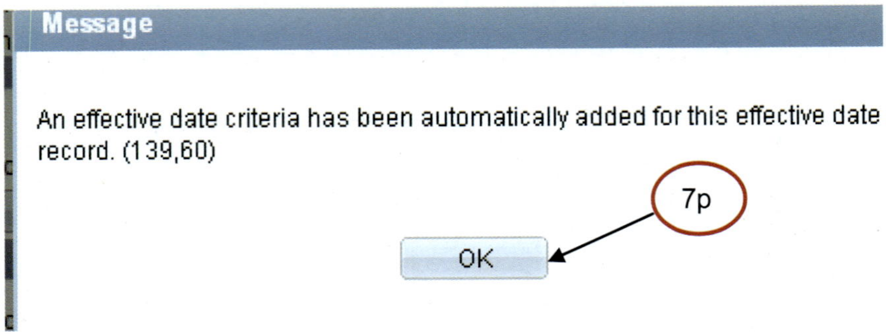

q. Click on *Check All* to select all the fields of the CURR_QUOTE_TBL record

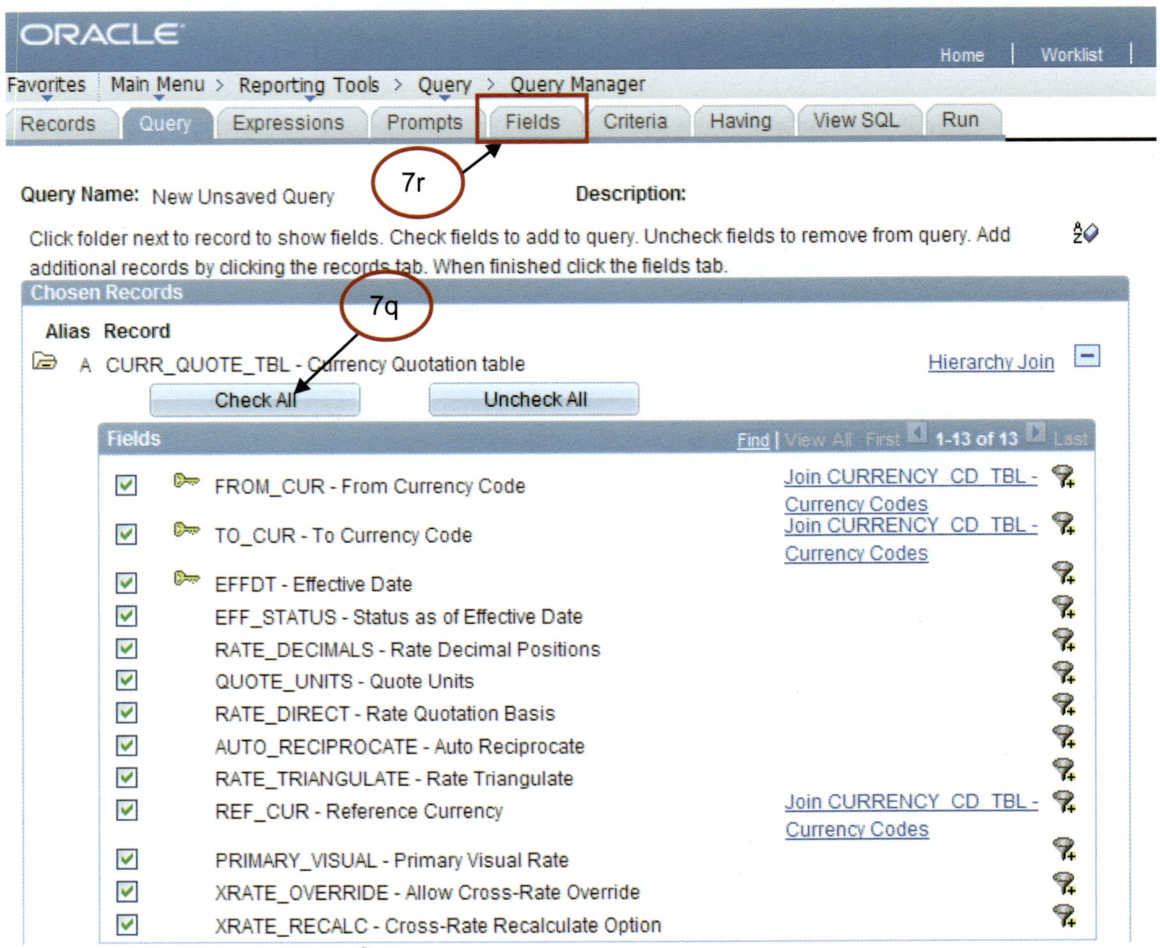

r. Click on the *Fields* tab and review the fields added

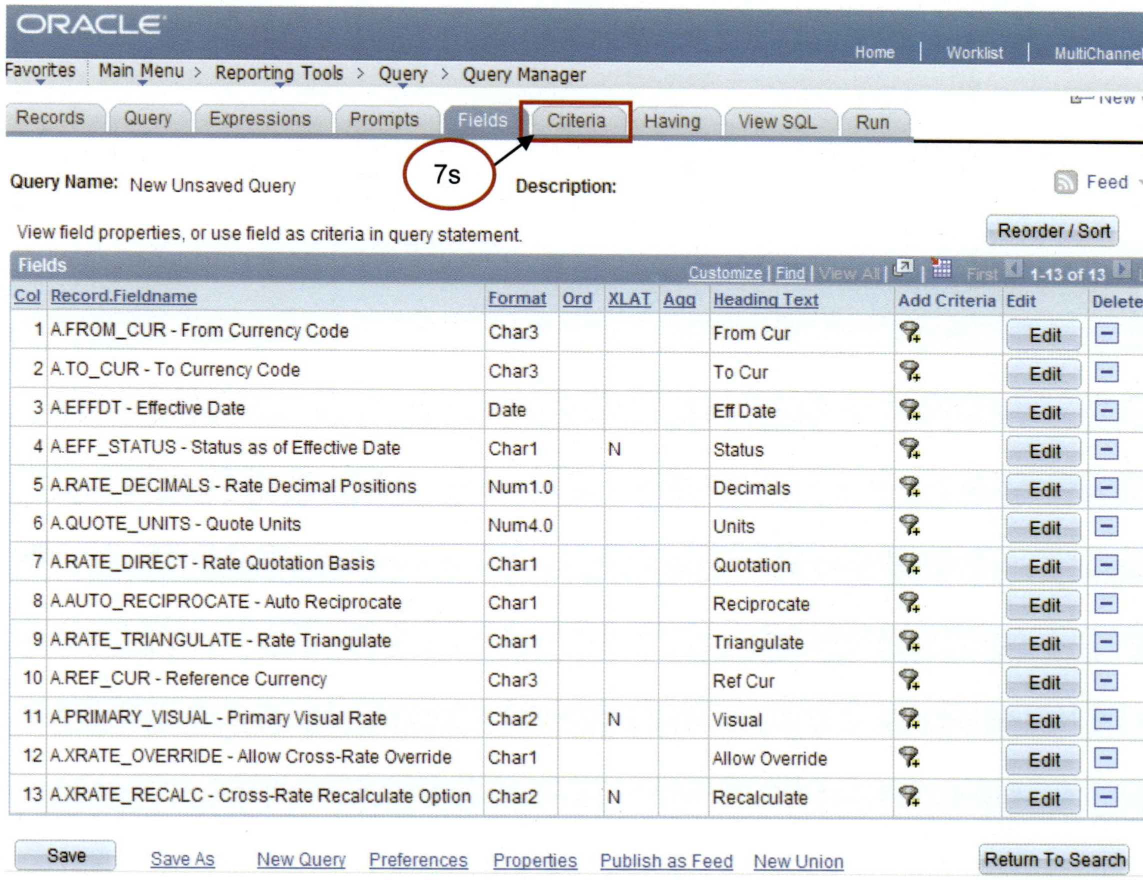

s. Click on the *Criteria* tab and specify the following:

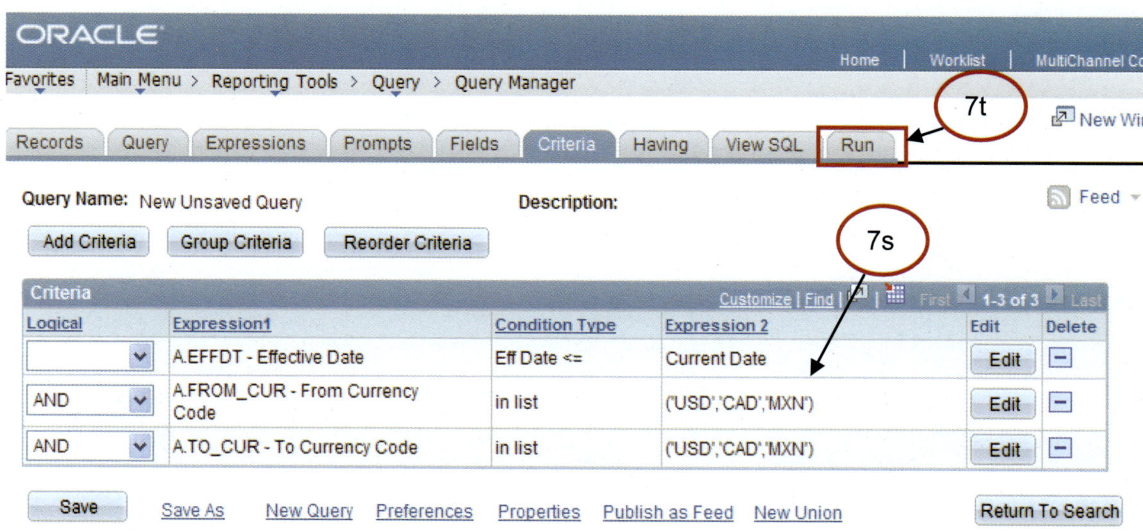

t. Click on the *Run* tab to view query results

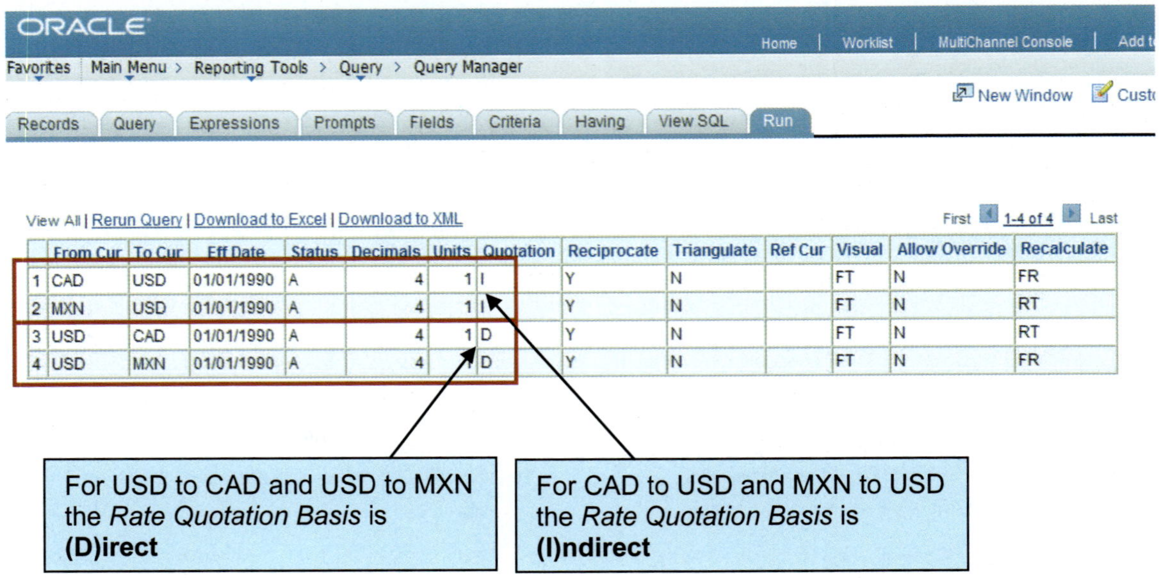

8. Define Market Rates

Next, you will manually enter market rates for the USD-CAD and USD-MXN currency pairs. Normally rates are uploaded using an automated daily batch process.

Add the following *Market Rates* referencing instructions in *Chapter 6: Step 6*. See the screen shots below for details.

From Currency	To Currency	Rate Type	Effective Date	Rate
USD	CAD	CRRNT	02/26/2010	1.15
USD	CAD	CRRNT	02/01/2010	1.10

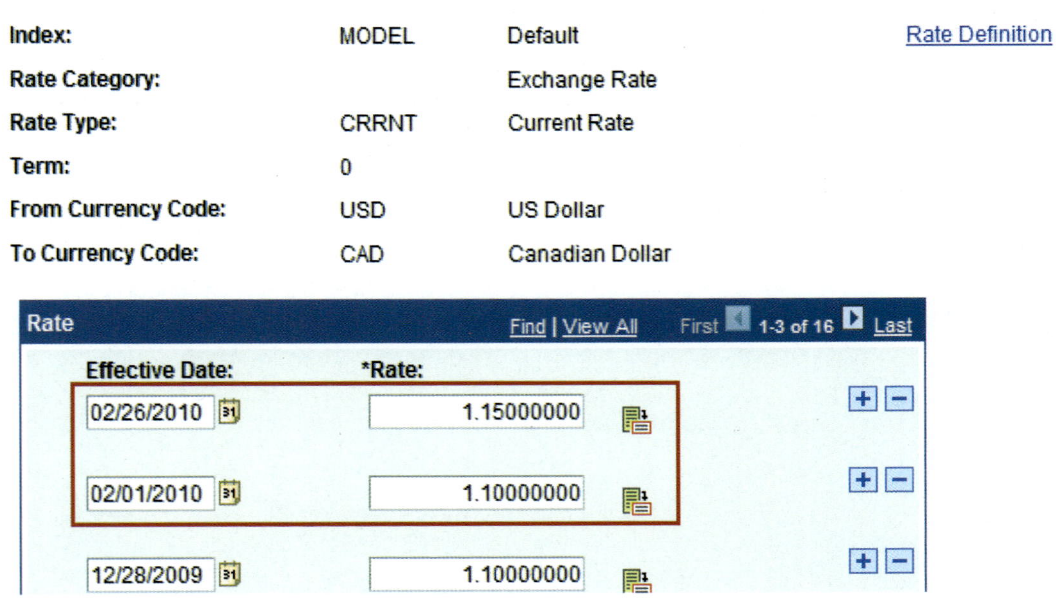

From Currency	To Currency	Rate Type	Effective Date	Rate
USD	CAD	AVG	02/26/2010	1.15

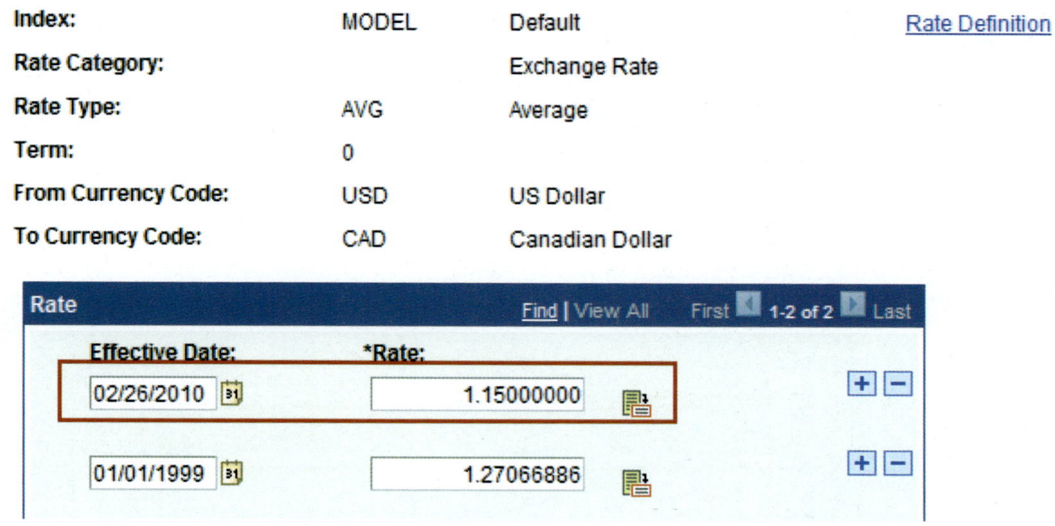

From Currency	To Currency	Rate Type	Effective Date	Rate
USD	MXN	CRRNT	02/26/2010	13.15
USD	MXN	CRRNT	02/01/2010	13.05

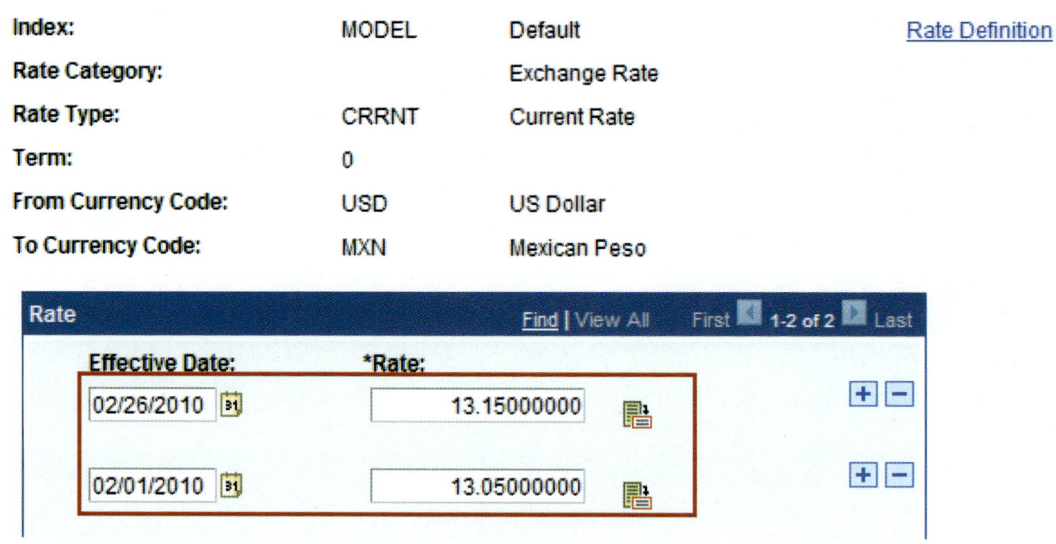

From Currency	To Currency	Rate Type	Effective Date	Rate
USD	MXN	AVG	02/26/2010	13.10

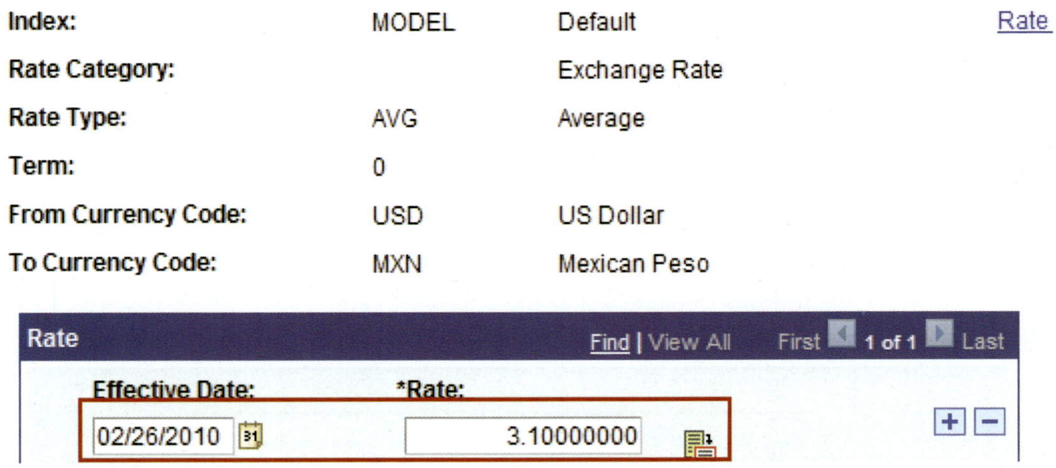

a. Use the screen shots shown below to query on record RT_RATE_TBL (database table: PS_RT_RATE_TBL) to examine how *Market Rates* are stored in the database:

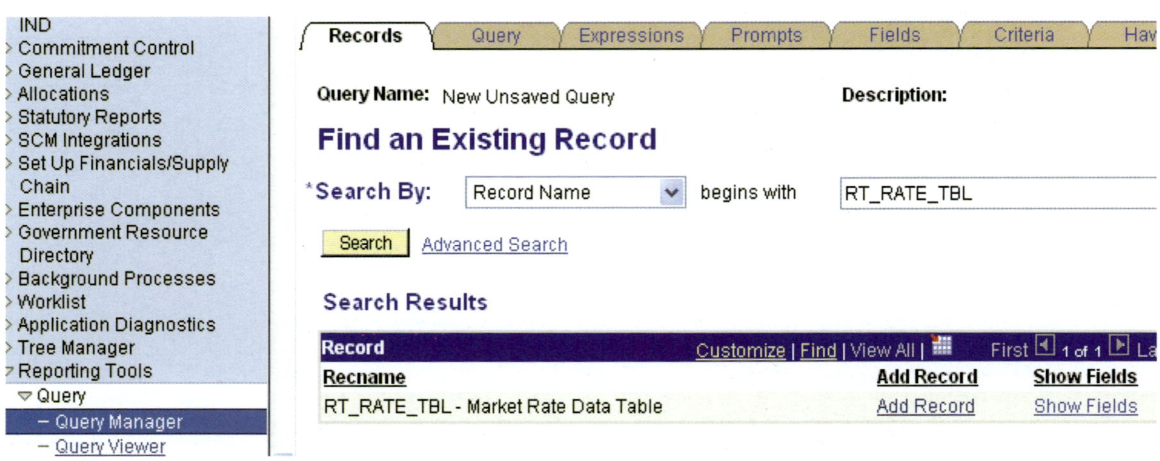

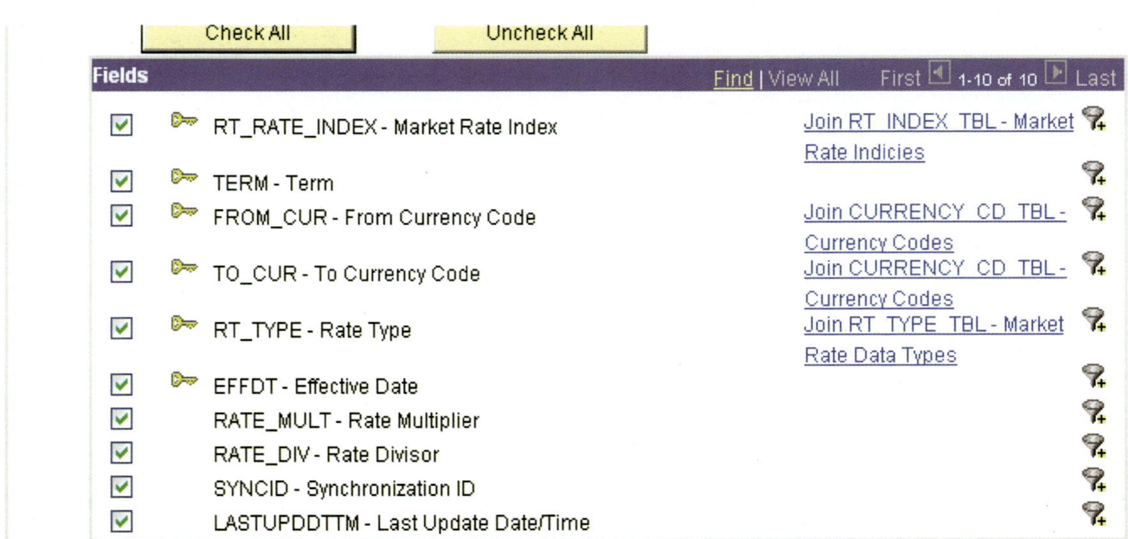

Edit Field Ordering

Reorder columns by entering column numbers on the left. Columns left blank or assigned a 0 will be automatically assigned a number. Change the order by number by entering numbers on the right. To remove an order by number, leave the field blank or enter a 0.

Edit Field Ordering — Customize | Find | View All | First 1-10 of 10 Last

New Column	Column	Record.Fieldname	Order By	Descending	New Order By
	1	A.RT_RATE_INDEX - Market Rate Index		☐	
	2	A.TERM - Term		☐	
	3	A.FROM_CUR - From Currency Code	1	☑	1
	4	A.TO_CUR - To Currency Code	3	☐	3
	5	A.RT_TYPE - Rate Type	2	☑	2
	6	A.EFFDT - Effective Date		☐	

Records | Query | Expressions | Prompts | Fields | **Criteria** | Having | View SQL | Run

Query Name: CURRENCY_RATES **Description:**

Add Criteria | Group Criteria | Reorder Criteria

Criteria — Customize | Find | First 1-5 of 5 Last

Logical	Expression1	Condition Type	Expression 2	Edit	Delete
	A.FROM_CUR - From Currency Code	in list	('USD','CAD','MXN')	Edit	−
AND	A.TO_CUR - To Currency Code	in list	('CAD','MXN','USD')	Edit	−
AND	A.RT_RATE_INDEX - Market Rate Index	equal to	MODEL	Edit	−
AND	A.RT_TYPE - Rate Type	in list	('CRRNT','AVG')	Edit	−
AND	A.EFFDT - Effective Date	between	2010-02-01 AND 2010-02-28	Edit	−

Save | Save As | New Query | Preferences | Properties | New Union | Return to Search

You added these six rows. Note that the currency exchange rates are in the *Multiplier* field

...rompts | Fields | Criteria | Having | View SQL | **Run**

View All | Rerun Query | Download to Excel — First 1-12 of 12

	Index	Term	From Cur	To Cur	Rate Type	Eff Date	Multiplier	Divisor	Sync ID	Last Upd DtTm
1	MODEL	0	USD	CAD	CRRNT	02/01/2010	1.10000000	1.00000000	9420	01/04/2010 9:19:00PM
2	MODEL	0	USD	CAD	CRRNT	02/26/2010	1.15000000	1.00000000	9420	01/04/2010 10:08:04PM
3	MODEL	0	USD	MXN	CRRNT	02/26/2010	13.15000000	1.00000000	21830	01/04/2010 10:09:05PM
4	MODEL	0	USD	MXN	CRRNT	02/01/2010	13.05000000	1.00000000	21830	01/04/2010 9:21:03PM
5	MODEL	0	USD	CAD	AVG	02/26/2010	1.15000000	1.00000000	9416	01/04/2010 10:08:26PM
6	MODEL	0	USD	MXN	AVG	02/26/2010	13.10000000	1.00000000	21832	01/17/2010 3:30:17PM
7	MODEL	0	MXN	USD	CRRNT	02/26/2010	1.00000000	13.15000000	21831	01/04/2010 10:09:05PM
8	MODEL	0	MXN	USD	CRRNT	02/01/2010	1.00000000	13.05000000	21831	01/04/2010 9:21:03PM
9	MODEL	0	MXN	USD	AVG	02/26/2010	1.00000000	13.10000000	21833	01/17/2010 3:30:17PM
10	MODEL	0	CAD	USD	CRRNT	02/26/2010	1.00000000	1.15000000	2603	01/04/2010 10:08:04PM
11	MODEL	0	CAD	USD	CRRNT	02/01/2010	1.00000000	1.10000000	2603	01/04/2010 9:19:00PM
12	MODEL	0	CAD	USD	AVG	02/26/2010	1.00000000	1.15000000	2599	01/04/2010 10:08:26PM

The system automatically generated these six rows. Note that the currency exchange rates are in the *Divisor* field

9. Enter Journals

Now enter journals to create test data for the revaluation process. For details on entering and posting journals refer to section *Enter Journal* in *Chapter 6: Step 7*.

a. Refer to the screen shots below to enter and post the following two journals:

Business Unit	Journal ID	Journal Date	Header	Lines				
			Ledger Group	#	Account	Dept	Currency	Amount
US003	MC3	02/01/2010	USD_ACT	1	620001		CAD	5000.00
				2	100003		CAD	5000.00
				3	620001		MXN	5000.00
				4	100003		MXN	5000.00
Use the *Copy Journal* feature to copy the above journal								
US003	MC33	02/15/2010	USD_ACT	1	620001	10200	CAD	5000.00
				2	100003		CAD	5000.00
				3	620001	10200	MXN	5000.00
				4	100003		MXN	5000.00
<u>Note</u> that 100003 is a balance sheet account and 620001 is an expense account. Also, in the second journal we have associated a department with the expense account 620001 for test data purposes. Also, exchange rates and base currency amounts will be automatically calculated by the system when you save the journal. Please do not key them in.								

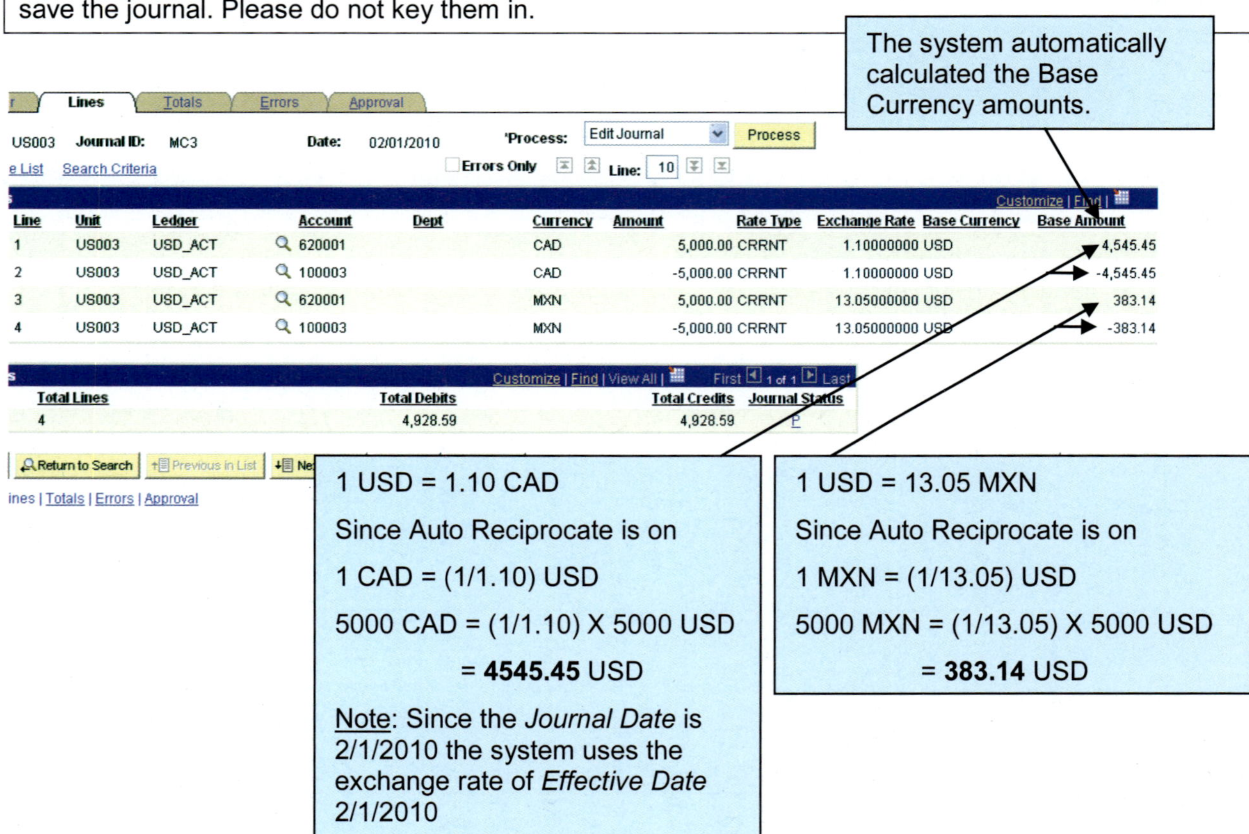

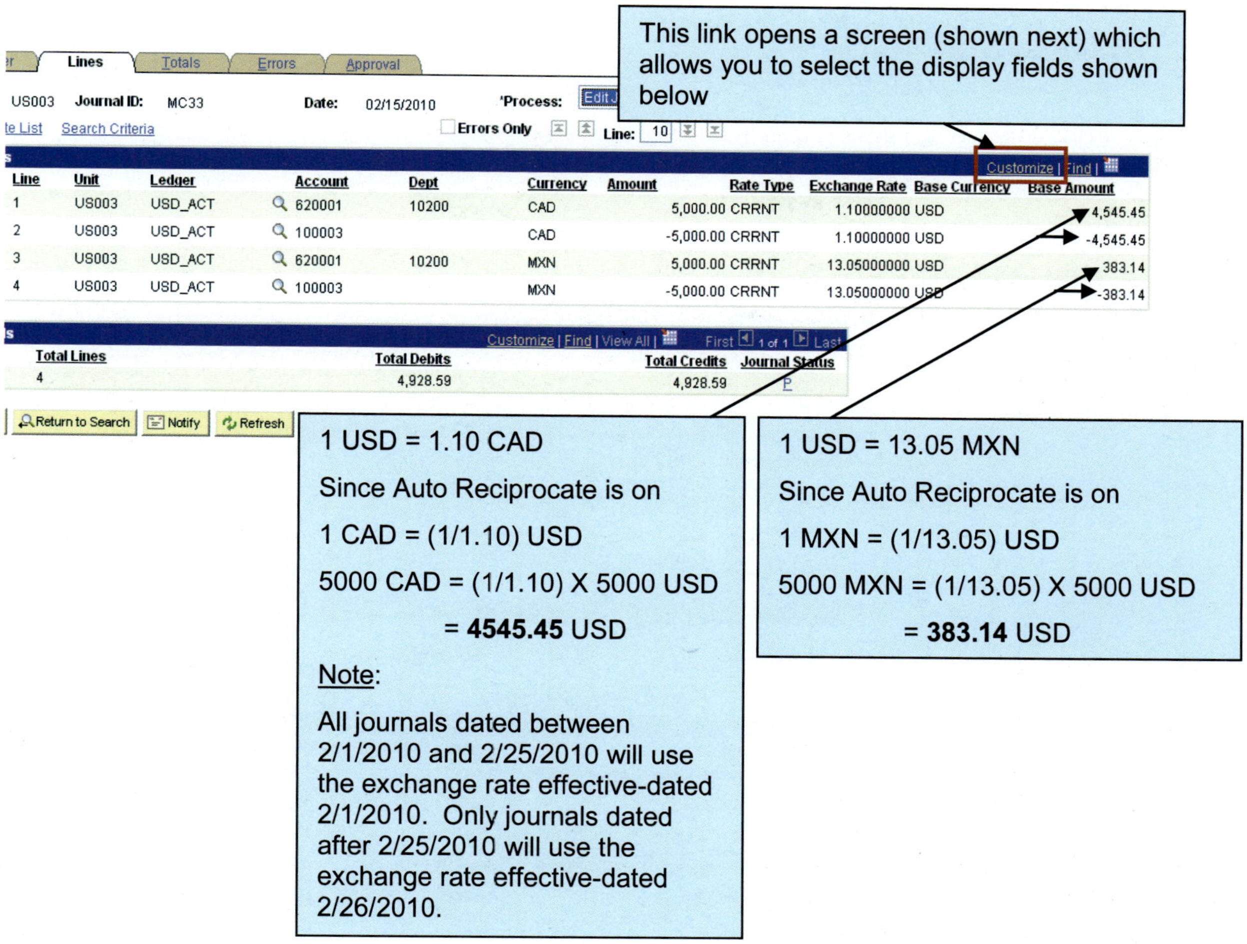

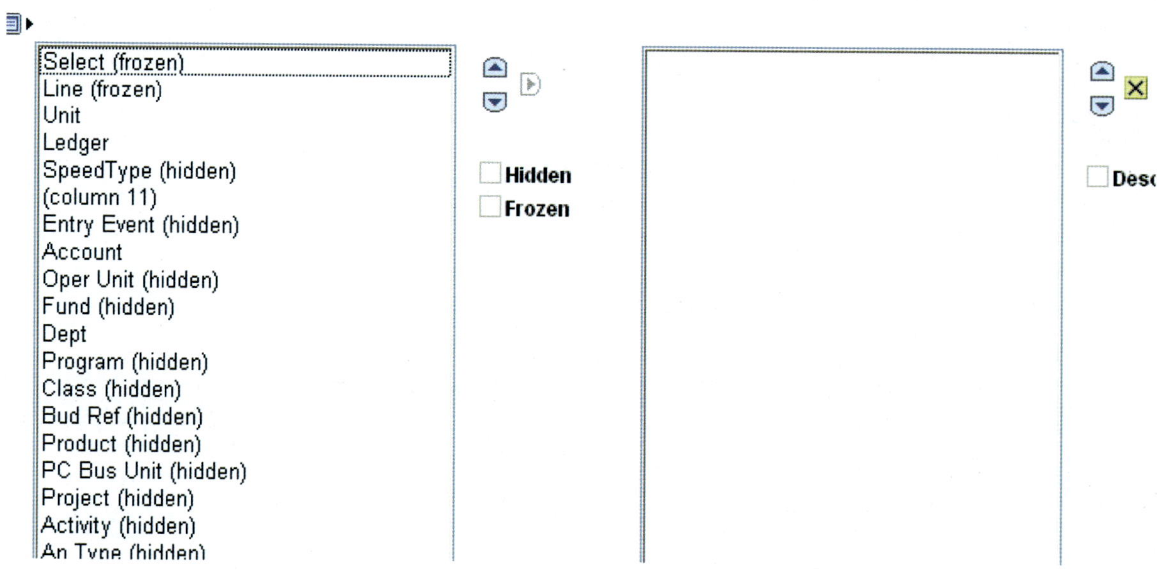

b. Next, use queries MC_JRNL_LN and MC_LEDGER (created in *Chapter 6*) to review the data in the PS_JRNL_LN and PS_LEDGER tables respectively. Refer to the screen shots below to add the `DEPTID` field, change the sort order, and specify the criteria shown below. First run the MC_JRNL_LN query and followed by the MC_LEDGER query.

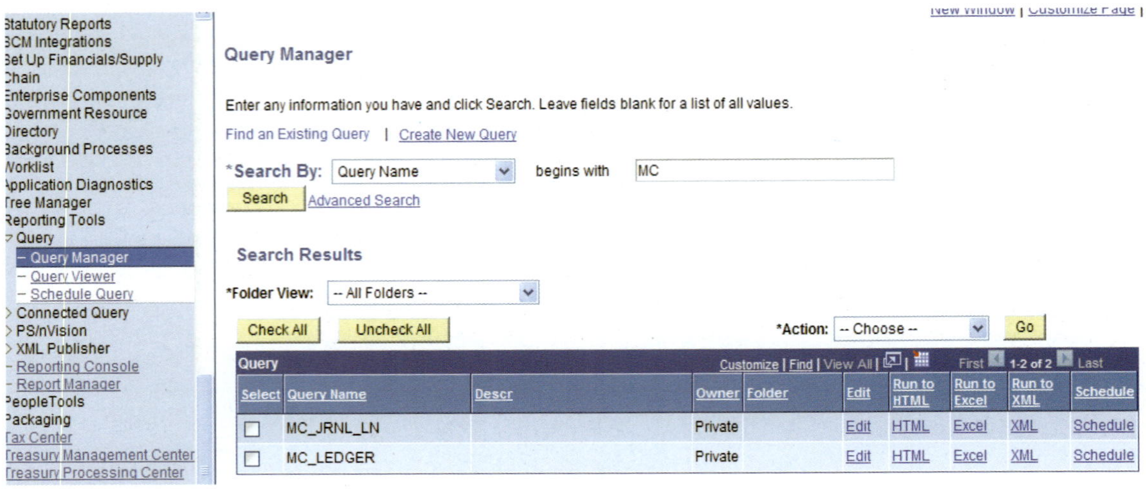
Query Manager
Enter any information you have and click Search. Leave fields blank for a list of all values.
Find an Existing Query | Create New Query
*Search By: Query Name begins with MC
Search Advanced Search
Search Results
*Folder View: -- All Folders --
Check All Uncheck All
*Action: -- Choose -- Go
Query
Select Query Name Descr Owner Folder Edit Run to HTML Run to Excel Run to XML Schedule
MC_JRNL_LN Private Edit HTML Excel XML Schedule
MC_LEDGER Private Edit HTML Excel XML Schedule

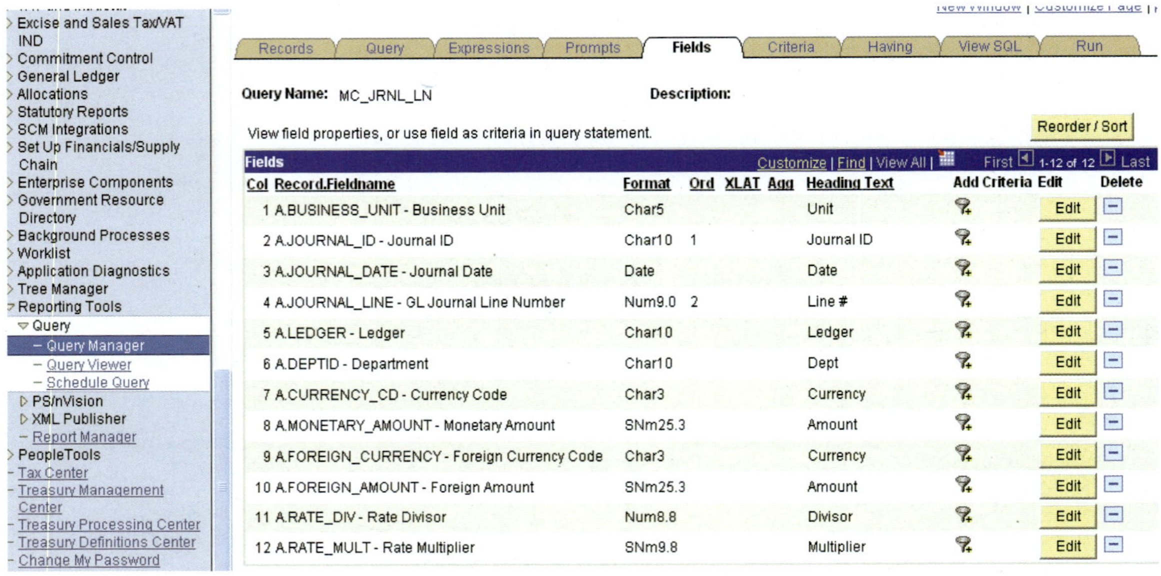
Records Query Expressions Prompts Fields Criteria Having View SQL Run
Query Name: MC_JRNL_LN
Description:
View field properties, or use field as criteria in query statement.
Reorder / Sort
Fields
Col Record.Fieldname Format Ord XLAT Agg Heading Text Add Criteria Edit Delete
1 A.BUSINESS_UNIT - Business Unit Char5 Unit Edit
2 A.JOURNAL_ID - Journal ID Char10 1 Journal ID Edit
3 A.JOURNAL_DATE - Journal Date Date Date Edit
4 A.JOURNAL_LINE - GL Journal Line Number Num9.0 2 Line # Edit
5 A.LEDGER - Ledger Char10 Ledger Edit
6 A.DEPTID - Department Char10 Dept Edit
7 A.CURRENCY_CD - Currency Code Char3 Currency Edit
8 A.MONETARY_AMOUNT - Monetary Amount SNm25.3 Amount Edit
9 A.FOREIGN_CURRENCY - Foreign Currency Code Char3 Currency Edit
10 A.FOREIGN_AMOUNT - Foreign Amount SNm25.3 Amount Edit
11 A.RATE_DIV - Rate Divisor Num8.8 Divisor Edit
12 A.RATE_MULT - Rate Multiplier SNm9.8 Multiplier Edit

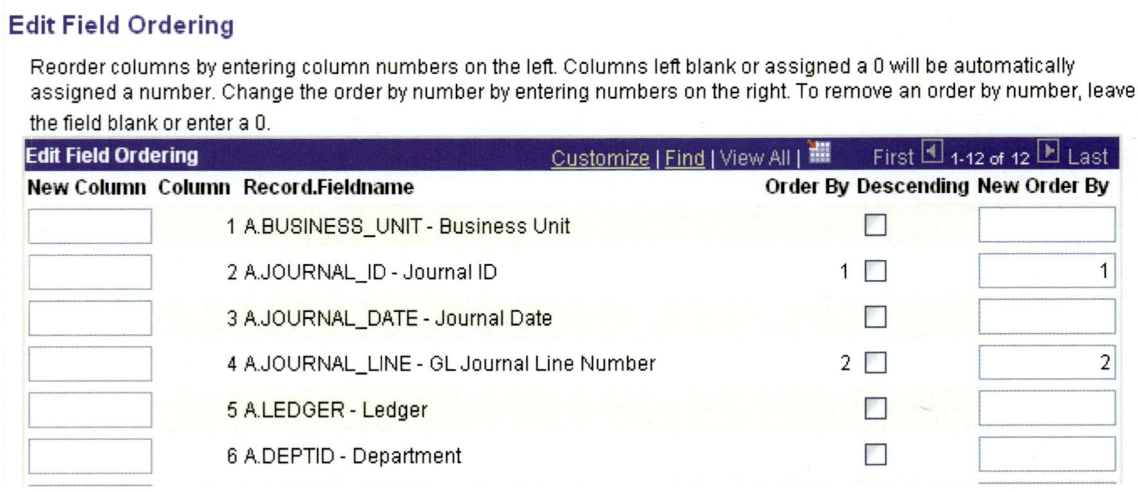
Edit Field Ordering
Reorder columns by entering column numbers on the left. Columns left blank or assigned a 0 will be automatically assigned a number. Change the order by number by entering numbers on the right. To remove an order by number, leave the field blank or enter a 0.
Edit Field Ordering
New Column Column Record.Fieldname Order By Descending New Order By
1 A.BUSINESS_UNIT - Business Unit
2 A.JOURNAL_ID - Journal ID 1 1
3 A.JOURNAL_DATE - Journal Date
4 A.JOURNAL_LINE - GL Journal Line Number 2 2
5 A.LEDGER - Ledger
6 A.DEPTID - Department

Records | Query | Expressions | Prompts | Fields | **Criteria** | Having | View SQL | Run

Query Name: MC_JRNL_LN **Description:**

Add Criteria | Group Criteria | Reorder Criteria

Criteria — Customize | Find | First 1-2 of 2 Last

Logical	Expression1	Condition Type	Expression 2	Edit	Delete
	A.LEDGER - Ledger	equal to	USD_ACT	Edit	−
AND	A.JOURNAL_ID - Journal ID	like	MC3%	Edit	−

Save | Save As | New Query | Preferences | Properties | New Union | Return to Search

Records | Query | Expressions | Prompts | Fields | Criteria | Having | View SQL | **Run**

View All | Rerun Query | Download to Excel — First 1-8 of 8 Last

	Unit	Journal ID	Date	Line #	Ledger	Dept	Currency	Amount	Currency	Amount	Divisor	Multiplier
1	US003	MC3	02/01/2010	1	USD_ACT		USD	4545.450	CAD	5000.000	1.10000000	1.00000000
2	US003	MC3	02/01/2010	2	USD_ACT		USD	-4545.450	CAD	-5000.000	1.10000000	1.00000000
3	US003	MC3	02/01/2010	3	USD_ACT		USD	383.140	MXN	5000.000	13.05000000	1.00000000
4	US003	MC3	02/01/2010	4	USD_ACT		USD	-383.140	MXN	-5000.000	13.05000000	1.00000000
5	US003	MC33	02/15/2010	1	USD_ACT	10200	USD	4545.450	CAD	5000.000	1.10000000	1.00000000
6	US003	MC33	02/15/2010	2	USD_ACT		USD	-4545.450	CAD	-5000.000	1.10000000	1.00000000
7	US003	MC33	02/15/2010	3	USD_ACT	10200	USD	383.140	MXN	5000.000	13.05000000	1.00000000
8	US003	MC33	02/15/2010	4	USD_ACT		USD	-383.140	MXN	-5000.000	13.05000000	1.00000000

Records | Query | Expressions | Prompts | **Fields** | Criteria | Having | View SQL | Run

Query Name: MC_LEDGER **Description:**

View field properties, or use field as criteria in query statement. Reorder / Sort

Fields — Customize | Find | View All | First 1-12 of 12 Last

Col	Record.Fieldname	Format	Ord	XLAT	Agg	Heading Text	Add Criteria	Edit	Delete
1	A.BUSINESS_UNIT - Business Unit	Char5				Unit		Edit	−
2	A.LEDGER - Ledger	Char10				Ledger		Edit	−
3	A.ACCOUNT - Account	Char10	2			Account		Edit	−
4	A.DEPTID - Department	Char10	3			Dept		Edit	−
5	A.CURRENCY_CD - Currency Code	Char3	1			Currency		Edit	−
6	A.FISCAL_YEAR - Fiscal Year	Num4.0				Year		Edit	−
7	A.ACCOUNTING_PERIOD - Accounting Period	Num3.0				Period		Edit	−
8	A.POSTED_TOTAL_AMT - Posted Total Amount	SNm25.3				Total Amt		Edit	−
9	A.POSTED_BASE_AMT - Posted Base Currency Amount	SNm25.3				Amount		Edit	−
10	A.POSTED_TRAN_AMT - Posted Transaction Amount	SNm25.3				Transaction Amt		Edit	−
11	A.BASE_CURRENCY - Base Currency	Char3				Base Curr		Edit	−
12	A.DTTM_STAMP_SEC - Last Update DateTime	DateTm				DateTime		Edit	−

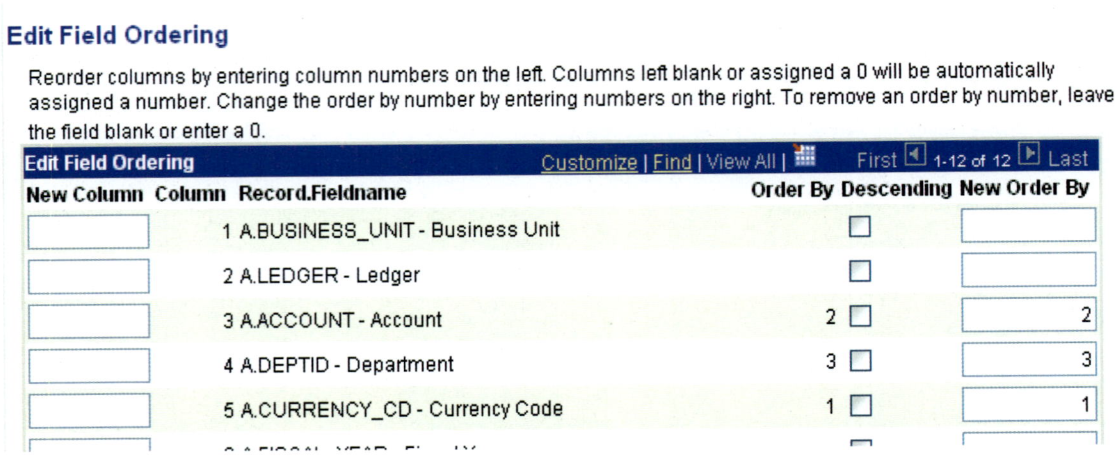
Edit Field Ordering
Reorder columns by entering column numbers on the left. Columns left blank or assigned a 0 will be automatically assigned a number. Change the order by number by entering numbers on the right. To remove an order by number, leave the field blank or enter a 0.
Edit Field Ordering
Customize | Find | View All |
First 1-12 of 12 Last
New Column Column Record.Fieldname
Order By Descending New Order By
1 A.BUSINESS_UNIT - Business Unit
2 A.LEDGER - Ledger
3 A.ACCOUNT - Account 2 2
4 A.DEPTID - Department 3 3
5 A.CURRENCY_CD - Currency Code 1 1

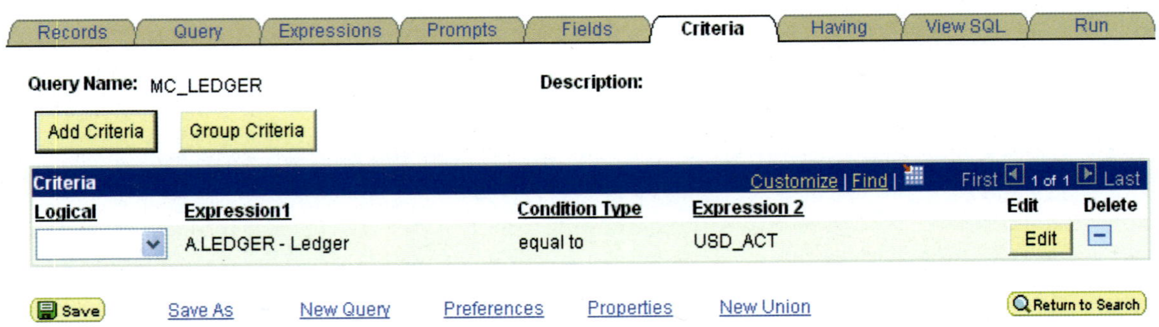
Records Query Expressions Prompts Fields Criteria Having View SQL Run
Query Name: MC_LEDGER
Description:
Add Criteria
Group Criteria
Criteria
Customize | Find |
First 1 of 1 Last
Logical Expression1 Condition Type Expression 2 Edit Delete
A.LEDGER - Ledger equal to USD_ACT Edit
Save
Save As
New Query
Preferences
Properties
New Union
Return to Search

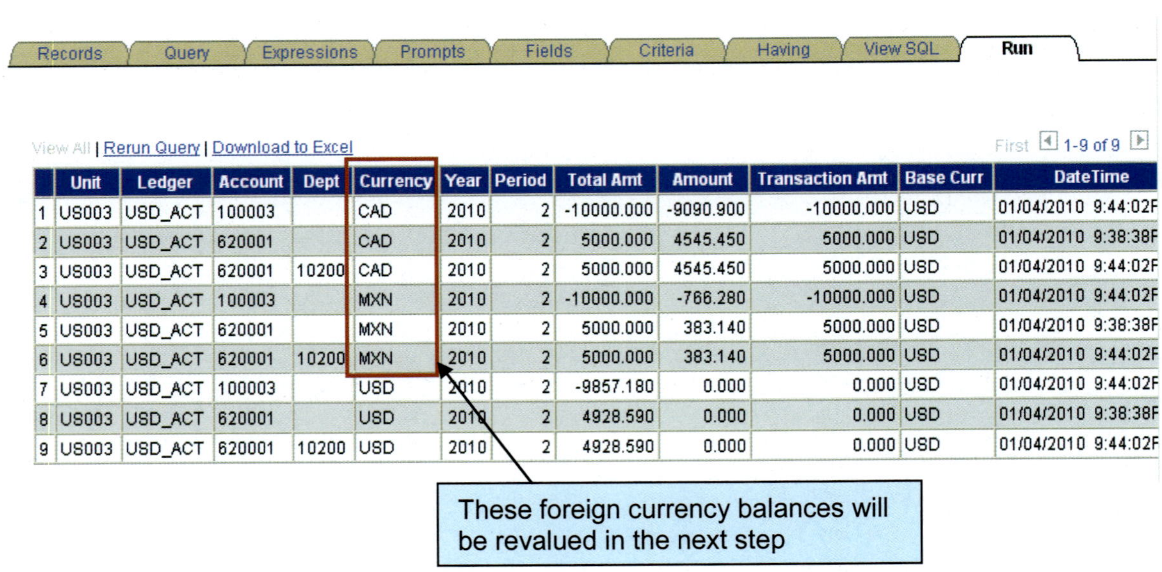
Records Query Expressions Prompts Fields Criteria Having View SQL Run
View All | Rerun Query | Download to Excel
First 1-9 of 9
Unit Ledger Account Dept Currency Year Period Total Amt Amount Transaction Amt Base Curr DateTime
1 US003 USD_ACT 100003 CAD 2010 2 -10000.000 -9090.900 -10000.000 USD 01/04/2010 9:44:02F
2 US003 USD_ACT 620001 CAD 2010 2 5000.000 4545.450 5000.000 USD 01/04/2010 9:38:38F
3 US003 USD_ACT 620001 10200 CAD 2010 2 5000.000 4545.450 5000.000 USD 01/04/2010 9:44:02F
4 US003 USD_ACT 100003 MXN 2010 2 -10000.000 -766.280 -10000.000 USD 01/04/2010 9:44:02F
5 US003 USD_ACT 620001 MXN 2010 2 5000.000 383.140 5000.000 USD 01/04/2010 9:38:38F
6 US003 USD_ACT 620001 10200 MXN 2010 2 5000.000 383.140 5000.000 USD 01/04/2010 9:44:02F
7 US003 USD_ACT 100003 USD 2010 2 -9857.180 0.000 0.000 USD 01/04/2010 9:44:02F
8 US003 USD_ACT 620001 USD 2010 2 4928.590 0.000 0.000 USD 01/04/2010 9:38:38F
9 US003 USD_ACT 620001 10200 USD 2010 2 4928.590 0.000 0.000 USD 01/04/2010 9:44:02F
These foreign currency balances will be revalued in the next step

10. Configure and Run Revaluation

Revaluation means accounting for the difference between the market value and book value. PeopleSoft allows you to revalue foreign currency balances (typically balance sheet accounts) by making journal entries to adjust the base currency ledger balances.

You will revalue the ledger balances (test data) from the previous step using the market rates from step 8.

← Test Data → ← Expected Results →

Account	Dept	Curr	Trn Amt A	Base Amt B	Rate for Reval C	New Base Amt = A / C D	Base Curr Adjustmnt = (D – B) E	Curr Gain/ Loss = - E
Revalue BS accounts at CRRNT rate								
100003		CAD	-10000.00	-9090.90	1.15	-8695.65	395.25	-395.25
100003		MXN	-10000.00	-766.28	13.15	-760.46	5.82	-5.82
Revalue P&L accounts at AVG rate								
620001		CAD	5000.00	4545.45	1.15	4347.83	-197.62	197.62
620001	10200	CAD	5000.00	4545.45	1.15	4347.83	-197.62	197.62
620001		MXN	5000.00	383.14	13.10	381.68	-1.46	1.46
620001	10200	MXN	5000.00	383.14	13.10	381.68	-1.46	1.46

Net, you will configure the revaluation items in the sequence listed below:

- Configure *Revaluation Steps*
  - Setup a *Revaluation Step* (RVL_BS) for balance sheet accounts to revalue at CRRNT rates
  - Setup a *Revaluation Step* (RVL_PL) for P&L accounts to revalue at AVG rates
- Configure *Revaluation Group* (or the *Process Group*)
  - Group the above two revaluation steps into a *Process Group* (RVL_BS_PL)
- Run revaluation
- Review journals created
- Run *Revaluation Calculation Log*

Follow these steps to configure and run the revaluation process.

a. Navigate to *Revaluation Step > Add a New Value* as highlighted below
b. Specify the following values:
   - `SetID: SHARE`
   - `Process Step: RVL_BS`
c. Click on *Add*

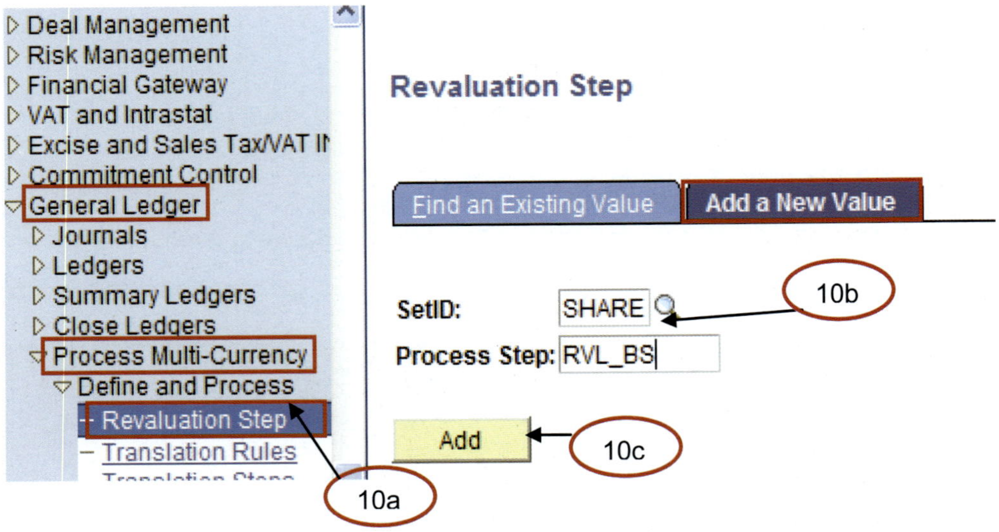

d. In the *Ledger and TimeSpan* tab, specify the *Ledger*, *TimeSpan* and *Rate Type* per details below:

- `Effective Date: 01/01/1990`
- `Status: Active`
- `Descr: Reval BS Accounts`
- `Description: Reval BS Accounts`
- `From Ledger Group: USD_ACT`
- `Ledger: USD_ACT`
- `TimeSpan: BAL` *(year to date)*
- `Rate Type: CRRNT`

e. Click on the *Source Chartfields* tab

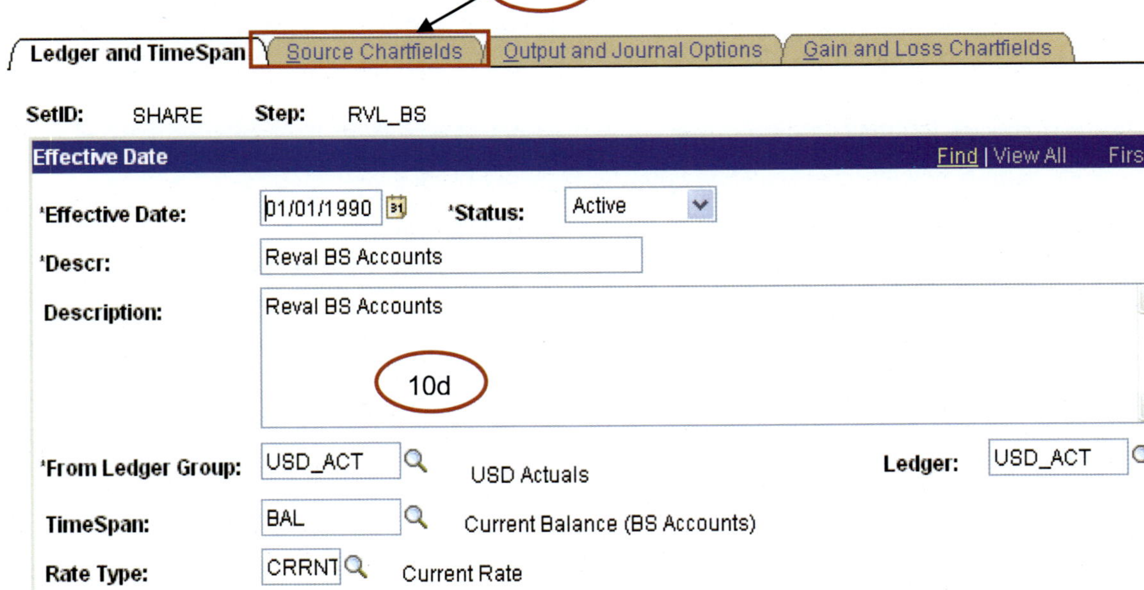

f. In the next screen specify the *ChartField* values for revaluation. You can select one or more ChartFields and specify values using either *Tree Nodes* or *Details*. Specify the following values for this example:

- `ChartField: Account`
- `How Specified: Selected Detail Values`
- `ChartField values/Tree nodes: 100003`

g. Click on the *Output and Journal Options* tab

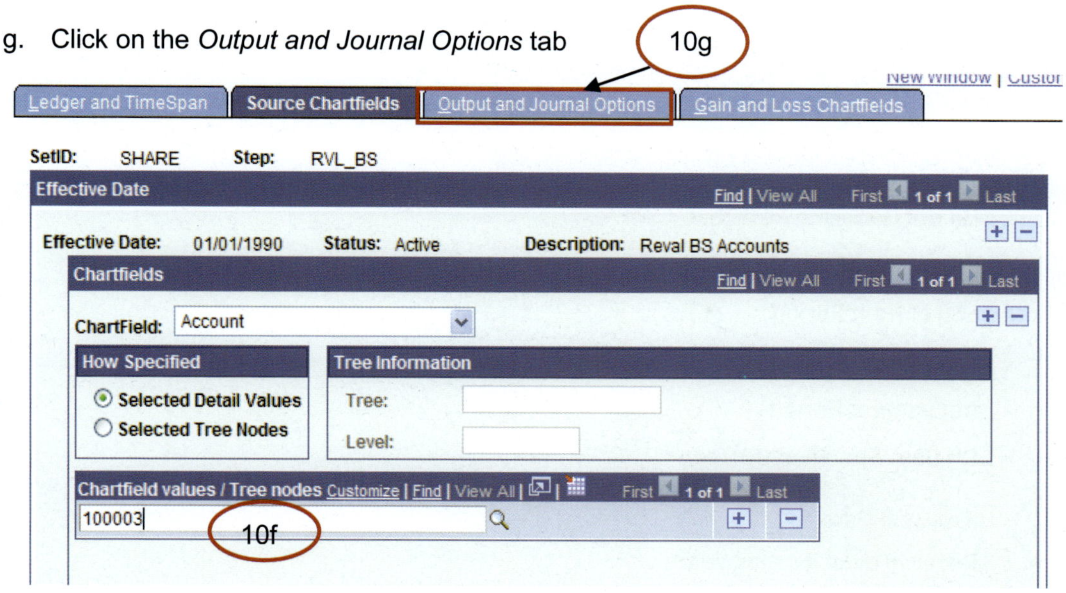

h. On the next screen, specify the output options for the journals that will be created when this revaluation step is run. Specify the following values:

- `Journal ID Mask: RVL`
- `Source: MCP` (Journal Source)
- `Description: BS Revaluation` (Journal Header Description)
- `Create Journal Entries: Checked`
- `Edit Journal(s): Checked`
- `Target ChartField: Account`
- `Retain Value: Checked` (this will cause the account values specified earlier in the *Source Chartfields* tab to be copied onto the output journal lines)

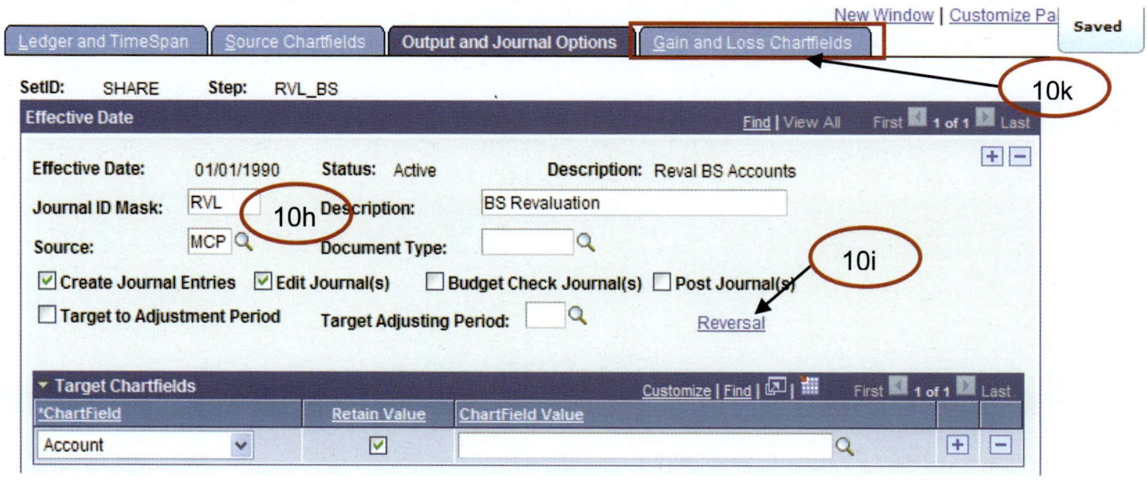

i. Click on the *Reversal* link and select the following value:

   a. `Reversal Code = Beginning of Next Period` (This will cause journals to auto-reverse at the beginning of the next period. If you do not want journals created for the last period of the fiscal year to reverse, then create a separate revaluation rule and select *Do Not Generate Reversal*)

j. Click on *OK*

k. Click on the *Gain and Loss Chartfields* tab

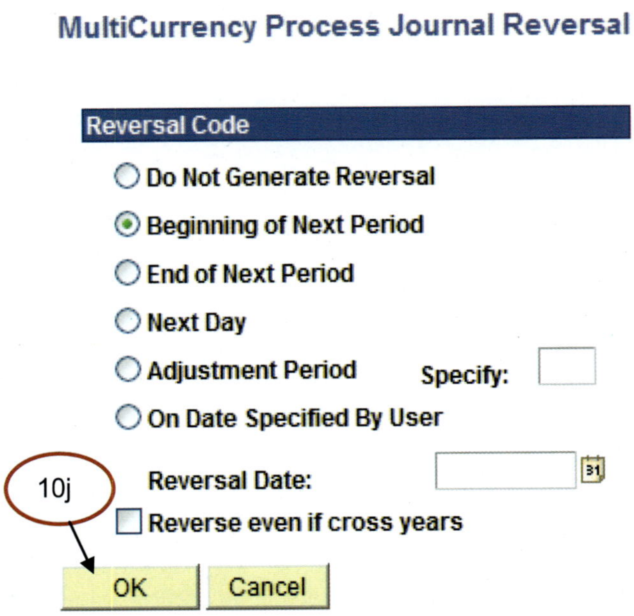

l. The system posts the offsetting credits to *Gain ChartFields* and debits to *Loss ChartFields*. Specify the following values:

- `Gain ChartKeys, Chartfield: Account, ChartField Value: 315000`
- `Loss ChartKeys, Chartfield: Account, ChartField Value: 315000`

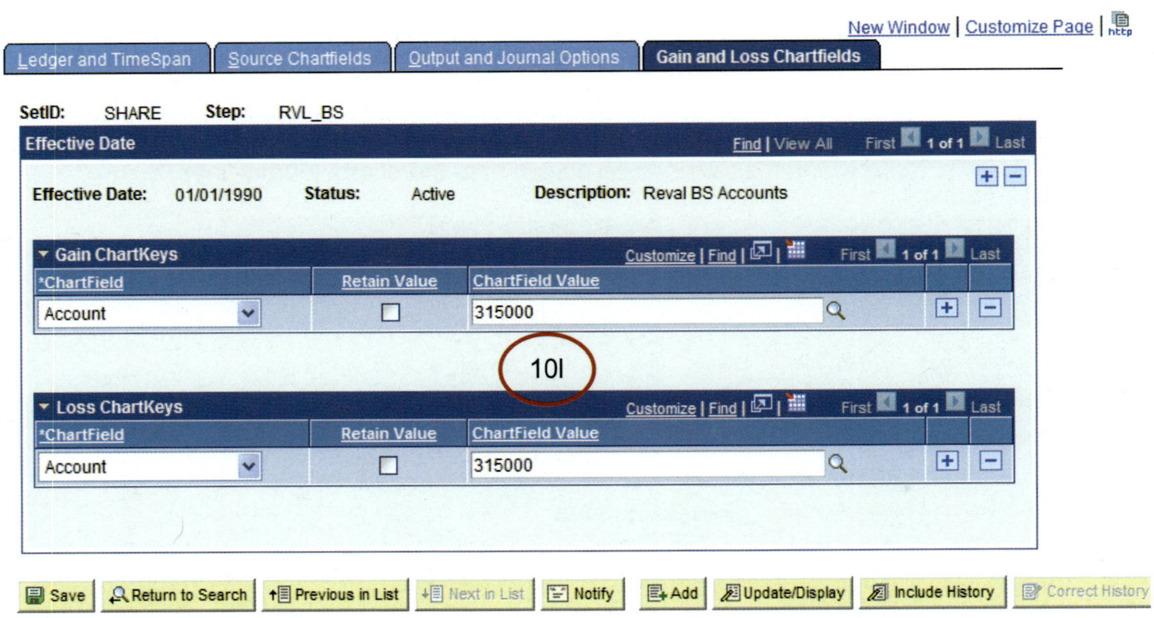

m. Click on *Save*

n. Refer to the screen shots below to setup the *Revaluation Step*, RVL_PL

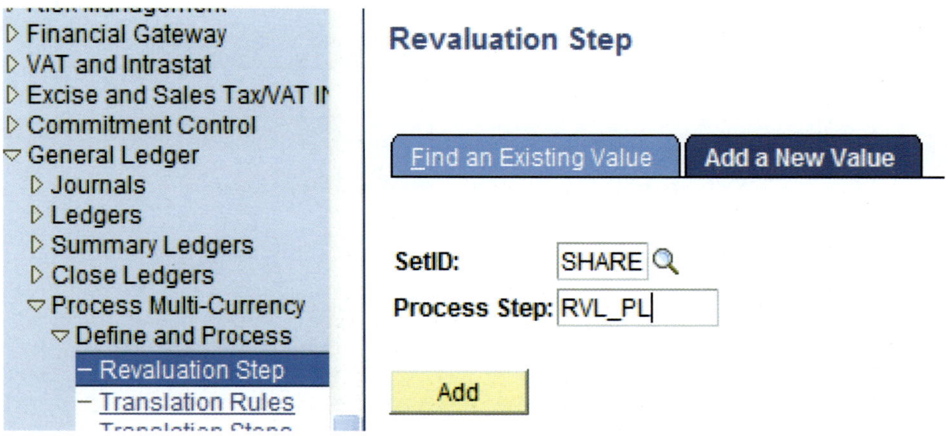
Financial Gateway
VAT and Intrastat
Commitment Control
General Ledger
Journals
Ledgers
Summary Ledgers
Close Ledgers
Process Multi-Currency
Define and Process
Revaluation Step
Translation Rules
Revaluation Step
Find an Existing Value
Add a New Value
SetID: SHARE
Process Step: RVL_PL
Add

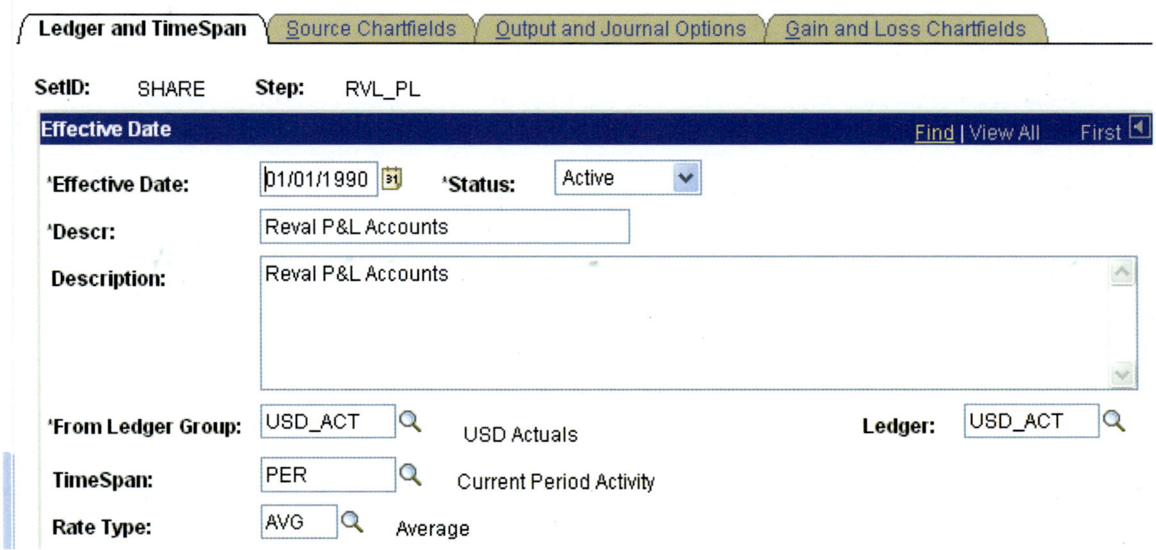
Ledger and TimeSpan
Source Chartfields
Output and Journal Options
Gain and Loss Chartfields
SetID: SHARE
Step: RVL_PL
Effective Date
Find | View All
First
*Effective Date: 01/01/1990
*Status: Active
*Descr: Reval P&L Accounts
Description: Reval P&L Accounts
*From Ledger Group: USD_ACT
USD Actuals
Ledger: USD_ACT
TimeSpan: PER
Current Period Activity
Rate Type: AVG
Average

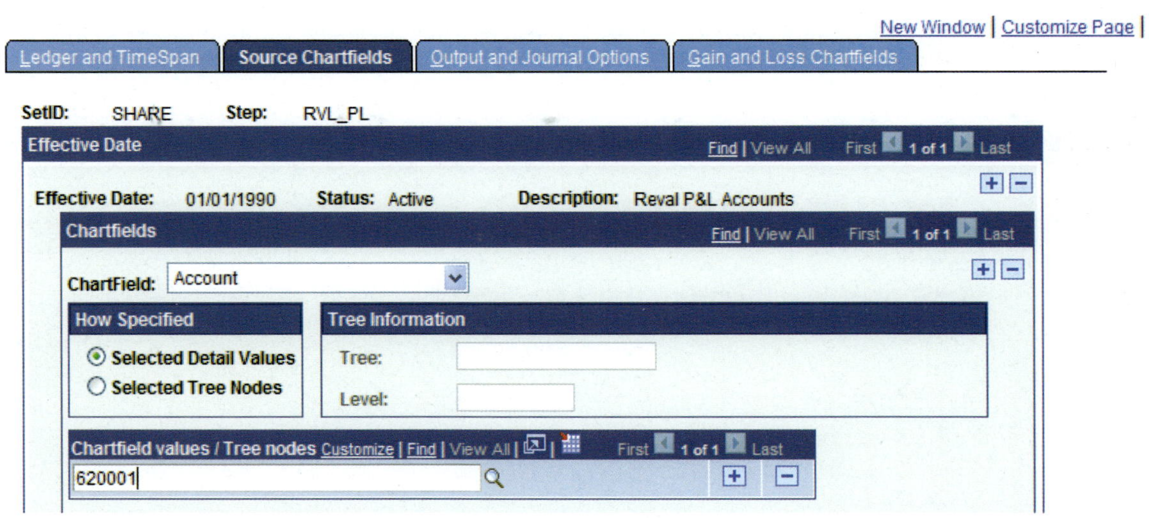
New Window | Customize Page |
Ledger and TimeSpan
Source Chartfields
Output and Journal Options
Gain and Loss Chartfields
SetID: SHARE
Step: RVL_PL
Effective Date
Find | View All
First 1 of 1 Last
Effective Date: 01/01/1990
Status: Active
Description: Reval P&L Accounts
Chartfields
Find | View All
First 1 of 1 Last
ChartField: Account
How Specified
Selected Detail Values
Selected Tree Nodes
Tree Information
Tree:
Level:
Chartfield values / Tree nodes Customize | Find | View All |
First 1 of 1 Last
620001

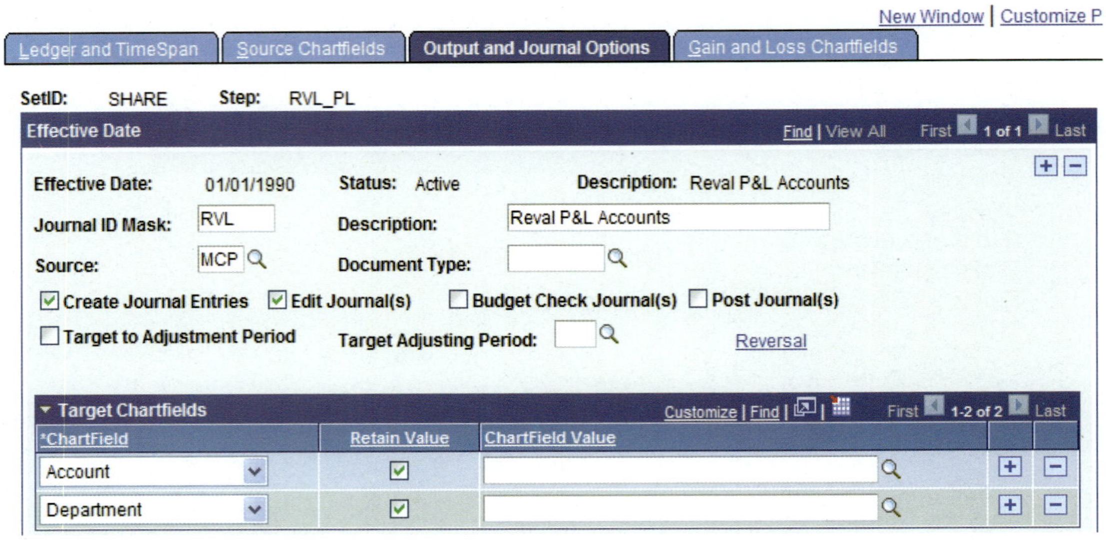
New Window | Customize P
Ledger and TimeSpan
Source Chartfields
Output and Journal Options
Gain and Loss Chartfields
SetID: SHARE
Step: RVL_PL
Effective Date
Find | View All
First 1 of 1 Last
Effective Date: 01/01/1990
Status: Active
Description: Reval P&L Accounts
Journal ID Mask: RVL
Description: Reval P&L Accounts
Source: MCP
Document Type:
Create Journal Entries
Edit Journal(s)
Budget Check Journal(s)
Post Journal(s)
Target to Adjustment Period
Target Adjusting Period:
Reversal
Target Chartfields
Customize | Find |
First 1-2 of 2 Last
*ChartField
Retain Value
ChartField Value
Account
Department

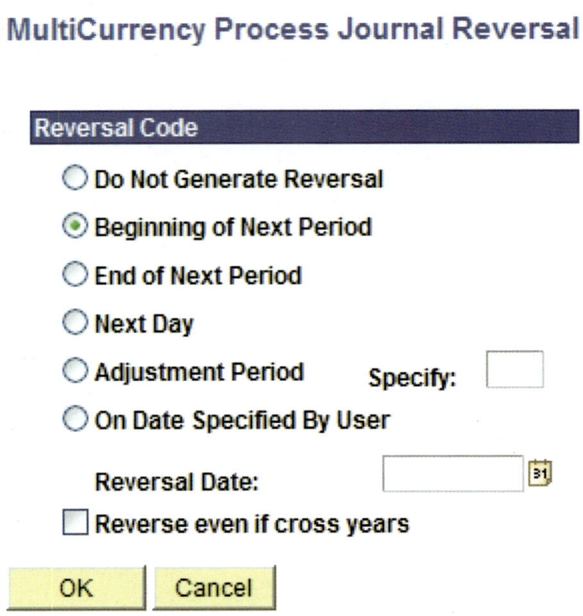
MultiCurrency Process Journal Reversal
Reversal Code
Do Not Generate Reversal
Beginning of Next Period
End of Next Period
Next Day
Adjustment Period
Specify:
On Date Specified By User
Reversal Date:
Reverse even if cross years
OK
Cancel

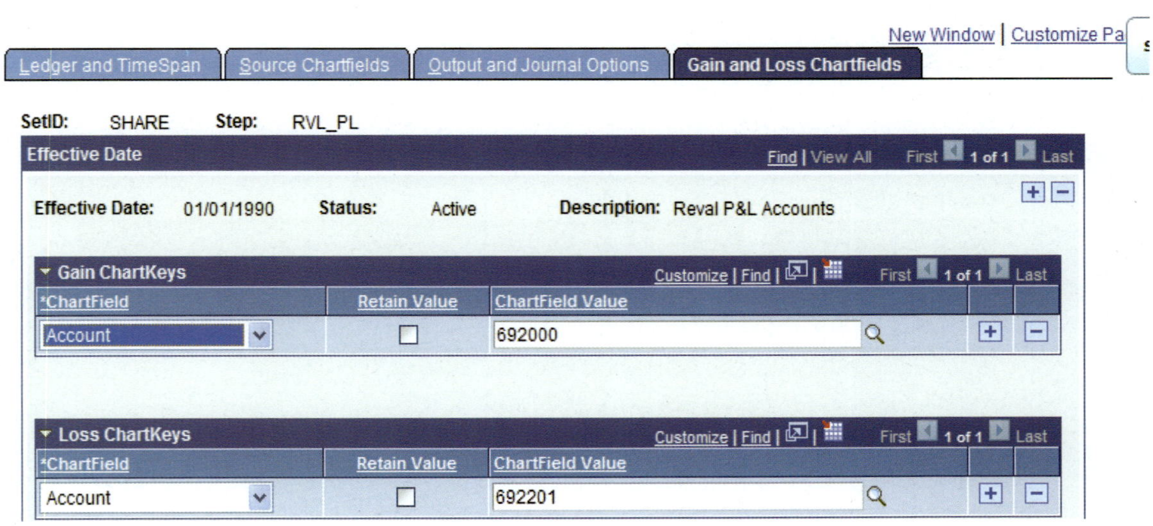
New Window | Customize Pa
Ledger and TimeSpan
Source Chartfields
Output and Journal Options
Gain and Loss Chartfields
SetID: SHARE
Step: RVL_PL
Effective Date
Find | View All
First 1 of 1 Last
Effective Date: 01/01/1990
Status: Active
Description: Reval P&L Accounts
Gain ChartKeys
Customize | Find |
First 1 of 1 Last
*ChartField
Retain Value
ChartField Value
Account
692000
Loss ChartKeys
Customize | Find |
First 1 of 1 Last
*ChartField
Retain Value
ChartField Value
Account
692201

o. Next you will setup the revaluation *Process Group*, RVL_BS_PL. Navigate to *Define Process Group* > *Add a New Value* as highlighted below and specify the following values:
   - `SetID: SHARE`
   - `Process Group: RVL_BS_PL`

p. Click on *Add*

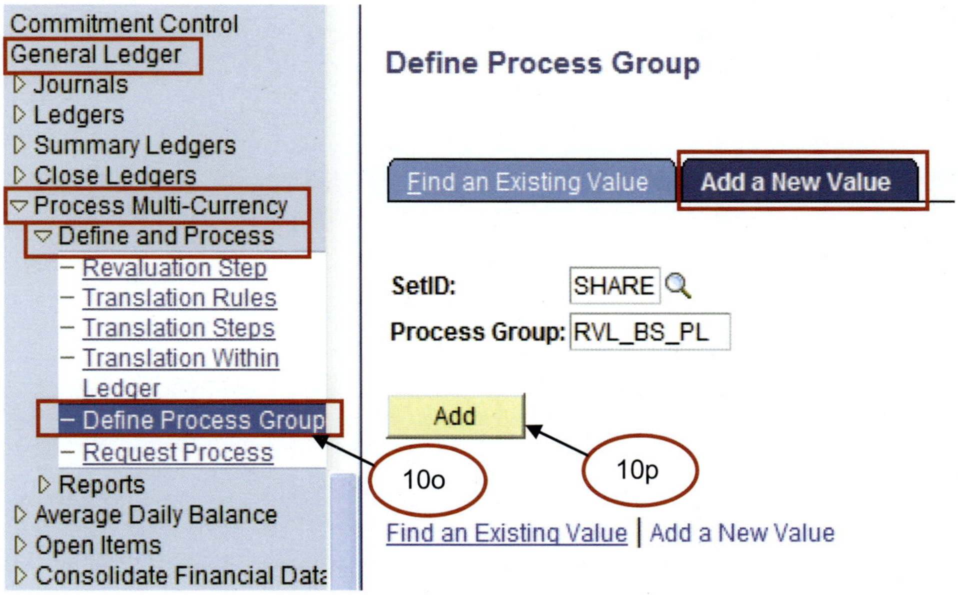

q. Add the two revaluation steps, RVL_BS and RVL_PL

r. Click on *Save*

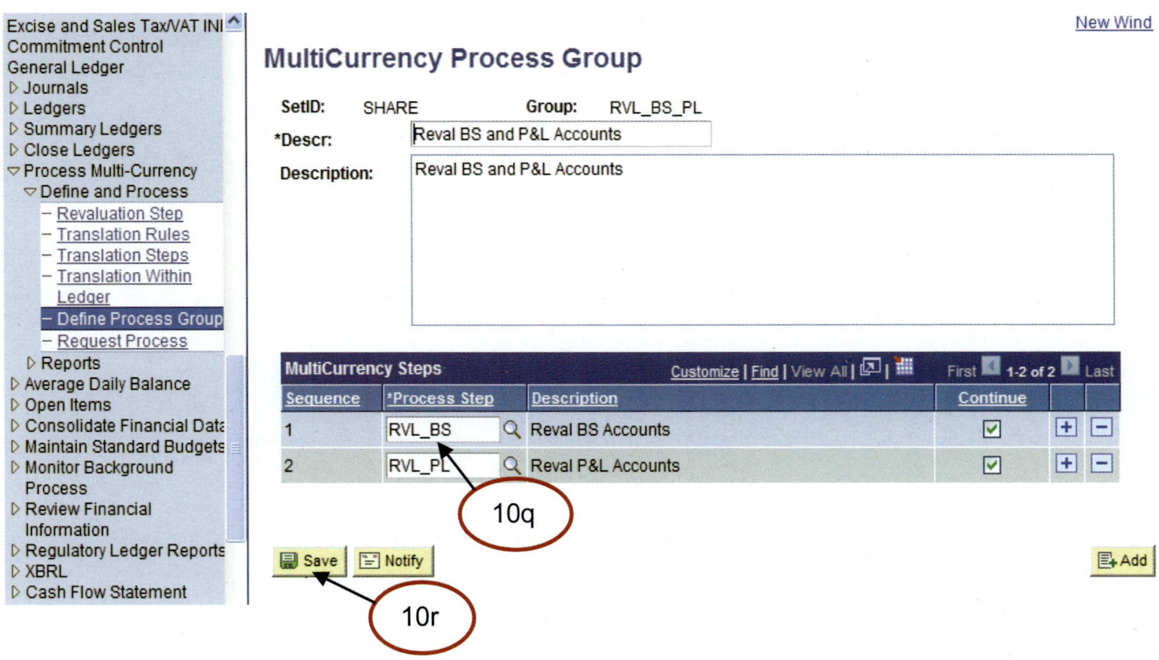

s. Next run the revaluation process to create the base currency adjustment journal entries. Navigate to *Request Process* > Add *a New Value* as highlighted below and specify the following value:
   - `Run Control ID: Reval`

t. Click on *Add*

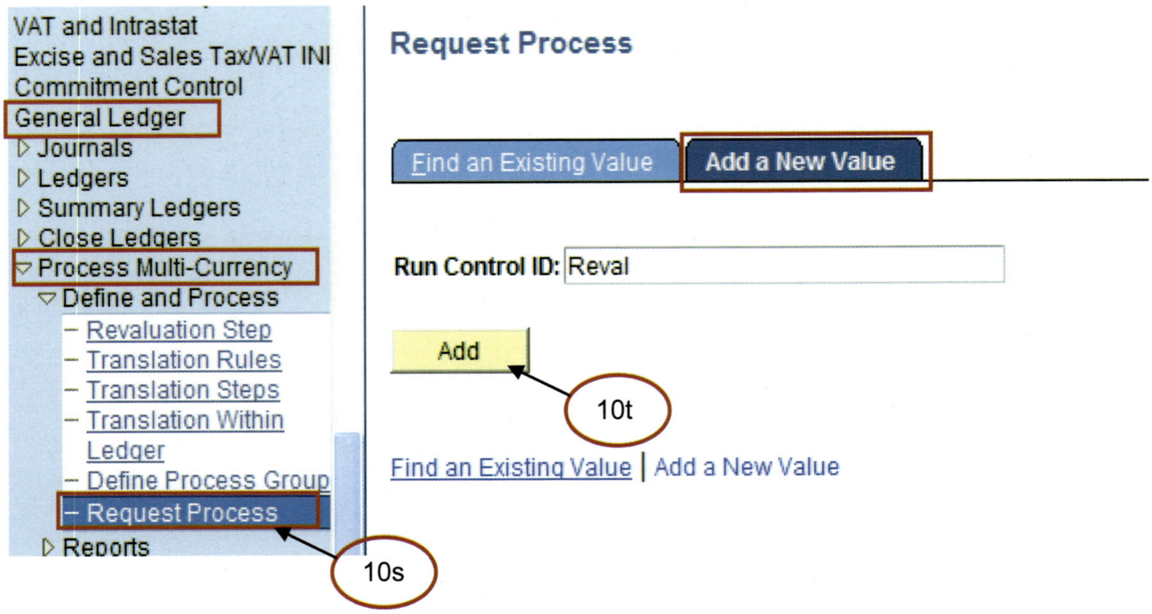

u. On the *MultiCurrency Process Request* page specify the following values:
   - `Process Frequency: Once`
   - `Unit: US003`
   - `Group: RVL_BS_PL`
   - `Calc Log: Checked`
   - `Request Date Option: As of Date`
   - `As of Date: 02/26/2010` (last business day of the month)

v. Click on *Save*

w. Click *on* Run

x. Click *on OK* on the *Process Scheduler* page. This will execute the FSPCCURR COBOL program.

y. You will be taken back to the *MultiCurrency Process Request* page. Click on the *Process Monitor* link at the top of the page and wait for the FSPCCURR COBOL program to indicate *Success.*

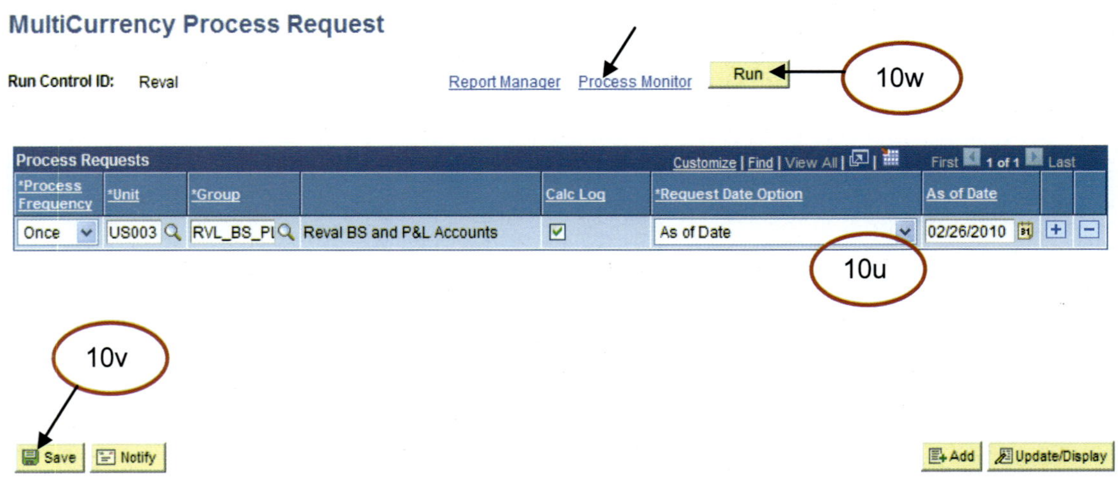

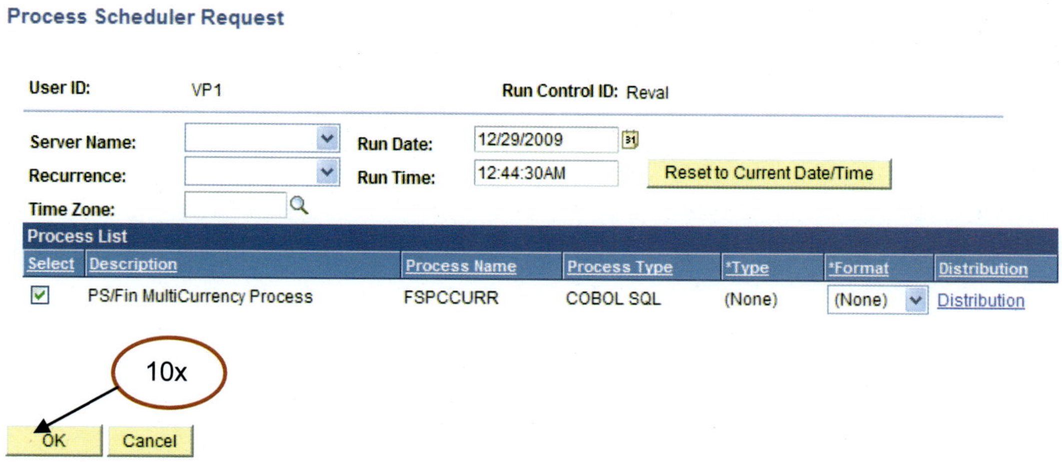

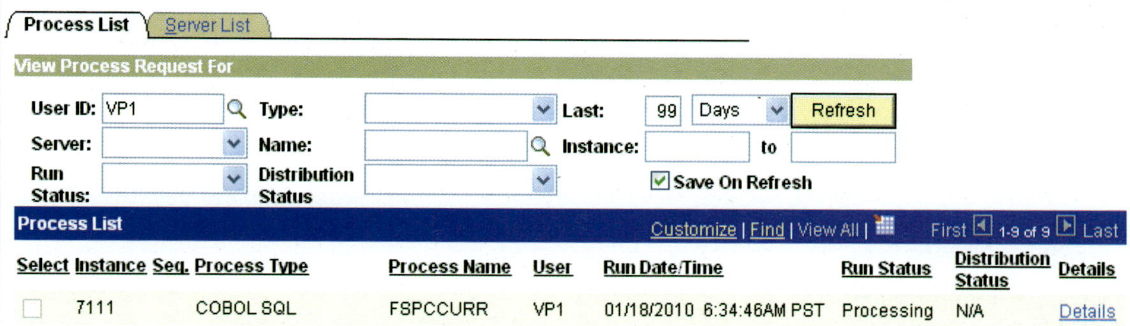

z. Now review the journals created by the revaluation process. Navigate to *General Ledger > Journals > Create/Update Journal Entries > Find an Existing Value* and specify the following values:

- `Business Unit: US003`
- `Journal ID: RVL`

aa. Click on *Search*. This should retrieve the two journals created by the revaluation process, one per each revaluation step, RVL_BS and RVL_PL.

bb. Click on the journals and see if data is as expected

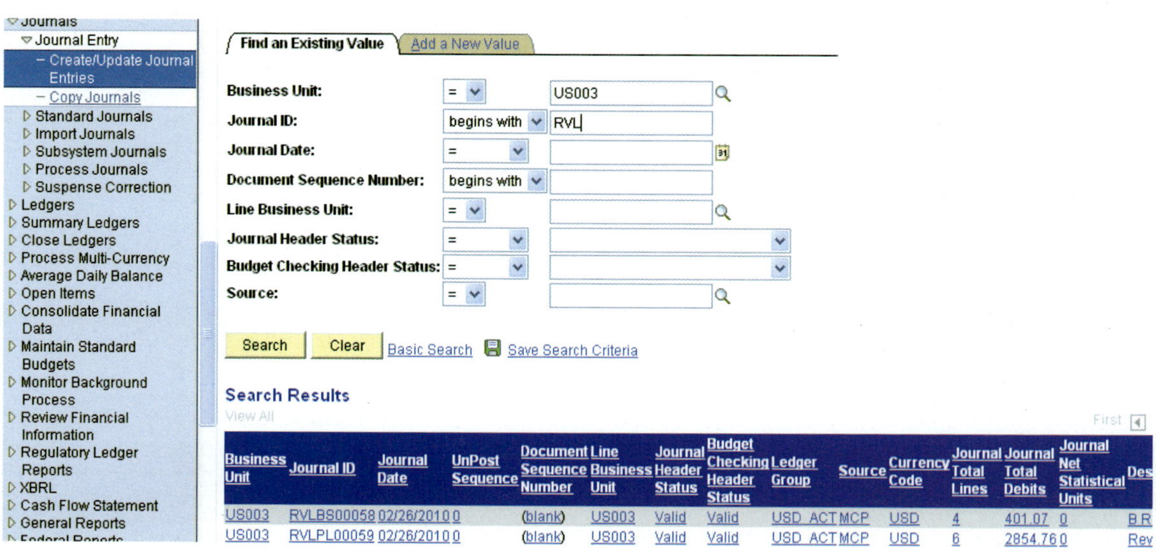

RVLBS is the journal ID mask, BS revaluation is the journal header description and MCP is the journal's *Source* that you specified on the RVL_BS revaluation step.

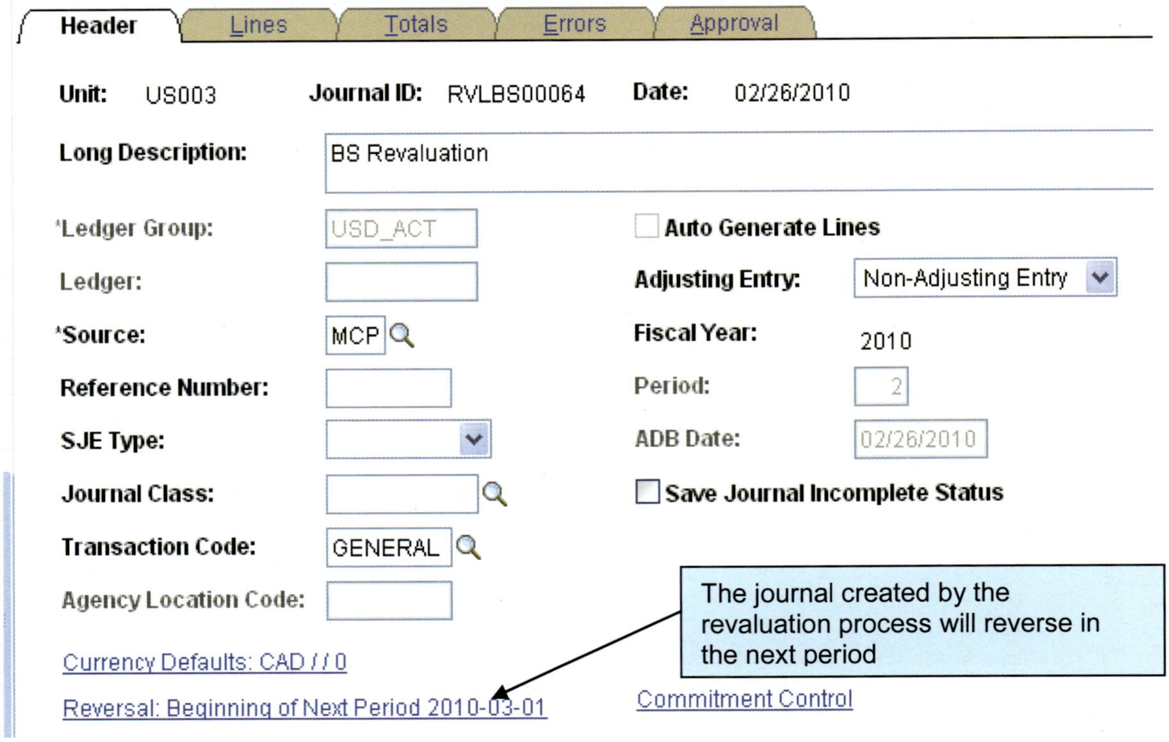
Header | Lines | Totals | Errors | Approval
Unit: US003 Journal ID: RVLBS00064 Date: 02/26/2010
Long Description: BS Revaluation
*Ledger Group: USD_ACT
Auto Generate Lines
Ledger:
Adjusting Entry: Non-Adjusting Entry
*Source: MCP
Fiscal Year: 2010
Reference Number:
Period: 2
SJE Type:
ADB Date: 02/26/2010
Journal Class:
Save Journal Incomplete Status
Transaction Code: GENERAL
Agency Location Code:
Currency Defaults: CAD / / 0
Reversal: Beginning of Next Period 2010-03-01
Commitment Control

The journal created by the revaluation process will reverse in the next period

Test Data / Expected Results

Account	Dept	Curr	Trn Amt A	Base Amt B	Rate for Reval C	New Base Amt = A / C D	Base Curr Adjustmnt = (D – B) E	Curr Gain/ Loss = - E
Revalue BS accounts at CRRNT rate								
100003		CAD	-10000.00	-9090.90	1.15	-8695.65	395.25	-395.25
100003		MXN	-10000.00	-766.28	13.15	-760.46	5.82	-5.82
Revalue P&L accounts at AVG rate								
620001		CAD	5000.00	4545.45	1.15	4347.83	-197.62	197.62
620001	10200	CAD	5000.00	4545.45	1.15	4347.83	-197.62	197.62
620001		MXN	5000.00	383.14	13.10	381.68	-1.46	1.46
620001	10200	MXN	5000.00	383.14	13.10	381.68	-1.46	1.46

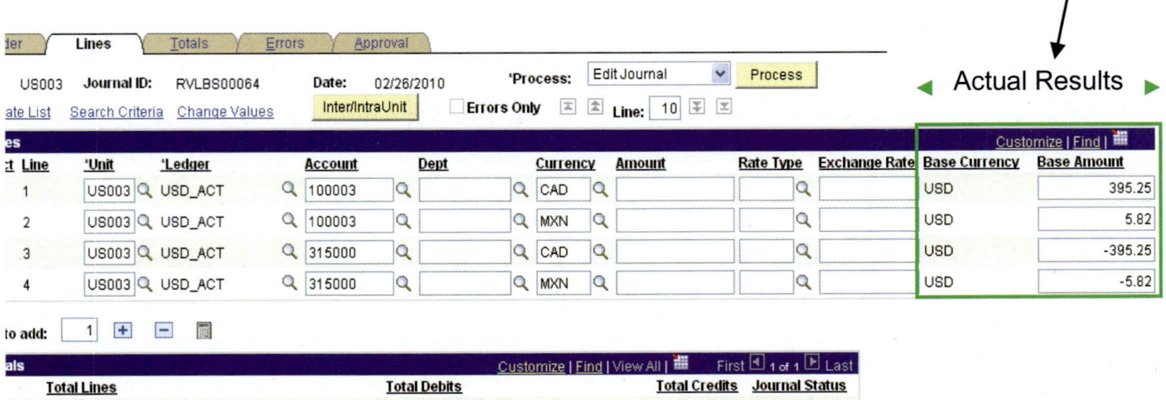
Lines | Totals | Errors | Approval
US003 Journal ID: RVLBS00064 Date: 02/26/2010 *Process: Edit Journal Process
Inter/IntraUnit Errors Only Line: 10

Line	*Unit	*Ledger	Account	Dept	Currency	Amount	Rate Type	Exchange Rate	Base Currency	Base Amount
1	US003	USD_ACT	100003		CAD				USD	395.25
2	US003	USD_ACT	100003		MXN				USD	5.82
3	US003	USD_ACT	315000		CAD				USD	-395.25
4	US003	USD_ACT	315000		MXN				USD	-5.82

Total Lines	Total Debits	Total Credits	Journal Status
4	401.07	401.07	V

Actual Results

RVLPL is the journal ID mask, *Reval P&L Accounts* is the journal header description and MCP is the journal's *Source* that you specified in the RVL_PL revaluation step.

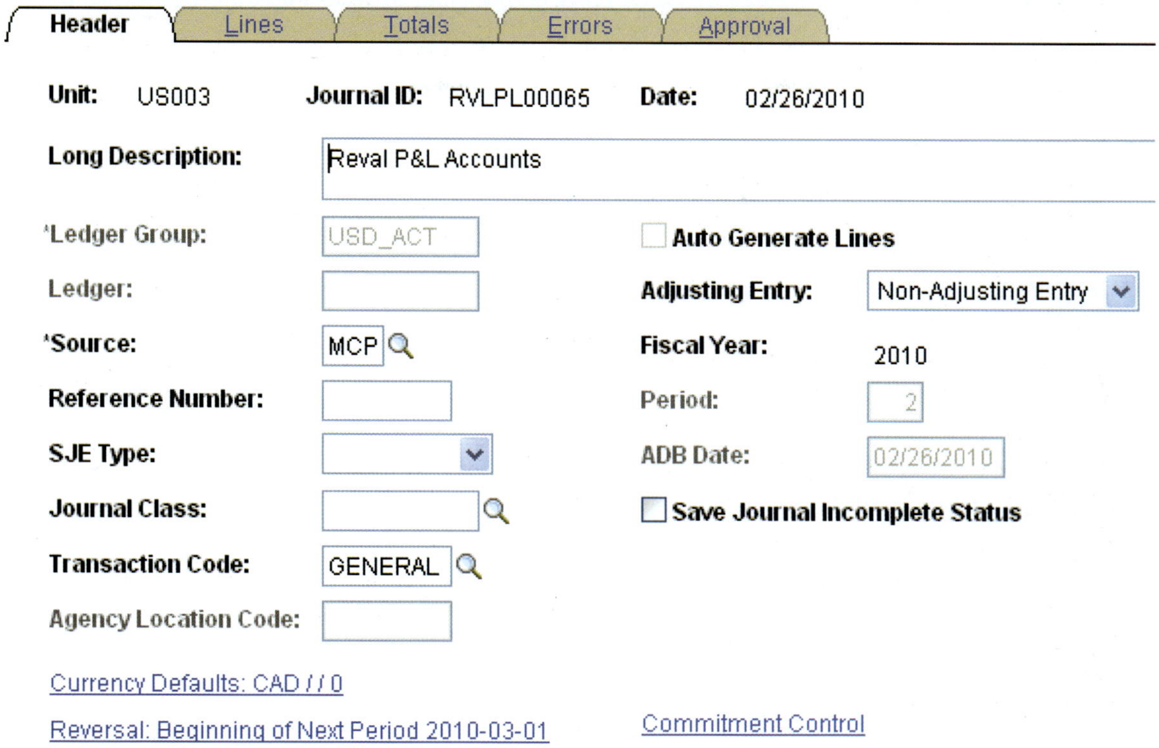

Test Data — Expected Results

Account	Dept	Curr	Trn Amt A	Base Amt B	Rate for Reval C	New Base Amt = A / C D	Base Curr Adjustmnt = (D – B) E	Curr Gain/ Loss = - E
Revalue BS accounts at CRRNT rate								
100003		CAD	-10000.00	-9090.90	1.15	-8695.65	395.25	-395.25
100003		MXN	-10000.00	-766.28	13.15	-760.46	5.82	-5.82
Revalue P&L accounts at AVG rate								
620001		CAD	5000.00	4545.45	1.15	4347.83	-197.62	197.62
620001	10200	CAD	5000.00	4545.45	1.15	4347.83	-197.62	197.62
620001		MXN	5000.00	383.14	13.10	381.68	-1.46	1.46
620001	10200	MXN	5000.00	383.14	13.10	381.68	-1.46	1.46

Actual Results

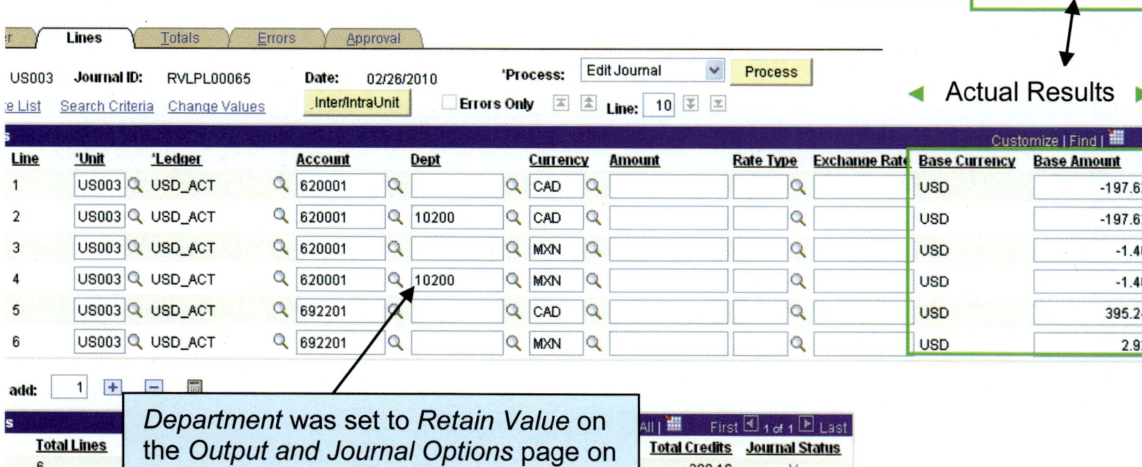

Department was set to *Retain Value* on the *Output and Journal Options* page on the RVL_PL revaluation step

cc. Finally, run the *Revaluation Calculation Log* report to verify the data on the journals created. Navigate to *Calculation Log > Find an Existing Value* as specified below and specify the following values:

- `Run Control ID: begins with: Reval`

dd. Click on *Search*

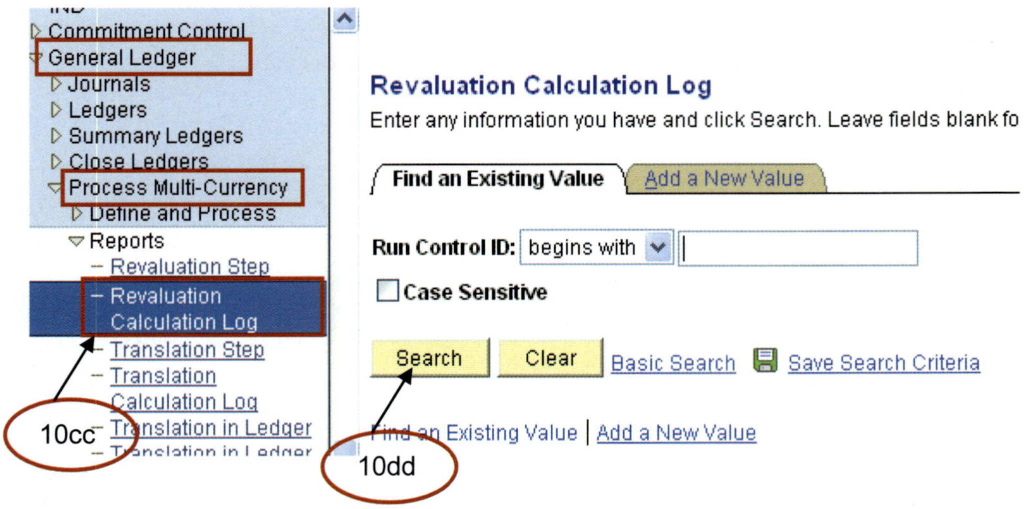

ee. In the *Revaluation Calculation Log Report* page specify the following values:

- `SetID: SHARE`
- `Beginning Instance: `*`<Process Instance ID of the Reval Process>`*
- `Ending Instance: `*`<Process Instance ID of the Reval Process>`*
- `Click on `*`Refresh`*` and select `*`Include CF`*` for `*`Account, Department,`*` and `*`Currency Code`*` ChartFields`

ff. Click on *Save* at the bottom of the screen (not shown in the screen shot)

gg. Click on *Run* on the top of the screen

hh. On the *Process Scheduler Request* select the following values:

- `Server: PSNT (or as appropriate in your installation)`
- `Type: Web`
- `Output: PDF`

ii. Click on *OK*

jj. The system will take you back to the *Revaluation Calculation Log Report* run control page. Click on the *Process Monitor* link on the top.

kk. When the report's run indicates *Success* in the Process Monitor click on *Details* > *View Log/Trace* to access the report's PDF output

ll. Review the report's output. It should match the data in your revaluation journals

Revaluation Calculation Log Report

Run Control ID: reval
Language: English

Report Manager | Process Monitor | Run

Report Request Parameters

SetID: SHARE
Revaluation Step:
☐ Prompt prcs instance from log
Beginning Instance: 7111
Ending Instance: 7111
☐ Sort By Currency ☐ Display Full Numeric Field

Refresh

ChartField Selection — Customize | Find | First 1-17 of 17 Last

Sequence	ChartField Name	Include CF	Descr
1	Account	☑	☐
2	Department	☑	☐
3	Currency Code	☑	☐

10ee

Process Scheduler Request

User ID: VP1 Run Control ID: reval

Server Name: PSNT Run Date: 01/18/2010
Recurrence: Run Time: 6:51:21AM Reset to Current Date/Time
Time Zone:

Process List

Select	Description	Process Name	Process Type	*Type	*Format	Distribution
☑	Revaluation Calculation Log	GLS5003	SQR Report	Web	PDF	Distribution

```
                                     PeopleSoft GL
Report ID:  GLS5003                  REVALUATION CALCULATION LOG                      Page No.  1
Process Instances:  0000007111 to 0000007111                                          Run Date 01/18/2010
Revaluation Step:   All                                                               Run Time 06:52:15

Process Instance:  0000007111  Revaluation Step:  RVL_BS  Business Unit:  US003  Ledger:  USD_ACT  Base Currency:  USD

Account   Dept    Currency   Exchange Rate  Currency  Posted Total Amount  Posted Base Amount  Revaluated Amount  Adjustment Amount


100003            CAD           1.15000000  CAD             -10,000.00          -9,090.90          -8,695.65             395.25

100003            MXN          13.15000000  MXN             -10,000.00            -766.28            -760.46               5.82

-----------------------------------
Revaluation Gain or Loss Adjustment:

315000            CAD                       CAD                                                                         -395.25

315000            MXN                       MXN                                                                           -5.82
```

```
                                     PeopleSoft GL
Report ID:  GLS5003                  REVALUATION CALCULATION LOG                      Page No.  2
Process Instances:  0000007111 to 0000007111                                          Run Date 01/18/2010
Revaluation Step:   All                                                               Run Time 06:52:15

Process Instance:  0000007111  Revaluation Step:  RVL_PL  Business Unit:  US003  Ledger:  USD_ACT  Base Currency:  USD

Account   Dept    Currency   Exchange Rate  Currency  Posted Total Amount  Posted Base Amount  Revaluated Amount  Adjustment Amount


620001            CAD           1.15000000  CAD               5,000.00           4,545.45           4,347.83            -197.62

620001    10200   CAD           1.15000000  CAD               5,000.00           4,545.45           4,347.83            -197.62

620001            MXN          13.10000000  MXN               5,000.00             383.14             381.68              -1.46

620001    10200   MXN          13.10000000  MXN               5,000.00             383.14             381.68              -1.46

-----------------------------------
Revaluation Gain or Loss Adjustment:

692201            CAD                       CAD                                                                          395.24

692201            MXN                       MXN                                                                            2.92
```

Ledger Translations

In *Chapter 6* we saw how to use the *Keep Ledgers in Sync* functionality to translate ledgers in real time. Although real time translation ensures most current data in the secondary ledgers, it may impact system performance. Alternatively you can use the *Translation* batch process to translate ledger balances into a separate ledger with different base currency. You can choose to run translation every night or every month-end depending upon business needs.

The primary ledger and secondary (non-translation) ledger's lines in a multibook are both populated with the foreign currency and foreign amount for all transactions. However, a secondary ledger of type *Translation* is populated with the foreign currency and foreign amount equal to the base currency and base amount of the primary ledger. Therefore, translation ledgers in a multibook have no more than one foreign currency (equivalent to the base currency of the primary ledger) at any given time. Like *Revaluation*, you can define multiple translation steps, and combine them into process groups.

Example: A fully owned US subsidiary of a Japanese company needs to translate its USD ledger into a JPY ledger at month-end for reporting purposes.

Solution: Setup two ledgers for the US GL business unit--a USD ledger and another JPY ledger--each in its own detail ledger group. You will record journals only into the USD ledger and run the multi currency process at month-end to translate the USD ledger into the JPY ledger. Follow these steps to implement the solution:

#	Step	Step Description
1	setup *Detail Ledgers*	setup two detail ledgers USD_ACT and JPY_REPORT
2	setup *Detail Ledger Groups*	setup detail ledger groups USD_ACT and JPY_REPORT
3	setup *Ledgers For a Business Unit*	attach *Ledger Groups* USD_ACT and JPY_REPORT to GL business unit US003
4	open periods	open fiscal year 2010 for ledger groups USD_ACT and JPY_REPORT for GL business unit US003
5	review *Currency Codes*	review USD and JPY currency codes
6	review *Currency Quotation Method*	review *Currency Quotation Method* for USD-JPY currencies
7	setup *Market Rates*	setup currency exchange rates for USD-JPY conversion
8	query PS_LEDGER Table	create a query to review the data in PS_LEDGER table for ledger USD_ACT
9	setup *Translation Rules*	setup a *Translation Rule* called ALL_ACCTS
10	setup *Translation Steps*	setup a *Translation Step* called JPY_LEDGER
11	setup *Process Group*	setup a multi-currency process group called JPY_LEDGER
12	run translation process	run the multi-currency process to translate ledger USD_ACT to JPY_REPORT
13	review translation results	query the translation results to confirm if USD_ACT translated correctly into JPY_REPORT
14	translate only MXN ledger Balances to JPY	modify the translation step JPY_LEDGER to convert only MXN currency ledger balances from ledger USD_ACT to JPY_REPORT

1. Setup Detail Ledgers

You will use two detail ledgers USD_ACT and JPY_REPORT. Re-use the detail ledger USD_ACT created in *Chapter 7 – Revaluation: Step 2*. Refer to the same step to setup the JPY_REPORT detail ledger. See the screen shot below for details.

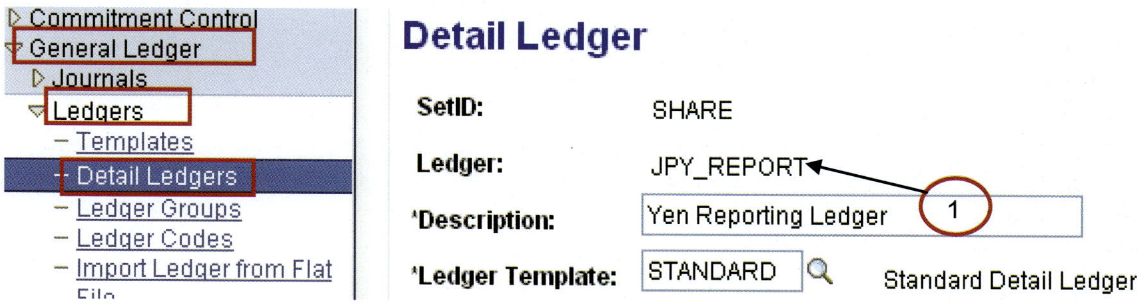

2. Setup Detail Ledger Groups

You will use two detail ledger groups USD_ACT and JPY_REPORT. The ledger group USD_ACT was already created in *Chapter 7 – Revaluation: Step 3*. Refer to the same step to setup the JPY_REPORT detail ledger group. See screen shot below for details.

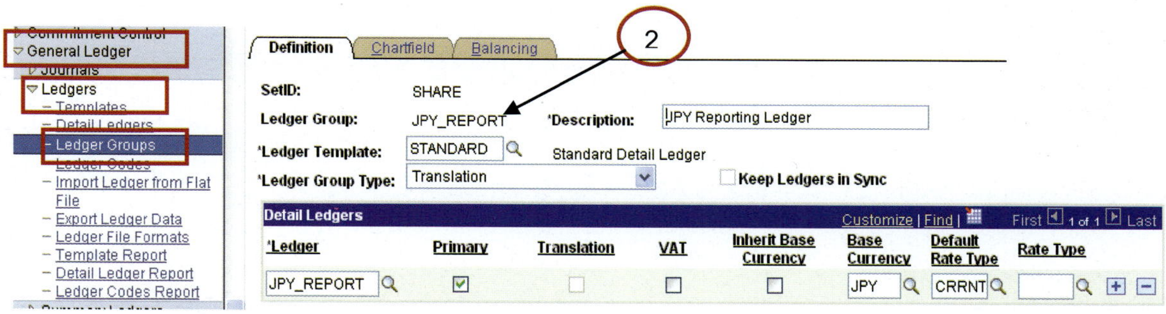

3. Setup Ledger For a Business Unit

You attached ledger group USD_ACT to business unit US003 in *Chapter 7: Step 4*. Refer to the same step to attach ledger group JPY_REPORT to business unit US003. See the screen shot below for details.

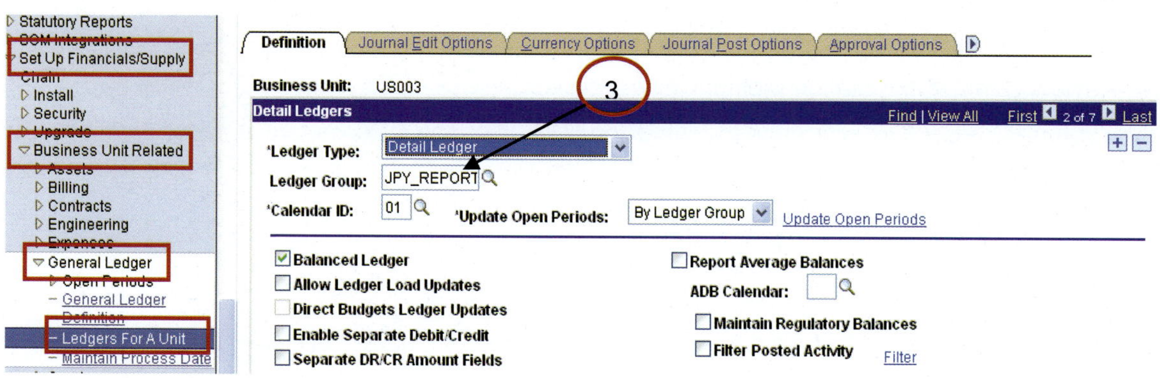

4. Open Periods

You opened periods for ledger group USD_ACT and business unit US003 in *Chapter 7: Step 5*. Refer to the same step to open fiscal year 2010 for ledger group JPY_REPORT and business unit US003. See the screen shot below for details.

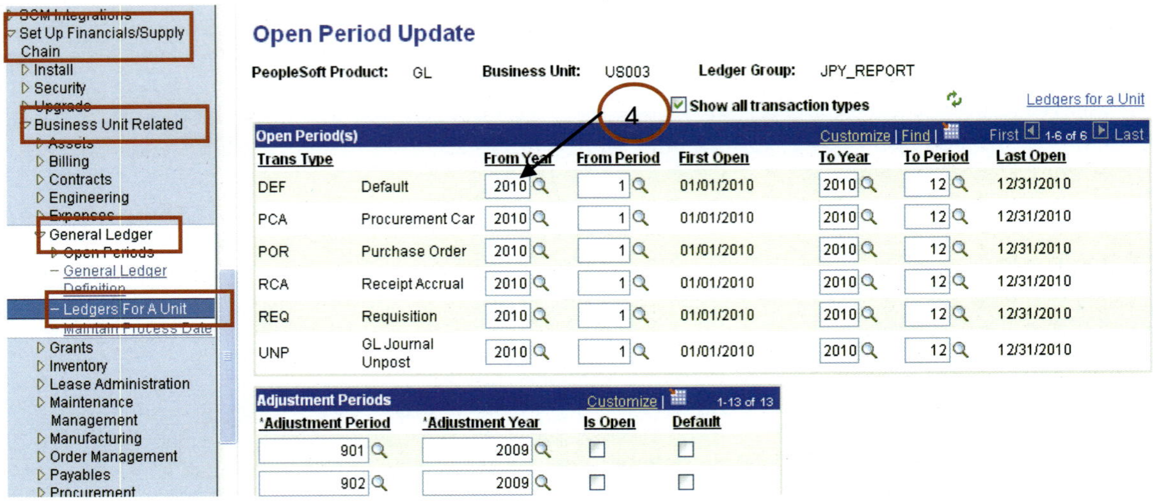

5. Review Currency Codes

Review the JPY currency using *Chapter 7: Step 6* as reference (where you reviewed the USD currency). See the screen shot below for the JPY currency.

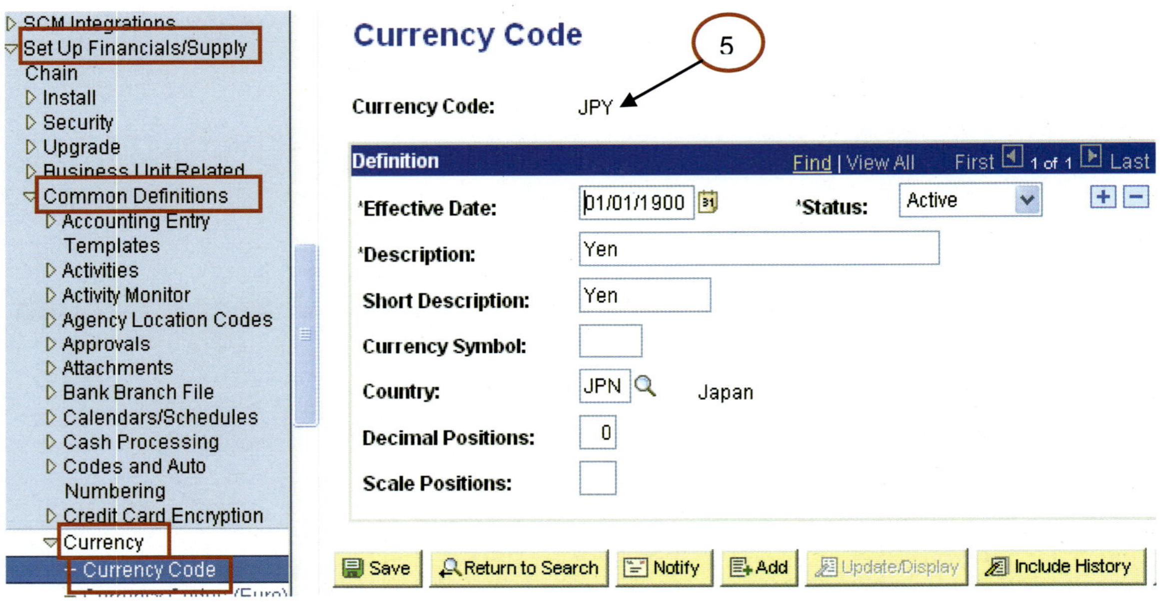

6. Review Currency Quotation Method

Use *Chapter 7: Step 7* as reference to review the USD-JPY pair's *Currency Quotation Method*. Ensure that it is set to *Direct*. See the screen shot below for details.

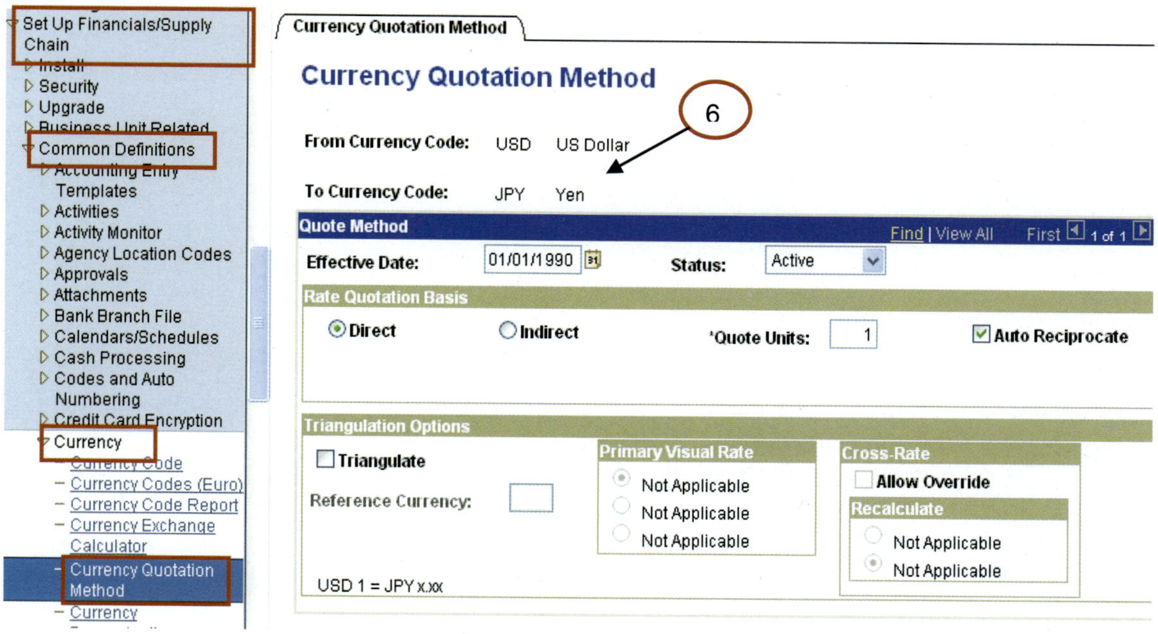

7. Setup Market Rates

Use *Chapter 6: Step 6* as reference to setup currency market rates for the USD-JPY currency pair. See the screen shot below for details.

From Currency	To Currency	Rate Type	Effective Date	Rate
USD	JPY	CRRNT	02/26/2010	89.58500000
USD	JPY	CRRNT	12/15/2002	198.40000000
USD	JPY	CRRNT	07/15/2002	79.08669545

8. Query Ledger data

Create and run a query on the LEDGER table to see the source data you will translate from USD to JPY. See the screen shot below for details.

- Select fields – `BUSINESS_UNIT, LEDGER, ACCOUNT, DEPTID, CURRENCY_CD, FICALYEAR, ACCOUNTING_PERIOD, POSTED_TOTAL_AMT, POSTED_BASE_AMT, POSTED_TRAN_AMT, BASE_CURRENCY.`
- Specify the following criteria – `BUSINESS_UNIT = US0003`, `LEDGER = USD_ACT` and `CURRENCY_CD = USD.`

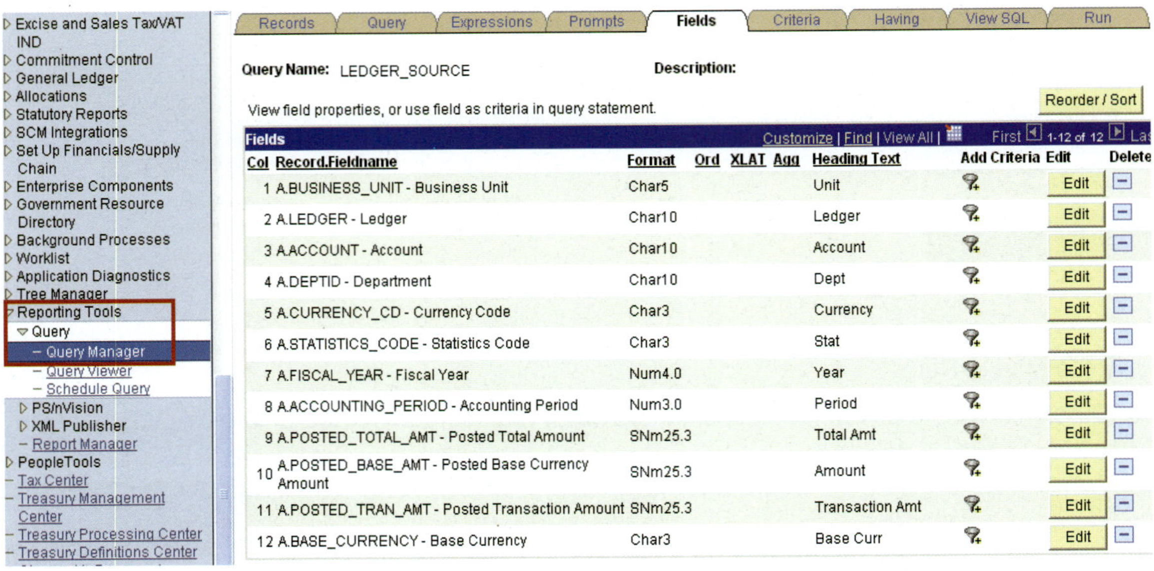

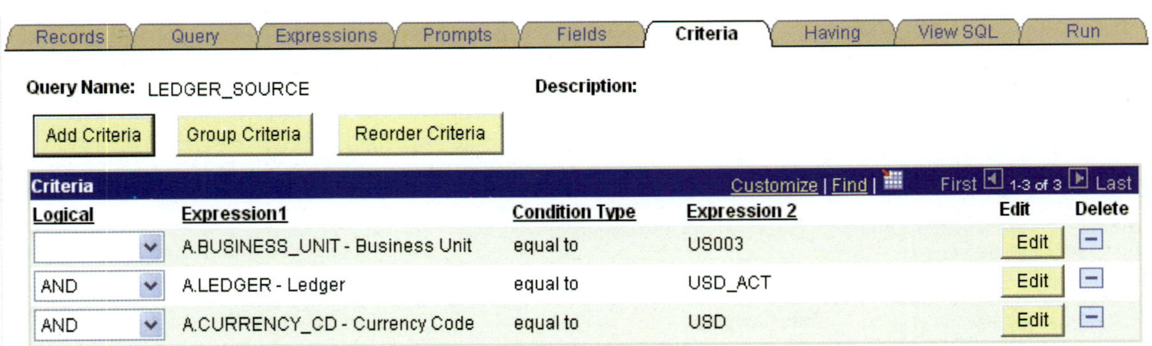

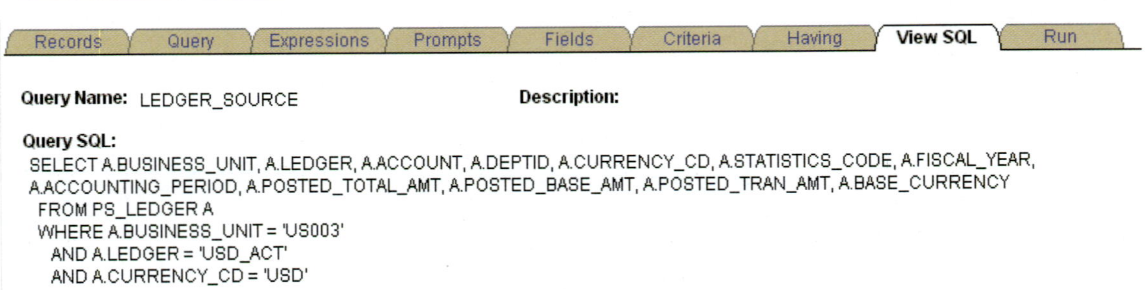

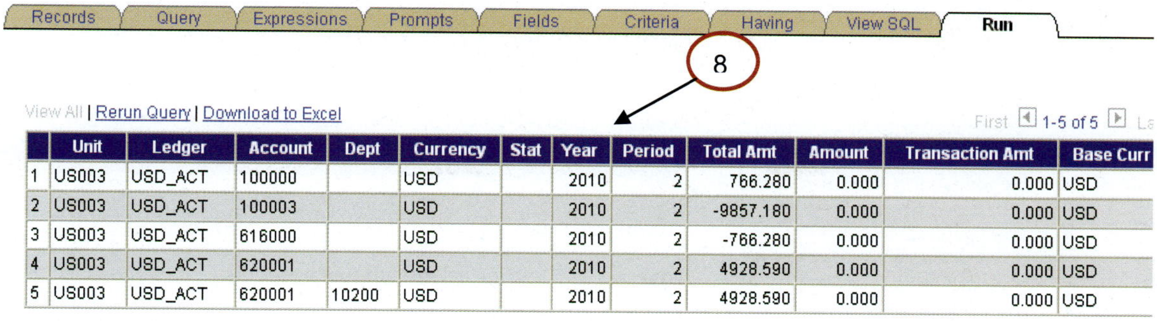

	Unit	Ledger	Account	Dept	Currency	Stat	Year	Period	Total Amt	Amount	Transaction Amt	Base Curr
1	US003	USD_ACT	100000		USD		2010	2	766.280	0.000	0.000	USD
2	US003	USD_ACT	100003		USD		2010	2	-9857.180	0.000	0.000	USD
3	US003	USD_ACT	616000		USD		2010	2	-766.280	0.000	0.000	USD
4	US003	USD_ACT	620001		USD		2010	2	4928.590	0.000	0.000	USD
5	US003	USD_ACT	620001	10200	USD		2010	2	4928.590	0.000	0.000	USD

9. Setup Translation Rules

In *Translation Rules* you identify the ledger data to be translated, which includes *ChartFields* and *TimeSpans*. Follow the steps below:

a. Navigate to *Translation Rules > Add a New Value* as highlighted below. Specify the following values and click on the *Add* button:
   - `SetID = SHARE`
   - `Translation Rule: ALL_ACCTS`

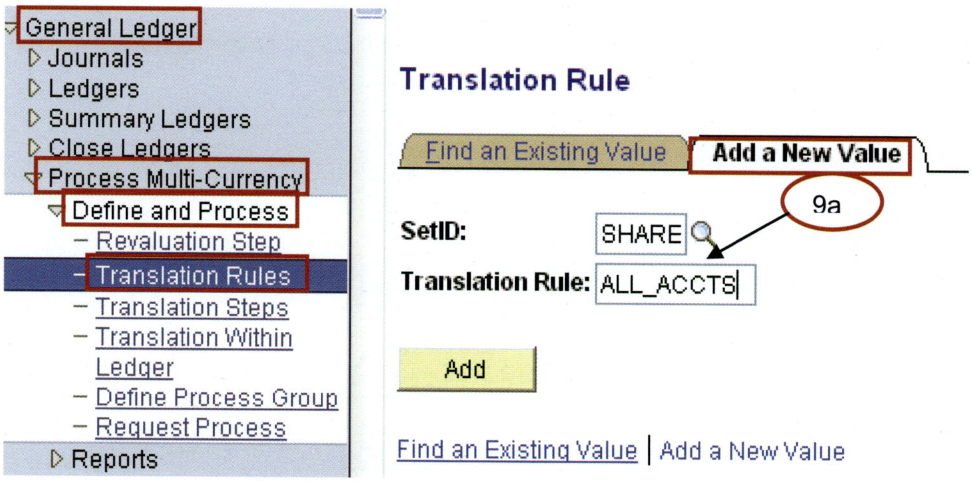

b. Specify the following values in the *TimeSpan and Rate* screen:
   - `Effective Date = 01/01/1901`
   - `Status: Active`
   - `Descr and Description: Translate All Accounts`
   - `Time Span: PER` (current period as determined by the *As of Date* specified on the *MultiCurrency Process Request* page, as discussed later in this chapter)
   - `Rate Type: CRRNT`

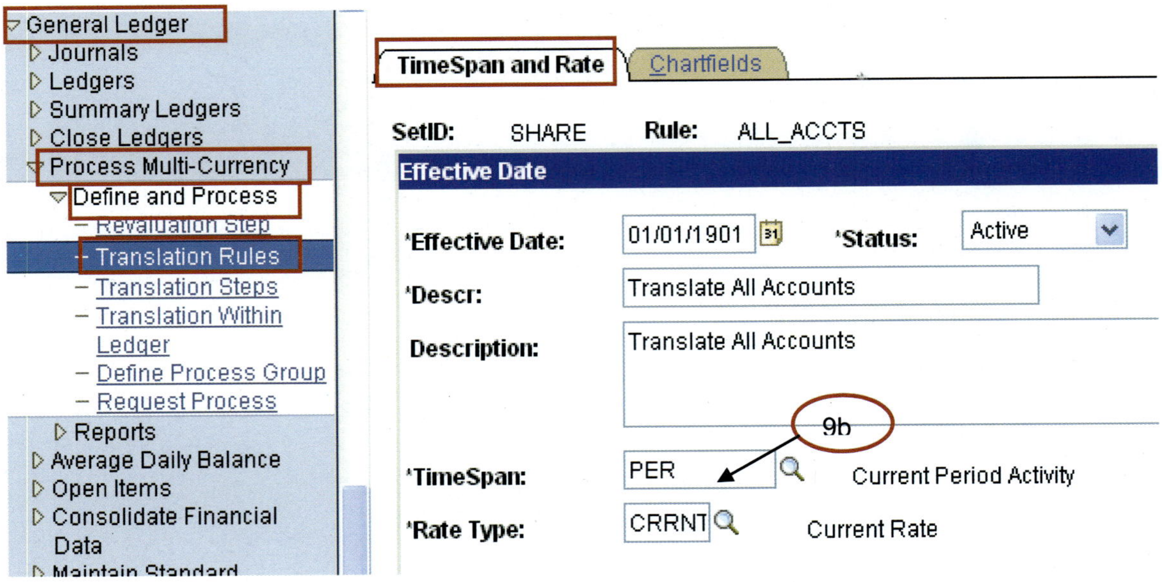

c. Specify the following values on the *ChartFields* tab and save the page.

- `ChartField = Account`
- `How Specified: Selected Tree Nodes`
- `Tree Information: Tree = ACCTROLLUP`
- `Chartfield values/Tree nodes: Select Value = ALLACCOUNTS`

If needed you can create separate rules with different *Rate Types* for different *ChartField* values. For example, you can create a rule that uses the CRRNT rate type for balance sheet accounts and the AVG rate type for P&L accounts.

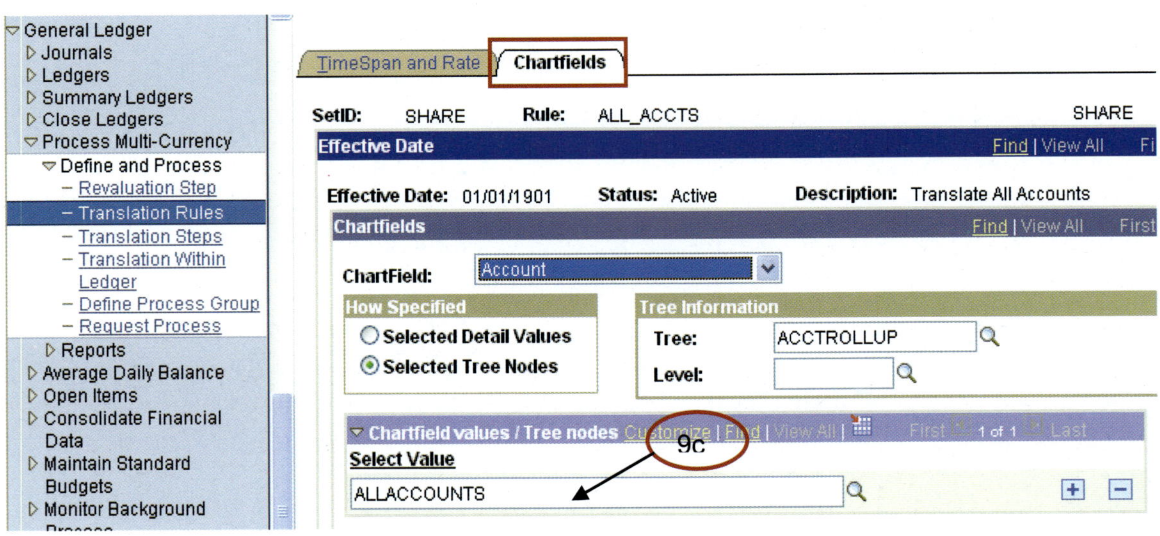

10. Setup Translation Steps

In *Translation Steps* you specify the *Translation Rules*, *Source & Target Ledgers*, *Output Journal details* (*Journal Source, Mask, Header Description* and if you want to edit/post into the journal) *and Gain/Loss ChartFields*. Follow these steps to setup the Translation Steps:

a. Navigate to *Translation Steps > Add a New Value* as highlighted below. Specify the following values and click the *Add* button:

- `SetID = SHARE`
- `Translation Rule: JPY_LEDGER`

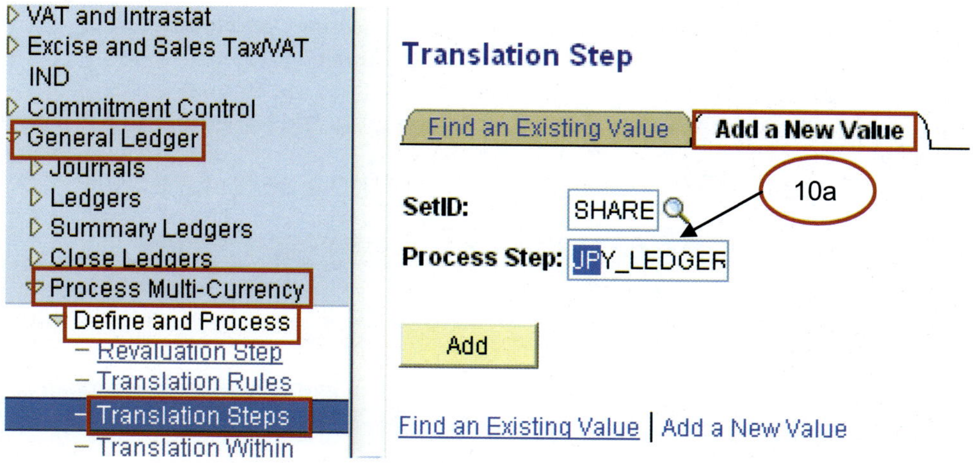

b. Specify the following values in the *Ledger* tab:

- `Effective Date = 01/01/1901`
- `Descr and Description: Translation into JPY`
- `From Ledger Group and From Ledger: USD_ACT`
- `Target Ledger Group: JPY_REPORT`
- `From Currency Type: L` (Ledger Base Currency)

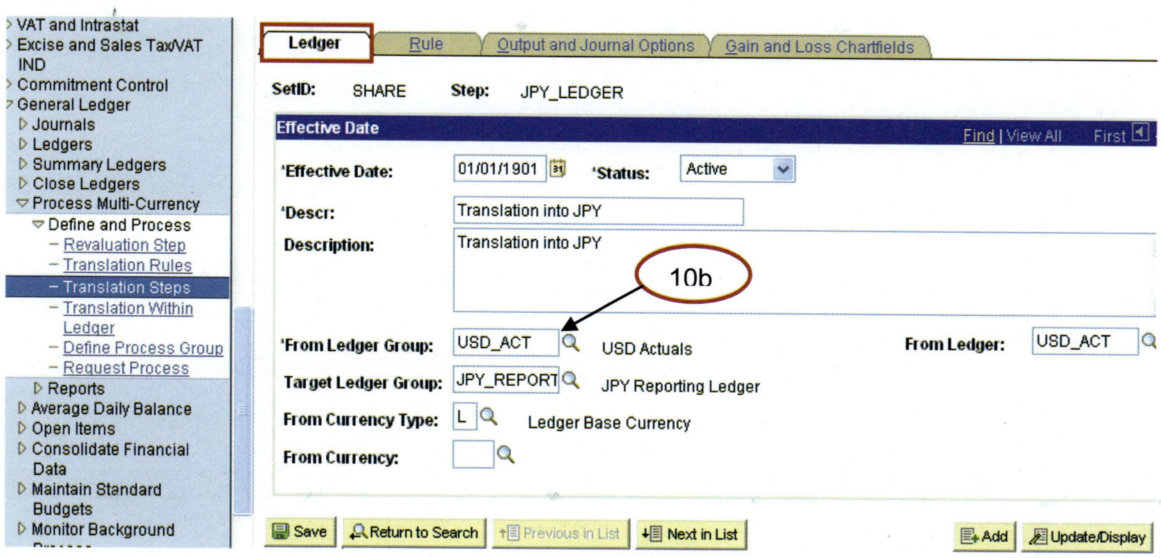

c. Specify the following values in the *Rule* tab:

- `Translation Rule = ALL_ACCTS` (you can specify multiple rules)

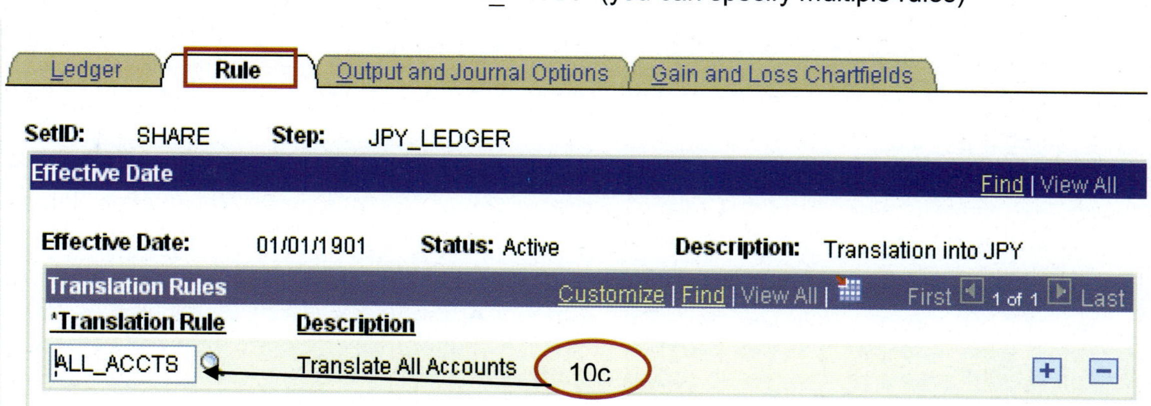

d. Specify the following values in the *Output and Journal Options* tab:

- `Journal ID Mask = TRN` (for translation), `Source = MCP`
- `Description: USD to JPY Translation Process`
- `Create Journal Entries: Checked, Edit Journals: Checked`
- `Target ChartFields: Account and Department` (i.e. *Account* and *Department Chartfield* values will be carried forward to the translated ledger)

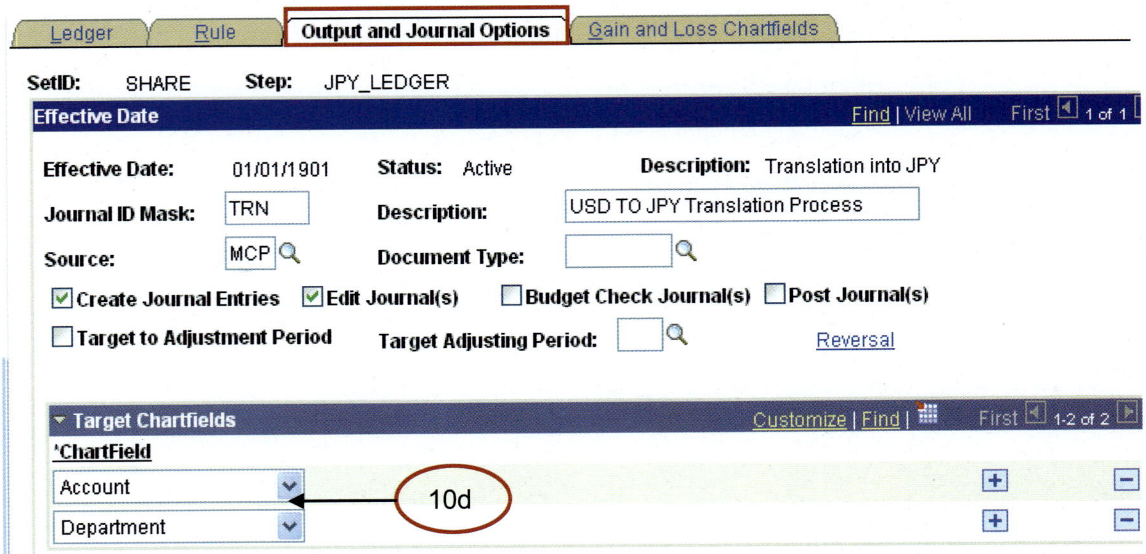

e. On the 'Gain and Loss Chartfields' tab specify the following values and save the step:

- `Gain ChartKeys: Account = 315000`
- `Loss ChartKeys: Account = 315000`

Any currency gain/loss during the translation process will be recorded in the *ChartField* values specified above.

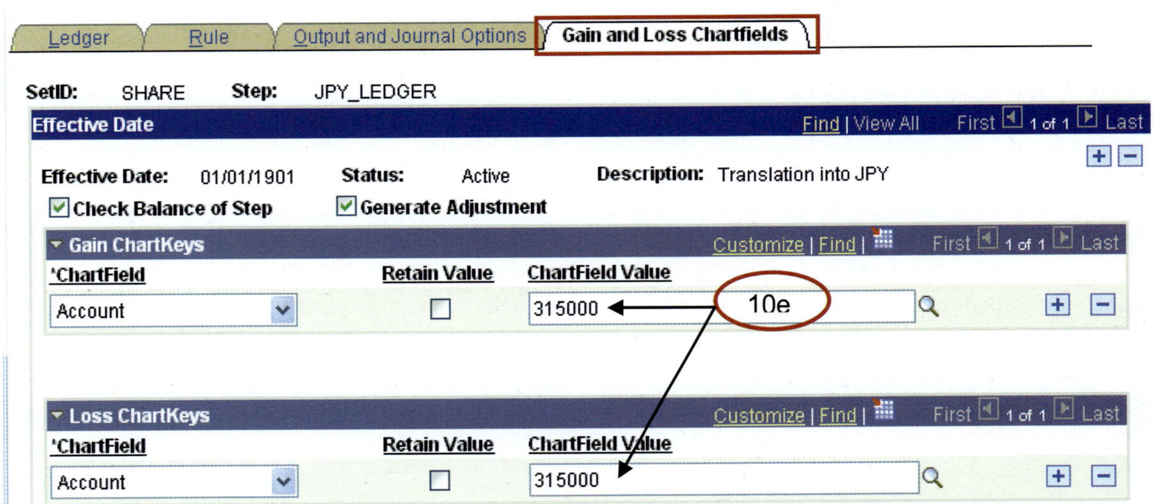

11. Setup Process Group

Next you will setup the *Multi-Currency Process Group*. You can group *Revaluation Steps* and *Translation Steps* into a process group and the system will run them sequentially. For this example, follow the steps below:

a. Navigate to *Define Process Group > Add a New Value* as highlighted below. Specify the following values and click on the *Add* button:

- `SetID = SHARE`
- `Process Group: JPY_LEDGER`

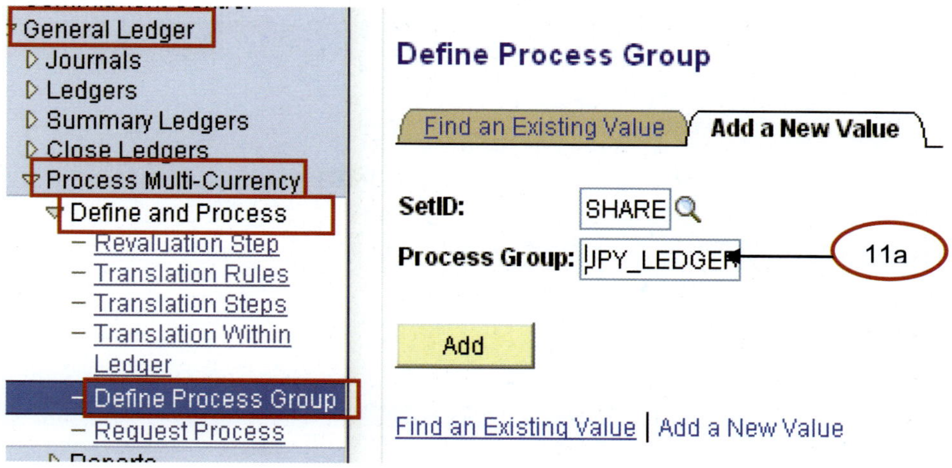

b. Specify the following values in the *Multi-Currency Process Group* screen and click on the *Save* button:

- `Descr and Description = USD to JPY Translation`
- `Process Step: JPY_LEDGER`

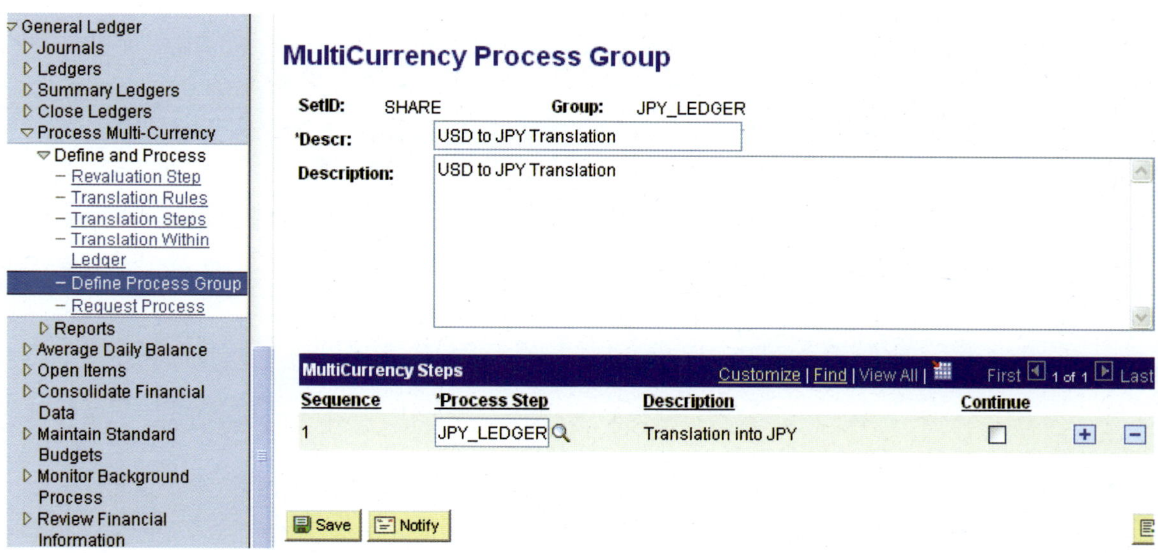

12. Run Translation Process

Next you will execute the multi currency process. Follow the steps below:

a. Navigate to *Request Process > Add a New Value* as highlighted below. Specify the following values and click on the *Add* button:

- `Run Control ID: JPY_Translation`

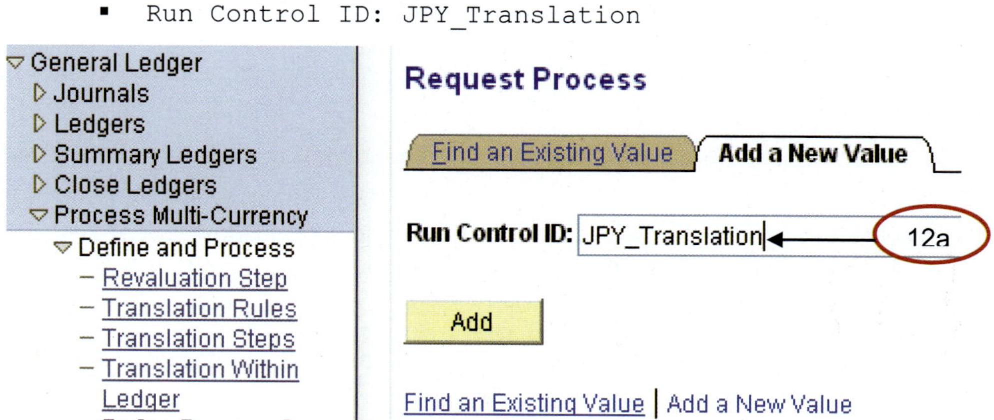

b. Specify the following values in the *Multi-Currency Process Request* screen. Save and click the *Run* button:

- `Process Frequency: Always`
- `Unit: US003`
- `Group: JPY_LEDGER`
- `Cal Log: Checked`
- `Request Date Option: As of Date = 02/26/2010`

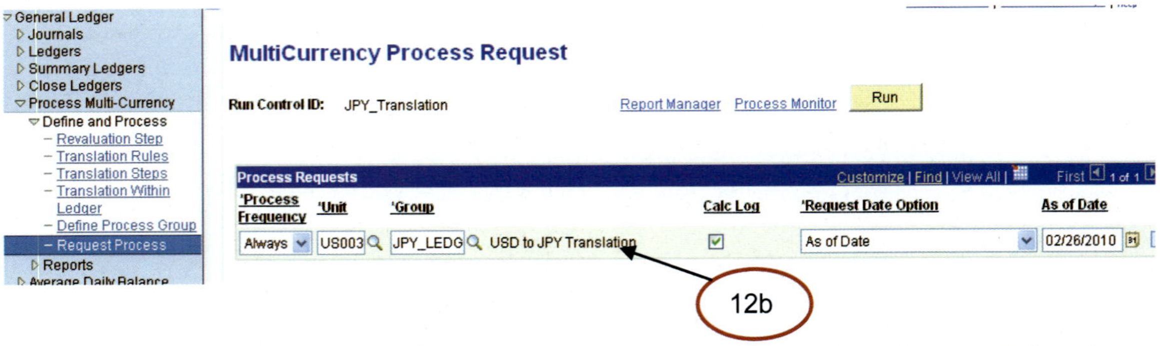

c. Select the *Server Name* (which is PSNT on this PC). Click on *OK* in the Process Scheduler Request screen.

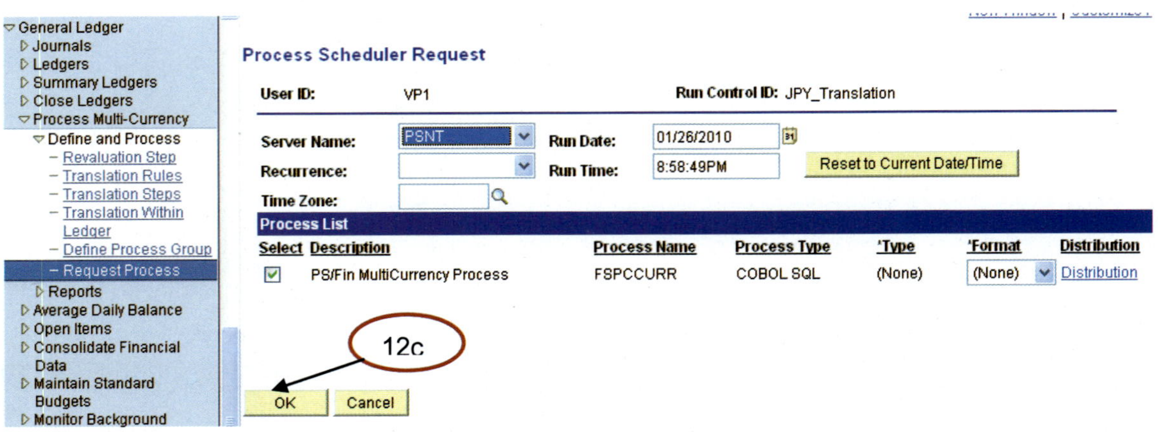

The COBOL process FSPCCURR is queued in the *Process Monitor*.

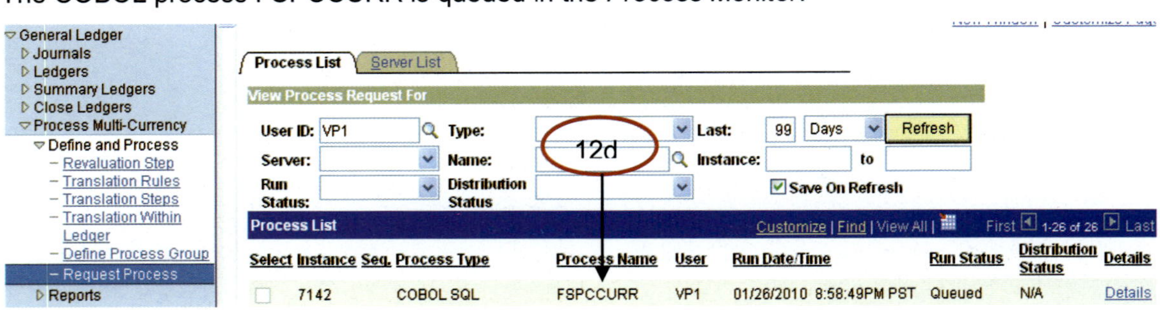

13. Review Translation Results

After the FSPCCURR process indicates *Success*, you must review the results of the translation process. Follow these steps:

a. Navigate to *Create/Update Journal Entries > Find an Existing Value* as highlighted below. Specify the following values and click on *Search*.

- `Business Unit: US0003`
- `Journal ID: TRN` (this is the Journal ID mask you specified in step 11d)

b. Click on the journal prefixed *TRN* (created by the multi currency process) and ensure that the *Long Description*, *Ledger Group*, and *Source* are same as you specified in step 10.

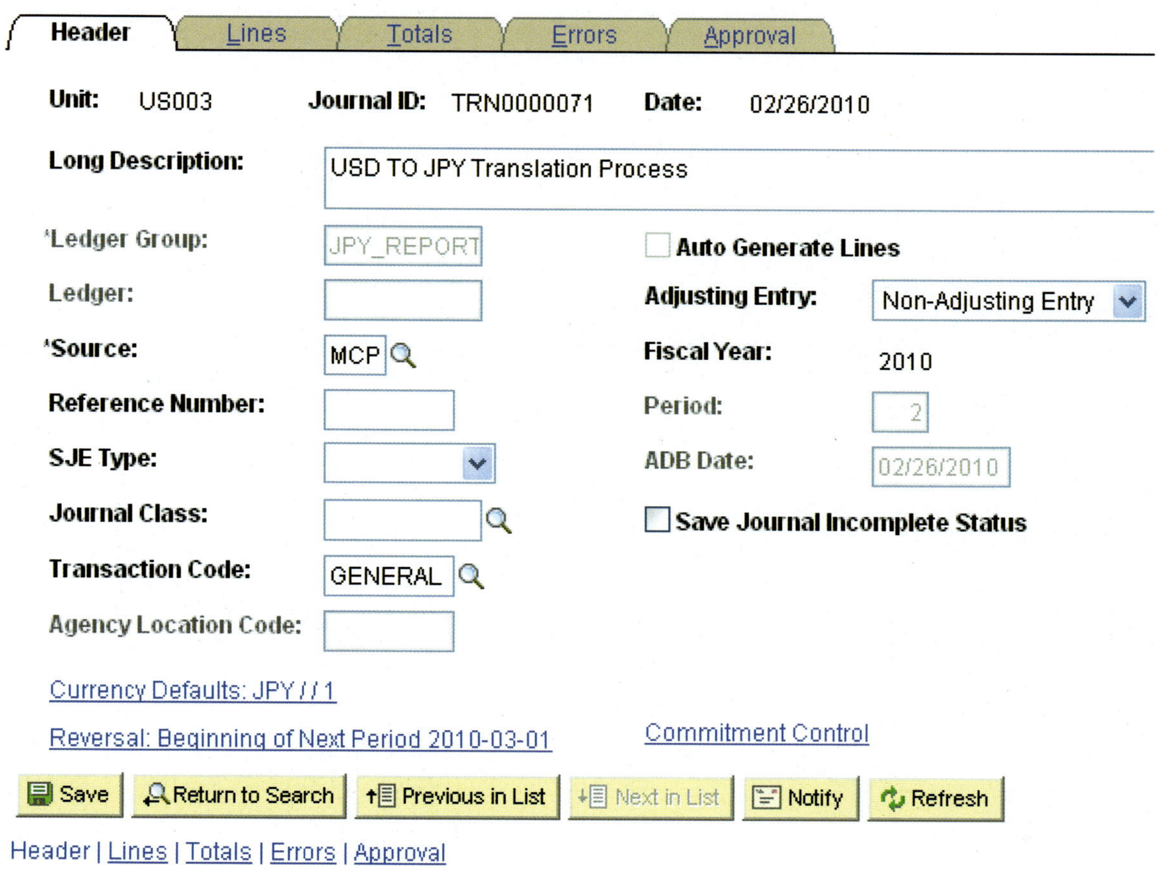

c. Click on the *Lines* tab and review the journal created.

Records | Query | Expressions | Prompts | Fields | Criteria | Having | View SQL | **Run**

View All | Rerun Query | Download to Excel — First 1-5 of 5 Last

	Unit	Ledger	Account	Dept	Currency	Stat	Year	Period	Total Amt	Amount	Transaction Amt	Base Curr
1	US003	USD_ACT	100000		USD		2010	2	766.280	0.000	0.000	USD
2	US003	USD_ACT	100003		USD		2010	2	-9857.180	0.000	0.000	USD
3	US003	USD_ACT	616000		USD		2010	2	-766.280	0.000	0.000	USD
4	US003	USD_ACT	620001		USD		2010	2	4928.590	0.000	0.000	USD
5	US003	USD_ACT	620001	10200	USD		2010	2	4928.590	0.000	0.000	USD

Test Data ← → Expected Results

Source Ledger	Account	Dept	Curr	Posted Total Amt A	Target Ledger B	Rate for Trans C	New JPY Base Amt = A X C D	Rounded JPY Base Amts
USD_ACT	100000		USD	766.28	JPY_REPORT	89.585	68,647.19	68,647
USD_ACT	100003		USD	-9,857.18	JPY_REPORT	89.585	-883,055.47	-883,055
USD_ACT	616000		USD	-766.28	JPY_REPORT	89.585	-68,647.19	-68,647
USD_ACT	620001		USD	4,928.59	JPY_REPORT	89.585	441,527.73	441,528
USD_ACT	620001	10200	USD	4,928.59	JPY_REPORT	89.585	441,527.73	441,528
n/a	315000				JPY_REPORT		0	-1

Lines | Totals | Errors | Approval

Journal ID: TRN0000071 Date: 02/26/2010 *Process: Edit Journal [Process]

Search Criteria Change Values [Inter/IntraUnit] Errors Only Line: 10

*Unit	*Ledger	Account	Dept	Currency	Amount	Rate Type	Exchange Rate	Base Currency	Base Amount
US003	JPY_REPORT	100000		JPY	68,647		1.00000000	JPY	68,647
US003	JPY_REPORT	100003		JPY	-883,055		1.00000000	JPY	-883,055
US003	JPY_REPORT	315000		JPY	-1		1.00000000	JPY	-1
US003	JPY_REPORT	616000		JPY	-68,647		1.00000000	JPY	-68,647
US003	JPY_REPORT	620001		JPY	441,528		1.00000000	JPY	441,528
US003	JPY_REPORT	620001	10200	JPY	441,528		1.00000000	JPY	441,528

Customize | Find | View All | First 1 of 1 Last

Total Lines	Total Debits	Total Credits	Journal Status
6	951,703	951,703	V

d. You can also run the *Translation Calculation Log* report (*General Ledger > Process Multi-Currency > Reports > Translation Calculation Log*) to verify the results. See report output below.

```
                                              PeopleSoft GL
Report ID:  GLS5002                     TRANSLATION CALCULATION LOG                      Page No.  1
Process Instances:  0000007144 to 0000007144                                             Run Date 01/26/2010
Translation Step:   ALL                                                                  Run Time 22:10:48

Process Instance:   0000007144  Translation Step:  JPY_LEDGER  Business Unit:  US003  Target Ledger:  JPY_REPORT  Target Currency:  JPY

Account    Dept      Currency        Currency  Year  Per  Exchange Rate   Posted Total Amount     Translated Amount

100000               USD             USD       2010  2    89.58500000                 766.28                68,647
100003               USD             USD       2010  2    89.58500000              -9,857.18              -883,055
616000               USD             USD       2010  2    89.58500000                -766.28               -68,647
620001               USD             USD       2010  2    89.58500000               4,928.59               441,528
620001     10200     USD             USD       2010  2    89.58500000               4,928.59               441,528

-----------------------------------
Translation Gain or Loss Adjustment:
315000               USD                                                                                        -1
```

e. Reference *Chapter 6: Step 7-J* to post the above journal into the ledger

f. Create and run a query on the LEDGER table to review the source data you will translate from USD to JPY. See the screen shot below for details.

- Select fields – `BUSINESS_UNIT, LEDGER, ACCOUNT, DEPTID, CURRENCY_CD, FICALYEAR, ACCOUNTING_PERIOD, POSTED_TOTAL_AMT, POSTED_BASE_AMT, POSTED_TRAN_AMT, BASE_CURRENCY.`
- Specify the following criteria – `BUSINESS_UNIT = US0003, LEDGER = JPY_REPORT.`

View field properties, or use field as criteria in query statement. Reorder / Sort

Fields — Customize | Find | View All | First 1-12 of 12 Last

Col	Record.Fieldname	Format	Ord	XLAT	Agg	Heading Text	Add Criteria	Edit	Delete
1	A.BUSINESS_UNIT - Business Unit	Char5				Unit		Edit	
2	A.LEDGER - Ledger	Char10				Ledger		Edit	
3	A.ACCOUNT - Account	Char10				Account		Edit	
4	A.DEPTID - Department	Char10				Dept		Edit	
5	A.CURRENCY_CD - Currency Code	Char3				Currency		Edit	
6	A.STATISTICS_CODE - Statistics Code	Char3				Stat		Edit	
7	A.FISCAL_YEAR - Fiscal Year	Num4.0				Year		Edit	
8	A.ACCOUNTING_PERIOD - Accounting Period	Num3.0				Period		Edit	
9	A.POSTED_TOTAL_AMT - Posted Total Amount	SNm25.3				Total Amt		Edit	
10	A.POSTED_BASE_AMT - Posted Base Currency Amount	SNm25.3				Amount		Edit	
11	A.POSTED_TRAN_AMT - Posted Transaction Amount	SNm25.3				Transaction Amt		Edit	
12	A.BASE_CURRENCY - Base Currency	Char3				Base Curr		Edit	

Records | Query | Expressions | Prompts | Fields | **Criteria** | Having | View SQL | Run

Query Name: TRANSLATE_RESULTS **Description:**

Add Criteria | Group Criteria | Reorder Criteria

Criteria — Customize | Find | First 1-2 of 2 Last

Logical	Expression1	Condition Type	Expression 2	Edit	Delete
	A.BUSINESS_UNIT - Business Unit	equal to	US003	Edit	
AND	A.LEDGER - Ledger	equal to	JPY_REPORT	Edit	

Save | Save As | New Query | Preferences | Properties | New Union | Return to Search

Records | Query | Expressions | Prompts | Fields | Criteria | Having | **View SQL** | Run

Query Name: TRANSLATE_RESULTS **Description:**

Query SQL:

```
SELECT A.BUSINESS_UNIT, A.LEDGER, A.ACCOUNT, A.DEPTID, A.CURRENCY_CD, A.STATISTICS_CODE, A.FISCAL_YEAR,
A.ACCOUNTING_PERIOD, A.POSTED_TOTAL_AMT, A.POSTED_BASE_AMT, A.POSTED_TRAN_AMT, A.BASE_CURRENCY
 FROM PS_LEDGER A
 WHERE A.BUSINESS_UNIT = 'US003'
   AND A.LEDGER = 'JPY_REPORT'
```

Records | Query | Expressions | Prompts | Fields | Criteria | Having | View SQL | **Run**

View All | Rerun Query | Download to Excel — First 1-6 of 6 Last

	Unit	Ledger	Account	Dept	Currency	Stat	Year	Period	Total Amt	Amount	Transaction Amt	Base Curr
1	US003	JPY_REPORT	100000		JPY		2010	2	68647.000	68647.000	68647.000	JPY
2	US003	JPY_REPORT	100003		JPY		2010	2	-883055.000	-883055.000	-883055.000	JPY
3	US003	JPY_REPORT	315000		JPY		2010	2	-1.000	-1.000	-1.000	JPY
4	US003	JPY_REPORT	616000		JPY		2010	2	-68647.000	-68647.000	-68647.000	JPY
5	US003	JPY_REPORT	620001		JPY		2010	2	441528.000	441528.000	441528.000	JPY
6	US003	JPY_REPORT	620001	10200	JPY		2010	2	441528.000	441528.000	441528.000	JPY

14. Translate only MXN Ledger Balances to JPY

Translation Rules also allow you to translate ledger balances in a specific transaction currency. In the example below you will translate the MXN currency balances in the ledger USD_ACT to the JPY_REPORT ledger. All the steps are the same as above except for how the *Translation Rule* is configured. Follow the steps below.

a. Modify and run the query created in step 8, changing the criterion from `CURRENCY_CD = USD` to `CURRENCY_CD = MXN`. See screen shot below for details.

Fields — Customize | Find | View All | First 1-12 of 12 Last

Col	Record.Fieldname	Format	Ord	XLAT	Agg	Heading Text	Add Criteria	Edit	Delete
1	A.BUSINESS_UNIT - Business Unit	Char5				Unit		Edit	
2	A.LEDGER - Ledger	Char10				Ledger		Edit	
3	A.ACCOUNT - Account	Char10				Account		Edit	
4	A.DEPTID - Department	Char10				Dept		Edit	
5	A.CURRENCY_CD - Currency Code	Char3				Currency		Edit	
6	A.STATISTICS_CODE - Statistics Code	Char3				Stat		Edit	
7	A.FISCAL_YEAR - Fiscal Year	Num4.0				Year		Edit	
8	A.ACCOUNTING_PERIOD - Accounting Period	Num3.0				Period		Edit	
9	A.POSTED_TOTAL_AMT - Posted Total Amount	SNm25.3				Total Amt		Edit	
10	A.POSTED_BASE_AMT - Posted Base Currency Amount	SNm25.3				Amount		Edit	
11	A.POSTED_TRAN_AMT - Posted Transaction Amount	SNm25.3				Transaction Amt		Edit	
12	A.BASE_CURRENCY - Base Currency	Char3				Base Curr		Edit	

Records | Query | Expressions | Prompts | Fields | **Criteria** | Having | View SQL | Run

Query Name: LEDGER_SOURCE **Description:**

Add Criteria | Group Criteria | Reorder Criteria

Criteria — Customize | Find | First 1-3 of 3 Last

Logical	Expression1	Condition Type	Expression 2	Edit	Delete
	A.BUSINESS_UNIT - Business Unit	equal to	US003	Edit	
AND	A.LEDGER - Ledger	equal to	USD_ACT	Edit	
AND	A.CURRENCY_CD - Currency Code	equal to	MXN	Edit	

Records | Query | Expressions | Prompts | Fields | Criteria | Having | **View SQL** | Run

Query Name: LEDGER_SOURCE **Description:**

Query SQL:

```
SELECT A.BUSINESS_UNIT, A.LEDGER, A.ACCOUNT, A.DEPTID, A.CURRENCY_CD, A.STATISTICS_CODE, A.FISCAL_YEAR,
A.ACCOUNTING_PERIOD, A.POSTED_TOTAL_AMT, A.POSTED_BASE_AMT, A.POSTED_TRAN_AMT, A.BASE_CURRENCY
  FROM PS_LEDGER A
  WHERE A.BUSINESS_UNIT = 'US003'
    AND A.LEDGER = 'USD_ACT'
    AND A.CURRENCY_CD = 'MXN'
```

Records | Query | Expressions | Prompts | Fields | Criteria | Having | View SQL | **Run**

View All | Rerun Query | Download to Excel   First 1-5 of 5 Last

	Unit	Ledger	Account	Dept	Currency	Stat	Year	Period	Total Amt	Amount	Transaction Amt	Base Curr
1	US003	USD_ACT	100000		MXN		2010	2	10000.000	766.280	10000.000	USD
2	US003	USD_ACT	100003		MXN		2010	2	-10000.000	-766.280	-10000.000	USD
3	US003	USD_ACT	616000		MXN		2010	2	-10000.000	-766.280	-10000.000	USD
4	US003	USD_ACT	620001		MXN		2010	2	5000.000	383.140	5000.000	USD
5	US003	USD_ACT	620001	10200	MXN		2010	2	5000.000	383.140	5000.000	USD

b. Setup the MXN-JPY *Currency Quotation Method* to *Direct* (if it is not already setup). Reference *Chapter 7: Step 7*. See the screen shot below for details.

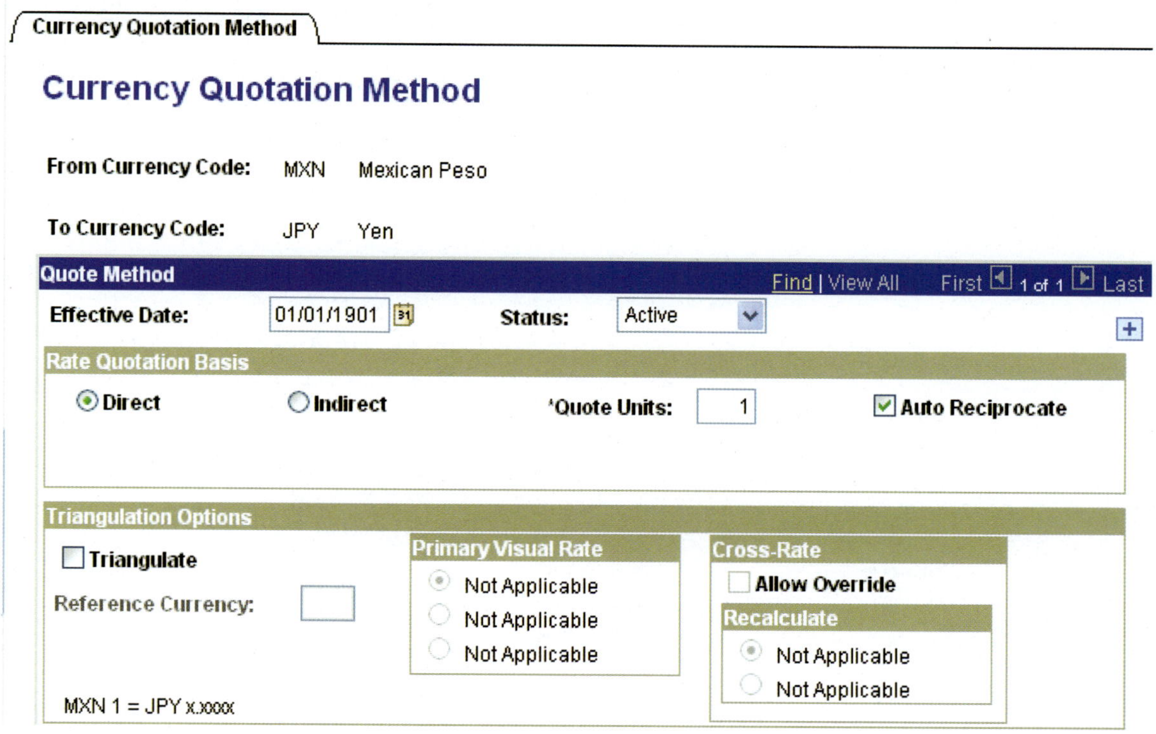

c. Use *Chapter 8: Step 8* as reference to setup MXN-JPY currency market rates. See the screen shot below for details.

From Currency	To Currency	Rate Type	Effective Date	Rate
MXN	JPY	CRRNT	02/26/2010	6.96351739

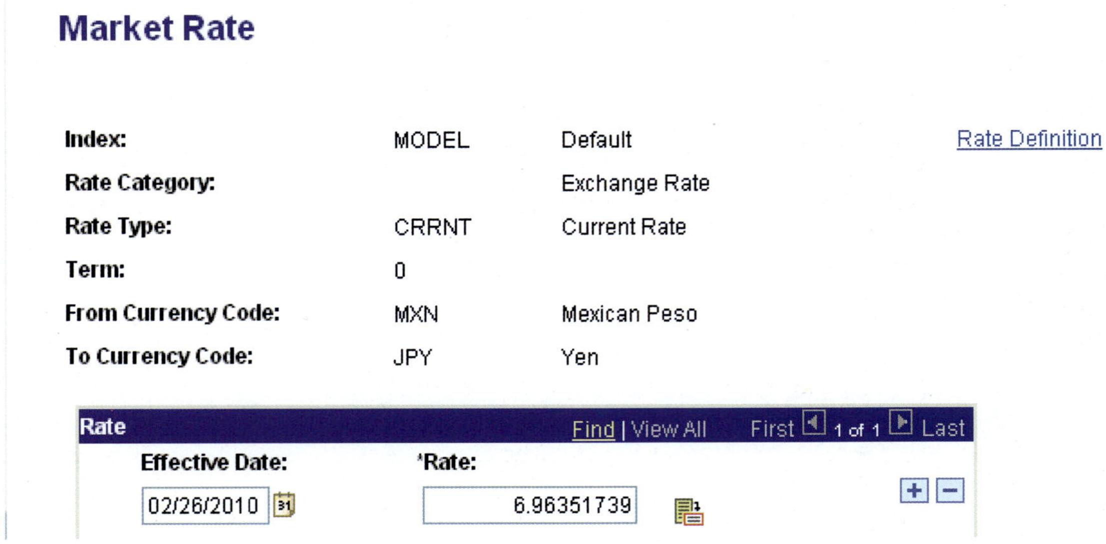

d. Modify the translation step JPY_LEDGER, you created in *step 10*, and specify the following values. Save the page.

- `From Currency Type: S` (Specify)
- `From Currency: MXN`

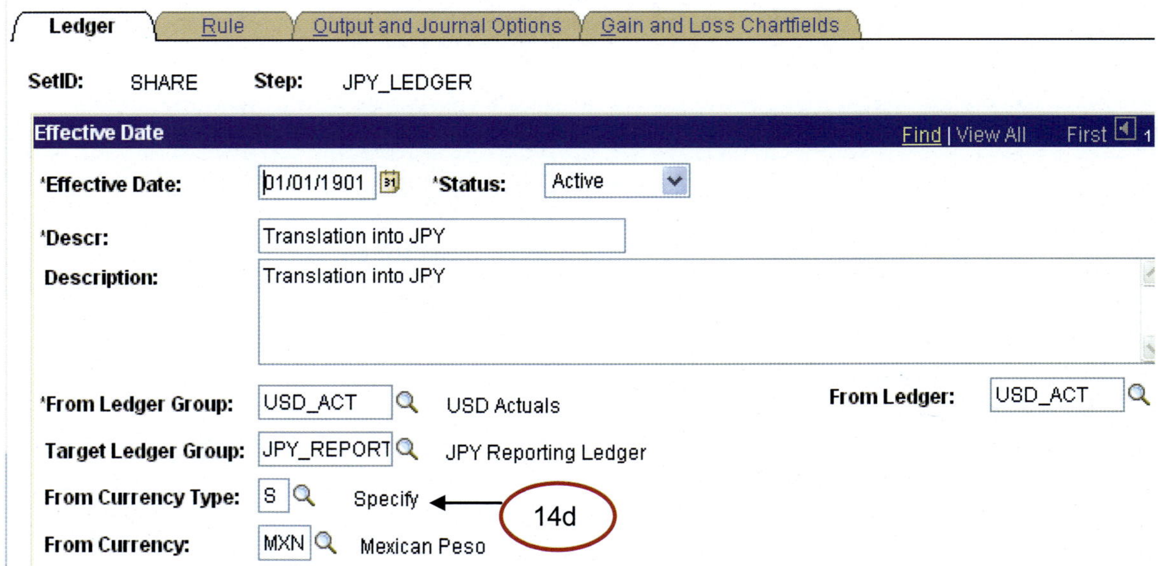

e. Repeat *step 12* to run the translation process.

f. Review the translation results below:

View All | Rerun Query | Download to Excel   First 1-5 of 5 Last

	Unit	Ledger	Account	Dept	Currency	Stat	Year	Period	Total Amt	Amount	Transaction Amt	Base Curr
1	US003	USD_ACT	100000		MXN		2010	2	10000.000	766.280	10000.000	USD
2	US003	USD_ACT	100003		MXN		2010	2	-10000.000	-766.280	-10000.000	USD
3	US003	USD_ACT	616000		MXN		2010	2	-10000.000	-766.280	-10000.000	USD
4	US003	USD_ACT	620001		MXN		2010	2	5000.000	383.140	5000.000	USD
5	US003	USD_ACT	620001	10200	MXN		2010	2	5000.000	383.140	5000.000	USD

← Test Data →   ← Expected Results →

Source Ledger	Account	Dept	Curr	Posted Transaction Amt A	Target Ledger B	Rate for Trans C	New JPY Base Amt = A X C D	Rounded JPY Base Amts
USD_ACT	100000		MXN	10,000	JPY_REPORT	6.9635 1739	69,635.51	69,635
USD_ACT	100003		MXN	-10,000	JPY_REPORT		-69,635.51	-69,635
USD_ACT	616000		MXN	-10,000	JPY_REPORT		-69,635.51	-69,635
USD_ACT	620001		MXN	5,000	JPY_REPORT		34,817.58	34,818
USD_ACT	620001	10200	MXN	5,000	JPY_REPORT		34,817.58	34,818
n/a	315000				JPY_REPORT		0	-1

Lines | Totals | Errors | Approval

Journal ID: TRN0000072   Date: 02/26/2010   *Process: Edit Journal   Process

Search Criteria   Change Values   Inter/IntraUnit   Errors Only   Line: 10

*Unit	*Ledger	Account	Dept	Currency	Amount	Rate Type	Exchange Rate	Base Currency	Base Amount
US003	JPY_REPORT	100000		JPY	69,635		1.00000000	JPY	69,635
US003	JPY_REPORT	100003		JPY	-69,635		1.00000000	JPY	-69,635
US003	JPY_REPORT	315000		JPY	-1		1.00000000	JPY	-1
US003	JPY_REPORT	616000		JPY	-69,635		1.00000000	JPY	-69,635
US003	JPY_REPORT	620001		JPY	34,818		1.00000000	JPY	34,818
US003	JPY_REPORT	620001	10200	JPY	34,818		1.00000000	JPY	34,818

Customize | Find | View All | First 1 of 1 Last

Total Lines	Total Debits	Total Credits	Journal Status
	139,271	139,271	V

PeopleSoft GL
TRANSLATION CALCULATION LOG

Report ID: GLS5002   Page No. 1
Process Instances: 0000007147 to 0000007147   Run Date 01/26/2010
Translation Step: ALL   Run Time 22:09:02

Process Instance: 0000007147 Translation Step: JPY_LEDGER Business Unit: US003 Target Ledger: JPY_REPORT Target Currency: JPY

Account	Dept	Currency	Currency	Year	Per	Exchange Rate	Posted Tran Amount	Translated Amount
100000		MXN	MXN	2010	2	6.96351739	10,000.00	69,635
100003		MXN	MXN	2010	2	6.96351739	-10,000.00	-69,635
616000		MXN	MXN	2010	2	6.96351739	-10,000.00	-69,635
620001		MXN	MXN	2010	2	6.96351739	5,000.00	34,818
620001	10200	MXN	MXN	2010	2	6.96351739	5,000.00	34,818

Translation Gain or Loss Adjustment:

Account	Dept	Currency	Translated Amount
315000		MXN	-1

Translate Within Ledger

The *Translation Within Ledger* batch process is used to revalue translation ledgers. This process works only for translation ledgers whereas the *Revaluation* process works only against secondary ledgers. You can run the *Translate Within Ledger* translation process at month-end to calculate currency gain or loss adjustments.

Example: A fully owned Australian subsidiary of a New Zealand company needs to translate its AUD Ledger into NZD at every month end for reporting purposes.

Solution: Setup a detail ledger group with two ledgers for the AUS01 GL Business Unit, one AUD Ledger and another NZD Ledger. The AUD Ledger will be the Primary Ledger. As a result, journal entries will be allowed only to the AUD Ledger. The two ledgers will be configured to always be *In Sync*. Consequently, when you post journals to the AUD Ledger the NZD Ledger will also be updated automatically.

Every month-end run the *Translate Within Ledger* process to adjust NZD Ledger balances to account for changes in currency market rates. Follow these step by step instructions to implement the solution:

#	Step	Step Description
1	setup *Detail Ledgers*	setup two detail ledgers 'AUD_ACTUAL' and 'NZD_REPORT'
2	setup *Detail Ledger Group*	group the two detail ledgers 'AUD_ACTUAL' and 'NZD_REPORT' in a multibook AUS_CORP
3	setup *Ledgers For a Business Unit*	attach *Ledger Group* AUS_CORP to GL business unit AUS01
4	open periods	open fiscal year 2010 for GL business unit AUS01 and Ledger Group AUS_CORP
5	review *Currency Codes*	review AUD, NZD and SGD currency codes
6	review *Currency Quotation Methods*	review *Currency Quotation Methods* for AUD-NZD and AUD-SGD currencies
7	setup *Market Rates*	setup *Market Rates* for AUD-NZD and AUD-SGD currency pairs
8	enter journals	to create test data, enter and post journals to business unit AUS01. Review journal lines created for the secondary ledger
9	setup *Translation Within Ledger*	create a step called NZD_TRNSL
10	setup *Process Group*	setup a multi currency Process Group called NZD_TRNSL and link the above translation step in this group
11	run the multi currency process	run *Process Multi-Currency*
12	review *Translation Results*	review created journals, calculation log, and confirm if results are as expected

1. Setup Detail Ledgers

Refer *Chapter 6: Step 2* to setup two detail ledgers 'AUD_ACTUAL' and 'NZD_REPORT'. See screen shots below:

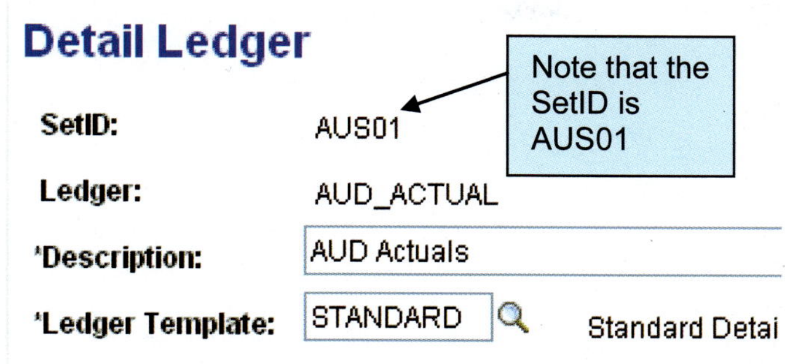

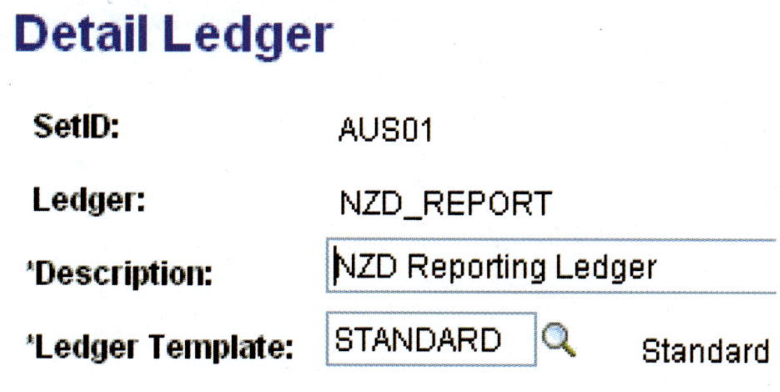

2. Setup Detail Ledger Group

Refer *Chapter 6: Step 3* to setup a ledger group called 'AUS_CORP'. See screen shots below:

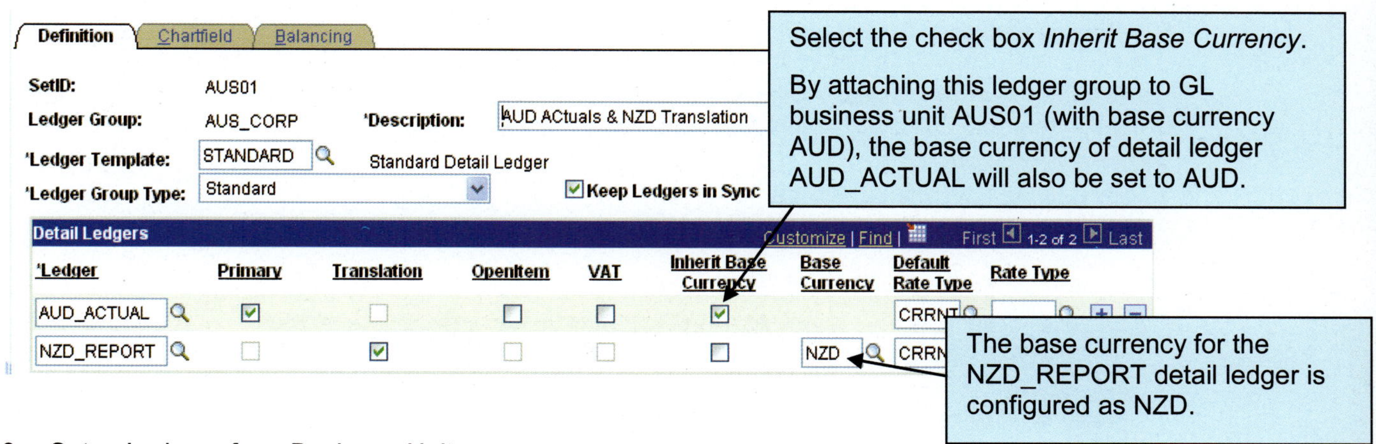

3. Setup Ledgers for a Business Unit

Refer to *Chapter 6: Step 4* to attach ledger group AUS_CORP to GL business unit AUS01. See screen shot below:

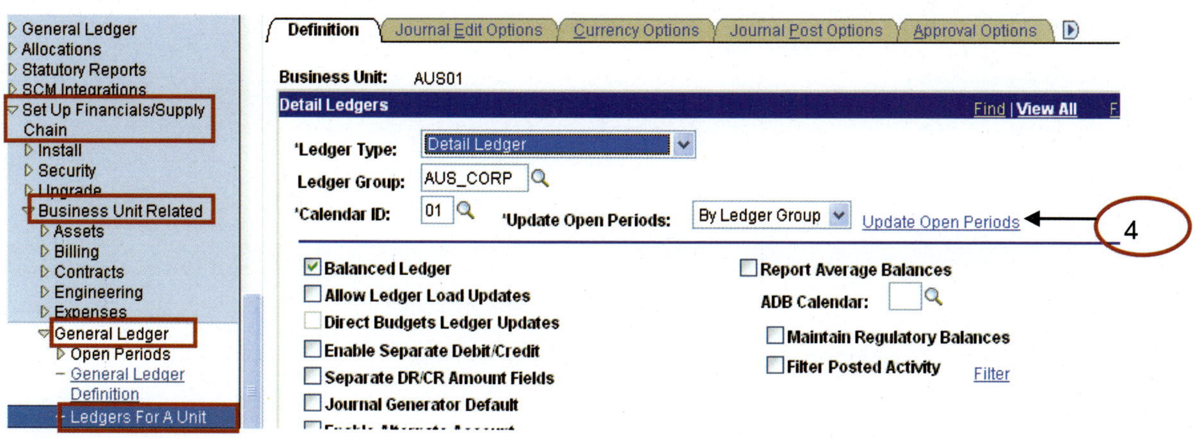

4. Open Periods

Click on *Update Open Periods* to open periods 2010/1 through 2010/12 for GL business unit AUS01 and ledger group AUS_CORP. See the screen shot below for details.

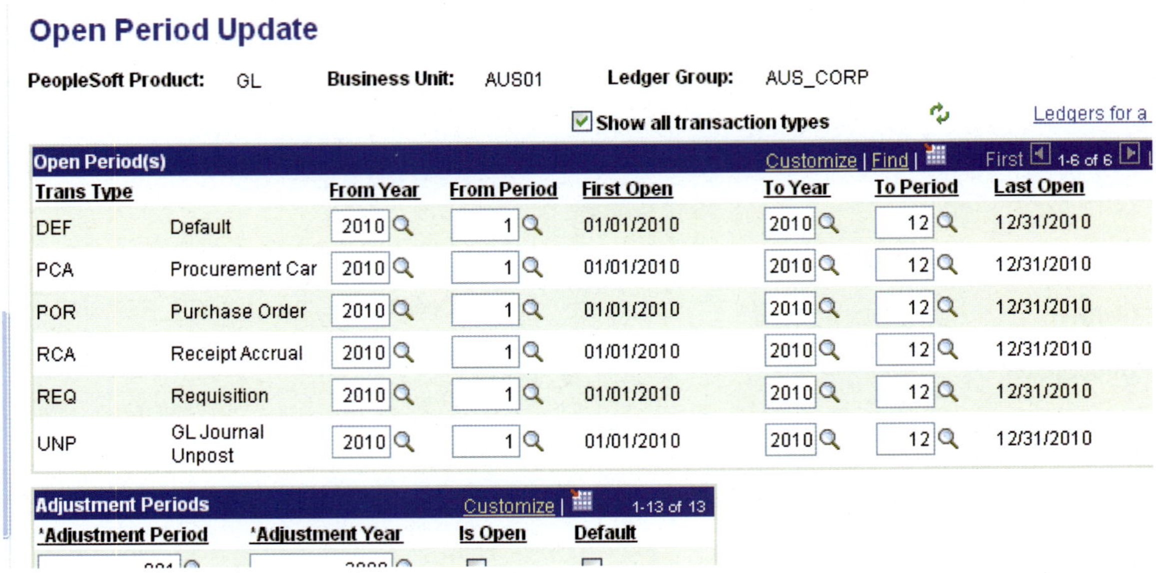

5. Review Currency Codes

Review the three currencies--AUD (Australian Dollars), NZD (New Zealand Dollars) and SGD (Singapore Dollars)-- that you are using in this example.

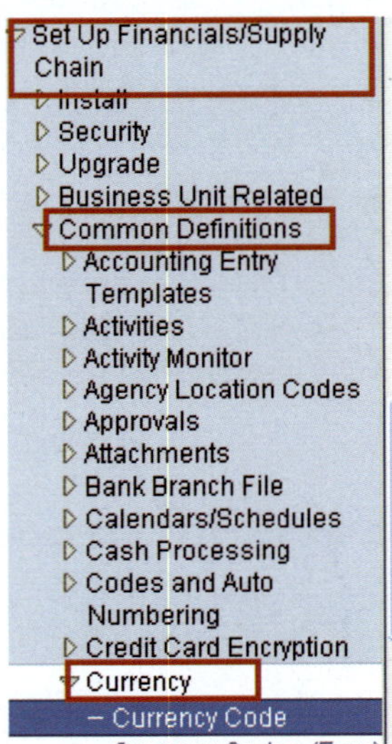

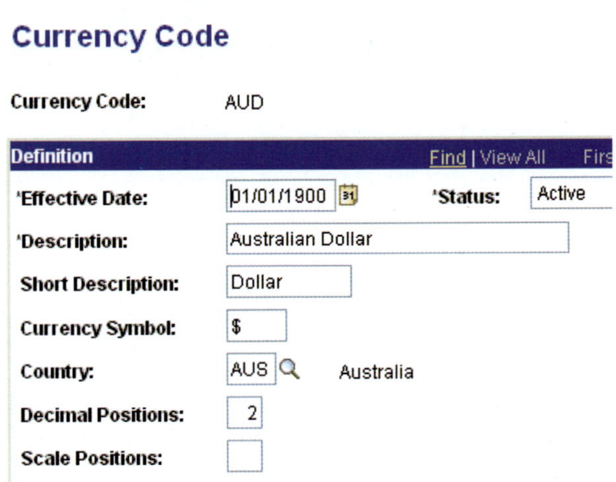

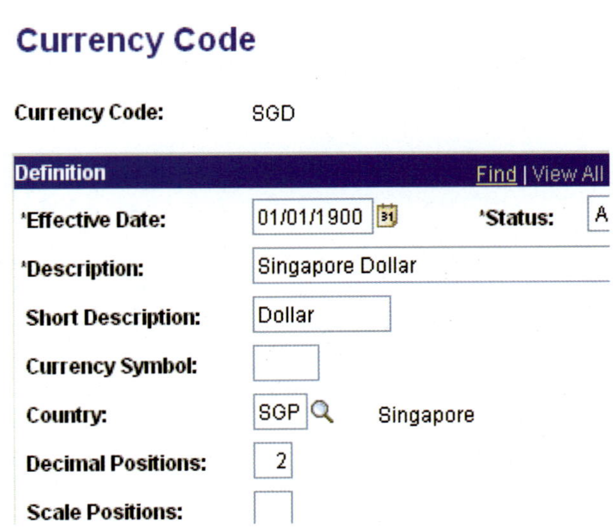

6. Review Currency Quotation Methods

Review (setup if needed) the following two pairs of *Currency Quotation Methods*: AUD-NZD and AUD-SGD. Note that the *Rate Quotation Basis* is set to *Direct*. Use menu navigation *Set Up Financials/Supply Chain > Common Definitions > Currency > Currency Quotation Method*. See screen shots below for details:

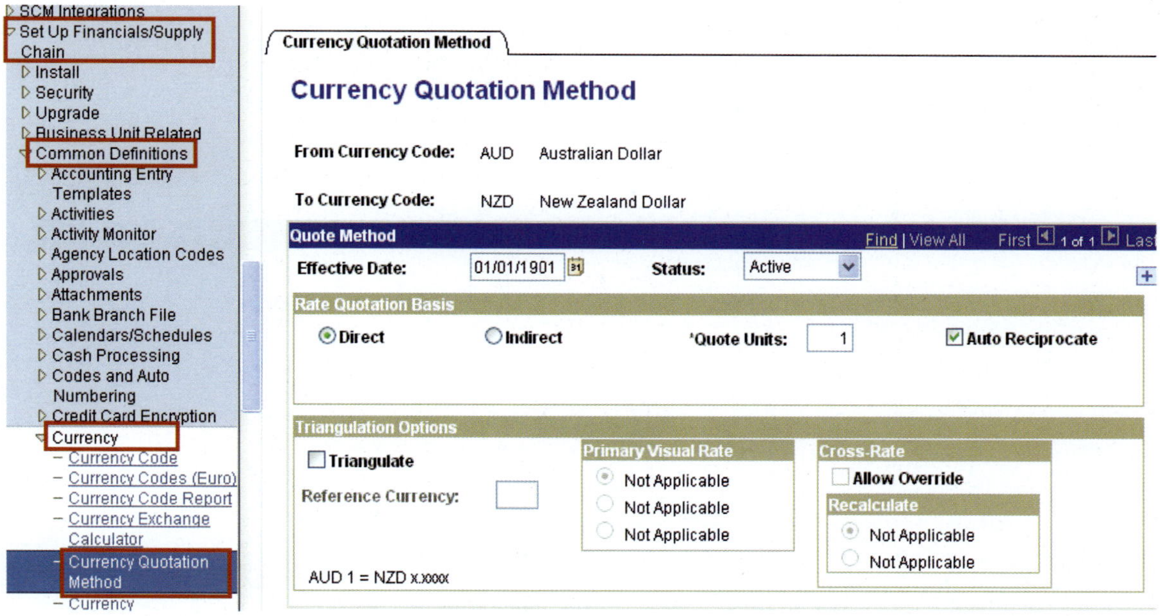

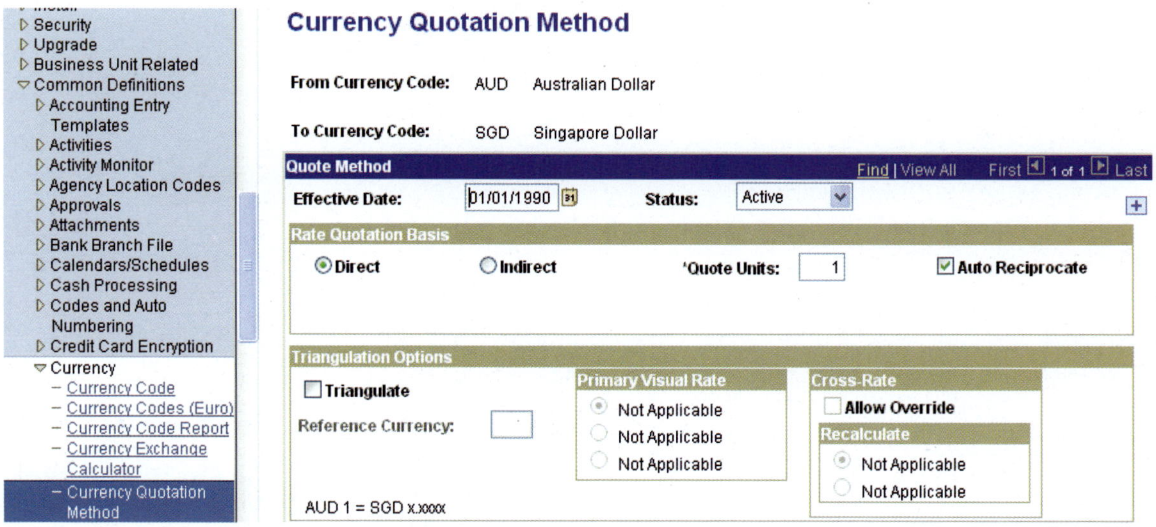

7. Setup Market Rates

Refer to *Chapter 6: Step 6* to setup the following market rates. See screen shots below for details.

From Currency	To Currency	Rate Type	Effective Date	Rate
AUD	SGD	CRRNT	02/26/2010	1.26500000
AUD	SGD	CRRNT	02/01/2010	1.26300000
AUD	NZD	CRRNT	02/26/2010	1.28120000
AUD	NZD	CRRNT	02/01/2010	1.27140435

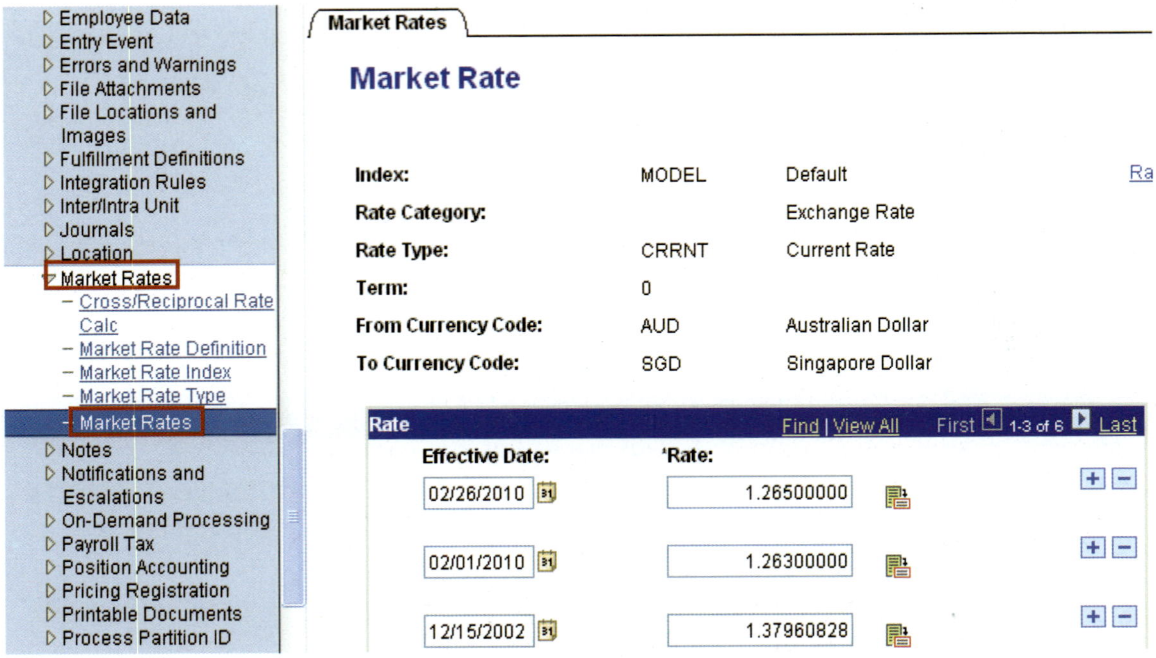

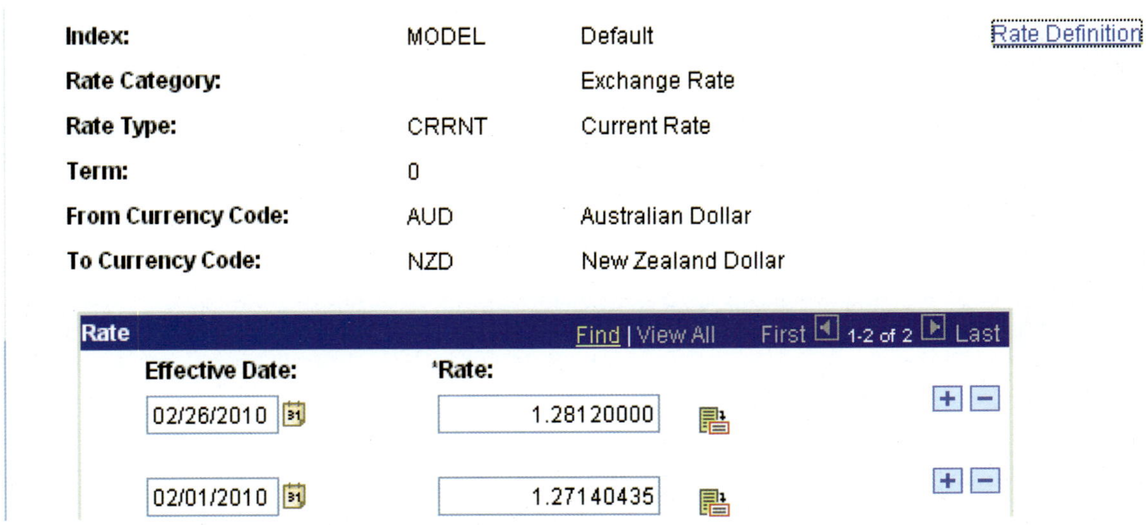

8. Enter Journals

In this step you will enter journals to create the test data. Follow the steps below:

a. Navigate to *General Ledger* > *Journals* > *Journal Entry* > *Create/Update Journal Entries* and specify the following values:
   - `Business Unit: AUS01`
   - `Journal ID: MC1`
   - `Journal Date: 02/01/2010`

b. Click on the *Add* button.

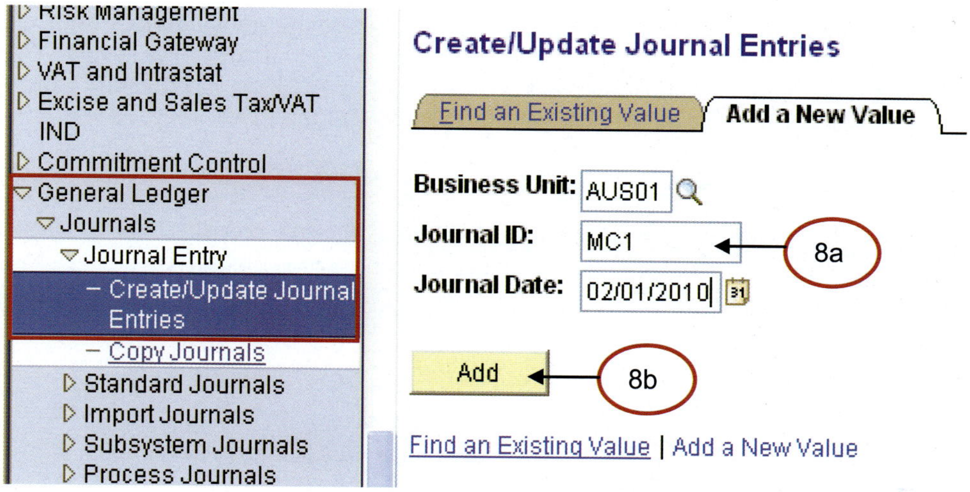

c. On the *Header* tab specify `Ledger Group = AUS_CORP`

d. Click on the *Lines* tab and specify the following values:

- Line `1: Account: 100006, Currency: AUD, Amount: 1000`
- Line `2: Account: 620003, Dept: 10200, Currency: AUD, Amount: -1000`
- Line `3: Account: 100006, Currency: SGD, Amount: 1000`
- Line `4: Account: 620003, Dept: 25000, Currency: SGD, Amount: -1000`

e. Save the journal. Review *Secondary Ledger Lines*

f. Post the journal

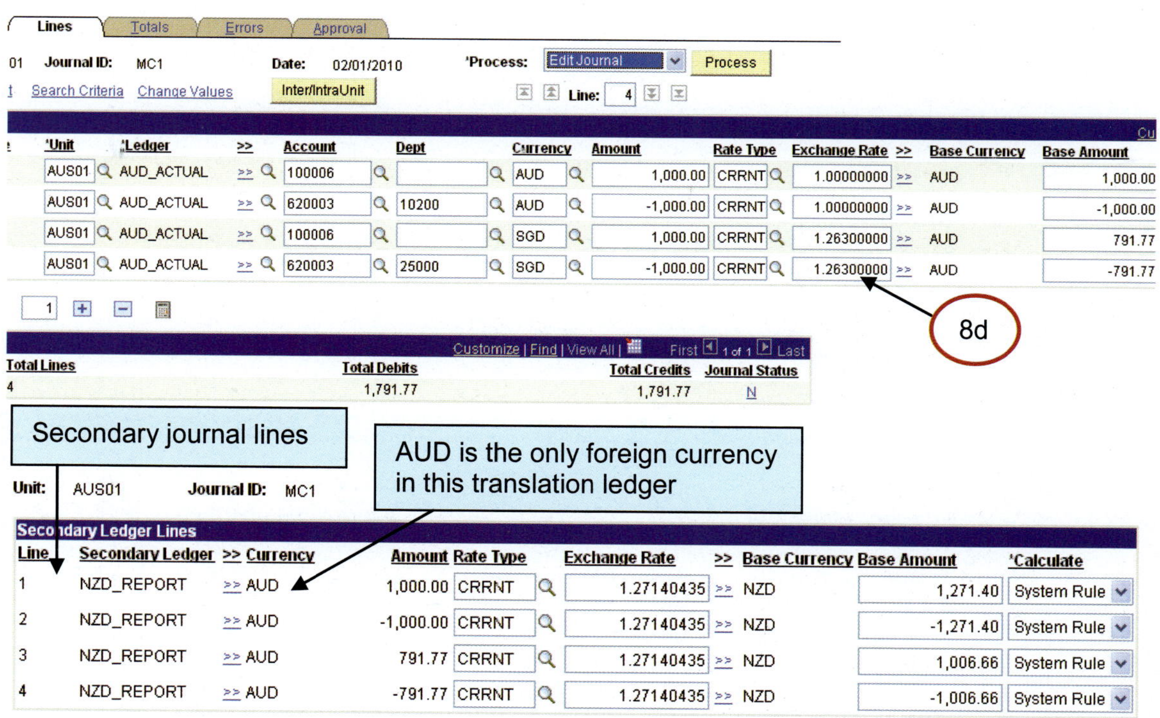

g. Create and run a query on the LEDGER table to see the detail ledgers data. See screen shots below for details.
   - Select fields – `BUSINESS_UNIT, LEDGER, ACCOUNT, DEPTID, CURRENCY_CD, FICALYEAR, ACCOUNTING_PERIOD, POSTED_TOTAL_AMT, POSTED_BASE_AMT, POSTED_TRAN_AMT, BASE_CURRENCY.`
   - Specify the following criteria – `BUSINESS_UNIT = AUS01, FISCAL_YEAR = 2010.`

Fields — Customize | Find | View All | First 1-12 of 12 Last

Col	Record.Fieldname	Format	Ord	XLAT	Agg	Heading Text	Add Criteria	Edit	Delete
1	A.BUSINESS_UNIT - Business Unit	Char5				Unit		Edit	
2	A.LEDGER - Ledger	Char10	1			Ledger		Edit	
3	A.ACCOUNT - Account	Char10	3			Account		Edit	
4	A.DEPTID - Department	Char10				Dept		Edit	
5	A.CURRENCY_CD - Currency Code	Char3	2			Currency		Edit	
6	A.STATISTICS_CODE - Statistics Code	Char3				Stat		Edit	
7	A.FISCAL_YEAR - Fiscal Year	Num4.0				Year		Edit	
8	A.ACCOUNTING_PERIOD - Accounting Period	Num3.0				Period		Edit	
9	A.POSTED_TOTAL_AMT - Posted Total Amount	SNm25.3				Total Amt		Edit	
10	A.POSTED_BASE_AMT - Posted Base Currency Amount	SNm25.3				Amount		Edit	
11	A.POSTED_TRAN_AMT - Posted Transaction Amount	SNm25.3				Transaction Amt		Edit	
12	A.BASE_CURRENCY - Base Currency	Char3				Base Curr		Edit	

Records | Query | Expressions | Prompts | Fields | **Criteria** | Having | View SQL | Run

Query Name: LEDGER_TWL **Description:**

Add Criteria | Group Criteria | Reorder Criteria

Criteria — Customize | Find | First 1-2 of 2 Last

Logical	Expression1	Condition Type	Expression 2	Edit	Delete
	A.BUSINESS_UNIT - Business Unit	equal to	AUS01	Edit	
AND	A.FISCAL_YEAR - Fiscal Year	equal to	2010	Edit	

Save | Save As | New Query | Preferences | Properties | New Union | Return to Search

Records | Query | Expressions | Prompts | Fields | Criteria | Having | **View SQL** | Run

Query Name: LEDGER_TWL **Description:**

Query SQL:

```
SELECT A.BUSINESS_UNIT, A.LEDGER, A.ACCOUNT, A.DEPTID, A.CURRENCY_CD, A.STATISTICS_CODE, A.FISCAL_YEAR,
A.ACCOUNTING_PERIOD, A.POSTED_TOTAL_AMT, A.POSTED_BASE_AMT, A.POSTED_TRAN_AMT, A.BASE_CURRENCY
 FROM PS_LEDGER A
 WHERE A.BUSINESS_UNIT = 'AUS01'
   AND A.FISCAL_YEAR = 2010
 ORDER BY 2, 5, 3
```

View All | Rerun Query | Download to Excel — First 1-11 of 11 Last

	Unit	Ledger	Account	Dept	Currency	Stat	Year	Period	Total Amt	Amount	Transaction Amt	Base Curr
1	AUS01	AUD_ACTUAL	100006		AUD		2010	2	1791.770	1000.000	1000.000	AUD
2	AUS01	AUD_ACTUAL	620003	10200	AUD		2010	2	-1000.000	-1000.000	-1000.000	AUD
3	AUS01	AUD_ACTUAL	620003	25000	AUD		2010	2	-791.770	0.000	0.000	AUD
4	AUS01	AUD_ACTUAL	100006		SGD		2010	2	1000.000	791.770	1000.000	AUD
5	AUS01	AUD_ACTUAL	620003	25000	SGD		2010	2	-1000.000	-791.770	-1000.000	AUD
6	AUS01	NZD_REPORT	100006		AUD		2010	2	1791.770	2278.060	1791.770	NZD
7	AUS01	NZD_REPORT	620003	10200	AUD		2010	2	-1000.000	-1271.400	-1000.000	NZD
8	AUS01	NZD_REPORT	620003	25000	AUD		2010	2	-791.770	-1006.660	-791.770	NZD
9	AUS01	NZD_REPORT	100006		NZD		2010	2	2278.060	0.000	0.000	NZD
10	AUS01	NZD_REPORT	620003	10200	NZD		2010	2	-1271.400	0.000	0.000	NZD
11	AUS01	NZD_REPORT	620003	25000	NZD		2010	2	-1006.660	0.000	0.000	NZD

9. Setup *Translation Within Ledger*

Unlike *Ledger Translation* both *Translation Rules* and *Translation Steps* are built into one *Translation Within Ledger* component. Follow the steps below to configure *Translation Within Ledger*

a. Navigate to *General Ledger > Process Multi-Currency > Define and Process > Translation Within Ledger > Add a New Value* and specify the following values. Click on the *Add* button:

- `SetID: SHARE`
- `Process Step: NZD_TRNSL`

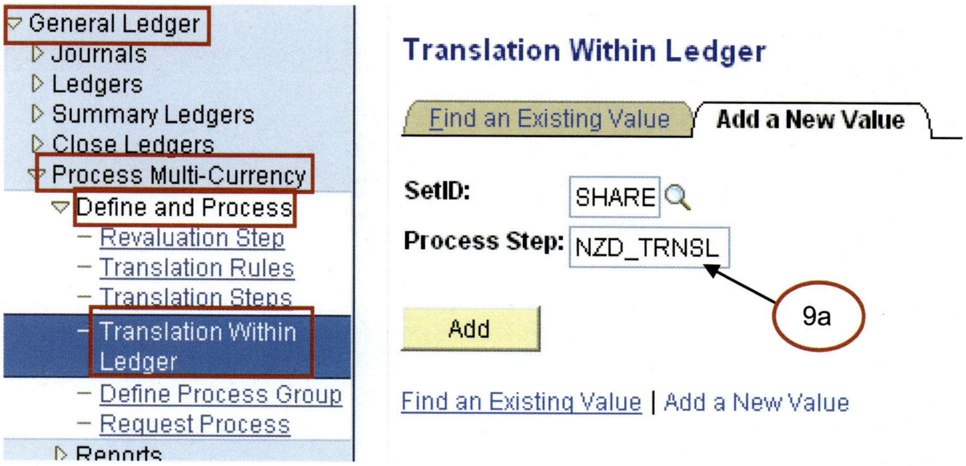

b. On the *Ledger and Timespan* tab specify the following values:

- `Effective Date: 01/01/1901`
- `Descr and Description: Translate NZD_REPORT Ledger`
- `From Ledger Group: AUS_CORP`
- `Ledger: NZD_REPORT`
- `TimeSpan: PER`
- `Rate Type: CRRNT`

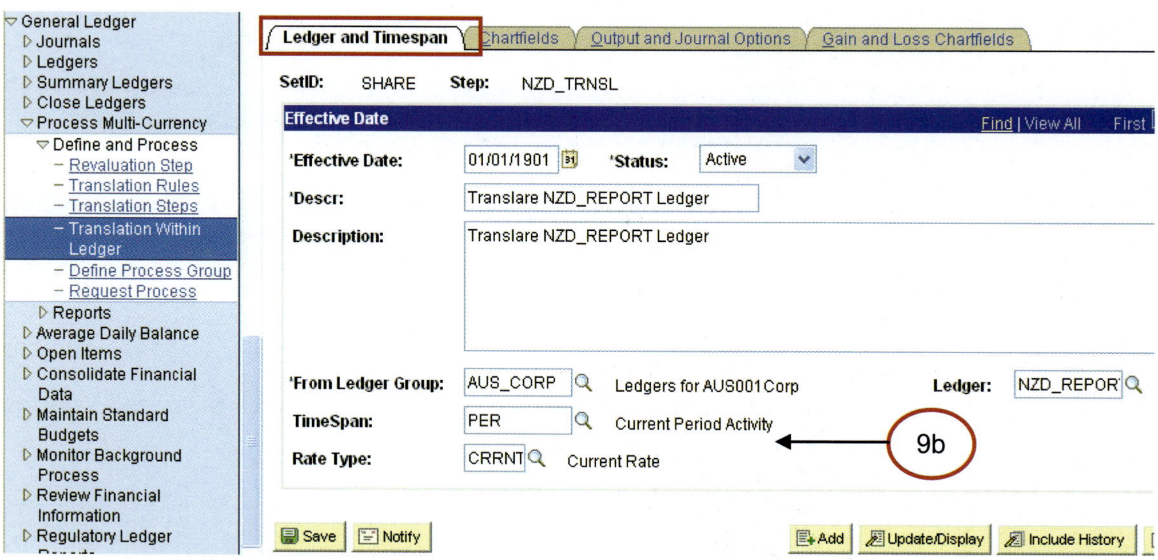

c. Specify the following values on the *Chartfields* tab:

- `ChartField = Account`
- `How Specified: Selected Tree Nodes`

- `Tree Information: Tree = ACCTROLLUP`
- `Chartfield values/Tree nodes: Select Value = ALLACCOUNTS`

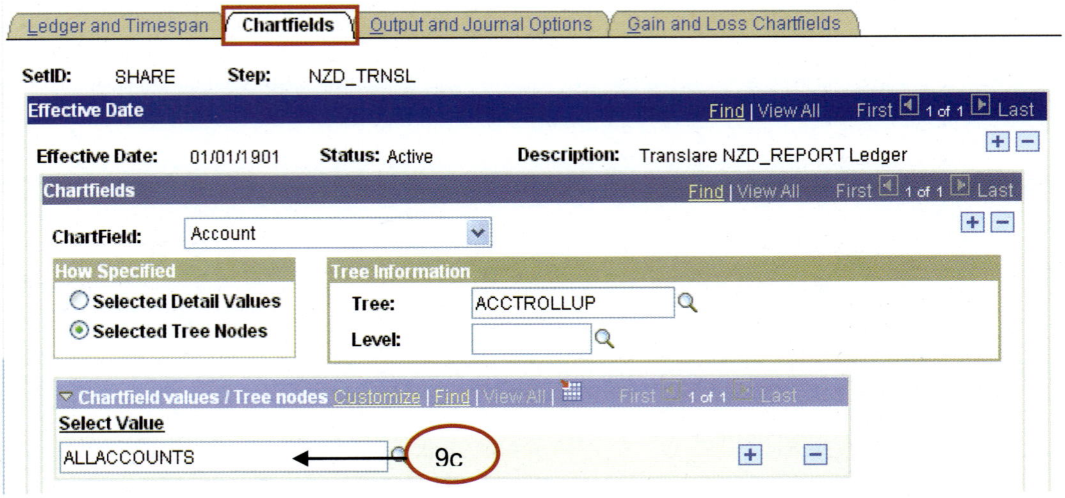

d. Specify the following values on the *Output and Journal Options* tab:

- `Journal ID Mask = TWL` (for Translation Within Ledger)
- `Source = MCP`
- `Description: Translate within ledger`
- `Create Journal Entries: Checked`
- `Edit Journals: Checked`
- `Target Chartfields: Account and Department`

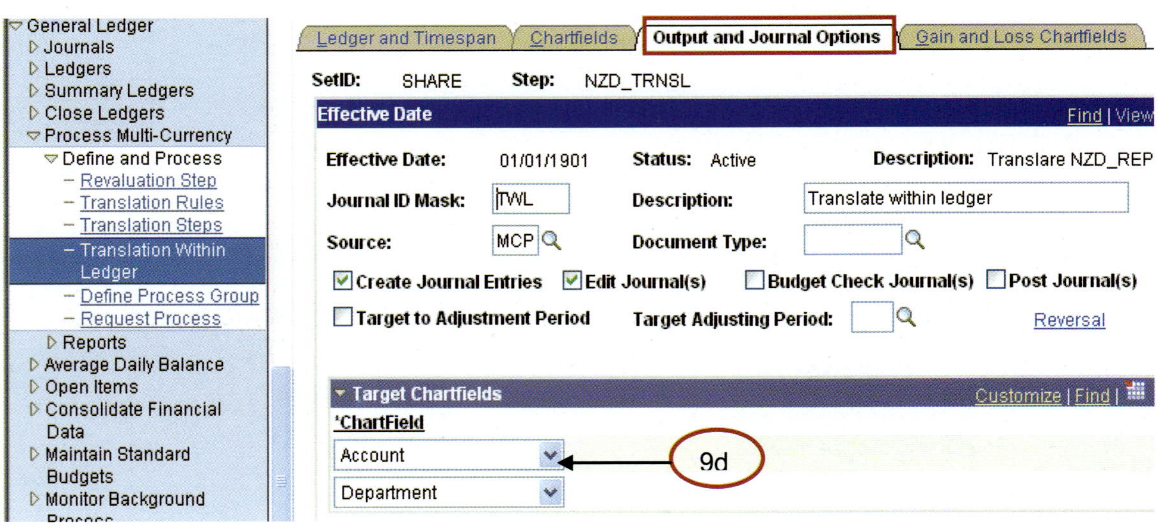

e. On the *Gain and Loss CharFields* tab specify the following values and save this configuration:

- `Gain ChartKeys: Account = 318000`
- `Loss ChartKeys: Account = 318000`

Any currency gain/loss during the translation process will be recorded in the *ChartField* values specified above.

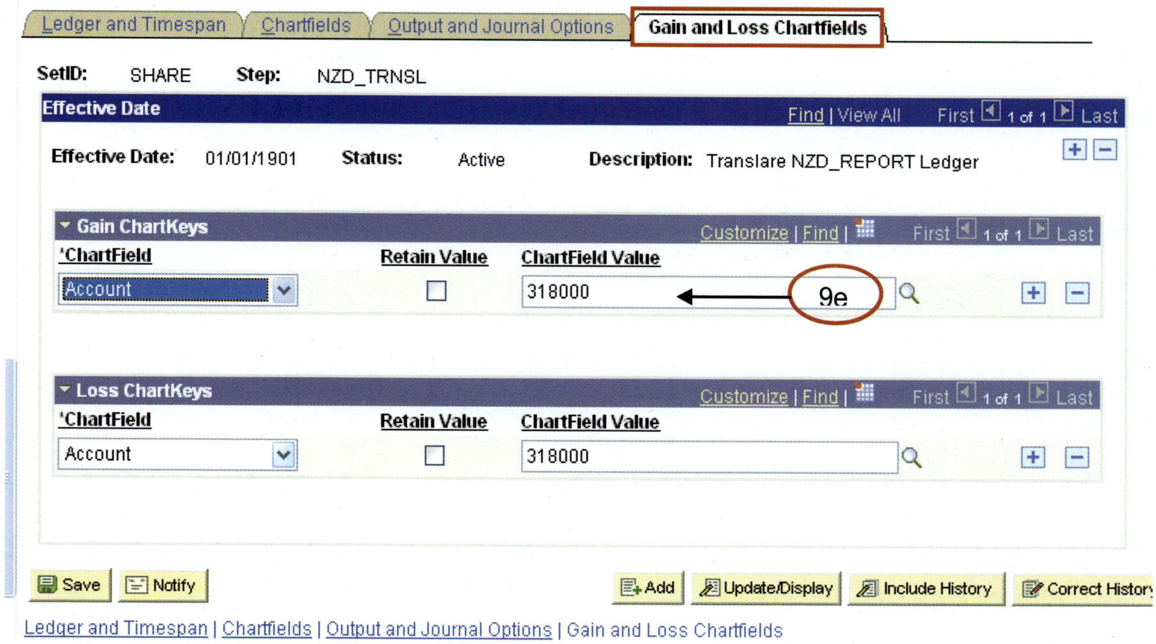

10. Setup Process Group

Next use the following steps to setup *Process Multi-Currency*.

a. Navigate to *Define Process Group* > *Add a New Value* as highlighted below. Specify the following values and click on the *Add* button:

- `SetID = SHARE`
- `Process Group: NZD_TRNSL`

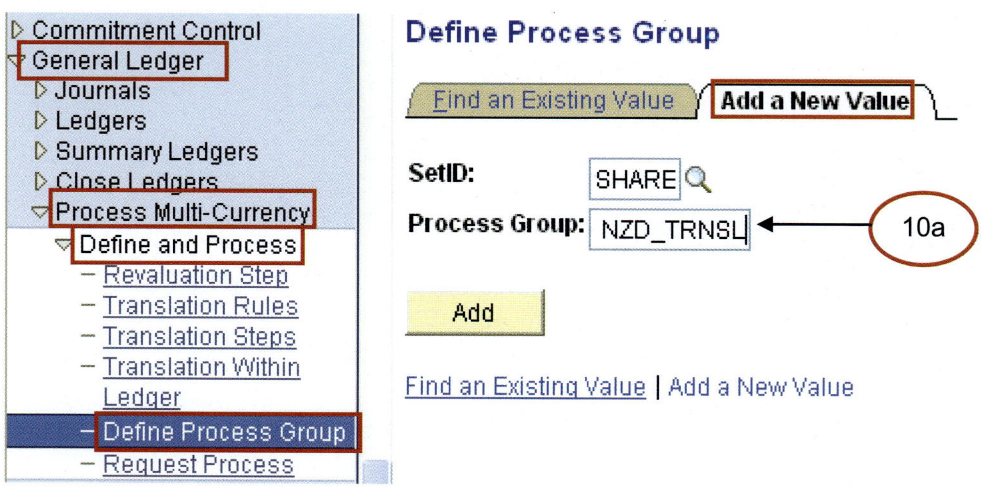

b. Specify the following values in the *MultiCurrency Process Group* screen and click on the *Save* button:

- `Descr and Description = NZD Translate within Ledger`
- `Process Step: NZD_TRNSL`

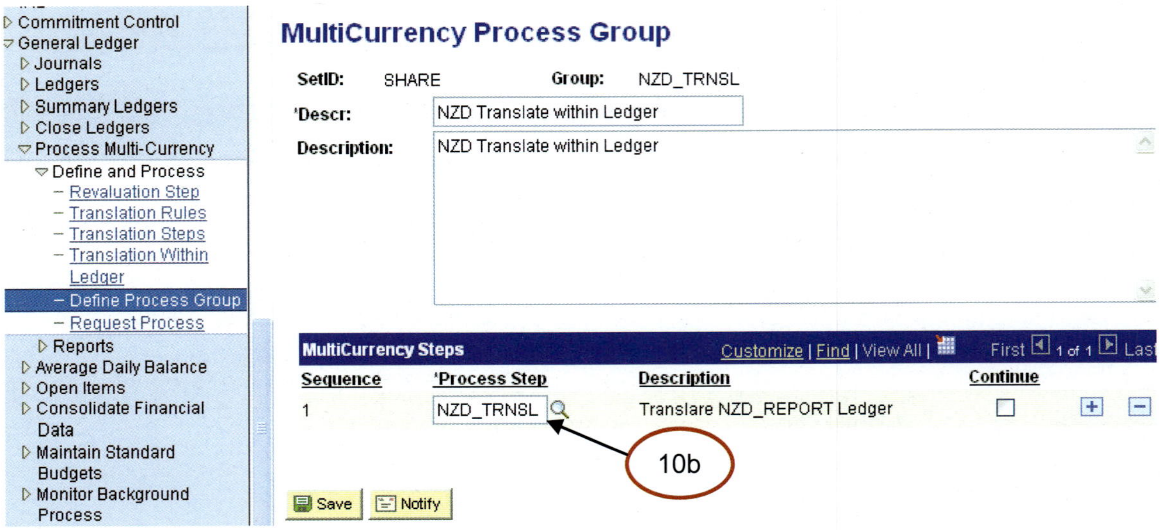

11. Run Multi Currency Process

Next you will execute the multi currency process. Follow the steps below:

a. Navigate to *Request Process > Add a New Value* as highlighted below. Specify the following values and click on the *Add* button:

- `Run Control ID: Translate_within_Ledger`

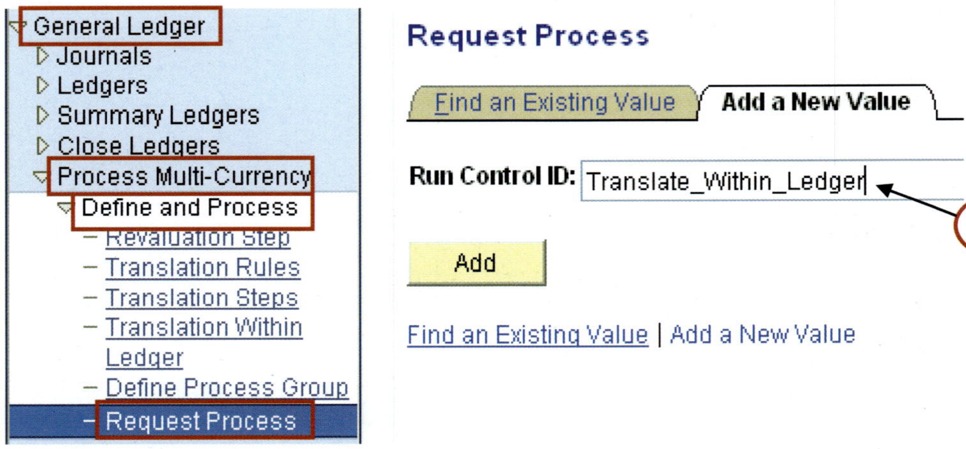

b. Specify the following values in the *MultiCurrency Process Request* screen. Save and click on the *Run* button:

- `Process Frequency: Always`
- `Unit: AUS01`
- `Group: NZD_TRNSL`
- `Cal Log: Checked`
- `Request Date Option: As of Date = 02/26/2010`

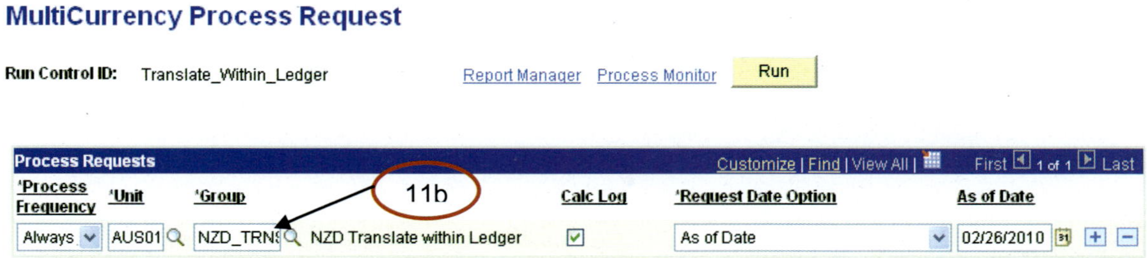

c. Select *Server Name*, which is PSNT on this PC. Click on *OK* in the *Process Scheduler Request* screen.

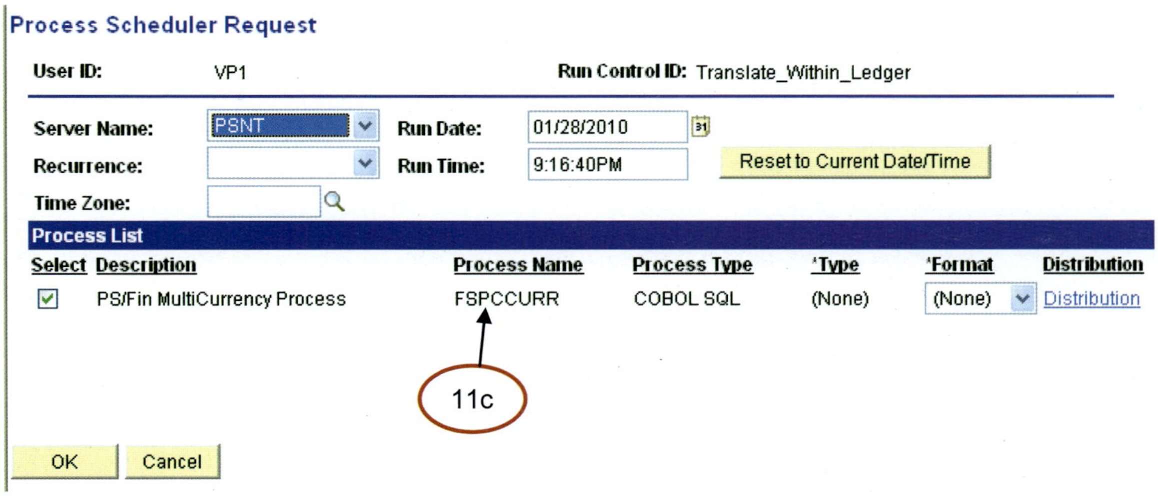

d. Note that the COBOL process FSPCCURR is queued in the *Process Monitor.*

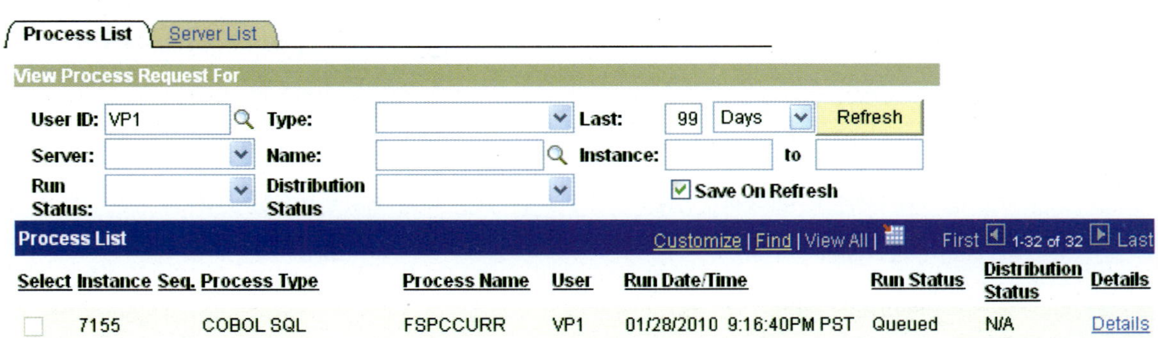

12. Review Translation Results

After the FSPCCURR process indicates *Success,* you must review the results of the *Translation Within Ledger* process. Follow these steps:

a. Navigate to *General Ledger* > *Journals* > *Journal Entry* > *Create/Update Journal Entries* > *Find an Existing Value* and specify the following values and click on *Search*:

- `Business Unit: AUS01`
- `Journal ID: TWL` (this is the Journal ID mask you specified in step 9d)

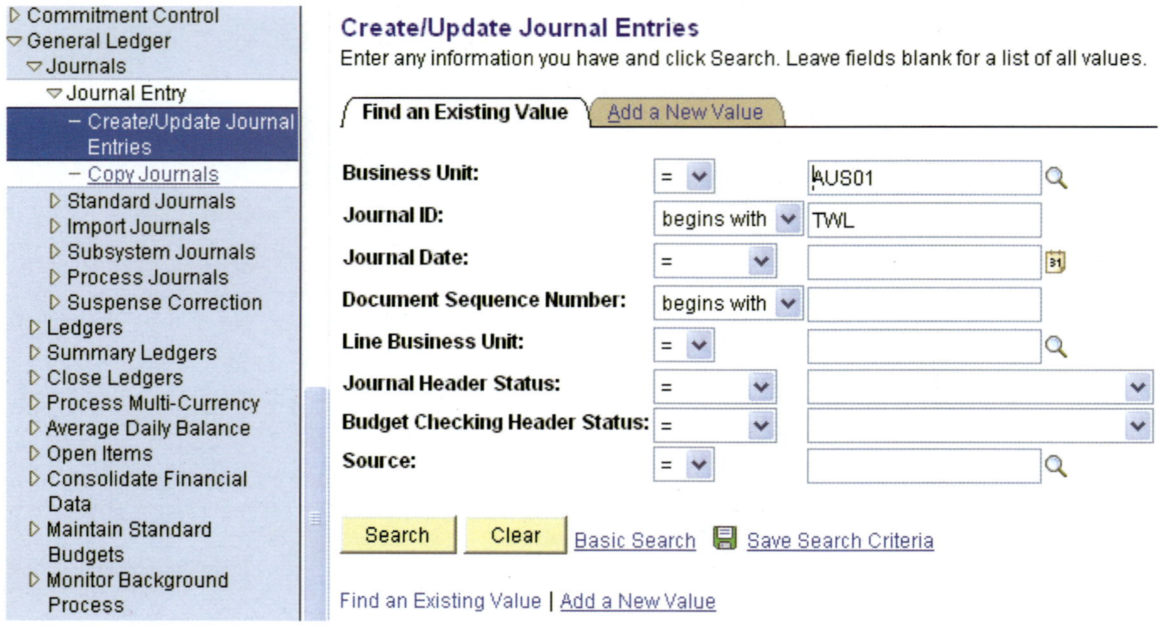

b. Click on the journal prefixed TWL, which was created by the multi currency process. Ensure the *Long Description*, *Ledger Group* and *Source* are the same as you specified in step 9d.

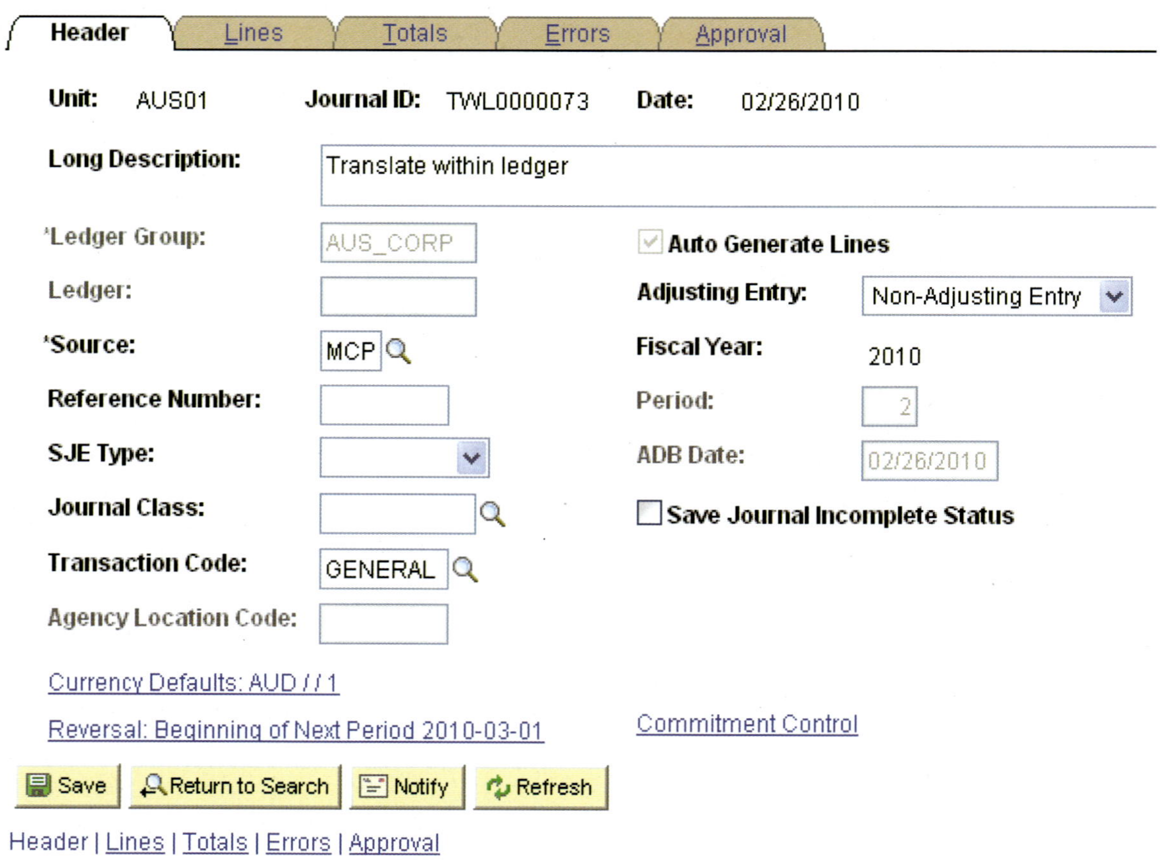

c. Click on the *Lines* tab and review the journal created.

Records | Query | Expressions | Prompts | Fields | Criteria | Having | View SQL | **Run**

View All | Rerun Query | Download to Excel   First 1-11 of 11

	Unit	Ledger	Account	Dept	Currency	Stat	Year	Period	Total Amt	Amount	Transaction Amt	Base
1	AUS01	AUD_ACTUAL	100006		AUD		2010	2	1791.770	1000.000	1000.000	AUD
2	AUS01	AUD_ACTUAL	620003	10200	AUD		2010	2	-1000.000	-1000.000	-1000.000	AUD
3	AUS01	AUD_ACTUAL	620003	25000	AUD		2010	2	-791.770	0.000	0.000	AUD
4	AUS01	AUD_ACTUAL	100006		SGD		2010	2	1000.000	791.770	1000.000	AUD
5	AUS01	AUD_ACTUAL	620003	25000	SGD		2010	2	-1000.000	-791.770	-1000.000	AUD
6	AUS01	NZD_REPORT	100006		AUD		2010	2	1791.770	2278.060	1791.770	NZD
7	AUS01	NZD_REPORT	620003	10200	AUD		2010	2	-1000.000	-1271.400	-1000.000	NZD
8	AUS01	NZD_REPORT	620003	25000	AUD		2010	2	-791.770	-1006.660	-791.770	NZD
9	AUS01	NZD_REPORT	100006		NZD		2010	2	2278.060	0.000	0.000	NZD
10	AUS01	NZD_REPORT	620003	10200	NZD		2010	2	-1271.400	0.000	0.000	NZD
11	AUS01	NZD_REPORT	620003	25000	NZD		2010	2	-1006.660	0.000	0.000	NZD

Test Data → ← Expected Results →

Account	Dept	Curr	Posted AUD Total Amt A	Posted NZD Base Amt B	Rate for Trans C	New Rounded NZD Base Amt = A X C D	Adjustment Base NZD Amt = C - B
100006		AUD	1,791.77	2,278.06	1.2812	2,295.62	17.56
620003	10200	AUD	-1,000	-1,271.4	1.2812	-1,281.20	-9.80
620003	25000	AUD	-791.77	-1006.66	1.2812	-1,014.42	-7.76
318000							-17.56
318000							17.56

Lines | Totals | Errors | Approval

Journal ID: TWL0000073   Date: 02/26/2010   *Process: Edit Journal   Process

Search Criteria   Change Values   Inter/IntraUnit   Errors Only   Line: 10

*Unit	*Ledger	Account	Dept	Currency	Amount	Rate Type	Exchange Rate	Base Currency	Base Amount
AUS01	AUD_ACTUAL	100006		AUD			1.00000000	AUD	
AUS01	AUD_ACTUAL	620003	10200	AUD			1.00000000	AUD	
AUS01	AUD_ACTUAL	620003	25000	AUD			1.00000000	AUD	
AUS01	AUD_ACTUAL	318000		AUD			1.00000000	AUD	
AUS01	AUD_ACTUAL	318000		AUD			1.00000000	AUD	

Customize | Find | View All | First 1 of 1 Last

Total Lines	Total Debits	Total Credits	Journal Status
5	0.00	0.00	V

Unit: AUS01   Journal ID: TWL0000073   Date: 02/26/2010

Secondary Ledger Lines

Line	Secondary Ledger	Currency	Amount	Rate Type	Exchange Rate	Base Currency	Base Amount	*Calculate
1	NZD_REPORT	AUD				NZD	17.56	System Rule
2	NZD_REPORT	AUD				NZD	-9.80	System Rule
3	NZD_REPORT	AUD				NZD	-7.76	System Rule
4	NZD_REPORT	AUD				NZD	-17.56	System Rule
5	NZD_REPORT	AUD				NZD	17.56	System Rule

d. Post the Journal created.

e. Rerun the query from step 8g to see adjusted ledger balances. See screen shot below.

Records | Query | Expressions | Prompts | Fields | Criteria | Having | View SQL | **Run**

View All | Rerun Query | Download to Excel — First 1-13 of 13 Last

	Unit	Ledger	Account	Dept	Currency	Stat	Year	Period	Total Amt	Amount	Transaction Amt	Base Curr
1	AUS01	AUD_ACTUAL	100006		AUD		2010	2	1791.770	1000.000	1000.000	AUD
2	AUS01	AUD_ACTUAL	620003	10200	AUD		2010	2	-1000.000	-1000.000	-1000.000	AUD
3	AUS01	AUD_ACTUAL	620003	25000	AUD		2010	2	-791.770	0.000	0.000	AUD
4	AUS01	AUD_ACTUAL	100006		SGD		2010	2	1000.000	791.770	1000.000	AUD
5	AUS01	AUD_ACTUAL	620003	25000	SGD		2010	2	-1000.000	-791.770	-1000.000	AUD
6	AUS01	NZD_REPORT	100006		AUD		2010	2	1791.770	2295.620	1791.770	NZD
7	AUS01	NZD_REPORT	318000		AUD		2010	2	0.000	0.000	0.000	NZD
8	AUS01	NZD_REPORT	620003	10200	AUD		2010	2	-1000.000	-1281.200	-1000.000	NZD
9	AUS01	NZD_REPORT	620003	25000	AUD		2010	2	-791.770	-1014.420	-791.770	NZD
10	AUS01	NZD_REPORT	100006		NZD		2010	2	2295.620	0.000	0.000	NZD
11	AUS01	NZD_REPORT	318000		NZD		2010	2	0.000	0.000	0.000	NZD
12	AUS01	NZD_REPORT	620003	25000	NZD		2010	2	-1014.420	0.000	0.000	NZD
13	AUS01	NZD_REPORT	620003	10200	NZD		2010	2	-1281.200	0.000	0.000	NZD

f. Navigate to *Reports > Translation in Ledger Calc Log* as highlighted below to run the calculation log report. See screen shots below for details. Note that the numbers on the report match with the journal shown in step c.

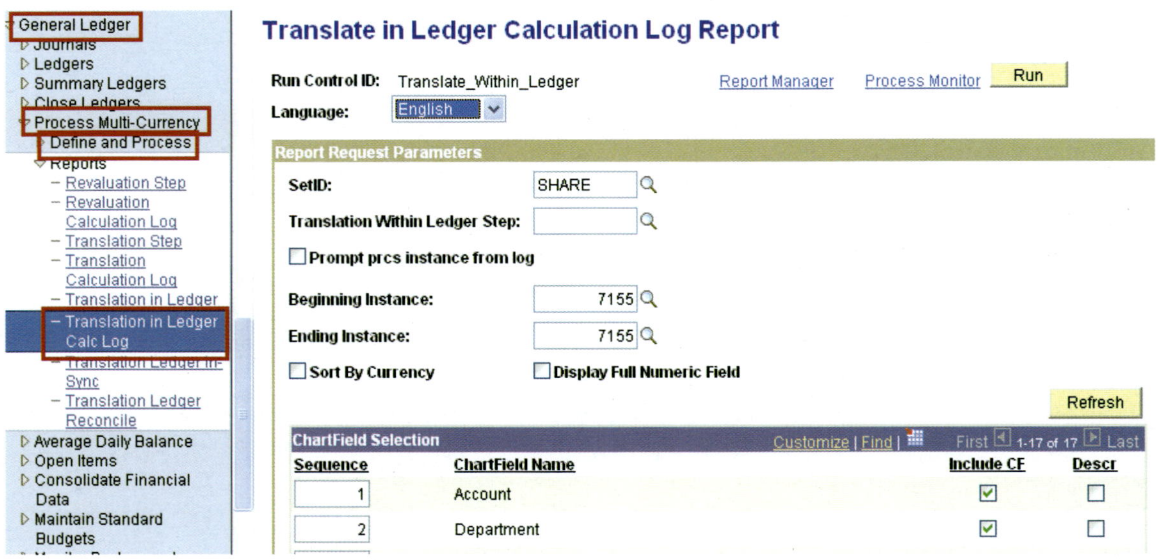

PeopleSoft GL
TRANS W/IN LEDG CALCULATION LOG

Report ID: GLS5004
Process Instances: 0000007155 to 0000007155
Translation Step: All

Page No. 1
Run Date 01/28/2010
Run Time 21:25:53

Process Instance: 0000007155 Translation Step: NZD_TRNSL Business Unit: AUS01 Ledger: NZD_REPORT Base Currency: NZD

Account	Dept	Adjustment	Exchange Rate	Currency	Posted Total Amount	Posted Base Amount	Translated Amount	Adjustment Amount
100006			1.28120000	AUD	1,791.77	2,278.06	2,295.62	17.56
620003	10200		1.28120000	AUD	-1,000.00	-1,271.40	-1,281.20	-9.80
620003	25000		1.28120000	AUD	-791.77	-1,006.66	-1,014.42	-7.76

Adjustment:

Account	Currency	Adjustment Amount
318000	AUD	-17.56
318000	AUD	17.56

Miscellaneous Functionalities

In this last chapter we will discuss some miscellaneous multi-currency functionalities in PeopleSoft applications:

Global display on/off of all multi-currency fields

You can turn on or off the display of all *multi-currency* fields on all PeopleSoft pages.

Turn the display of multi-currency fields on or off by checking or un-checking the *Multi-Currency* check box on the *PeopleTools Options* page. The menu navigation to the page is: *PeopleTools > Utilities > Administration> PeopleTools Option*s. In a strict single currency environment, you can choose to de-select the *Multi-Currency* checkbox.

The global display (on or off) applies only to fields of type multi-currency. Fields are flagged as multi-currency on a page by selecting the *Multi-Currency Field* check box on the *Page Field Properties* dialog box.

Follow these steps to gain a detailed understanding of this functionality:

a. In the Application Designer open page JOURNAL_ENTRY2_IE. Right click on the *Amount* field and select *Page Field Properties*.

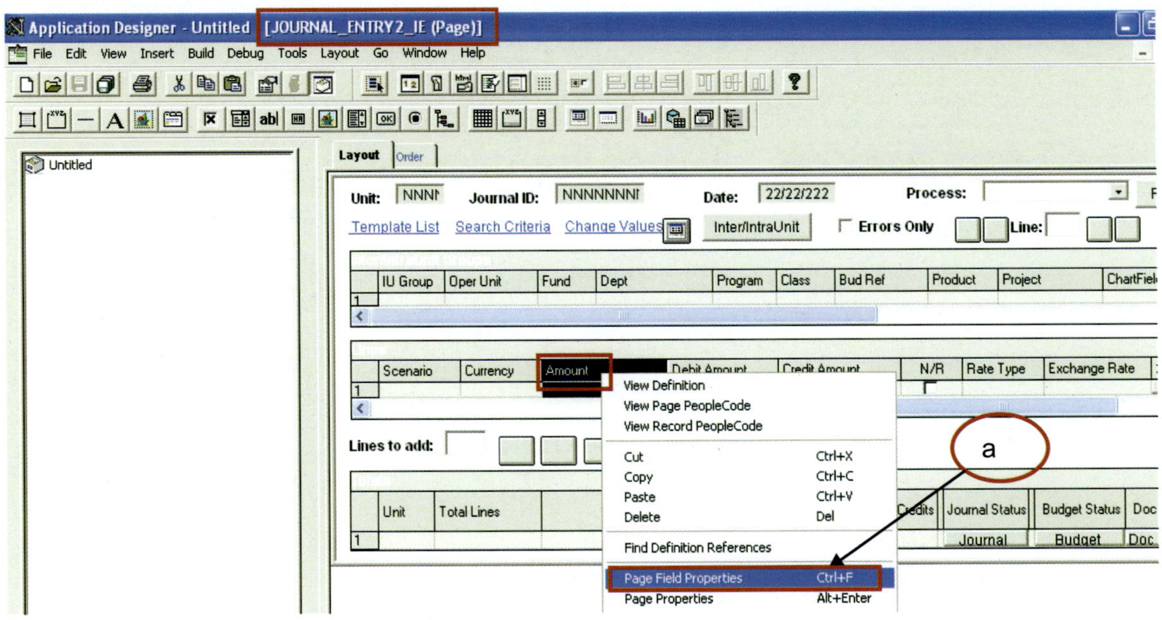

b. On the *Use* tab select the *Multi-Currency Field* checkbox and click on *OK* (not shown in the picture). Save the page. This makes the Amount field *multi-currency*.

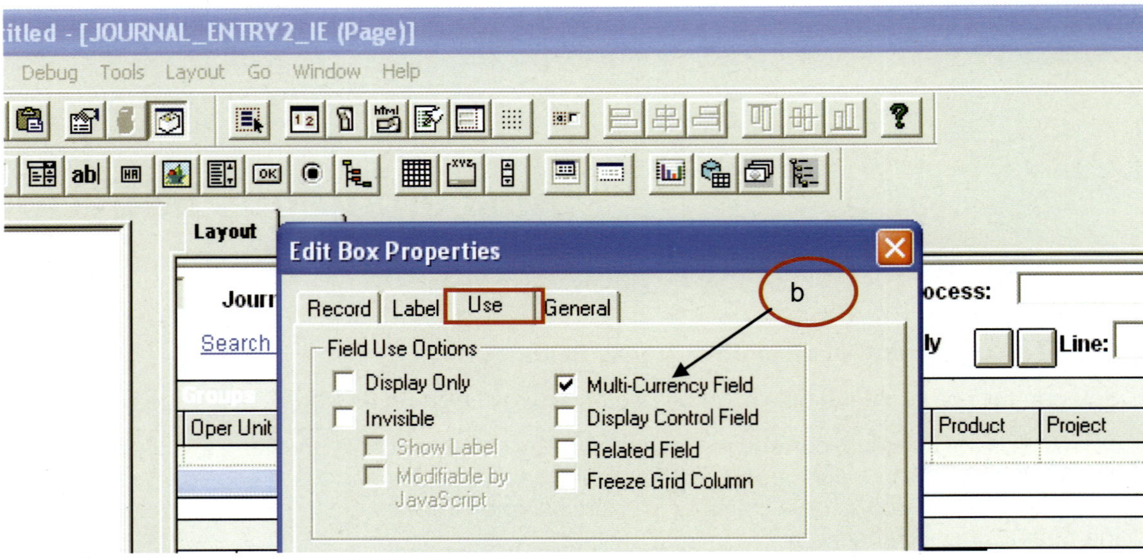

c. Next, navigate to *PeopleTools* > *Utilities* > *Administration* > *PeopleTools Options*. Select the *Multi-Currency* checkbox if not already selected.

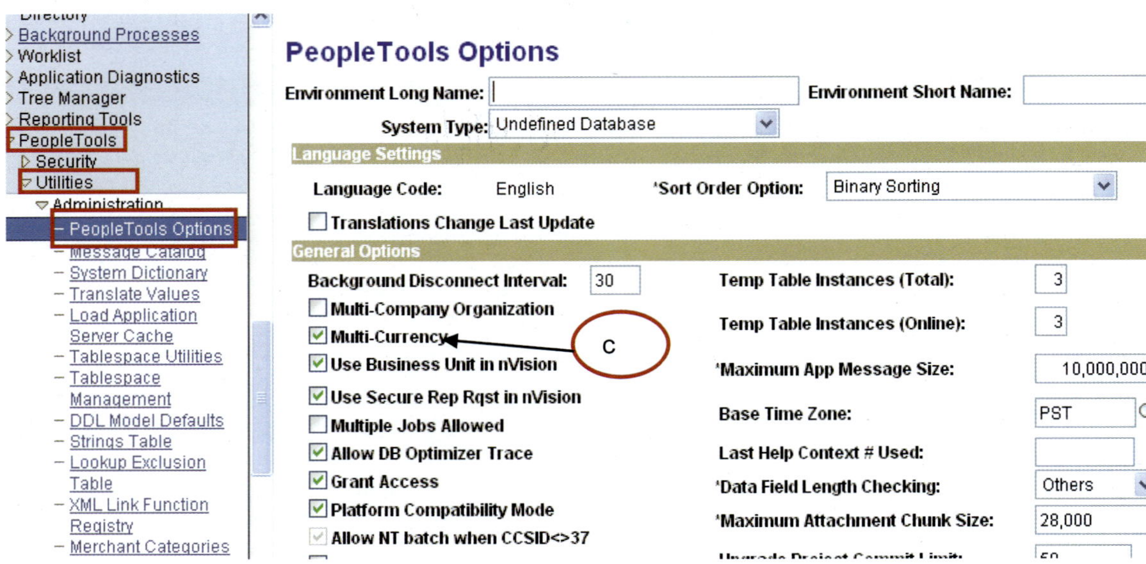

d. Sign out of PeopleSoft and restart Application Server. Sign in as user VP1. And then enter a journal. Note that the Amount field is visible on the Lines tab.

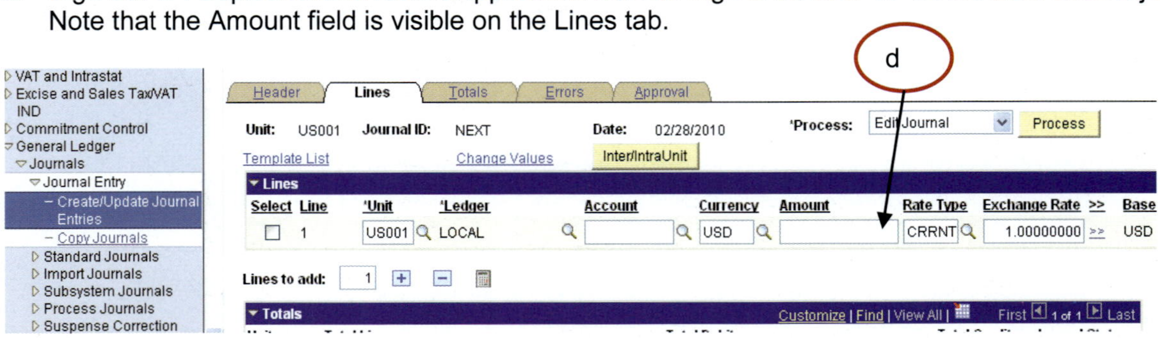

e. Navigate to *PeopleTools* > *Utilities* > *Administration* > *PeopleTools Options*. Deselect the *Multi-Currency* checkbox.

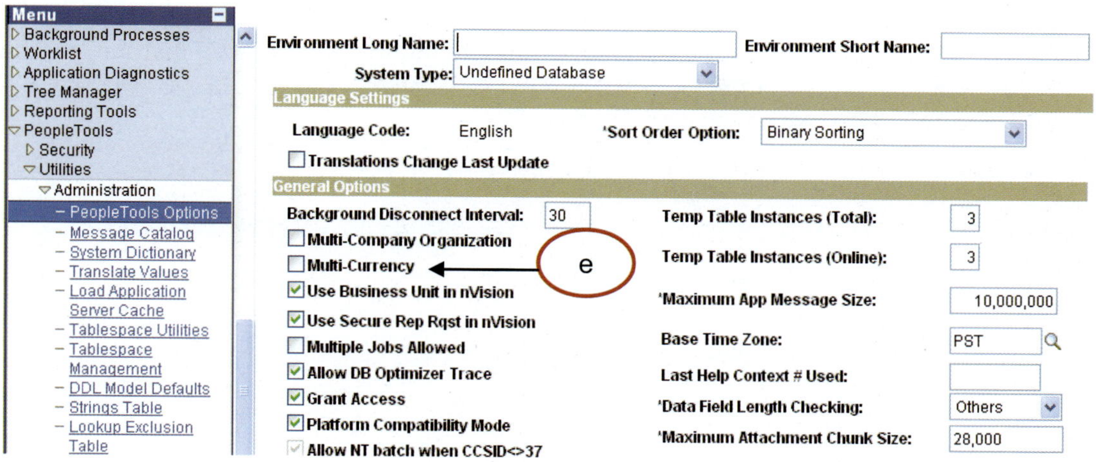

f. Sign out of PeopleSoft and restart Application Server. Sign in as user VP1. And then enter a journal. Note that the Amount field is <u>not</u> visible.

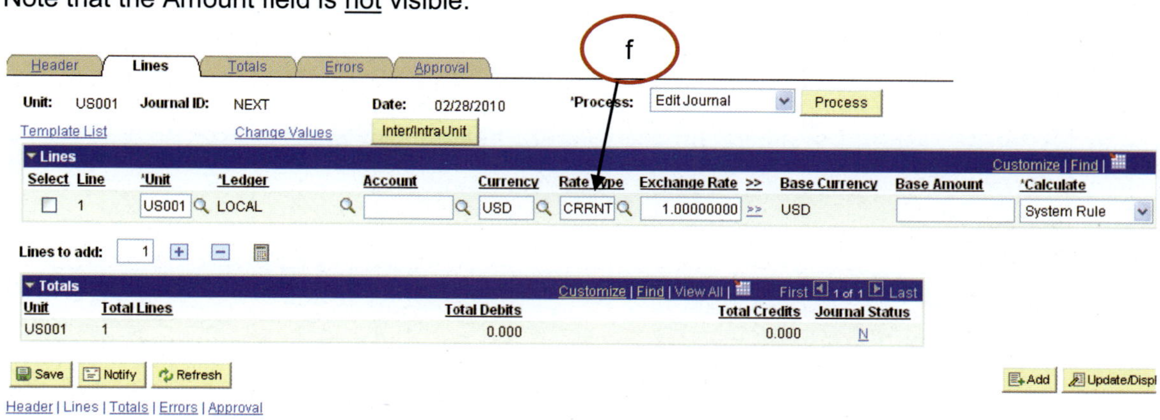

g. Repeat steps c and d

h. The grid below summarizes display of multi currency fields:

<table>
<tr><th>Multi Currency field on Page Field Properties dialog box</th><th>Multi Currency field on PeopleTools Option page</th><th>Impact on field's visibility</th></tr>
<tr><td rowspan="2">checked
(field's visibility is controlled by PeopleTools Options page)</td><td>checked</td><td>All multi currency fields will be visible</td></tr>
<tr><td>unchecked</td><td>All multi currency fields will be hidden</td></tr>
<tr><td rowspan="2">unchecked
(field's visibility is <u>not</u> controlled by PeopleTools Options page)</td><td>Checked</td><td rowspan="2">No impact on field's visibility</td></tr>
<tr><td>Unchecked</td></tr>
</table>

In addition, the *Multi-Currency* check box on the *PeopleTools Options* page enables the following:

- Automatic formatting of currency sensitive amount fields (i.e. amount fields which have associated currency control fields)
- Validation of user entries against the currency's defined decimal precision

Displaying Currency symbols and thousand separators

You can turn on (or off) the display of currency symbols and thousand separators in individual fields on a page. The following steps explain this.

a. Note that in the journal below the amount fields do not display the USD currency symbol of $.

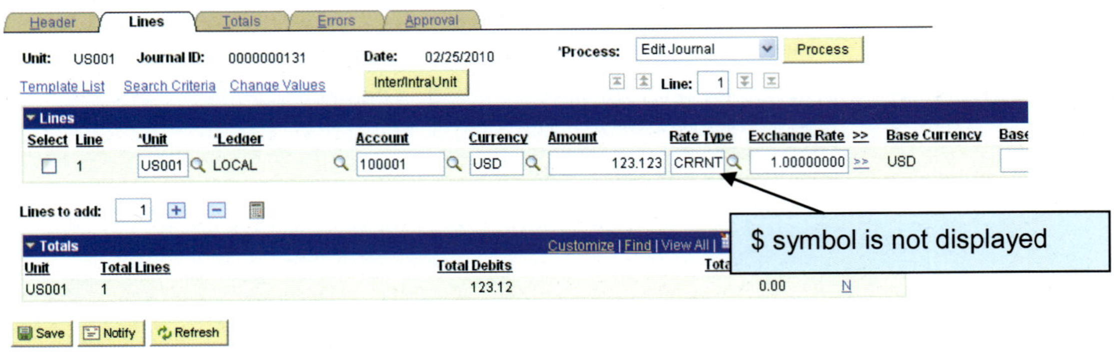

b. In the Application Designer open page JOURNAL_ENTRY2_IE. Right click on Amount field and select *Page Field Properties*. On the dialog box that opens up select the *Currency Symbol* checkbox on the *Record* tab. The *1000 Separator* checkbox should already be selected. Click on *OK* and save the page.

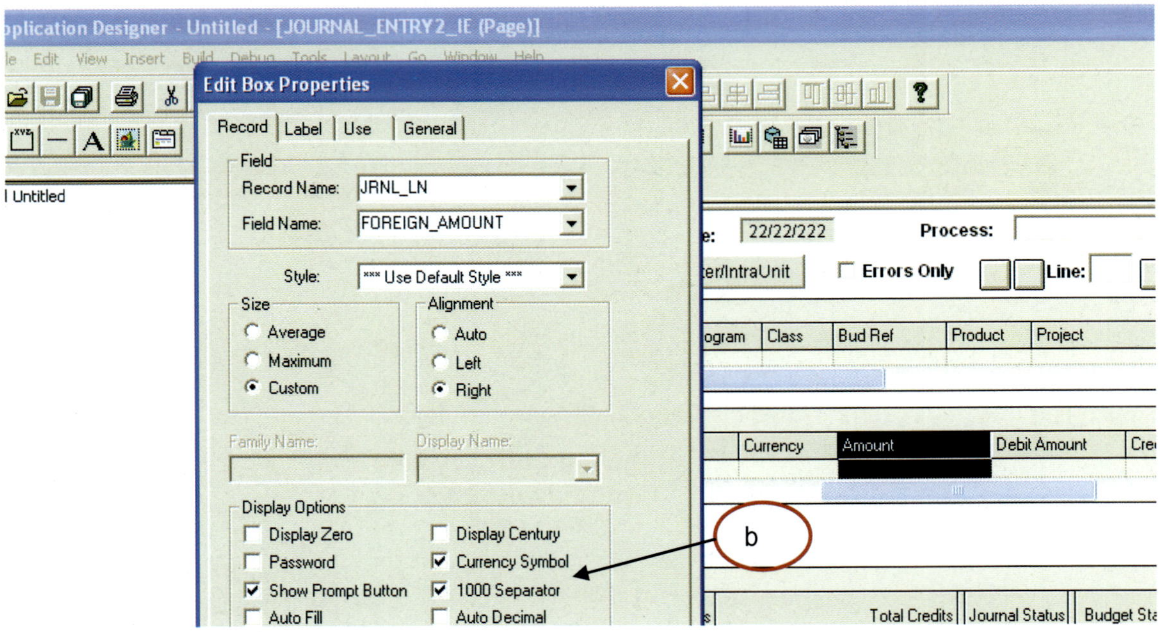

c. Now when you enter a journal with the Amount field displays the $ sign. The Base Amount field does not display the $ sign because it was not formatted to display currency symbols.

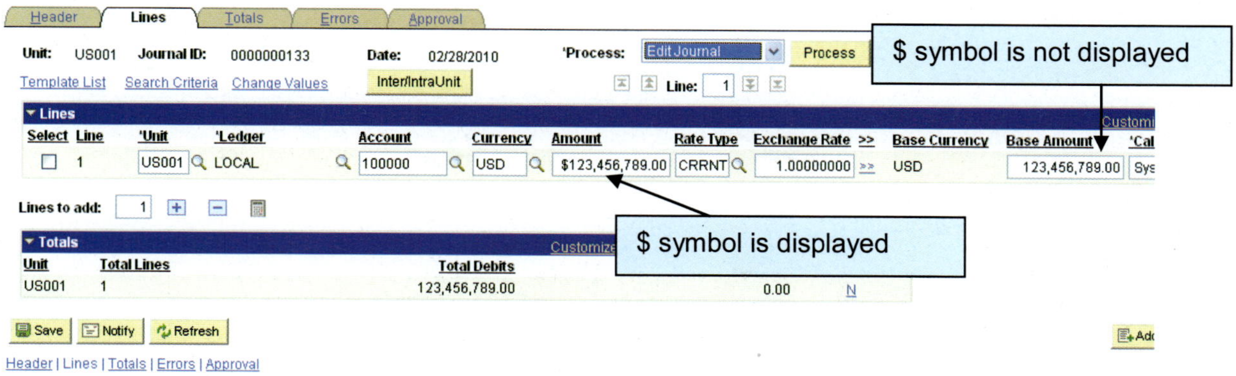

Scale

This defines the how many numbers are displayed to the left of decimal. For example, if you want to scale dollar amounts by a million (i.e. not display the trailing six zeros), then specify *Scale Positions* of 6. Thus, 36,000,000 is displayed as 36, but is stored in the database as 36,000,000.

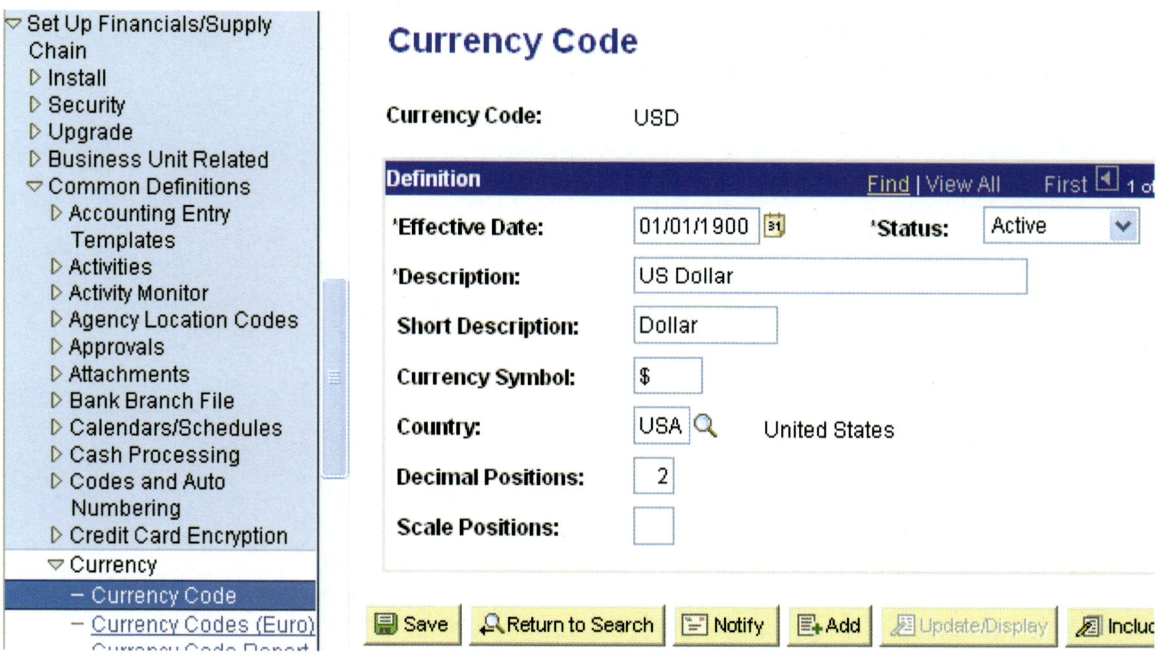

Loading Market Rates

To load market rates from a flat file into PeopleSoft tables, set up your parameters on the *File Inbound* page, then run the load process from the inbound file page. Refer PeopleBooks (*PeopleBooks > PeopleSoft Enterprise Global Options and Reports 9.1 PeopleBook > Processing Multiple Currencies*) for more details.

You can also write a custom SQR program to load the market rates. Use the flowchart below as a reference.

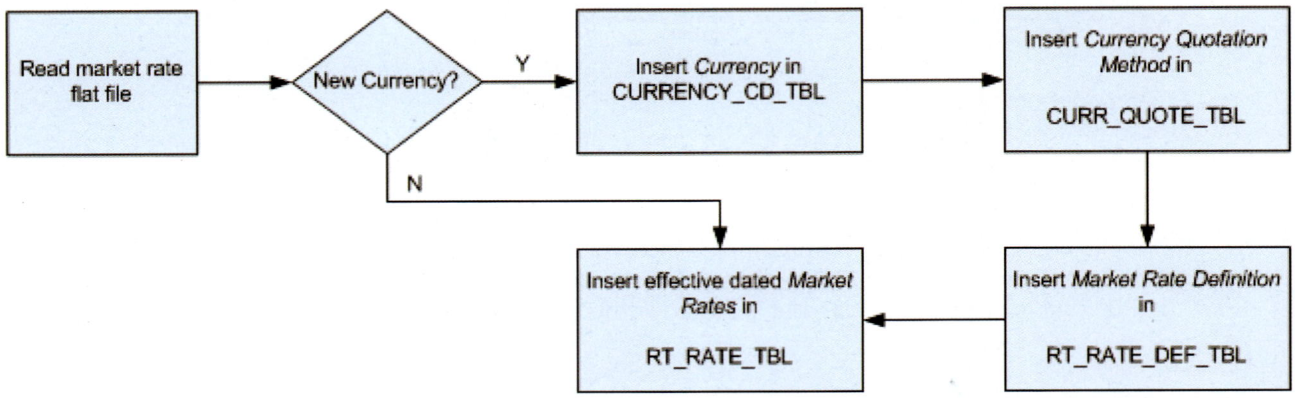

APPENDIX A

PeopleTools Objects

Multicurrency related PeopleTools Objects are tabulated below:

Screen	Navigation	Menu	Component	Page	Records
Currency Code	Set Up Financials/Supply Chain > Common Definitions > Currency > Currency Code	DEFINE_GENERAL_OPTIONS	CURRENCY_CD_TABLE	CURRENCY_CD_TABLE	CURRENCY_CD_TBL
Currency Code (Euro)	Set Up Financials/Supply Chain > Common Definitions > Currency > Currency Code (Euro)	DEFINE_GENERAL_OPTIONS	CURRENCY_EURO	CURRENCY_EURO	CURRENCY_EURO
Currency Code Report	Set Up Financials/Supply Chain > Common Definitions > Currency > Currency Code Report	DEFINE_GENERAL_OPTIONS	RUN_FIN0035	RUN_FIN0035 **Crystal - FIN0035**	RUN_CNTL_FS
Currency Quotation Method	Set Up Financials/Supply Chain > Common Definitions > Currency > Currency Quotation Method	DEFINE_GENERAL_OPTIONS	CURR_QUOTE_PNL	CURR_QUOTE_PNL	CURR_QUOTE_TBL
Currency Denominations	Set Up Financials/Supply Chain > Common Definitions > Currency > Currency Denominations	DEFINE_GENERAL_OPTIONS	CURR_DENOM_TBL	CURR_DENOM_TBL	CURR_DENOM_TBL
Cross/Reciprocal Rate Calc	Set Up Financials/Supply Chain > Common Definitions > Market Rates > Cross/Reciprocal Rate Calc	DEFINE_GENERAL_OPTIONS	RUN_EO9030	RUN_EO9030 **SQR - EO9030**	RUN_EO_RT_GEN
Market Rate Definition	Set Up Financials/Supply Chain > Common Definitions > Market Rates > Market Rate Definition	DEFINE_GENERAL_OPTIONS	MARKET_RATE_DEF	RT_RATE_DEF_TBL	RT_RATE_DEF_TBL
Market Rate Index	Set Up Financials/Supply Chain > Common Definitions > Market Rates > Market Rate Index	DEFINE_GENERAL_OPTIONS	MARKET_RATE_INDEX	RT_INDEX_TBL	RT_INDEX_TBL
Market Rate Type	Set Up Financials/Supply Chain > Common Definitions > Market Rates > Market Rate Type	DEFINE_GENERAL_OPTIONS	RT_TYPE_TBL	RT_TYPE_TBL	RT_TYPE_TBL
Market Rates	Set Up Financials/Supply Chain > Common Definitions > Market Rates > Market Rates	DEFINE_GENERAL_OPTIONS	RT_RATE_PNL	RT_RATE_PNL	RT_RATE_TBL
Revaluation Step	General Ledger > Process Multi-Currency > Define and Process > Revaluation Step	MAINTAIN_LEDGERS	REVAL_STEP	REVAL_STEP_LED_TM, REVAL_STEP_CF, CURR_STEP_OUT_JR, CURR_STEP_GN_LS	CURR_STEP_TBL, CURR_STEP_RVALF, CURR_STEP_RVALV, CURR_STP_TGTF, CURR_STPGN_TBL, CURR_STPLS_TBL
Translation Rules	General Ledger > Process Multi-Currency > Define and	MAINTAIN_LEDGERS	TRANS_RULE	TRANS_RULE_TIME_RT, TRANS_RULE_CF	CURR_RULE_TBL, CURR_RULEF_TBL,

Screen	Navigation	Menu	Component	Page	Records
	Process > Translation Rules				CURR_RULEV_TBL
Translation Steps	General Ledger > Process Multi-Currency > Define and Process > Translation Steps	MAINTAIN_LEDGERS	TRANS_STEP	TRANS_STEP_LED, TRANS_STEP_RULE, CURR_STEP_OUT_JR, CURR_STEP_GN_LS	CURR_STEP_TBL, CURR_STPRL_TBL, CURR_STEP_TBL, CURR_STP_TGTF, CURR_STEP_TBL, CURR_STPGN_TBL, CURR_STPLS_TBL
Translation Within Ledger	General Ledger > Process Multi-Currency > Define and Process > Translation Within Ledger	MAINTAIN_LEDGERS	MBXLAT	MBXLAT_STEP_LED_TM, MBXLAT_STEP_CF, CURR_STEP_OUT_JR, CURR_STEP_GN_LS	CURR_STEP_TBL, CURR_STEP_RVALF, CURR_STEP_RVALV, CURR_STEP_TBL, CURR_STP_TGTF, CURR_STEP_TBL, CURR_STPGN_TBL, CURR_STPLS_TBL
Define Process Group	General Ledger > Process Multi-Currency > Define and Process > Define Process Group	MAINTAIN_LEDGERS	CURR_GROUP	CURR_GROUP	CURR_GROUP_TBL, CURR_STEP_TBL
Request Process	General Ledger > Process Multi-Currency > Define and Process > Request Process	MAINTAIN_LEDGERS	CURR_REQUEST	CURR_REQUEST **COBOL - FSPCCURR**	CURR_REQUEST
Ledger Group	General Ledger > Ledgers > Ledger Groups	MAINTAIN_LEDGERS	DETAIL_LEDGER_GROUP	LEDGER_GROUP	LED_GRP_TBL, LED_GRP_LED_TBL
General Ledger Definition	Set Up Financials/Supply Chain > Business Unit Related > General Ledger > General Ledger Definition	ESTABLISH_BUSINESS_UNITS	BUS_UNIT_TBL_GL	BUS_UNIT_TBL_GL3	BUS_UNIT_TBL_GL
Ledgers For A Unit	Set Up Financials/Supply Chain > Business Unit Related > General Ledger > Ledgers For A Unit	ESTABLISH_BUSINESS_UNITS	BUSINESS_UNIT_LED	BUSINESS_UNIT_LED3	BU_LED_GRP_TBL, BUL_JE_RA_SET, SRC_JE_BS_CFS
Source (Journal)	Set Up Financials/Supply Chain > Common Definitions > Journals > Source	DEFINE_GENERAL_OPTIONS	SOURCE	SOURCE3	SOURCE_TBL
Report – Revaluation Step	General Ledger > Process Multi-Currency > Reports > Revaluation Step	MAINTAIN_LEDGERS	RUN_GLS5001	RUN_GLS5001 **SQR - GLS5001**	RUN_CNTL_GL
Report – Revaluation Calculation Log	General Ledger > Process Multi-Currency > Reports > Revaluation Calculation Log	MAINTAIN_LEDGERS	RUN_GLS5003	RUN_GLS5003 **SQR - GLS5003**	RUN_CNTL_GL
Report – Translation Step	General Ledger > Process Multi-Currency > Reports > Translation Step	MAINTAIN_LEDGERS	RUN_GLS5000	RUN_GLS5000 **SQR - GLS5000**	RUN_CNTL_GL
Report – Translation Calculation Log	General Ledger > Process Multi-Currency > Reports > Calculation Log	MAINTAIN_LEDGERS	RUN_GLS5002	RUN_GLS5002 **SQR - GLS5002**	RUN_CNTL_GL
Report – Translation in Ledger	General Ledger > Process Multi-Currency > Reports > Translation in Ledger	MAINTAIN_LEDGERS	RUN_GLS5005	RUN_GLS5005 **SQR - GLS5005**	RUN_CNTL_GL

Screen	Navigation	Menu	Component	Page	Records
Report – Translation in Ledger Calc Log	General Ledger > Process Multi-Currency > Reports > Translation in Ledger Calc Log	MAINTAIN_LEDGERS	RUN_GLS5004	RUN_GLS5004 **SQR - GLS5004**	RUN_CNTL_GL
Report – Translation Ledger In-Sync	General Ledger > Process Multi-Currency > Reports > Translation Ledger In-Sync	MAINTAIN_LEDGERS	RUN_GLS1006	RUN_GLS1006 **SQR - GLS1006**	RUN_GLS1006
Report – Translation Ledger Reconcile	General Ledger > Process Multi-Currency > Reports > Translation Ledger Reconcile	MAINTAIN_LEDGERS	RUN_GLS1005	RUN_GLS1005 **SQR - GLS1005**	RUN_GLS1005

APPENDIX B

TableSet Control

The multi-currency record group is GL_06.

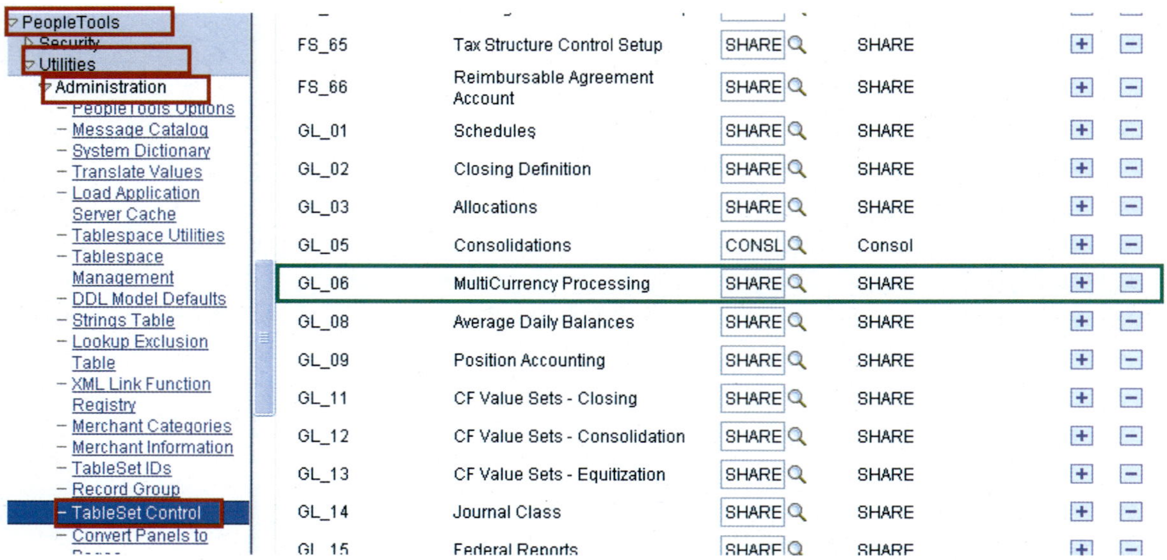

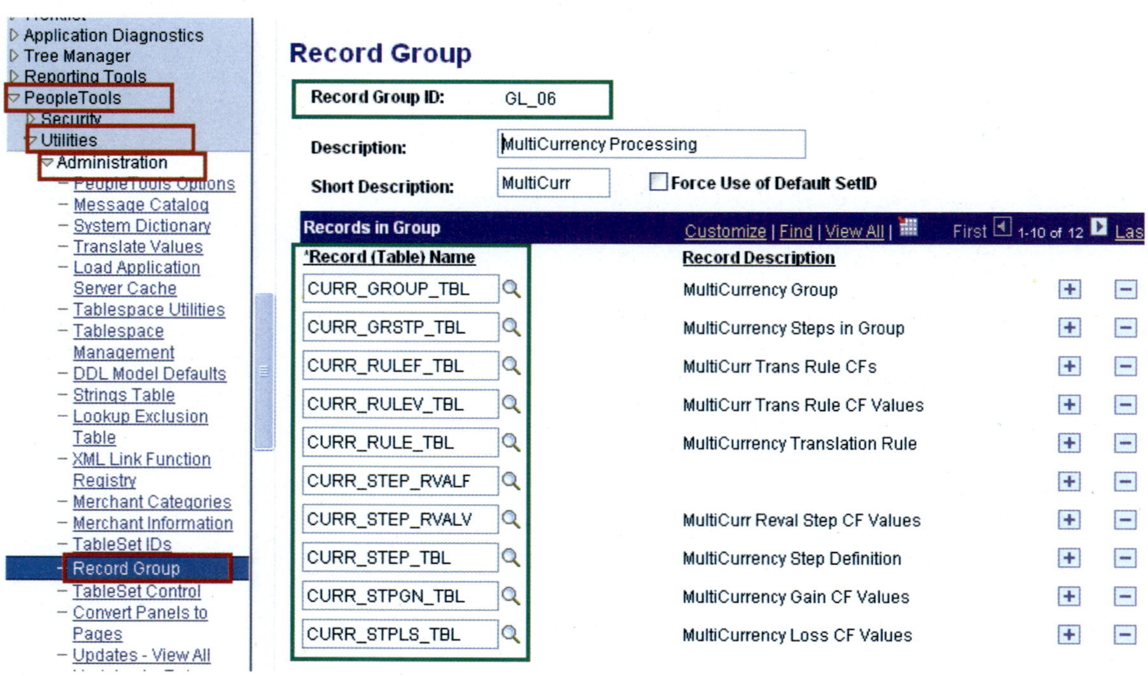

The table below is a query on record REC_GROUP_REC. It lists twelve records in the GL_06 group.

Group ID	Record
GL_06	CURR_GROUP_TBL
GL_06	CURR_GRSTP_TBL
GL_06	CURR_RULEF_TBL
GL_06	CURR_RULEV_TBL
GL_06	CURR_RULE_TBL
GL_06	CURR_STEP_RVALF
GL_06	CURR_STEP_RVALV
GL_06	CURR_STEP_TBL
GL_06	CURR_STPGN_TBL
GL_06	CURR_STPLS_TBL
GL_06	CURR_STPRL_TBL
GL_06	CURR_STP_TGTF

APPENDIX C

Message Catalog

The table below is a query on table PSMSGCATDEFN and lists *Message Catalog* entries for multi-currency. Message Catalog can also be accessed by menu navigation: *PeopleTools > Utilities > Administration > Message Catalog.*

Set	Msg	Message	Description
5870	1	GL MultiCurrency processing has begun.	GL MultiCurrency processing has begun.
5870	2	GL MultiCurrency processing complete.	GL MultiCurrency processing complete.
5870	3	Step %1 in Group %2 for Business Unit %3 was not processed due to errors.	GL MultiCurrency processing for the specified Step was incomplete. See the log for additional information about possible errors.
5870	4	Beginning processing, Step %1 in Group %2 for Business Unit %3.	An informational message stating the identifiers for the GL MultiCurrency Step which is being processed through the batch program. Subsequent messages which are issued prior to the next Step, are in reference to this GL MultiCurrency Step specification.
5870	5	PSPSQLRT error in GL MultiCurrency Processing: %1.	An error message that the GL MultiCurrency Step encountered an error while executing an SQL command. The specific program location is given. Contact the PeopleSoft Help Desk for more information on this error.
5870	6	Batch MultiCurrency processing has begun.	Batch MultiCurrency processing has begun.
5870	7	Batch MultiCurrency processing complete.	Batch MultiCurrency processing complete.
5870	20	SQL Statement buffer overflow; unable to build statement.	Dynamic SQL statements such as SELECT and INSERT are built in the program. The area in the program is not big enough to contain the current statement.
5870	21	Program buffer area too small for fields and constants. Stopped on Field %1, Step %2.	The program reads all data elements for a Step into a large memory area. This buffer area must be increased in size to process this Step (Copy Member FSCCBUFF.CBL). After increasing the buffer array, all MultiCurrency programs (FSPC*.CBL) should be recompiled.
5870	22	Record Field array overflow adding field %1.%2 in Step %3.	The program contains a table with one occurrence for each field defined in one or more of the records involved in GL MultiCurrency Processing. If the records (as defined in the Data Designer) have more fields than expected, this table may not be able to contain them. Check the Step definition to ensure it is correct, and does not involve superfluous ledger references. A program change is required to process this Step as currently specified.
5870	23	Too many SELECT variables. Stopped adding Field %1 in Step %2.	The program's capacity for SELECT items in a dynamic statement has been exceeded.
5870	24	Too many BIND variables. Stopped adding Field %1 in Step %2.	The program's capacity for BIND items in a dynamic statement has been exceeded.
5870	25	Array overflow error on %1. Occurrence count totaled %2.	An error message which indicates that an array overflow error occurred on the specified array name. The total number of occurrences indicates the array size required to successfully execute this request. Changing the array size will require a change to the source code. Contact the PeopleSoft Help Desk for more information on this error.
5870	26	No PSRECFIELD definitions for record %1.	There were no definitions found on the PSRECFIELD table for the named table. The program must be changed. Contact the PeopleSoft Help Desk for assistance.

Set	Msg	Message	Description
5870	40	Ledger %1 is not defined for SetID %2 or BU %3, Step %4.	One of the Ledgers (i.e., 'From Ledger' or 'Target Ledger' for Translation, or 'Ledger' for Revaluation) is not defined in the specified SetID or not established for the specified Business Unit.
5870	41	Target Field %1 is not defined in the Target record, Step %2.	Each ChartField in the Target definition must be defined on the Target Ledger record and, if Target Journals are being produced, on the Journal record which updates the Target Ledger.
5870	42	For Ledger %1, record %2 must contain fields for debits and credits, or a net amount field, Step %3.	The Ledger used in the indicated GL MultiCurrency Step does not contain the required amount fields. A Ledger must have either a single Net amount field or both Debit and Credit amount fields. Change the Ledger Record Definition and the corresponding Ledger Definition.
5870	43	Calendar %1 defined in SetID %2 does not have an entry for the As-Of Date used with Step %3.	Either the Calendar is not defined in the indicated SetID, or periods have not been defined through the As-Of Date.
5870	44	Time Span %1 not defined in SetID %2. Unable to process Step %3.	Verify that the Time Span is defined and spelled correctly. Also check TableSet options to ensure the correct SetID is being used for Time Spans.
5870	45	Tree %1 not defined or inactive in SetID %2, Step %3.	The indicated Tree does not exist, is not Effective, or is set inactive on the As Of date specified on the GL MultiCurrency Request. Also, check the SetID to verify that the Business Unit which requested this GL MultiCurrency Process is sharing this tree via the correct SetID.
5870	46	Account value %1 is not defined for SetID %2.	The stated Account value is part of the GL MultiCurrency Step specification. It needs to be entered for the stated SetID in PS/GL.
5870	47	Detail Field %1 for Tree %2 not found in field catalog.	Check the definition for this Tree and determine that the detail field specified in the tree structure is still valid.
5870	48	The target ChartField, %1, is not on the Process From ledger in Step %2.	Target ChartFields must be on the Process From ledger. The target ChartFields represent the level of detail for the output. Therefore in order to restate the amounts for these ChartFields, they must be part of the Process From ledger.
5870	49	The 'NEXT' journal id could not be assigned for Step %1.	An error message which indicates that a journal id could not be assigned for this GL MultiCurrency step. The NEXT journal id mask indicates that the system should assign the journal id value.
5870	50	A reversal date could not be determined using detail calendar %1.	An error message which indicates that a reversal date could not be determined using the referenced detail calendar.
5870	52	No primary ledger found from SetID %1 and ledger group %2.	There is no primary ledger defined for the specified SetID and ledger group. Define a primary ledger for the specified SetID and ledger group.
5870	53	Ledger group %2 is not a ledger group defined for business unit %1 or the calendar id is undefined.	The specified ledger group is not defined as the ledger group of the specified business unit or the calendar defined for the business unit ledger group panel is undefined.
5870	54	The ledger template specified for SetID %2 and ledger group %1 is not defined.	The ledger template for the specified SetID and ledger group is not defined. Define the ledger template and run the process again.
5870	55	SetID %1 ledger group %2 and ledger %3 is not defined.	To correct the error, define the specified ledger for the specified SetID and ledger group.
5870	56	No ledger is defined for SetID %1 and ledger group %2.	To correct the error, define one or more ledgers for the specified SetID and ledger group.
5870	57	Post journal fails for Business Unit %1 and Step %2.	The post journal process fails for the specified Business Unit and Step. The post journal process is done by calling GLPJEDT2. This error happens either when the fiscal year and period are not open or there are some system errors.
5870	58	Edit journal fails for Business Unit %1 and Step %2.	The edit journal process fails for the specified Business Unit and Step. The edit journal process is done by calling GLPJEDT2. This error happens either when the fiscal year and period are not open or there are some system errors.
5870	60	Time Span %1 defined in SetID %2 crosses fiscal years. Unable to process Step %3.	The accounting periods in the GL MultiCurrency Processing TimeSpans must fall within a single fiscal year.

Set	Msg	Message	Description
5870	61	Target Ledger Group %2 is balanced - Journal Entries must be created. Unable to process Step %1.	Journal entries must be created when the specified Target Ledger Group is balanced.
5870	62	ChartKeys in Rule %1 are specified for translation in other rules in Step %2.	The ChartKeys in the specified rule have already been translated according to other rules in this Step. Verify that the Rules do not duplicate the translation of ChartKeys and that the Target ChartFields include sufficient detail to differentiate the Rule ChartKey specifications.
5870	63	Untranslated ledger amounts for ChartKeys specified in Step %1 do not balance.	The untranslated ledger amounts for the specified step do not balance. The translation gain/loss calculation will not be accurate. Verify that all active Balance Sheet and Income Statement ChartKeys are included in the Rules specified for this step. One common error is only current period's Income Statement ChartKeys are included. If all ChartKeys are included in the rules then verify that your exchange rate table contains rates for the specified exchange rates and that the rule TimeSpans are appropriate for the period that you are translating. You could select 'Calculation Log' output option in your MultiCurrency definition. Although this error will terminate your MultiCurrency processing, the selected ChartKeys will still be populated to the calculation log table. Then, you can check the ChartKeys in the calculation log table to see if some ChartKeys are missing.
5870	64	The MultiCurrency work table has no data for this process instance, Step %1.	Batch MultiCurrency Processing is unable to select data from the work table. There may not have been any data entered for the specified process or the program is unable to locate data for the process instance. Verify that ledger balances are present for the period being processed, the exchange rate table contains entries for the exchange rate types in your rules, that the from and to ledgers and currencies are specified correctly and that the TimeSpans are appropriate for the period you are processing.
5870	65	Step %1 fails but the MultiCurrency Group continues.	MultiCurrency Step fails due to errors. However, since the continue flag is set on, the next MultiCurrency Step within the MultiCurrency Group will continue.
5870	66	Target ledger group %2 is balanced. An adjustment must be generated for step %1	Target ledger group %2 is balanced. An adjustment must be generated for step %1.
5870	67	Journal ID %1 already exists.	Journal ID %1 already exists.
5870	68	Doc Seq option enabled for Business Unit %1. Document Type in step %2 in Group %3 must be defined.	Document type is not defined on MultiCurrency journal option panel. This is required for running allocations for business units with document sequencing enabled.
5870	69	Calendar %1 with SetID %2 is not defined for year %3.	The specific calendar is not defined for the mentioned SetID, year. Please define the calendar before running MultiCurrency process.
5870	70	Calendar %1 with SetID %2 do not have specific adjustment period defined for time span %3.	The adjustment period defined in the time span is not defined in the calendar. Please verify the adjustment period against the calendar.
5870	71	Step %1 not processed in group %2.	The step may not be active by the as of date when the process was executed.
5870	72	No suspense ALTACCT provided.	No suspense ALTACCT is provided in the ledgers for a unit definition page.
5870	73	No suspense ACCOUNT provided.	No suspense ACCOUNT is provided in the ledgers for a unit definition page.
5870	74	ACCOUNT and ALTACCT not mapped in Step %1.	Account and ALTACCT has to be mapped before using them in pairs in target, gain, or loss ChartFields.
5870	75	Both ACCOUNT and ALTACCT are missing in step %1	Either ACCOUNT or ALTACCT has to be used in defining the step.
5870	76	Accounts with different book codes were used in step %1	
5870	77	Accounts with different balance sheet/off balance sheet indicators were used in step %1	
5870	78	ACCOUNT %1 not active.	

APPENDIX D

PeopleBooks

The link to Oracle hosted PeopleBooks is:

http://www.oracle.com/pls/psft/homepage

The screen shot below highlights multi-currency related topics.

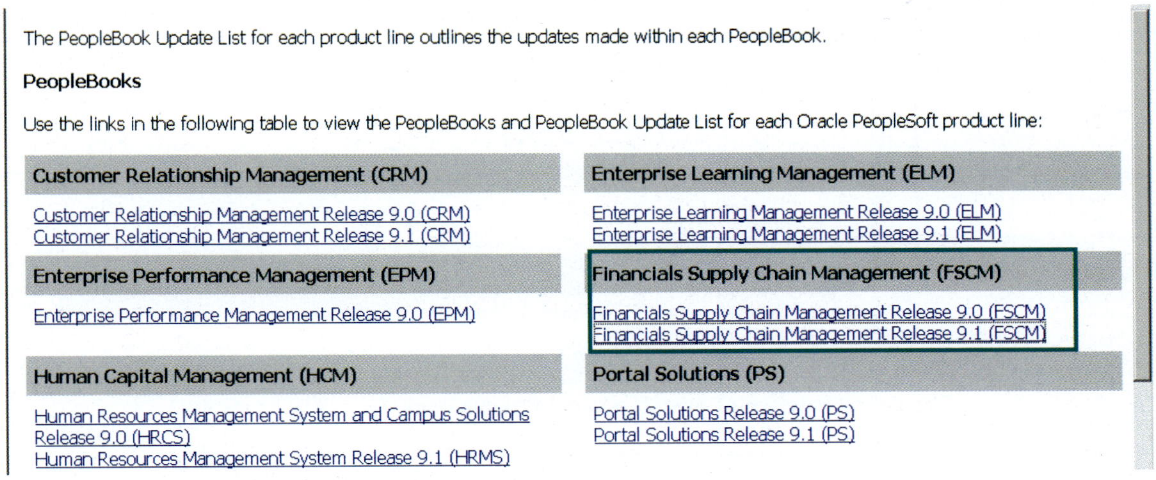

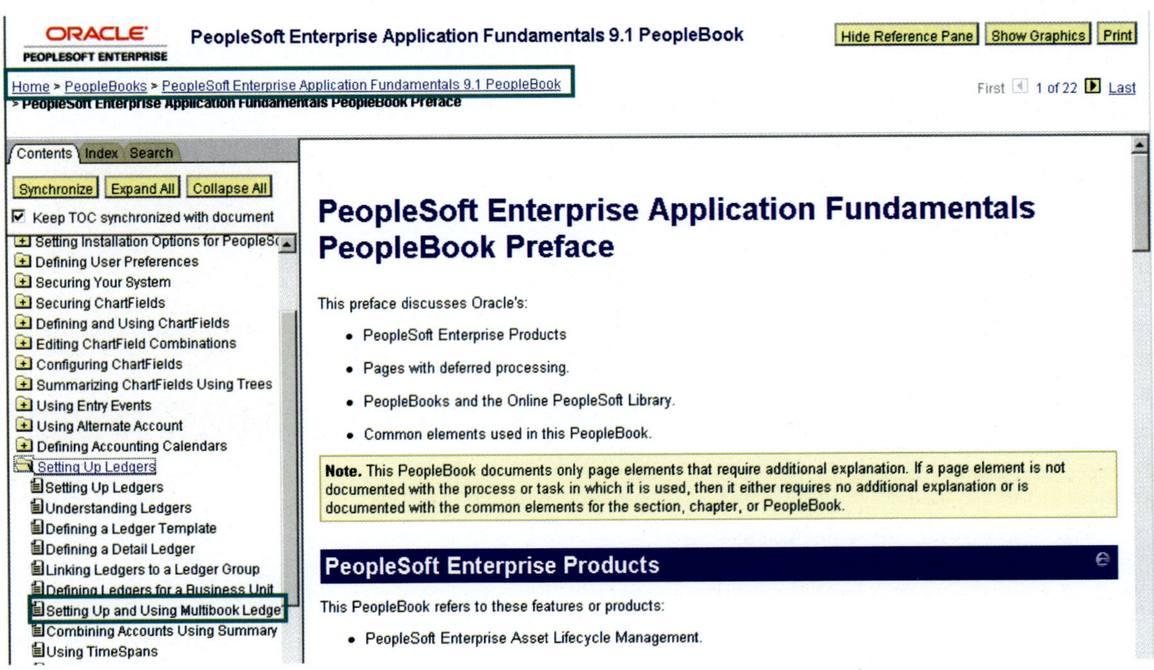

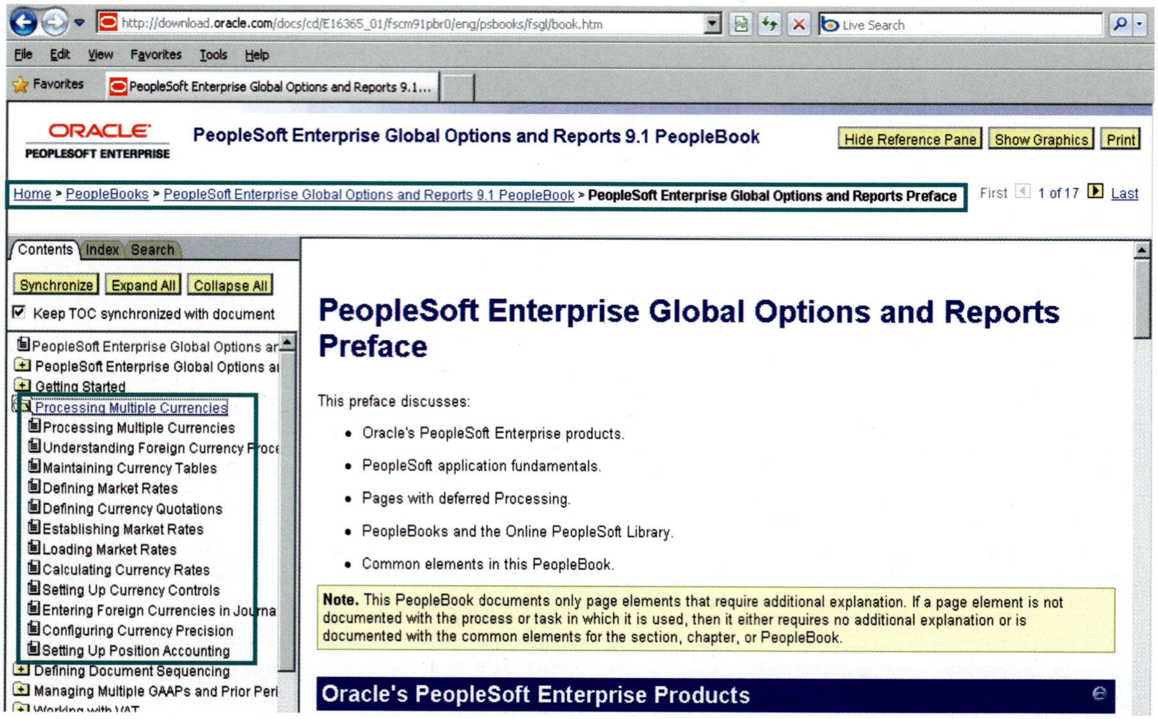
http://download.oracle.com/docs/cd/E16365_01/fscm91pbr0/eng/psbooks/fsgl/book.htm
Live Search
File Edit View Favorites Tools Help
Favorites
PeopleSoft Enterprise Global Options and Reports 9.1...
ORACLE
PEOPLESOFT ENTERPRISE
PeopleSoft Enterprise Global Options and Reports 9.1 PeopleBook
Hide Reference Pane
Show Graphics
Print
Home > PeopleBooks > PeopleSoft Enterprise Global Options and Reports 9.1 PeopleBook > PeopleSoft Enterprise Global Options and Reports Preface
First 1 of 17 Last
Contents Index Search
Synchronize Expand All Collapse All
Keep TOC synchronized with document
PeopleSoft Enterprise Global Options ar
PeopleSoft Enterprise Global Options ar
Getting Started
Processing Multiple Currencies
Processing Multiple Currencies
Understanding Foreign Currency Proce
Maintaining Currency Tables
Defining Market Rates
Defining Currency Quotations
Establishing Market Rates
Loading Market Rates
Calculating Currency Rates
Setting Up Currency Controls
Entering Foreign Currencies in Journa
Configuring Currency Precision
Setting Up Position Accounting
Defining Document Sequencing
Managing Multiple GAAPs and Prior Peri
PeopleSoft Enterprise Global Options and Reports Preface
This preface discusses:
Oracle's PeopleSoft Enterprise products.
PeopleSoft application fundamentals.
Pages with deferred Processing.
PeopleBooks and the Online PeopleSoft Library.
Common elements in this PeopleBook.
Note. This PeopleBook documents only page elements that require additional explanation. If a page element is not documented with the process or task in which it is used, then it either requires no additional explanation or is documented with the common elements for the section, chapter, or PeopleBook.
Oracle's PeopleSoft Enterprise Products

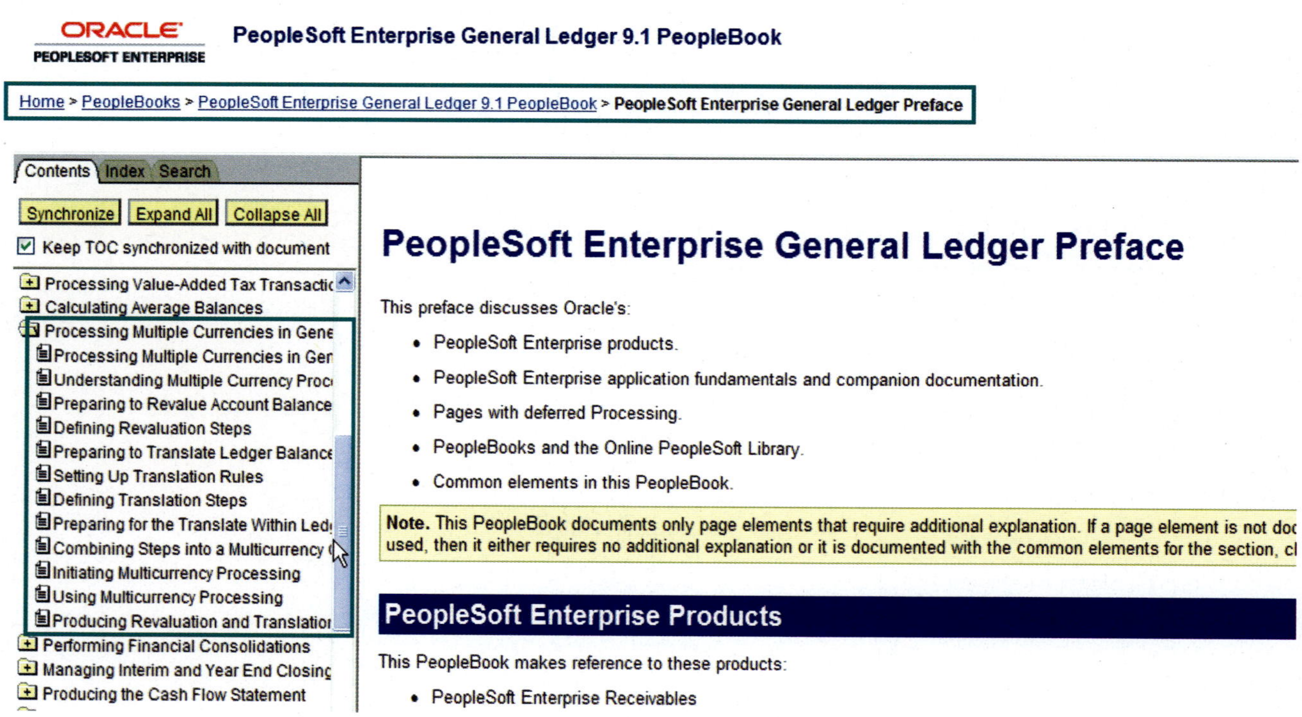
ORACLE
PEOPLESOFT ENTERPRISE
PeopleSoft Enterprise General Ledger 9.1 PeopleBook
Home > PeopleBooks > PeopleSoft Enterprise General Ledger 9.1 PeopleBook > PeopleSoft Enterprise General Ledger Preface
Contents Index Search
Synchronize Expand All Collapse All
Keep TOC synchronized with document
Processing Value-Added Tax Transactic
Calculating Average Balances
Processing Multiple Currencies in Gene
Processing Multiple Currencies in Ger
Understanding Multiple Currency Proc
Preparing to Revalue Account Balance
Defining Revaluation Steps
Preparing to Translate Ledger Balance
Setting Up Translation Rules
Defining Translation Steps
Preparing for the Translate Within Led
Combining Steps into a Multicurrency
Initiating Multicurrency Processing
Using Multicurrency Processing
Producing Revaluation and Translatio
Performing Financial Consolidations
Managing Interim and Year End Closinc
Producing the Cash Flow Statement
PeopleSoft Enterprise General Ledger Preface
This preface discusses Oracle's:
PeopleSoft Enterprise products.
PeopleSoft Enterprise application fundamentals and companion documentation.
Pages with deferred Processing.
PeopleBooks and the Online PeopleSoft Library.
Common elements in this PeopleBook.
Note. This PeopleBook documents only page elements that require additional explanation. If a page element is not doc
used, then it either requires no additional explanation or it is documented with the common elements for the section, cl
PeopleSoft Enterprise Products
This PeopleBook makes reference to these products:
PeopleSoft Enterprise Receivables

Index

Calculation Rules 24
Crystal Reports – Currency Precision 41
Currency Code 31, 35, 36, 40, 41, 103, 135, 153
Currency Control Field 39
Currency Controls 56
Currency Precision 41, 43, 46
Currency Rounding 47
Currency Quotation Method 10, 48, 49, 50, 52, 54, 105, 135, 148, 154
Currency Symbols 169
Currency Triangulation 48
Detail Ledger 32, 87, 102, 134, 152
General Ledger Definition 37, 57, 59
Journal Entry 10, 16, 34, 40, 65, 92, 115, 155
Journal Source 57, 63, 64
Ledgers For A Unit 33, 57, 60, 89, 102, 134, 152
Ledger Groups 32, 58, 81, 88, 102, 134, 152
Ledger Template 86
Market Rates 10, 17, 19, 20, 21, 49, 51, 91, 111, 136, 149, 154
Market Rate Definition 21
Marker Rates – upload 171
nVision – Currency Precision 46
Open Periods 33, 63, 91, 103, 135, 152
PeopleTool Options 167
Process Group 126, 141, 160
Request Process 127, 142, 161
Revaluation Calculation Log Report 131
Revaluation Step 120
Rounding Adjustment ChartFields 62
Query 37, 95, 107, 113, 116, 137, 146, 157
Scale 170
SQR – Currency Precision 41
Thousand Separator 169
Translation Calculation Log 145
Translation in Ledger Calc Log 165
Translation Steps 140, 149
Translation Rules 138
Translation Within Ledger 158
User Preferences 14, 15, 16